A SAILOR'S TALE

1893-----1898

MISS JUDITH MISS MOLLY

Edward G. Hlusko

ISBN 978-1-959071-26-6 (paperback)

Printed in the United States of America

ACKNOWLEDGEMENTS

To my mother, who put me on this path. Her name,
and loved ones, will always be in that "Family History."
Seaman 1st, USN, my father. His quiet words,
that guided me to my future.
My dear wife, for her patients at this endeavor,
and putting up with me.
A "Lady of the Castle," Scottish Lassie.
Too shy to want to be named.
A man whom always thought of his daughter as.
"His Princess."

FROM THE AUTHOR

I have received varying comments toward the first revision of Miss Judith 1888-1893. "We had to chew on some the sailor said." True. That is why, how I got thrown into this project by Mrs. Bracken. He was abrupt in his language, and you had to re-read some things, at times, to get his meaning. I have, in some cases, added in sentence structure, for the read. He was never vulgar, writing to his niece or younger cousin. I can speculate on either term, to not give a good answer to you.

He graduated from secondary school at 16. At the time, that was the end of the state's curriculum of education. Only later were the 11th and 12th grades added. Ask any man who had the honor of entering the US service will tell you that they got a whole new vocabulary of terms to deal with, whether in the Army, Marines, or Navy. I can personally say I had to be careful of me language, at home, after my indoctrination at Navy Boot Camp. Patton said he used it to get the troops attention. The first day of Navy Boot Camp caught up my attention.

For this 3rd Revision I added a Table of Content/Date Index to the front of the manuscript. It contains letter dates, where he was when he wrote them, and key personnel he was dealing with, like a Captain or Admiral. I tried to set his timelines to order. He wrote in a, "Roundy, Roundy," fashion, as you would do in a letter. A thought would come to mind and set it to paper. It was another thing, "To chew on."

In the same regards, I have specially underscored when he digresses to his earlier ventures. He was, "Catchin ya up to how I became a sailor." He didn't start to write her until he had been in the Navy for a number of years. By then he'd been to Alaska, Charted the Missouri River, and had some horrific life experiences. I smoothed out his sentences, so it is easier for the reader. No, I changed none of the content or the situations he encountered. I hope I took his word from hard rum to smooth whiskey. I may have used an Old Whiskey barrel for this. Some wood flavor to it, aged a bit too much.

E.G.'L.

IN THE YEAR 2001:

PRELUDE: AND SO THE STORY GOES ON.

As I said in Volume 1 of this, 'A Sailor's Tale,' I got involved in this work when I was doing geological research at the local County Historical society. I can always say, "My mother started this." I became intrigued with the letters, from this late 1800's sailor, whom I could never tie to my research. I thought it was because of misplaced files, short obituaries, or any number of reasons, as I found compiling my family histories.

The only certain aspect of my research was Mrs. Bracken bringing me that box of letters, hovering around like a buzzard. She was guardian of those letters. Out of that box, to my hand, watched like a hawk as I copied them, then carefully tied together in thin ribbon, and placed back. It was like they were hers. I asked and got, "No. And you are careless in your work. You overlook the obvious, but, do pick up little details." She'd give me those teacher eyes, finger waving, like being chastised for a poor report.

Mrs. Bracken, I thought, would have made a good 'Used Car Salesman." I paid 5 cents to copy each page. I only had so much time available for this copying, after I did what research was on my list. It was still a cost I grumbled at. So, she says if I buy a copy machine printer cartridge and ream of copy paper, I'd get a discount on printing. "2 cents!" Nice smile, bright eyes I got, and brought them to her. No, she gave me the exact items to buy. Next time there and got the same deal. It took some time, but I figured out it would have been cheaper to pay the 5 cent rate.

One small problem was she wasn't always there when I made a visit. I'd ask about the box of letter and get a questioning look. "Oh, I don't know where she places them. I'll call her and have her come in tomorrow afternoon. She volunteers her time." Next afternoon I find her with bright smile. Box hits the table and angry teach looks she had. She be smiling, hummed this tune I never heard of, as she put envelops together with that ribbon. I had to laugh, later, as she'd turn, seen me watching, and I'd get teacher eyes.

At night, Dad would be watching TV. I'd be at the kitchen table going over my notes and Mom would read the letters I copied. Mom would be laughing, sad, have her hand over her mouth, at different times, reading the letters.

I was a member of "The Modern Navy." Nuclear carrier and cruisers. Ships with guns and missiles. "Old Navy" men talked of Fram 2 destroyers and boilers in carriers, with affection. This sailor served at the time of "Tall ships, with sails." The period just before the transition to iron ships. The era of, "Wooden Ships, and Iron Men!" No, I have no desire to "Time Warp" back and step into his position.

May you enjoy reading about an "Old Salt, or Sea Dog," and his ventures!

E.G.H.

CONTENTS

IN THE YEAR 1893, 16 JULY: MEDITERRANEAN

Dear Miss Judith,

The ship left Gibraltar on Monday, 12 June, 93. We was to leave on Sunday, but the officers were aboard the Frigate, all afternoon. I got another afternoon with me Beer Tender. The evening brief to get underway was the usual. I figured Little, Mac, and Mr. Hanna could do it. I just stood at the Capt'n door.

Mr. Smith outlined our next cruise. There was to be minor repairs in Toulon and waterin in Gaeta. I'd get to see Monic. A check at Palermo for a Frigate. On to Cyprus, Crete, and give stuff to the Frigates off Africa. Nothing unusual. I wondered why I was present.

We left that Frigate there in Gibraltar, ahead of us at the pier, Thank St. Christopher. Little, Mr. Hanna, Mr. Pontus, and Warrant Silvis did a good sail of the ship. Mr. Smith was real involved in the ships calls. "Unmoor Ship. Cast Off." Mr. Hanna gave the signal for the salute and Mr. Pontus gave eyes to him at callin early, for sails. Smith pays no attention to the flag atop Gibraltar mount, the Consultants place nor at that Commissionin Pennant, hangin limp.

Came a lee gun from two Spanish Frigates afore our whey point to North, and Toulon. Smith gave the signal to haul up. I don't know all in that book but, it was a strange reply. Even the Middie had to look at. Next whey point and was that Spanish Frigate I recognize. Smith went over, back, and we head to Toulon.

After that transit, well, Mr. Smith seemed to want to, "Helm Up" or, "Helm Down, Tack The Ship!" That be to take the ship into the wind to change the ship course. Smokin Lamp Lited and I could give no good reason for his actions. I didn't care as we got to Toulon and me second story place to have some drinks and quiet.

We shot the straights of Corsica and Sardinia under top Gallants and full sails, like the Devil himself was ahind us. Mr. Smith even did ok with helm orders. Little's finger touched them up. Oh, even Mac and them 3 stripper eyes wondered some.

The crew are on liberty by divisions, so I got to see Monic. She set up the others I brought along. She be like that. We was in, watered, shore liberty, and out in two days. That broke lots of hearts. Mostly the women, for money lost. But, I ain't sayin.

It was two days to Palermo. Yes 2. Mr. Smith played in the wind with the ship. No, I don't mind. It gives the 3 strippers and QM Mac practice. Pontus and BM2's crew got real good at sifting sails and all. We didn't find no Frigate, so stopped in that little town just East of it. Aspra. Just one liberty per division.

We went west around Sicily. Mr. Smith didn't want to get tied up in the Straights of Messina. He had a "Social" meeting in Valletta, Malta. The crew didn't mind the liberty. We haven't seen a Frigate yet. Nothing goin on, but something is goin on.

• • •

In 1884, after the stop in Kodiak town, it took another week to 'Round' the Upper part of that island. Marmot Bay should have been called Mammoth Bay. Plus, The East side of Afognak Island and then the North Side, Deep bays. Mr. Rose and Mr. Lydick argued, again, about goin into the bays. Me, George, McCoy, Jeffreys, and crew sure did fly along. The only easy part was Marmot Island.

Friday, 29 August, 84, by log entry, we crossed over to main land Alaska. 500 miles or so to Cold Bay, Alaska. Lookin at the Chart, it would take 'No Time At All!' That Chart was smeared, like at Shuyak Island. Them smears was like someone took an axe to the land. We got trapped in Hallo and Kukak Bay. The wind, rain, and the waves came just straight out of the South East.

Stuck in the bay, Talig, with nowhere to go, get Mr. Chips to rig this big, bigger than Weaver, structure with netting over it. It has an entrance on both sides. He takes some real nasty smellin stuff, smears it on an old piece of fur, for bate, and the 'Cage' goes over the side on a line on a block of the boom. The next day, 'Stuck,' well, up come some spiders inside that was 6 feet across. I mean it. Talig takes them out, hits these things on the head, pulls off the leggs, yep at least 8 of them, and the heads go into a pile. Leggs as big as your arms to the Cook to boil.

Our table got to try them first. Talig showed us how to take a Mallet and smash the outside shell. It was boiled in salt water, so it had that taste. Soft, not quite mushy meat. Not fishy. Not anything I ever ate. Others of the crew tried them. It was better than salted beef or pork. Only the officers enjoyed them. Soo, every time we got stuck in a bay, often it was, we'd haul up a couple cages full.

Up to Anchorage, then around Kodiak, sure set us up for this last leg of our cruise. Me hands were thick with skin from rowing. I could hardly open me hands the whole way. When our crew ran ahead, Weaver or me could start the fire to warm up our pails. Sextant to measure mountains to our log. I got a taste for Talig muscle and sweet root kettle stuff. Talig would find something to shoot to add to his pot. He shot some seals.

Them seals had a fishy taste, as they ate fish. By now, as I said, we had eaten lots of fish. The seal fat had that odder, which we figured out was that smell in his kayak. We told Talig to not bring them bring them back. He'd shoot them, skin them, and leave them. He'd go back, as he often just went off, night or day, and shoot the bear that came to feed on it. Bear was good eatin.

Salmon was goin up streams to spawn, Talig said so, to lay their eggs. The bears stayed close to the fresh water streams, so we saw few on the Beach. The exception was a beach where seals hung about. A pistol shot and the bear ran off. Deer! Talig had the time to go to brush for them. Oh, just beautiful place to look at. We did what was to be logged, found muscles, sweet roots, and tended the fire.

At a couple of places, odd places, the deer would come to the shore and seemed to be sniffin at the fire. They about ignored me, tendin the fire. If I stood, then they'd run. Ifn I just sat, tending the pot, well, Talig liked I shot them in the head. I got pepper from the cook and by the time the crew came for lunch, well, it added to the pails. The rest went back to the ship for supper.

It was at Sutwik Island that Talig went over in his kayak to, "See you later!" Well, it took a week to shoot all that and Chignik Bay. Talig did come back for more pepper, which the sacks contained. He brought back hides for his store. Every time the ship stopped that crab pot went over the side. Overdue salted pork, beef, or them Crab heads went into the cage.

Wind, rain, blowin, tide, currents and all sure tied us up all September getting to that Chignik Bay and all. Oh, as long as waves weren't much, over we went to places. Weather gear on and off we went. Came back to Mr. Newhouse yelling about water on his, already wet deck. I never figured out that one. I guess he just needed to vent about something.

Alaska has some stuff do deal with, on a ship. Wind, of course. Next was the sun. Ya can't shoot it at noon through clouds. Clouds and rain come together. Them 5 Quartermasters and Mr. Rose kept a tight chart were we was. Two minded the angles to the land we shot and our speed log over all the time. George and me just watched them, down at the galley tables, figuring the Latitude and Longitude each day, without sun, lots of them days and no stars at night neither. Oh, there was lots of time after the sun down to look.

26 Sept, 84, the wind got us out of that big bay. That smear of a Chart said 200 miles to Cold Harbor. We'd hit that first known land and skip down some. Oh, guns, lunch pails, fire goin, and we waited for the gig. Times came the gig landed and got a meal from the fire we made. Talig was some there and not. It is just a rugged land to see, shoot angles to mountains, sit and wait.

You'd have said a beautiful place. After All this beauty, it was hard to see it, after so many places. The boat crew would come in wet and hungry. They ever liked that muscles and sweet root boil Talig or me made. Just time and again we went back to the ship tired.

Half way to Cold Bay we found the smear of land was not All dry. More islands, rocks, juts of land, and what not. Even Lydick gave up on complainin to Mr. Rose. Talig had no names for some of them islands. At some he was over the side and off to, "Maybe back in a day or two."

It was two weeks round them islands, with no names, well, some of them. The West ones Talig could put a word to them. He did trading with the people, what were there. Them East ones we just called, "More Ptui islands." Few places to land and no animals we saw.

From Unga Island to Dolgoi Island, I can't make up these names, Mr. Rose and Mr. Lydick got into it again. The latter wanted to Explore Pavlof Bay. The former gave him, "one day, one boat, one crew. Stay Overnight. No more!" Talig had warned of, "bad winds and stuck for a week."

Good old Jeffreys and McCoy bet them both we could shoot the place using a mountain on each side of the bay, hit the major Points, and back by dark, starting at sunrise. We took Nor-Easter gear, food for three meals, and our guns. It was a trip to remember. Even worse than that island place we did before. We touched land only to take them mountains to shore and used the oars to back off the land.

The wind kept the ship right there that next day. Oh, the boat crew, me and George, got to explain all the shots, angles, compass reading, and soundings. The Cartographers even made a model of it with wood. So, Me and George got lots of thanks? No. Was accused of making up some compass readings and poor sextant angles.

We make this King Cove October 20, 1884. It is outside that Cold Bay place. Talig said the bay had bad winds. He loaded up his kayak and off he went. We anchored and liberty boats went over. It was a 2 mile pull in the barges. Oh, Jeffreys and McCoy set up the sail of the gig so we got to be the first to this town of two places to drink. It was expensive to drink. Talig was there so got a couple on his money and bought him one each. We towed him back.

So, we was done? NO! South of King Cove was more chunks of rocks above water. Then, Talig mentioned this "False Pass." The natives take it into the Bearing Sea! Sunrise off Ikaton peninsula over we went in that gig. Lydick wanted to go. Jeffreys said only ifn he rowed. Mr. Rose thought that was funny. I asked and, "No, Mr. Lydick cannot take your place!"

The next day we made it back just at supper time, Mr. Rose watched them Cartographers makin some part of what they had to match to what we found. There was bad winds so we couldn't go anywhere. Came the Same complaints of bad shots. Me and George finally said, "Don't like them, go do them yourself."

Me log says 24 October, 1884 we did the last landings on an Alaska Peninsula. A big mountain was at that end. Snow covered more than most of it and it was getting cold out. Captain Hullenbaugh had the cook made this desert of plums, crushed ships biscuits, bits of meat, other fruit, and rum. Cookin burned off some. I saw the Bos'n add some straight from the bottle when it came out. Oh, such good eating.

We turned about and didn't stop till Kodiak Island and town. Two days of liberty and Talig went nowhere without one of us with him. See, the bars had a bell. Pull that rope on the clapper and ya bought a round for the house. We got him in a corner table and would not let him out. George and me had enough money to wet his thirst. Talig bought some for us. Come the time, well, poured him into his kayak. Oh, we went back inside as that bell kept sounding. Free drinks always have a better taste to thems. Free!

The ship got to Sitka, Alaska on 2 November and Talig was over the side with first load of, ah, stuff. He came back three times. The last time, well, the gig crew got an invite to his place. No, we had to go, per Mr. Lydick. We went into his wife, older children, Grandpa and Ma. They served food I hardly recognized, 'cept for the muscle and sweet roots. They talked native and we all got lots of points, and laughs. Talig was telling stories.

Oh, drinks! We got plain mugs. The bottle came to each and as the English would say, "Filled to the Bumpers," top, with strong Whiskey! We sipped to the family drinkin it like, straight down. It was Mr. Lydick who stood first, sorta. We sipped that good stuff. He tried to keep up with them.

Talig mentioned presents for us. He came out with a figured walrus Tooth for Mr. Lydick. The crew got seal skin gloves, "So you don't wear out your hands, rowing!" Nice gloves. Out came this neckless of two bear canine teeth and front bear claws 'atween for George. I got three canine teeth and them 6 inch long claws. Talig said some strange words and all them got a good laugh. "Told them I give this to mighty White Hunter," with words in his language to more laughs, "That fills the Hides with holes!" Well, we all had another laugh at that. We rowed back to the ship about dry and had to help Mr. Lydick up that Port side.

So, we just sailed to Frisco? No. We skipped some places goin up so as to miss the winter cold in Alaska and got to 'Survey' all them places down that coast of Alaska. I found out the State of California flag had a bear on it. I didn't see nary a one. We made Frisco 15 February, 1885. 11 months gone by.

• • •

Oh, this last cruise of 1893? Mr. Smith had a time of it in Valetta, Malta. We all did. That local woman made sure we got what we wanted. Me and 3 strippers was shown a local place. Best, cheap drinks.

It wasn't till after that place in Cyprus that we met a Frigate. Well, their sail rigged barge and some thirsty looks. I didn't take a day for them to lead us to it. They needed green stuff. They took some barrels of cabbage and water, also. Gave the water as next was our stop in Crete.

At the place in Crete, all were social. I still can't 'Parley' all they say. Oh, the shop owner greeted us and got good wine and food for our Liberty coins. Ship got filled with water. The crew got good wine, food, at the landing and the Marines didn't take but a few back to the ship.

Capt'n Smith was makin a bee line for Malta, and, shush, his social, when we met second Frigate cutter. The Chart said it be a straight line from Libya and Tunis, Tunisia is not a day sail. Mr. Smith across and we gave them what they wanted. Wanted Greens! Well, Purser gave out what we could spare and that pickled cabbage went over in barrels. I saw some barrels of water go over. Round the smokin lamp the talk was of something goin on.

We spent three days in Valletta, Malta. Two was official and ain't sayin nothin about the last one. The crew got that day of liberty and didn't say a word. The all officers meeting with the local Governor was unusual. Oh, it came down to the main deck that the Governor wanted to thank all thems, being the last cruise. The pier woman is Nora. I asked her. She is the daughter of the bar owner she took us to. Part Brit.

It was to be 6 days to Gibraltar. Capt'n likes them Top Gallants, now. In light breezes they pushed us to 8 good knots, which is why I could figure on the 15th of July. Mr. Smith must have been reading them old English books of sailin. He'd give an order and I, havin read some of Uncle Curtis stuff, could about translate. They'd had a 'Parley' and we went back to what was understood.

Mr. Smith held quarters on Sundays. Oh, the crew shined them shoes, uniforms just so, and the ship ready for, almost, for Admiral Inspection. Come 10 AM we lined up by divisions and Mr. Smith did an inspection of the ship. He mixed the volunteer to the crew so they'd feel like a part of it. I'd be at the helm as Fitz recorded any infractions. After, he'd say some words. We had no Chaplin aboard. Done by 11AM and the crew could lounge around till Noon meal. That is after the sun was shot at noon.

Sunday, 09 July, 1893, the inspection party went down the forward hatch, 10:15, and the lookout said, "On Deck! Galite Island on Port Fore Quarter." It should not have been there, by me calculations. Just mid ship in an hour. Next comes, "On Deck, sail, Larboard Fore Quarter!" Same place. OK. I can 'Adjust Course 1 point,' that be 10 degrees to you, and steady up. I saw that island peak, not 5 minutes later, so I gave the ship another point North, again. I saw two rocks above water, Port side, some way of so, and add another Point to the compass, North.

Come 10:30 and up come Mr. Smith, and party, through the aft ladder. He gets settle to the Poop Rail, center, for his say and the lookout said, "Ship, Mid, Full Sail. No Flags." Smith, Pontus, and Hanna went to the Taft Rail, to see this ship. I shuffled their feet as I gave the ship another 'Point' North.

It came up hand over fist, doin 12 or more to our 8, or so. Well, Little, at the Port Chart Table logged the time they put a gun to wind and hauled up, 'Sir, Stop To Be Boarded!' Officers there at the Taft Rail and I got eyes to me 'nother Point North. From the mast comes, 'That Barkey got more crew than us, Sir.' To make the point, I gave the ship a point, or so, North, along our line. I shifted the deck to make thems give a look. The next time, well, Nor West waves, with Nor Nor-East wind, so, I planted the nose of the ship into that wave with a, ah, two point shift of the rudder and put the ship on course. I got bad eyes from this 'War Council.'

It must have been that puff of smoke from that ship that got some attention. The ball was way short, Port. Comes the second puff, the ball cane to Starboard and short. Mr. Smith gets out, "Gen," and that Marine at the ships bell sure made me ears hurt.

The council ended so I grab Mr. Mack, gunner, and said, 'At 200 Yards grape is best.' I got, "So, a QM is sayin what a Gunner should do?" I said, 'Yes!' Back was, "You turn this Barky around two times," he looks at Mr. Smith, "and, I'll let you pull the trigger on that gun!" I said, 'No. Three times around if I get Full Jibs and just Fore Sails!' I got eyes and off he went. I caught up Silvis and told him what I needed, to Bad eyes, but a nod.

I didn't take no time for that ship to come up ahind us. Came a ball to Port, close, and the next just to Starboard. Came them words to mind, from Forest. "Got our Range." So, Mr. Smith called out to, "Commence Fire!" I jinxed the ship to Port and them 2 aft Port Nine Pounder went off as one. I gave a finger and the 3 strippers and Mac sat on the deck to mind the helm. I jinxed to Starboard and other two shot.

Gunner was there to watch this. He and Mr. Smith kept given me the eye. The 9 pounders were reloaded and I jinxed the ship to Starboard with a small wave so ship didn't move fast. The port side officer's privy took the hit. Gunner comes by me, given an eye to Mr. Smith, and say, "Grape it is, Laddie!" I caught up Silvis about that Aft mast spanker sail.

When I jinxed the ship that other would follow. Mr. Smith finally said, "Up Helm!" I waited for Silvis and Mr. Pontus to give the sail orders, and the ship turned to Starboard. I saw the other one do the same! I heard our guns go off as they bore to the other. Somewhere in this noise I heard a shot come to us Forward, Mid, and next I was over on the Port bulwark.

I tried to get up, to me left leg hurtin. There was three sticks of wood there. Oh, I just pulled them out, got up and, me left arm sure hurt. I looked at some sticks in it. I took me right hand and just bushed them off, to, pain! They was stuck into me arm. The poop, helm deck was all down, 'cept for Little and Hanna about. Bosn's, the aft ones, come up to mind the spanker. Told them to take the wounded below. Mr. Smith was one of them.

The helm was jammed to Starboard as the 3 strippers, Mathew and Luke, got blown under the ships wheel. Mac and John was just layin there. The Bosn's took them below as me and Mr. Hanna kept it hard to Starboard. Oh, Susquehanna came through that wind like she was born to do it. The other ship? Well, her port side didn't look good and the sails were flappin around. It missed Stays. That crew didn't mind the sails and wind didn't allow it to come about.

We got a puff or two of smoke from her and Mr. Mack sure gave it all 6 Port guns. That aft pusher sail, with the wind, turned us some. Jib sails, and, never saw so many set, turned us again.

We came around, West, with some fore movement, don't know how, and put the Starboard side to this ship again. Pontus and Silvis got whistles to the sails. I heard little of it. Oh, Bang, BABAbang, Bang, down our Starboard side. The helm was still at full Starboard. The last shots I heard was from George and Pete on them fore 9 pound chasers. Pontus called, 'Helm Amid, set small sails."

The other ship was dead in the water and some smoke from places. I swear to MaMa, two Marines dragged half dead Mr. Smith up to the Poop just then. He looked like an Egyptian mummy for the bandages on his head, right arm, body, well, all over. Came his, "Small sails, Mr. Pontus. Caution to approach." Engle brought up a chair and brandy. Mr. Smith just got a sip of that mug, seated, and that other ship blew up, right there.

Our boats pulled some 12 people off the fore deck wreckage, floating. Another few came from aft section. I watched as a piece of the ship, aft, came into view. There was 4 woman on a grate, with two thrashing the water with swords. The Marines got close them went swords just thrashed the water. They wouldn't let them get close to the grate. Shot dead.

Them 4 woman didn't take kindly to the chains Bos'n put on them. Such screechin and screaming I never heard. It took two Marines to keep thems separate them from the men in the brig. They calmed down, some, after a while.

Mr. Chips was all over the area and, "Scuse me, Captain," tryin to fix the bulwark. Next was some Real Bad words to his mates as to, well, bad words, "Scuse Me, Captain." Engle had him, Mr. Smith, seated on pillows, blanket, and about coddled him like his first born son. He could not get him to go to his cabin.

Mr. Smith, gray, said, "QM1, you are drippin blood on My Deck." I had put that silk neckerchief to me thigh. 'Doc says I have big feet, where most of my blood is, Commander!' No one, not even Mr. Smith likes me jokes.

I passed out about then and woke up to Doc Johns pouring that acid to me leg wounds. Nice guy. Personable. "Lucky you plucked out

'Most of the Wood,' QM1. Oh, rest will just come out in time." Me arm to his desk and more acid to it. Such nice words of, "Oh, easy ones." I got acid, cut, splinter out, to the next one. I was last on his butcher bill so I got good treatment. Slow, and painful. He'd sown up me head gash afore I woke!

We met the last Frigate off Algiers with Admiral Taylor aboard. Mr. Smith was still too hurt to go over. Admiral came to us. Fitz had the "Action" report already written. Mr. Smith said he remembered little of happened. As the whole fight lasted not 10 minutes, it read like our "Captain" had directed the action, "till he blacked out, relieved by Mr. Pontus."

Oh, I got a visit from him also. Admiral Taylor. I could only say, 'Yes, the Captain made all the calls.' Got his bad eyes, I did. It was no direct lie! Mr. Smith called for the sails, gave the helm that order to Starboard. That Mathew and John were down, keeping the helm over, well, no more orders were needed!

We got here, Gibraltar, yesterday, 15 July, right on schedule. Oh, them prisoners went over to the Frigate. Word around was Admiral took them into Algiers and saw the Sultan. It took some time to hobble to that first bar I go to. Phoebe, beer tender, said the scar on me head just might improve me looks. Oh, everyone laughed! They never laugh at me jokes.

We be stuck here for a few more days till the Admiral arrives. I got liberty as I want so, only me money is that problem! The other is hearin. I was standin there at the helm indicator when that explodin shell went off. I have to say, 'What,' a lot. People should learn not to whisper at me!

By Your Leave, Missy,

An Old Salt,

IN THE YEAR 1893, 12 AUGUST: ATLANTIC CROSSING

Dear Miss Judith,

Yes, your letter went in the Packet that came in Monday, 17 July. Admiral Taylor was right there at the same time. I got mail, Thank you. There was an officers meeting aboard that Frigate. Mr. Smith is feelin a bit better. He just walks slow, like me. It was about that ship that blew up. No, none aboard died from our little action. Lots of splinter wounds. It seems the ball that hit the poop exploded and took out 3 feet of railing. Mr. Smith, it seems, got hit with most of it.

18th, July, we had a big ceremony aboard with all dressed up. Admiral inspection and Promotions. It seems Fitz had saved me list. Yep, Bothel to 1st class and Wagner to 2nd. Now they can take care of 'Their Own' problems. Lots were on that list and now more Petty Officers than we need. Mr. Hanna was promoted to Lieutenant. That surprised him. Shush. Commander Smith will get Captain stripes once that action report gets to Norfolk. Mr. Pontus will get Commander stripes. An admiral bird said so. Admiral gave out them good words, letters to about all. Me? I got a note from Admiral to see Doc. Shush. I have to see him daily for "Miracle Medicine!" It is for the blood loss and to prevent another attach of Gaul fever!

When we get back I'm supposed to get leave to see you and MaMa. So why am I writing? Been through this 'Denied' afore. I hobbled me way to that shop and got that knife and marlin spike. Only me interested in them. I had to 'Register' them with Mr. Pontus and have me orders stamped three times for, "Personal Weapons." Don't ask me. Just like with them guns at home.

The 19th we left Gibraltar with a "Dignitary" to take to Azores, Bermuda, and Norfolk. A nice guy. Politician. He spends more time in a hammock than botherin us. No sailor leggs. Ya, both of thems. Bermuda is a nice place. Ptui on Azores. It smells of sheep. 'Scuse me.' The new minted Lieutenant is bothering me to use the Chart Table.

27 July, I smelled the Azores a day afore we anchored in llha de Sao Miguel Island, Punta Delgada, again. A barge for the dignitary

and gig for Mr. Smith. He still walks odd. I warned that new Bos'n 1st about money. It was George, Pete, them 3 strippers in the gig. Oh, it took all afternoon for that meeting. No, I smelled the sheep sausage and took the other. Bos'n 1st was lookin hard at us gigs eatin, sippin, ah, colored water. I gave that cute waitress a Silver dollar and nodded at them misfitss. He, He! Two ss's as was more than one.

Afore this, when the weather was nice, Ambassador McKnight got to sit at the poop rail, in a chair. He is still not a good sailor, watched the crew do 'Boarding Practice' drills. He asked about officers and Mr. Smith caught up his ear. "Oh, Understand, Captain."

After that place, most splinter wounds had healed so Gunner got to demonstrate our guns. Oh, that butcher bill was 36 with splinters, broken bones and such. The 3 strippers? By the time we got to Gibraltar they was playin monkey in the tops. We set McKnight to the poop, and put 4 old barrels to a distance to shoot at.

Mr. Smith wanted to do three turns. Well, come the time he yells out, "Prepare to about ship!" Ok. Whistles from Mr. Pontus and Silvis and before, "Ready" comes, Mr. Smith yells out, "Helm Full To Starboard!" Petty Officer 2nd Little, yes promoted, froze at the helm indicator. The correct thing. I jumped there and yelled, 'I Have The Helm, Captain! Orders, Sir?' Pontus and Silvis yell out, "Ready, Captain," about then. Oh, I got more evil eyes than Forest or Taylor ever gave me.

Well, them 3 strippers and Mac, promoted to QMSM, just kept lookin at me finger in the air, twirling around. "Helm full to starboard, QM1." Me finger hit that piece of iron and I held it there for them 3 full turns. Gunner and crew just banged, banged them guns to no end. Me eyes and Mr. Smith never turned from each other that whole time. No test of Will. I was awaiting orders. Mr. Hanna yelled out, as hard to hear, "Back On Course, Captain!" I got, "Helm amid!" McKnight just laughed and clapped to the ruckus.

The day after, I get Mr. Smith at the wheel. Oh, he had a time with it, not asking to take it. I kicked off the wheel stop and he about took them spokes to the deck. There be lots of pressure on his side. By the Binnacle light I caught his bad eyes, "I should Mast You And Little for not following orders!" I said, 'Could. But not with Mr. McKnight aboard.' I wrinkled me nose and said, 'Might look bad, Captain. Orders read to watch over the crew and ship safety.' I still got bad eyes. 'Turn before the sails handlers are ready and the sails get blown out by the sail holes, Sir. Makes Ya look bad, like dirty laundry flappin in the breeze, Captain!' He didn't correct me to them being, "Clew Holes."

Mr. Smith didn't like that we'd be in Bermuda the late afternoon of 3 August, 93. I don't make the wind. Oh, I got lots of desires to man the gig and barge. Capt'n to former and Ambassador to other. I said each crew member had to show a Silver Dollar Liberty, to be aboard. Well, there was grumbles about that dollar and less to choose from. BM1 Bothel chose his own 12 man crew. I got BM2 Wagner as Coxswain. Yep, 3 strippers, George, Pete, and QMSN McFeature. I reminded Bothel about costs of berthing in Bermuda. Now, his crew.

It was 4PM, to you, when we rowed away from the ship. The gig had Mr. Smith, Mr. Pontus, and me people. The barge had the Ambassador, Marine Saltsgiver, 6 Marines and 6 crew to row, and Bothel. No, was no Red Sky in the night. Still light out. However, last night I briefed, 'that the Barometer was rising, Fast. Winds from the North tomorrow.' I got no words.

It was a pier to see. Brit Marines, Governor, staff, and all. Mr. Smith to it, barge tied up, our Marines over and Bothel piping to the stomp of us and their Marines. Off this procession goes and I see that flag up on the Governor place go straight south. I told George, Pete, Mark, and John to check on rooms. They know the places. I point to the flag to Bothel and get, ah, "We be back by hammocks down, QM1." Equal rank now, so, it ain't me worry, sorta. He forgot about no goin back after sunset. Not into a North wind.

The governor staff took good care of us. We went up to the kitchen for evening supper and refreshments. Water. Bothel and me sat at that same bench and watched the ship out there in the water. Oh, the Governor gave a fine dinner, which started at 8PM. The sun be setting, lamps lited around, and the party went on. About then Saltsgiver came and said we'd be spending the night.

This Petty Officer, Brit, took my gig crew Silver dollars and exchanged them for Brit crowns. Bothel, crew, and Marines? Saltsgiver and Pontus had to ask the governors assistant for funds, "to lodge the men." Well, them Marines and Bothel crew. Bothel got to assign men to guard the boats for the night.

Edith yelled out, "Got Company, Alfa!" It was no surprise as George, Pete, Mark, and John had already been there. Alfa sure made a fuss with each one. Oh, she kissed thems, to lots of red faces. Me? She caught up me face in her hands, turned it side to side and said, "All them scars remind me your Uncle Curtis. Ugly that he was!" Oh, that got lots of laughs! Beer all around and I, at the bar, got whiskey. Edith and me turned in about 10 PM, to singin, and laughin, such to hear down the street from the locals and the gig crew carryin on.

I let the boat crew sleep in till 6AM as I already knew about the time the governor place got awake. Eggs, sausages, tators, and Alfa givin winks and eyes to all them crew members. No, I didn't ask what went on. I just remember red faces and bein shy. George and Pete included. The 3 Strippers? They never looked up to Alfas rubbin their head hair, sayin something, like MaMa would, to tease us boys. I ain't sayin more.

At the pier I saw such a motley crew as I'd never seen. The barge crew and the Marines about looked like they'd slept, well, in that barge. It was the first time I'd seen Marines look so rumbled. Bothel and Marine Saltsgiver gave me, crew, bad looks, us being so cheerful. Nope, not a word from me. I did need to shush me crew up, some.

It was not till 10AM that McKnight, Capt'n, and Mr. Pontus come to the pier. A quiet row back to the ship. Aboard, well? I got to stand afore the Capt'n as he said bad word to the barge crew as to how they looked. "Pitiful," was the least he called them. Me? He threw thems out and I got the next words about, "Taking care of Ashore Crews, QM1!!" Yep, two exclamations. Twice said. Marines? Thems got to march around the deck, in nice uniforms, for 4 hours. BM1 and me had some words of understanding. Like, 'When I say Silver dollars, No one goes over without them.'

It was when Uncle Curtis came to live that summer. Shush. Some afternoons or evenings he'd take me with him to them saloons, till time for bed. Come time to pay he reached up into that blouse and come out with cost. Nope, never reached into his pockets. He said, "When they roll a Sailor, they go for your pockets. He! He!" He showed me that cloth around his midsection, with pockets. A finger to one and out came a Liberty. 10 cents.

I had one, there in Bermuda and could have paid for both crews, 'cept I warned them. It was good that we rowed back that next day. I can't predict the wind all the time. Now, ifn we'd have needed to stay another day, then I'd have paid. I always some gold coins in me hidden vest.

The Packet Ship had been there and said we'd be stopping. The town ain't that large. Alfa had been to the Governors place and said she would take in crew at half a crown. That Petty Officer Brit thought that was excessive so, the barge crew got the Flop house for half, of half Crown he allowed them.

At the evening brief, of course, Gunner wanted to shoot the guns, "One last time, Captain." Mr. Colligan wanted to do another boarding party exercise as the rest of the time would be to, "Pretty The Ship!" Mr. McKnight asked if he could participate in these activities. Gunner said he'd be glad to have him pull a lanyard on a gun. I jumped into this and said I'd, 'Personally show Mr. McKnight how to use a weapon, Captain! McKnight is not an "Officer' Sir!'

Gunner made sure Mr. McKnight didn't get his toes run over when that gun recoiled. Such a grin on his face. Mr. Smith was not thrilled, but clapped at his excitement. Guns stowed, Mr. Colligan started his stuff with the crew. I got two wood halberds, 6 feet long polls with axe and spikes at the end, for him and me. For a time I had Mark and Mac do play attacks with swords, so he could see me hands. I used mine left handed. Oh, it just came natural to him. The thrust, catch the sword, back real quick, and thrust again.

I had McKnight and me defend for the attach stage, on the left flank, Port side. Now, most just rushed to the center and tried to hack their way through. So, come the attack, he'd get a sword and I'd stab the opponent. Just repeat this a bunch of times till we were actually behind the attackers and just stabbing them from behind. Mr. Colligan just grinned from ear to ear at us. He called a halt the attack. McKnight sure had a grin. Oh, we had to do three Hurzays for Mr. McKnight! Mr. Colligan came to me, slapped me on the back and said, "I always thought you was Left Handed, QM1!" Capt'n? I got only his bad eyes.

Mr. Smith seated, that Pilot and jackass tugs tucked us all nice and safe there at the North side of the South pier, Wednesday, 09 August, 93, in the afternoon. The whole thing was lined with carriages and people. Admiral Forest was first to be piped aboard. I recognized Squadron officers and none after that. Thems could hardly fit all in Capt'n cabin. OUT? Oh, we got all them officers inspecting us up and down the line. Saltsgiver would salute, turn, me and Nichol would salute, and follow ahind them Admirals and Officers. August and hot. We sweated there through this. Come the podium and drippin more. Came long words as to our, "Fine cruise."

First off was those ship company on leave. Next came Doc Johns list. 15 for evaluation at the hospital. I said some got broke bones and some bad splinter wounds. Me 10 'Volunteers' were last. I will say Gunner, Mr. Chips, Mr. Colligan, Mr. Hanna, and Mr. Pontus made sure to thank us.

Marine Lieutenant Saltsgiver and Corporal Nichol lined them 10 up and the first song they sang was the Marine Hymn. Oh, the looks from all. Last off the ship and I got Warrant Silvis there to salute and an invite to Friday dinner at his place. I looked down that pier and hoped to see Mr. Smith inspecting the lines. Maybe a discrete word from him? He weren't there.

It was not till Friday morning, the 11 August, that I got called in to see Admiral Stevens. Mr. Stills has been ignoring me request for leave. I got to sit as was just him and me. Real social able he was and asked about MaMa. Oh, no need to go on and on. There was a stack of letters there he gave me, one at a time. First was from the Susquehanna officers. Nice words about the volunteers and me. Last, from Mr. Smith, he read to me. It was like them words Admiral Forest said, comin to greet us in the brig aboard Monongahela. Fine words for a bunch of ragged sailors.

So, he put down the paper and asks if I was the last wounded to leave the Navigation deck. 'course I was. Capt'n Smith called out the orders for battle? Yes, he initiated the action and returned to the deck afore the ship blew up. True. Refused to go below, though obviously in distress. 'We could have just picked up that chair, but, yes.' He picked up a letter and read, "Would be honored to go into action with QM1 and his volunteers, at next occasion, Admiral." I was told to return after at 1PM for another meeting.

I got to go back to his office and had a "Visit" with Admiral Forest. Well, Forest, Stevens, two more admirals I ain't never seen, Captains and all to fill the room. From the ships log, yep, one from the ship, I had to go over the times, jinxing, other ships position and all I could remember. It ended to all thems dismissed, but me. Forest finger said to sit. I had to laugh as I looked around to see if my siblings and Dog were there. It was like PaPa's voice.

The first question from him, just him and me, "How is your Mother?" Fine, from her letters. "Why did you jinx the ship?" To keep the other ship off guard, hoped they miss with the chasers, 'And work us up to windward more.' He asked about Mr. Smith. I don't lie to Forest, so told him I told Smith it was a buffet in the wind. I said the quarter galley went over the side as it was a small bow wave and the aft end didn't move much, to his bad eyes.

Out came a letter Admiral Stevens didn't show me. It was from Ambassador McKnight. No, he read it. A true politician the Ambassador be. The only ones left out were Cook Fiscus and Old Tom, the cat. The words just flowed along and give pleasure to ears. The last part was his pleasure at getting to, "Fire a Fine Navy weapon of war!" The 18 pounder. "And, the delight in QM1 and myself, defending the ship, in time of Crisis." Boarding practice. Out came me order for leave, from his hand. No dates on it.

Right here he shouts out, "CLERK! PAPPERS!" Now Admiral Stevens, his clerk, Mr. Stiles, Fitz, and who knows in the room. That blue service record, me used one, and a pen come to that desk. Still his real bad eyes and, "Well, QM1! Time to decide if you extend your enlistment or, go home and be a farmer?" Oh, I Forgot. That time of year!

I put 1 in the box and signed me name. Forest, Stevens, Mr. Stiles sighed to witness. I looked at the paper for those who signed from afore. Came, "Return to duty, Gentlemen." All jumped up and out. The last word didn't apply to me. His eyes to me and over comes a 5 dollar gold coin. "Take your," and you don't want to hear them words for us, "out for a night liberty one me." Oh, never argue with an Admiral. See, the volunteer orders have that cost taken care of. Shush. That Gold went under me blouse, for the future.

I put this to the Post on Saturday, 12 August, 1893. Hope to see you soon.

By Your Leave, Missy,

An Old Salt,

IN THE YEAR 1893, 30 OCTOBER:

Dear Miss Judith,

I got your letter, Thank you. Yes, it was a joy to see you when I was on leave. And, you didn't squeal on me letters. MaMa is such a worry wort. She still refuses to go to the "Hooligan" place of PaPa's relatives. Him, Uncle Curtis, and hers also. There was lots of fun nights at the "Founding Fathers" meetings. It seems they meet more often when I'm there. With the scars on me face I have to tell of our 'Fight At Sea!" The same looks from MaMa, goin and commin.

It was still two days going and two getting back. MaMa met me at Cresson and went to Ebensburg to stay the night there. The change was more children. I put the pocket bottle to that lemonade as boring men and a cackle on that porch. I found them navy recruits there at Cresson station. No, a different guy. The same boring sights up and back. Yes, trains are best for travel. I spent enough time on them to know.

Old horse was still there. PaPa uses him only to go to the Blacksmith shop. He has a new filly for the long distances he must go for work. Old horse pulled that little buggy around to close places MaMa took me. I tied him down in the corrals to talk with horse there. No, I couldn't pull out me pocket bottle for the lemonade.

We did that long haul down South. Old horse would never have made it. The new one just pulled along. I finally got the name of Princess father. He still looks sad. His mother yelled it out when he did something. Benjamin John. He helped with settling the horse and asked where I'd been. Nowhere new. Oh, there was lots of new children around. The family is growin. A couple years and thems will be in the pond, like we was, long ago.

I got back here on 1 September. MaMa said I was bored and should go back. After that place South, well, even she got bored tryin to visit. We'd seen about everyone around. No, no women in distress or such on the trains. I looked around and found none! He! He!

I have me little room on the barracks second floor and liberty when I want. The Beer tender, Ella, is tryin to get Harrold sent aboard a ship. Is a joke atween us. Maybe! Oh, they have their moments. Don't ask me about their love for each other.

Warrant Silvis, well wife, Regina, still tries to set me up. Most Fridays or Saturday nights I get invited for supper. Fitz is there some. I wonder where she knows these women from. The local business, I think. Me problem is our ships schedule. We are supposed to go to the Caribbean in November. Not much time to get to know someone. Oh, nice women. They like the Sea Stories! Me thinks Regina has me, us over for Silvis evening company.

Doc Johns told Squadron, Admiral Stevens, that Mr. Smith was slow in healing up, from about being blown apart! Oh, Admiral Forest had promoted him and Mr. Pontus when I was on leave. It seems Captain Smith got ill at a celebration party. Forest and Stevens was present. He was bed ridden, as I heard from Fitzsimmons. Commander Pontus was temporary Commanding Officer. No problem as the ship is pier side till the end of October or November.

It was Monday, 18 September, 93, that Admiral Stevens and Lieuy Stiles came in all dressed up afore noon. Fitz neglected to tell me, that at Noon, a new Commanding Officer of Susquehanna was to be installed. "Not our ship. Not our concern!" True, sorta. It is not goin anywhere or loadin out and no requests for men.

That afternoon Warren Silvis caught me ear with him havin been relieved as Bos'n. It seems, "New Commanding Officer had brought his own Ships Bos'n, clerk, Coxswain, and such." I said, 'Not my ship. Not my concern!' To tease him I said, 'Carney,' a local squadron supply ship, 'needs a Bos'n!' No one likes me jokes.

Friday, 22 Sept, afternoon muster, I got my usual and Marine Saltsgiver there with 10 from Susquehanna. "Bos'n threw them off the ship." Bothel, Wagner, George, Pete, two Oldsters, fore masters. 3 of me 3 strippers and another lookin like they got into a bad fight and lost. Bothel said new Bos'n had them, "Race the Mast. Last down to get a beating." His hand up to, "We tried to stop him." That was when I noticed George and Pete had head wounds.

I told Captain Saltsgiver his medical type needed to evaluate all their bruises, 'Just so I can't claim you beat them, Sir. I need that report to give to Mr. Stiles. Soon, would be nice, Sir.' He gave me bad eyes, looked at his charges, as he had to provide beds for them.

The Romp and Stomp of them Marines marched them away. Those from Fran and Carney were in the barracks. It only holds so many. It must be that time of year for throwin sailors off ships and send them to Squadron to be reassigned.

Saturday and Sunday I got more from Susquehanna. A couple gunners and storekeepers. Unusual. Monday morning, the 25th, Mr. Stiles didn't like me new list of people under his command. His eyes sure got big when I handed over the Marine medical report of Friday's men. I saw the Marine Major put a little note along with it. Oh, I'd already read it. There was some Fine Words to give to the Admiral.

In return, I got his daily work list of things that needed men. It seems Carney, Fran, and Susquehanna wanted the same type of men, that they threw off. I said, 'Usual work detail orders signed by the Admiral. The men are not gonna volunteer to sign on to these ships, Sir.' Came, "Fitz, get in here!"

Saltsgiver, me, and two marines took men to each ship. Comes Susquehanna, well, I had 4 Marines as escorts. Susquehanna Bos'n was not happy with, "Captain to sign, Lieutenant," from Saltsgiver. There was words atween them and that "Romp and Stomp" of the Marines. We turned arounds and we made it to the brow when this Bos'n agreed. Somehow, I got to present the list to this Captain, in his cabin, with Saltsgiver and Bos'n there.

Behind that desk is an older Captain, that looks as sick as Mr. Smith was, two weeks healing. Three piles of papers around and his clerk looked no better. I said about volunteers, Captain, and, lookin worse, signed and says, "Another Paper Works Left by Captain Smith!" Well, he just might as well as spit.

I, ahind him, can see stores lists, requisition list, for new stuffs to come. His clerk had more papers in his hand. 'Captain, I have a ships clerk that has done this before. He's at Squadron, one of my men. He could help out with the paperwork, on a daily basis.' I got a mean look from him. 'Daily basis, mornings or afternoons, to help out. I need him to keep track of Squadron men, but.' Fitzsimmons had been a bit uppity, lately. It will give him something to occupy his time.

Bos'n was a different problem. A big voice. Shouting stuff and stompin his stick, to make a point. Saltsgiver Marines gave him two romps, stomps and he could only be up at the Poop Rail. Bothel and Wagner bein there just might have set him off. 'Sir, you say what is need to be done and My Men will do it.' Oh, me and Saltsgiver stayed that morning. Bothel was forward and Wagner on aft work party. I threw in the gunners just to get some work out of them.

Back, after lunch, I dragged Fitzsimmons with me. Oh, such words he had. Not his ship, not his concerned. 'Be friendly. Help out the clerk and be nice. I have your liberty card!' Well, that settled that. And, it was only for part of the days. I still needed him back at the office.

Friday, 29 September I went aboard to Mr. Hanna, the former Navigator, now 1st Lieuy, at the Starboard side of the Poop. That Bos'n was grumbling, at Port side. Oh, Hanna just had to go around and get saluted by all the former Susquehanna volunteers. I got to meet the new Navigator, Ensign Curry, fresh minted by the gleaming gold on his bars and hat. Come the end of the work day, well, Captain Stutter comes out and said some nice things to me volunteers. It took Fitz till that morning to get the papers all organized and signed.

Friday evening me and Fitz was at Warrant Silvis place for supper to two new ladies. He grumbled the whole way there till he got introduced to his evening partner, Zoe. Mine be Carrie. A nice women. Fitz took a shinnin to Zoe right off, as the same age. I thought Regina bribed Carrie to be there, at first. No, no instant spark but we could talk.

Monday, 02 October, I be in front of Mr. Stiles and give him the new list of Squadron men available. Sunday morning me and Fitz put names to Carry and Fran. No, J.E. Williams wasn't in, to see Skully and company. George, Pete, the 3 strippers and the other wanted a change of ships. I don't ask. Fitz scratched up orders for them all, real nice. By the time I was in front of Mr. Stiles, well, Marine Captain Saltsgiver was marchin thems to the south side of the North pier. Both ships are to leave on Thursday tide.

Stiles said me list was short. I divided up the men as requested by Fran and Carry, which came Friday. Admiral had already signed them lists and the men gone. Oh, such looks when I get handed a list of men Susquehanna wanted to, "Sail with The Tide on Tuesday, 03 October." Oh, no QM1 requested nor a ships clerk! To his looks

I just said, 'I can get volunteers but, Marine Saltsgiver has to be in charge of them and signed aboard as his charges, Sir!' His mouth moved twice and heard, "Fitzsimmons! Get in here!"

A work party of some men were there came their underway that time. I sat on a bollard at the end of the pier to watch this getting underway. I was watchin that channel buoy and Captain Sutter at that Taft rail. Came that moment and my mind shouted out, 'Cast Off!' That buoy moved North and Captain had still not moved. Too late, he give the orders and me workers helped throw off the lines.

Oh, there was words to hear all around. Susquehanna yard arms hit Fran to that stick pounding, somewhere, and shouts from poor Fran. She was last ship on the North side and took the brunt of the hit. Foul words was on both ships Poop decks. Susquehanna lost some outside yard arm belayin lines and Fran about beat up her side wood with them spars to push her off. Poor Sutter just stood there like his world had ended. But, eventually his ship did get into the channel.

I don't know who gave the order but Susquehanna turned counter clock wise and the bow hit the pier and the bow sprint end hit the building on the North side, where ships stores are warehoused. Oh, I just heard that stick on the Poop Deck and Saltsgiver Marines doin a romp and stomp. Not me ship, not me concern. It seems Captain Sutton forgot to order them Jackass tugs. Most especially what with the contrary winds.

Come Thursday, 05 October, I was on that same bollard and watched Susquehanna come back down the channel. Silvis was there, "Nothing better to do." It came on the front of the incoming tide, with much sail. The bow hit the pier end of the South side of the pier. Silvis and me got their hawser over a bollard and some spring lines over so it didn't end up down river. I heard lots of words, that cane from the Poop deck, and the Romp and Stomp of them Marines. There was no happy faces at the rail.

Come slack tide the ship made it to the actual pier and Saltsgiver slammed that volunteer list to me chest, as I was standing at the end of the brow. His charges, now mine, sure sang that Marine hymn real LOUD down that pier. They was there, in ranks, as that Marine

Major went in the Admiral building door. Na, me ears are too blown out to make out the actual words he said.

Oh, Fitz and me took the evening down on the strip to see Ella, the beer tender. I put Gold to the bar as me 'Volunteer' were there, at me expense. The words I got were to no be heard by you. It was an interesting voyage. Saltsgiver, in charge of the volunteers, had repeated words with the Bos'n to the extent Bos'n couldn't step but so far on the main deck. 1st Lieuy, Hanna, about put the Bos'n under charges. I wondered they made it back to the pier. Bos'n and Hanna had some words about mooring. I never knew Hanna knew about sails. He'd called for reducing them, up river, to be over ruled by Bos'n. It was an earful of stuff to hear.

Friday, 10 AM, Squadron place, saw more gold stripes than afore around. I stood there in front, with Corporal Nichol, as me men went in to this proceeding. I don't know why I was there, other than for my men, as all got called, but me. Bein October, so was not as hot, but I hate just standing. At 11:30 Nichol marched us to lunch. 1 PM, after lunch, and was just me standing outside that building, as ordered.

Squadron Clerk jerked his finger to me to come in. I go into Admiral Stevens room to, only Admiral Forest ahind a desk. I got his finger to a chair in front. "Well, QM1, what happened?" I wasn't there was not to be said. So, it took some time to say what I observed, aboard, and the men sent to Squadron, just said the facts I knew and what me crew said, to his cold eyes. I mentioned the Bos'n stick and Saltsgiver warning him off the deck. Bothel and Wagner knew their trade and sails. 'Just tell them what was wanted and it would be carried out, Admiral.'

'Captain Sutter was sailing like he was going to a Frigate anchorage down in Portsmouth. At the front of the tide, drop anchor, and turn on the tide, like a war ship. 'Cept, it is a supply ship to a pier, Admiral.' I still got his eyes only.

"Captain Sutter is a good officer. He left a lot to ships handling to his Bos'n and 1st lieutenant. The 1st officer, ah, declined to follow him, QM1." Well, flags went off in me mind. "Court Martial, this morning, found him not negligent in duty."

Fitzsimmons already told me, over lunch, what went on. Marine Captain Saltsgiver gave bad words to ships Bos'n actions. The Marine Major brought up past items of men assigned and physical conditions. Mr. Hanna had some words for the ships movements. The new navigator had no idea what to do. The romp and stomp of the Marines kept that Bos'n off the deck and from hitting men, as I heard.

"Captain Sutter, whom I know personally, is a good officer. Just relied on his ships Bos'n, too much, to sail. He needs a good Navigator to look after the safety of the ship and men, QM1." I gave, 'Former Susquehanna Bos'n, Silvis, would like to exchange with your Warrant Office Bos'n, for a change, Admiral,' to no good nor bad eyes. 'My Squadron Ships clerk, Fitzsimmons, being a Captains Clerk, needs to be a 3rd class, Admiral,' to bad eyes from him. I just stood to him standing.

The new ships bos'n is Lunger. A BIG voice. Silvis introduced us during load out. From the Poop deck he sounds like he is next to you on the foredeck. Not kidding. Silvis gave him a whistle to try. It is better than his voice but drives me ears crazy.

Fitz got advanced to 3rd. Ya couldn't wipe the grin off his face for two days. He wrote the "Volunteer" paper real well and hid more stuff in there than I thought possible. Admiral Stevens just put his name to the line and handed it over. Fitz is about heartbroken that we are leaving with Susquehanna. He is sure is fond of Zoe.

Last night, 26 October, I got to take last liberty at Ella and Harold place with me 'Volunteers." No, the Admiral paid this time. It is in the orders. Nichol and Saltsgiver was invited. We had a right good time of it.

Sea chest is aboard to just a small bag for stuff in me room. We will miss the cold and snow, bein in the Caribbean. I will miss some, but not the cold. I date this as 30 October, 1893, and drop it in the mail goin to Squadron to muster the volunteers.

By Your Leave, Missy

An Old Salt,

IN THE YEAR 1893, 26 DECEMBER: CARIBBEAN

Dear Miss Judith,

Monday morning at Squadron is always hectic. Weekend tally's to address and letters from all over. Muster by Corporal Nichol was of, "All troops present and somber, QM1." Two, in the back, just went face to dirt about that time. Nichol just said, "Ah, present, QM1." They snuck off base and got back early. Nothing unusual.

We didn't go aboard till the afternoon. Come 10 AM, to you, well, Admiral Stevens gave them some fine words to, "And a fine Hearty Shore meal before I send you to your ship!"

Somewhere after this Fitz come up with 4, 1 Strippers. New from Boot Camp. Crew calls them, "Fresh Meat." They know nothing and get the brunt of lots of jokes. 'Add them to the volunteer list. Add two of the Oldsters to be their charge.' He gave me a bad look as the Admiral should sign them onto the ship.

The Marine Major led us down that pier to Susquehanna. After the other Bos'n issue and beat men, word was he wanted to personally have the men signed for. It was a formal affair. The crew was lined up, us formin up in front. Captain Sutter, Major, Saltsgiver at the end of each line of men, and back. Sutter and he signed three sets of papers. Done! Them Marines romped and stomped the Major over the side.

I mentioned to Mr. Hanna, now 1st Lieuy, about a 'Brief' of getting underway on Wednesday, 01 November. I don't need to worry about ships on the North side of the pier but. The ship was fully loaded out and three stakes lower. That is the planks on the side of the ship.

Afternoon of the 31st all ships officer are in Sutter cabin. Line officers to Starboard and the rest to Port. A status thing in the Navy. Gunner, Mr. Chip, Armoror, Purser, and Mr. Hanna give a report of ships condition. Sutter was like he'd never been at a brief afore. He looked like a rat given 5 kinds of cheese to eat. Last was me and Ensign Carry. I give time to the outgoing tide, expected weather, winds, and all on that report. Times were 'To be Determined,' including that

'North Wall' current. He never heard of it! My saying the time for tugs got his attention. I got just his "Sniff" and dismissed.

It was Fitz who said Mr. Sutter wanted a, "Private Meeting In his cabin." No such thing aboard this ship. I caught up Captain Saltsgiver to be Me Aide de Camp. Oh, I just said that Saltsgiver and I had no secrets. He would catch me up ifn I said incorrect things, 'To You, Captain.' I smelled a trap for me words. Sutter said, "Good. Two birds with one stone."

Sutter went through me service jacket and over the "Volunteer" paper real good. "The Board of Inquiry, about our leaving and entering port, said our Navigation staff was lacking." Admiral Forest said Court Martial, but. On to, "I like a well disciplined ship! The Board felt the Bos'n was, ah, harsh with his training." Marine Major's letter said more than that. "QM1. Squadron, as you are most senior in Navigation, assigned you to the ship." I thought Admiral Forest about ordered me aboard.

His eyes to Saltsgiver and, "Bos'n and you had some words, about the men assigned." He and Mr. Hanna. "I asked for another marine office to be aboard. Your Major," he about spit the last out, "stated I accept you or he would be aboard for this cruise, with adequate quarters for his rank." So much for being social. "I had to accept you as the ship could not accommodate him."

Saltsgiver, a Marine, saluted him and turned on his heels, gone. I about made it to the door and got, "Someone, I don't remember who, said if you're are asked a question, proper, you never lie." I turned to that. Only Forest knows that for a fact. I got, with a smile, "I heard you don't like a stick used for discipline!" I just nodded and said, 'Good Officers Lead, from the front. Men recognize it and follow. No need for a stick, Sir.'

"The volunteers yours or mine, QM1?" I said, 'Old Navy saying is, "A hand for the ship and one for the Mate, Sir.' He knew the words. 'Men sign onto a ship 'cause they like the ship or Captain, Sir.' Came, "I hear they only signed on because of you!"

"I hear you can take this ship out of this pier, down the Norfolk Channel, turn to the Chesapeake Channel, to the sea, without tugs, QM1?" Forest, again. 'A good tide, trained crew, and good winds, ah, possible.' I got, "Today, QM1?" I said, 'You put that as a written order and I'll try. No guarantee, Captain.'

01 November, 93, Mr. Sutter sure didn't like sittin on that chair on the Starboard side. The usual Pilot just gave me a wink as them 4 1 stripper yelled out his helm orders. BM1 Bothel helped Lunger with the sail whistles. BM2 Wagner stood with Mr. Hanna handling the aft sail and spanker. Ah, back at sea again.

The next problem was Engle, ship's Captain Steward. Sutter brought his own and forgot his cook, or the cook refused to come aboard. Either way, Engle got, in writing from Fitz, to do the cookin, cleanin, as a Steward only knows about serving and worshin, which worked out well, sort of.

Once in deep water I had Armoror bring up me speed and current weights. Mr. Chips brought up the wood thing he made for the bulwark. Bothel and Wagner had the yard men rig the halyards to yardarms. Lunger just stood by. The entire crew, nothing to do, was there. Sutter called for Top Gallant sails to get us South fast. Winds of 25 knots, even for a lugger, the speed log said 10 or so knots we was makin. I worked on them weights as I showed 11. I gave the time to that current and the crew just about to normal business.

The crew eats at 5 PM and officers at 6. The Captain calls for his meals when he feels like it. The skylight said Engle laid out chipped supper ware and an old mug. I'd come from the smokin lamp, to be at the Chart Table for that current. All hands were there, in the dark, as it gets dark early. A North wind, Top Gallants, and it was like a stage performance, set, and waitin for the curtain to come up. Fitz warned Engle, who took the wine off the table.

The Marine struck that quarter hour bell and be darned if the bow went straight West. The wind caught them sails and next we be slanted at 20 degrees. Through that skylight I saw Sutter Steward reach over him and grab that chipped dinner plate. Well, the mug, butter cup, and all but his plate got thrown to the Starboard side.

Now, the Bos'n didn't care for the crew cheering. His whistle and the belaying pins got pulled out, so the ship came on even keel. Sutter came out on deck like a bear was chasin him and, oh, the words he yelled out. He must have thought the ship was sinkin under him. Mr. Hanna yelled out from the Poop rail, "Just the North Wall, Captain. On the Daily Sailing Report, Sir."

And, ya be sayin I set him up for this, Captain Sutter. No. I warned him and had Fitz find that book about the current, in ships books, right there, at his hand. Oh, the officers to his cabin and words to us ya not want to hear. All got dismissed, 'cept me.

Oh, fine words about Captain Mast and such I got. "Any Words, QM2!" I said, 'Pardon, but it was in the Daily Sailing Report, Captain.' That got me evil eyes. 'The entire crew knew of it, even Engle, Sir. Please consult Marine Captain Saltsgiver about Captain Mast, Sir. I'll be in the Ships Brig, awaiting word, Captain.'

I got me hammock rigged to them rings and settled when Mr. Hanna comes to bother me. The Marine guard didn't bother to lock the door, so in he walks. "QM1." I said, 'QM2, by the Captain.' From Hanna, "Well," and gave me bad words to me health, character, blood line, and more that I remember. Finally was, "Your Duty At The Helm!"

The Poop men deserted when I caught up that helm. Ya got a light forward so men can see the foremast. One amidships, so can see the Main and a Binnacle light to see the compass. I saw stars, like home, and that ships wheel in me hand. I figure I'll be leaving when we get to Nassau De Bahama's. I never saw that figure 'ahind me.

"Your orders are to take care of the ship and men, QM1." Captain Sutter. 'First orders of a good Petty Office, Captain.' Came, "And your Captain, QM1. I heard someone said him also, QM1."

Well, I tied of this round about Who is Who. 'Admiral Stevens orders say ship and men. Admiral Taylor is in the Med, Sir.' I got, "Admiral Forest said you would try my mantle, QM1. This experience did that. I told Mr. Hanna to be more forceful, at times, to get my attentions in manners affecting the ship and men."

There was no good light to see his eyes when I said about knowin their names and stations. Givin good words to them, bein on deck to watch them. 'You have a good ship and crew. Lead them, encourage them, and they will follow you, Captain. Else, Saltsgiver walks off with 30 men. 15 for discharge and medical reasons, Captain.' Just a shadow went down that ladder.

The next problem was Sutter gig crew. They didn't mix much with the crew and didn't do much for the ship either. Ate, slept, and sat separate. Bothel and Wagner got no good words from them, tryin to be friendly. His gig lead, a BM2, objected when I assigned them to 'Waisters' positions. "Don't scrub Decks. Captain Crew." Come time for meals, well, Warrant Cook Fiscus told them to, "Eat with the Captain!"

Yes, I was in front of Sutter for that. 'Ship's crew, Captain.' Assigned, by me, through Sutter, they got week of thems scrubbing the forward, port, and Captains heads. Then I assigned pumpin out the ship ballast deck. Soosh. Mr. Chips would open the underwater Sea Cocks to put water in the lowest hold, that the pumps ended in. I had them man them pumps three times a day. 'Don't want the ship to sink, Do Ya?' Come time, BM2 thought scrubbing decks was OK. Helpin with the sails and Bos'n stuff was better than cleaning the heads or mannin the ships pumps.

We had the evening brief for Nassau on 09 November. Mr. Curry gave it. He just had to read from the sheet of entries we already went over. I had a map of the place on Capt'n desk. Indifferent winds got us here, comin South. I recommended we anchor off the light house by no less than a cable length, about 3 hundred yards or so, and a barge and 12 to row. Nor Easter gear to be at hand for all.

Now, I don't know ifn Captain has been here afore. He wanted to go into, "Inner harbor. Close to the Governor residence. Gig only and weather gear not required." I took the paper from Mr. Curry, scratched through those spaces, wrote his wishes at the bottom and gave it to Mr. Curry, who handed it to him. I saw us stuck in that Inner Harbor for a number of days. The crew would like that. Sutter said he'd, "Mind the wind and decide in the morning."

Come 10 November, afore lunch, we set out the forward anchor with a ketch and dropped another ketch aft. The lighthouse be 600 yards astern. Oh, some have nice rollin waves. Sutter called for his gig. Engle handed him Nor Easter gear, which was refused. He and gig crew got drenched not 50 yards from the ship. Nope, no foul weather gear aboard.

Was brave, drenched men who rowed Sutter back through them waves. It took some time to reach the ship. Drowned Rats would have looked better. There was a trail of water from the quarterdeck to Capt'n cabin. Oh, Engle just gave him sweet words as to his condition. I didn't know Engle could make him feel that bad. No, no liberty and two days for the wind to shift, to up anchors.

• • •

George and me got lots of liberty in San Francisco, February, 1885. We was not a member of the ship's crew. The ships old crew going and new members were commin aboard. Such activity. We could walk off and on as we pleased and about walked through two pairs of shoes, we did. We never went outside the Army Presidio without BM1 McCoy. The wharfs, piers and places close, we never went near. Go into a bar there and ya wake up on a ship to China, ya could.

Best was we got caught up in mail! Oh, I got a postal card from MaMa, in Anchorage, delivered in that Army dispatch pouch. The next was in Sitka when we was goin south. Another Army dispatch pouch, to Mr. Lydick hand. I read the letters and postal cards over and over and caught up about a year from home.

McCoy did take us to the outside of that China town area. It was something you'd want to see. It looked like the Chinese world got transplanted to here. Street venders had charcoal stands, on wheels, and cooked up stuff you'd wonder what it was. All them different smells in the air. The ally's so crowded with people, not wide ones, and full of shops and more food places. Three story high buildins and their laundry all hung out to see. 'Course, all were in Chinese garbs and talking that language.

On the outside board walk, McCoy had us get little snacks. It was grilled, bread wrapped, or at one place we found a vender that almost made Talig kettle, muscle, and root boil. It was a paper cone he put that kettle stuff to. Oh, Hot! We got wood sticks to pick out stuff. Best was to just take a sip and get a bit of the muscles. Oh, I still remember that taste.

It was Friday, 27 February, 1885, that Mr. Lydick bought us our orders. That cable length line, range finder, and sextant went to a box Mr. Chips made. I asked about a compass and time piece to no answer. The ships Armoror said the Trapdoor rifle and pistol was mine and George's. He made up a box for each of us. The rifles was broken down, to make the box small. He divided up the cartridges to each of them and sniffed at the bird shot stuff Talig showed us how to make from brass we shot. We only used them shells when a rabbit or ptarmigan, like a grouse, was spotted.

Mr. Lydick was to stay a bit. Mr. Dias, yes, from the bear, got to escort us back to Philly. Well, eventually. The orders, he read, said we was to stop in Kansas City, Kansas, board a, "Navy procured Vessel, Proceed up the Missouri River to First waterfall, at Pierre, South Dakoda." Between, well, "Verify the River Depths, Location, and Note Anomalies found." We got a 4 inch roll of the river Charts, each, and "Only 500 or so miles long." Oh, Lydick gave us a smile and got handed us 5 new log books apiece.

Sunday morning, 01 March we headed for the ferry to Oakland. Mr. Dias hired a wagon for our stuff. He had two sea chests and stuff. George and me put in sea bags, the box with sextant, and our boxes of guns. No, he got to ride in that buck board. At least we didn't need to lug that stuff around. It would have taken two trips.

Luckily, the drover to take the wagon on the ferry and hauled our stuff to the train station. Boxes and guns went into the baggage car. Nope, kept our sea bags, we did. We got them into our berthin room to, three high, again. We put the locks to our bags and got escorted to the, first, stinking, coach car! Cheap tickets again with last lunch and luckily I had, shush, in Oakland, filled up them pocket bottles. It was strong enough to kill the water and food taste!

The land to Sacramento is just flat and the Telly poles was the only thing goin by. We got there just afore dinner time. I hoped they loaded on some good food. I was wrong. The same old tasteless stuff the pocket bottle fixed. Dias said I couldn't sleep early. We all had to sleep at the same time. Soo, I stuffed meself into that front seat corner, blanker over me, and hugged that sea bag, a pillow atop. No damsels in distress to cuddle to. I gave the steward 2 Liberty's to put some fire to the stove two times. It was March and still cold, at night.

The train got us to Reno, Nevada, the next afternoon. We made Salt Lake by the 4th and Denver on the 5th. Topeka, Kansas was at 10 AM on the 6th. All the meals were the same. Tasteless. Shush! In

Reno, when Dias wasn't lookin, I bought a full bottle, topped off the pocket ones, and sure hugged that sea bag because of that. It was just after noon we got into Kansas City. It smelled to high heaven 'cause of them cattle cars headed for Chicago.

If I thought any train station was a big place then this sure topped that. The rails just converged to more rail yards. We got to pass them goin to Union Station, Kansas City. Big, like Pittsburg. Dias went off to get the baggage as Weaver and I sat around. Dias comes back with a, ah, scruffy, older guy, who smelled worst than us. Yep, worst. Dias introduced him as Gay Lloyd, Captain of J. Garman.

Oh, he caught up a wagon for our stuff and we got to sit in the back of the wagon. Two horses took us over, around, right, left, and ended up at the Missouri River. Pier? No. They drove posts into the side of the river and put some boards atop. Oh, the gang plank was just that. Two boards, wood planks to the, ah, ship, or boat.

We found out it was a big tug. A 6 man crew of 2 line handlers, 1 coal stoker, one ships mechanic, cook, and the boiler man. Normally it hauled barges up and down this river. Bein a slow time of year they took the Navy offer to take us up this river.

We got, "The Grand Tour." More than half of it was the boiler/engine room. It was a warm and smelled of oil. The roof of this place had louver boards to let out the heat. It was just making steam to get us underway tomorrow. I didn't want to be there when the boiler was full up.

Main deck, forward, was the galley stove and table to eat at. The crew slept down one deck in a windowless, smelly space. Below that was ships stores. I didn't need to see either. Oh, we got the second story. Mr. Lloyd called it guest berthing. 4 small rooms. His room was in the front of the ship. Well, we each did have a port hole to look out of. I opened mine to air out the place. It needed the bedding aired out, like years ago. It did have a water pump, wash basin, and sit down place in the Privy. Water for the sit down place was a pail on a hook next to the pump.

George and me was forward main deck when came, "Eats is UP!" Not 15 steps to the door and by the time we got there the 6 crew was around. We had to wait for second serving. A plate of stew, thick bread, and butter. I asked about salt and pepper and cook, McGinity, gave me bad looks. I just said I liked pepper!

Round that same table we tried to "Make a plan" for this "Mapping" thing. We sorted out the Charts order. No real Chronometer so we had to rely on the Charts for Latitude and Longitude. No books for sunrise nor set nor stars. Ya can't put "Big Tree" as a reference. It came down to good points on the Charts, distance, and angles from thems. Two deck hands could do depth of the water.

So, our "Venture" started at the base of North and South railroad bridge on the Kansas River. A place that never moves. The tug could about go up on the bank of the river for us to use its compass and the range finder for distance. We shot the Noon sun to set the ships clock time in the log. We used one log book for daily notes. Come after supper we was around that table to set all things proper to the log and verify the Charts.

The first day was slow going to get things set. By the time the sun set we made it but 20 miles upriver. The Dang river was like a snake in motion. Only 480 more to go, that day. Dias had the Chart up on the bridge to see where we was when the lead man called out dept of water. One marked the dept while other, and Cook, fished over the side.

Best was to see a named creek. Ya can use it as a reference point on the Chart. I said the Missouri winded around. Some measurements might have been off, a bit. Noon sun shot said the ships clock drifted with Mr. Lloyds winding.

We tie up in Omaha, Nebraska. The crew was about to mutiny. Ah, they ran out of beer and stuff to kill the taste of the bad river water. Dias did take a blind eye to George and me bringing a hogs head of cheap rum, each, aboard. We didn't notice his. It took a day to load on coal.

Now, to supplement the coal, we'd tie up to a bank and do some work on a snag of a dead tree or one that fell over. Me and George could do some cutting with a two man saw. Gloves was required. Mates, Donahue and Lewis sure could split the pieces of a trunk up. The first time we hit a bank, George and me put on our pistols, to the Capt.'s looks. We saw some local deer but, out of range of our pistols. Next time he gave big eyes to them 45 carbines.

Come one day and we got 4 deer over some, watchin us. George and me ducked ahind that trunk and put the carbine sights to them. Two went down and two jump over and looked around. The Cooks stew was better. It just needed more salt and pepper, to me getting his evil eyes. We was getting tired of fish stew, that needed lots of pepper.

The tug stopped at Sioux City, Iowa for repairs to some worn iron parts in the engine room. No purser for pay so no saloons for us. The mercantile store had hogs heads, so we stocked up on real cheap stuff. Rum, whiskey, or local stuff was fine. The trick was to put some water in a bucket and let stuff settle out. The clear water on top went to that empty hogs head. Clear was a sorta thing. We filtered that through cloth we bought.

Oh the hours we spent at that table with charts and making out that log. A break was sawing up them trees or rowing the boat to places the tug couldn't get to the bank. Best was to see some deer way off and trying to hit them with the carbines. Sometimes we got two or three shots afore the deer ran off, or we'd hit some.

• • •

Ifn ya be wonderin about this Caribbean cruise, then go back and read me other letters. Be the end of the second round and in Barbados for some shore time. I spend most time at the bar where the woman has those boyfriends on the Frigates. Such stories she tells.

It took the first round for the crew to come together, volunteers and gig crew. Mr. Hanna now has the foresails and jibs. BM2 Wagner watches him, over his shoulder. BM1 Bothel is watched over by Lunger, on the Main and Aft mast. The Navigator, Mr. Curry is doing well. I stand ahind him during evening briefs. This last round, well, I didn't need to be there. Capt'n Sutter still gives me the eyes.

First time here in Barbados, I called for barge. He didn't like that till Mr. Johns, doctor, Navigator, and Mr. Saltsgiver needed to talk with their opposites here. After that he took me words at my Evening Brief.

Sutter has been out on the deck lots. Oh, even after inspections and such. No, no Capt'n Mast, so far. The crew has been civil and the Marines catch up those that might be tipsy or looking or trouble. No, Sutter hasn't caught me up from behind on the Poop. It is almost too perfect a cruise. Well, 'cept for somes in Cozumel. That little place off the Yukatan we get some days ashore. Shush. Some got rowed back with "Food Poison." Doc even said so. It was the fruit in that punch they drank. Castor oil and three days pumpin water cured that!

The venders in Cartagena, Columbia, know our schedule, so have extra for the Purser to buy them vegetables and fruit. We did some hull scraping and Bos'n stuff in that little bay where ya get fruit punch and them pollo or jambo corn rolls. Trujillo. We got water in Puerto Rico. Sweet water, it be. No, no Spanish Frigates are around. I wonder about that. The Packet arrived so I sign this to you 26 December, 1893.

Hope you celebrated Christmas real well. Have a Happy New Year!

By Your Leave, Missy

An Old Salt,

IN THE YEAR 1894, 17 FEBRUARY: CARIBBEAN

Dear Miss Judith,

Capt'n was in no hurry to leave Barbados. Only 3 frigates and lots of time to find thems. Oh, no worries about tide there, about in the Atlantic Ocean. We left the morning of the New Year, 01 January 1894. Happy New year to you.

I take first head of the line for lunch. That way I can relieve the helm so they can catch up with their meal mates. No need for Little or Mac so I sent them off. Next I got Mr. Sutter ahind me. It is never good, us alone. Come to me ear, "QM1. Why is it I haven't had a Captain Mast since we left Norfolk?" I said, 'You had your chance with me, Captain. The crew heard of it so are on best behavior, Sir.' Came, "And, the fruit poison, Fore master in sick bay on his birthday, and shall I go one, QM1."

Well, I may have not mentioned stuff, to you. Things goes on. 'You'd need to ask Dr. Johns about sickbay and his medical opinion. Mr. Saltsgiver or Corporal Nichol know about Liberty stuff, Sir!' I hear, "Admiral Forest said any ship you go aboard, Masts are few, QM1. Is he correct?" I said, 'I don't know about other ships, Sir. A good ship and crew is all I know.'

He came to the Chart Table soes to look at me. "Why have no volunteer come to me to sign on, QM1." I gave, 'First, Captain, you haven't asked them about that.' Oh, no words to that. Second,' and give him a cheeky smile, 'You haven't shown them a test of your mantle, Captain.' Oh, that got eyes. 'A good ship, good crew, fine voyage, but.' He didn't like that, 'But.'

'The crew didn't take a shinin to Captain Smith till after that time with that Arab ship off Africa. He came up not good from sick bay, but sat, commanding the ship. A couple signed on as crew. Most knew he'd be replaced in Norfolk.' I couldn't see what a man is thinking.

'Some who signed on were the ones your Bos'n threw off the ship. Makes the men wonder, Captain.' He asked, "And you would have defended the men from the Bos'n, QM1?" I said, 'Best you should ask Admiral Forest about that, Captain.' That challenge paper be only in that "Formal" blue jacket. That, and some others.

Armoror, Mr. Colligan has had boarding practice often as the crew is bored. Mr. Mack insists we fire the guns once a week. Capt'n looks on as the guns fire, with no interest in his eyes. He watches Boarding Practice. He takes interest when I and Mr. Colligan practice. I know Armoror moves by heart but got that padding on to play along with him. No, no officer allowed over that line. He asked. Denied by Armoror. Capt'n asked about this at an evening briefing. Colligan said it might, "cause some concerns to the crew. Regulations, Captain. No!"

Ya say Colligan allowed it once. That was when I shot them two officers with the wooden pistols. Yes, I did that after I swore to Colligan I would not hit them. I Didn't! Oh, he gave me some bad words for the trick I did. It is allowed, by the rules.

• • •

It was a week in Sioux City, Iowa for repairs. We caught up on the Charts and logs. It was too expensive for much liberty. Mr. Dias had our cloths laundered. It cost him extra as the lady said they smelled to high heaven. Last, is me word for it. He had to buy us new skivvies. No, they were beyond boiled worshed. She, ah, had words for thems we showed her. He bought some soap type powder for us. The tug looked like a laundry line for the airing out of bedding and all from our rooms. Clean water to a bucket and we scrubbed down our rooms. Yep, ceiling, walls, and floors to the wood. I kept that Port Hole open for the new smell. We left on 10 April, 85.

I know you like names of places or towns. Well, that shore line was empty of those till Yankton. That doesn't mean we wasn't busy. Left, right curves like a snake that river was. Sholes, islands, and places Old Lloyd took to the bank ya would have not thought.

Tween Springfield and Santee it was like a marsh. Only the helmsman, Lloyd, knew the main channel through. We marked the main river on that Chart. Two pages of angles from, no, not "The Big Tree!" Anyone reading our angles and stuff would say we was drunk. Rivers change, over time.

After thems we stopped in Williamson Gulch. It was on the Chart. The town was Pickstown. Old Lloyd wanted to on load coal. There was nothing much to see 'cept polls sunk into the bank and boards atop. A boy was there to take orders. Given, he ran off and sometime later a wagon of that stuff shows up. The coal was in sacks. Oh, no, the line handlers and coal stoker, Shaffer, got that job. The ship had a pole, cross member atop, and line attached. Ya turns it and the cross member goes over the pier with a hook on the line through halyards attached. The hook snatches up a bag, up it comes, turn pole so the cross member is over the ship, and lower that bag into the hold. The dangdest thing I ever saw.

Some mile up river was a left hand turn in the river. Boat over, Weaver, me, and Dias to steer, went to the north bank, set a pole for McCoy to get distance and angle. I had to dump bilge water, so I went through the brush, for privacy. I turned around and not 50 yards away are 2 deer lookin left. Two was staring straight away. One had its head and neck turned to me. There wasn't much of a rise in the land, as the carbine was level, and I shot it. It went right down.

Eyes on that deer, I got half to it when George and Dias caught up with me. Oh, the deer was wigglin so shot it with my pistol. We carried guns when off ship to the land. George elbowed me and pointed to this open field. There was 4 men on horses lookin down at a horse, layin in the grass, and this man standin over it.

Next, I heard a clatter of yelling and whoopin to the left. I could see a couple men with something in their hands, oh, just shouting. It was Dias that said, "Indians!" Oh, I went to dirt, flipped up that tang sight and moved it to 300 yards. I didn't know if they was friendly or not so I put the sight on the lead horse nose and shot. That horse jumped 3 feet in the air, came down, and switched ends. Gone!

I reloaded and told George to shoot in front of the next horse head. I lined up, like afore, and shots went off as one. BOOOOM! That horse came up on hind legs, straight up, and fore hove's just a pawin the air. The rear ones was stompin the ground to run. The front hove's came to dirt with the horse facing around. Well, it disappeared.

That brush was just alive with heads moving. I couldn't count how many was there for the movement. I do know thems sure raced in the direction the first two horses went. Me eyes saw movement in the field and here them 4 horsemen had swords out and was racing to that brush. Dias started the next excitement.

He got us ahind him and he walked to that downed horse and man. Not 20 feet from this and he got rigid and salutes. Weaver and me do the same and got such a flurry of bad words for it. Oh, just mean stuff. When his left hand crossed to his pistol, well, mine came out cocked, and pointed. I weren't just gonna stand there and be shot. This guy sees my gun and his hand went off that gun of his.

I have been chewed on with words afore. Especially in Boot Camp. Well, they couldn't put a match to this guy. Dias made me holster the pistol and called this guy, "Colonial." It is an Army word for a Captain and they walk off to talk. I went over and looked at the horse. That big bullet hit smack 'tween the eye and ear. Oh, for sure it was dead when it hit the ground. I shot the deer in the neck muscle, it went straight through, and hit that horse.

The 4 Army guys came back with two skinny young boys no older that 16 or so. Their arms tied in front, rope around neck, and tied to the saddles. One was an Army Captain, Navy Lieutenant. The second one had upside down marine stripes. Sargent? Anyway, they talk to this Colonial and hold up a Winchester repeater, like Talig had, and a shoulder belt of cartridges. Those got that officer attention.

The Colonial did come over to us, to our salute, and thanked us for drivin off the, "Indian War party." His eyes was as hard as a rock. He looked back at his dead horse, to us, and walked off. Dias quick walked us back to that deer, picked it up and into the boat. We made quick time back to the tug. Dias never said a word.

Me and Weaver just started to take out the innards when Cook McGinity comes out with two knives and his meat cleaver. Oh, we was terrible at this, he said. We retrieved two pots as he did his butcherin. He used that coal contraption to hoist it up. He put salt and pepper to the hide, now his. It was a site to see how he cut it up. The clever took the head off right at the ears. He said, "Oh, neck stew tonight!" It was better than Navy provided salt mystery meat.

Captain Garman then come and give us bad words for, "Blood On His Deck!" We had to scrub it with big bristle brushes on long wood handles. Oh, the line handlers provided the water, from the river. Two scrubs later I got some of that stuff we used to clean the rooms and sprinkled it about. It was the first time that wooden deck saw daylight in years! The rear deck was so clean Lloyd ordered us to clean the fore deck.

After that deer neck stew, with added salt and pepper, we took to the Chart and the smooth log for the day. No, no thanks from the crew for fresh meat. They grumbled when we didn't shoot a deer each day. It came to, 'We chart the river and not be a hunting party!' Anyway, the Army guys was from Fort Randall. It was close by.

The river widened after that. Read, slower goin and more angles to put to paper. It had a little creek here, big creek there, and more stuff to shoot then, 'A big Tree!'

We made that Chamberland, South Dakota, place on 24 April, 1885. There was on loading coal and I heard a 'Bad' noise below. A broke engine. It was not much of a town. A couple saloons, one mercantile, and a Blacksmith shop. The Blacksmith and engine mechanic, Yohe, had a time fixin the problem. The only thing louder than the bangin was them words they used.

Oh, we did laundry with that soap powder. It worked real good. We caught up on the Chart work and did lots of fishing over the side. The Cook came up with strips of cloth dipped in bacon grease. We caught some ugly stuff he called, 'Mud Cats." They didn't look like a cat but had a muddy taste to it. Oh, the crews thought they was in heaven, for the big slices and not stew.

We left there 24 April and went past Fort Thompson and after Lower Brule the river about turned on itself. We could see where we was goin and then where we'd been. After that was just days of angles, distance, put a stick to a bank, row back to tug and so one. Oh, if we hit dirt I'd look around for deer. We didn't see many. I hated that salt whatever meat Cook cooked.

It was 15 May, 85 when we hit Pierre, South Dakota. It took two days to Chart the islands, shoals, and such around that place. That was the biggest town we hit, asides Kansas City, and Omaha. I didn't mention Omaha as we only loaded on coal, at a mud bank.

Mr. Dias escorted us, and seabags, to the first laundry, bath house. Yep, new skivvies. The worsh lady just threw ours in the fire to heat bath water. The bath woman took one look at me and Weaver and we took first bath in 3rd used water and got fine words from her when we got out! We left a ring in the water for her to scrub out. Next was fresh heated water. I got all soaped up, brush to scrub with, just leaning back, she comes in with some course brush, and shoos us out. No modesty is a sailors first name. We got her bad eyes and towels to dry off and wear.

The mercantile was right there so we just used towel to pick out skivvies. Dias paid for a course shirt and cheap pants for us. Oh, it came out of our pay, later. He listed it to our charge sheet. The same as a hogs head of cheap whiskey to take back. That water is still hard to drink.

Capt'n and crew took that Saturday and Sunday of to relax. Read that as get stinkin drunk, both days. The Cook? He lay in 4 hogs head of whiskey, and then joined thems. Oh, me and George could cut up that old meat and make a stew. The ship had cans of vegetables to add. A little salt, some pepper, add some flower to thicken, well, Talig muscle boil tasted better.

We left there 18 May, 85. Lloyd was in no rush to get us to Kansas City. The head of steam just enough to go 5 knots. Come his thought, he got anchor over the side and tied to a tree on the bank. Me and George would go on land to see a deer. At sun down and we were back aboard. Especially down to that Fort.

We asked Dias about getting off in Omaha, Nebraska. It was right on the river. No, Kansas was on the orders. So, we just sat wherever and watched that river bank go by. We'd go to the bridge, bored, just to see where we was or fished with the crew. We caught little. Them mud cats like to sneak up on that bait. No sneaking at 5 knots. They had to swim for it. Didn't.

May 26, Weaver and me did laundry with that powder. The tug looked like a laundry shop. We packed up the carbines and pistols to them wood boxes. Oh, we put that line, range thing, and sextant to wood afore that. No need for them. If we ran aground, well, the Chart said where we were! Broke down was another issue. That maybe why Lloyds had the tug goin slow.

Come the 28th, McGinity gave us fried tators stuff with bacon and eggs. That came aboard at the stop we started our laundry and ate that breakfast since. I guess he wanted us to say what good food the tug served. We tied up to that same pier and seabags, wood boxes, and all to that shaky pier. A drover and wagon was right there. I asked him how he knew we was commin? He drove up and down the land path and met ships that tied up, to see if they wanted a wagon.

Unlike with MaMa, there was no hugs and kisses from the crew. Ok by me. We got a wave. Mr. Lloyd and Garman did shake Dias hand. Gear loaded up and off we was to the Union Station, Kansas City, Missouri. I think. There weren't no line in the dirt to tell.

We got to that station, sssllllooowwwlllyyy. That drover horse was about dead on its feet. We tied up at around 10 AM and by the time we got to that station the Noon train was loaded out. So, we had to wait till 4 PM one.

Brickell, the ship, didn't pay us out for the time aboard. The Purser gave us a small portion of our pay, to go on liberty. He gave us the same when we left the ship. The Army post Paymaster stamped our orders with, "$5 Dollars Paid." That ran out in Pierre. We hit Dias up for some cash to send a telly home, when we was to arrive.

That Station Master about spit on that Navy Script thing, but. Weave and me got $1 cash to hand and, spit, 5 of them Navy Scripts to use to get to Philly. It was 1o cents to send a telly to home station. "Kansas Stop," shush, less than Missouri, "Home 30th Stop Last Berg Train Stop." This was a guess on making it by the 30th, but for a train broke down, Chicago?

There was no better sleepin stuff on that train. Meals? No salt or pepper on that table. It was end of May so just a blanket kept me warm. I was saving money. Ahh, train travel.

We got to Chicago at 7 PM on the 29 May, 1885, and just got the last sleepin berth on the 9PM train to Pittsburg. Not mine. Theirs. I slept in the front seat of that stinking coach. I figured that train stopped at every turn of the track and got woke to all them stops, yes, in the night. We got to Canton, Ohio by 1 PM on the 30th. That was Weavers stop. A hand shake to him and, 'See you in Philly.' I had one month leave by me papers.

Pittsburg station was at 4 PM. Whew. Me gag and box to a dolly and I got a ticket on another train to home, through Blairsville. I saluted Mr. Dias and stepped onto that train. The sun set on them mountains as we got to that station. It was the last train for the night. The milk train. See, it goes up to Home, Pa, for the night. Come 4 AM, it returns back to All them places to pick up milk and goods for Pittsburg.

At 8 PM, that 30 May, 1885, I got off that train on the North side track, as we called it, to Ma and Pa under that coal oil lamp at the station. Whew! Home! Not 30 minutes later I was stripped to naked and cloths to a wash tub. MaMa was kind enough to put water to the stove earlier. It was too cold for a bath in that horse trough. I worshed, scrubbed, and got a drop of Lavender oil in. Pa gave me some of his old cloths to put on as I had grown, a bit, in that year. It was Saturday, so got to talk around that table till 10 PM.

• • •

Oh, this Caribbean Cruise, ya ask. After our last conversation on the Poop, the Navigation deck, Capt'n decided to be personable with the crew. He just stepped right on that deck and, well, caused a near riot. The crew was working stuff so buckets of water hit the deck as the sailors had to salute. A man at a belayin pin forgot to let go of the line and got about heaved up to the yard arm. Another saluted and fell down the Amidships ladder.

To save lives, hands, and heads, Capt'n would mention to an officer when he was to walk around. That officer to be at that "White Line" and shout, "Attention On Deck!" Those not doing something dangerous would then salute him. After that, "No Saluting!" By the end of the 3rd time around he was accepted, to do this. He was startin to learn most of their names.

This last round, well, all was goin good till he decided, as we was ahead of schedule, the crew could get some liberty in Cartagena. I'll say the officers grumbled at that. None had been there afore, 'cept for the Purser and some of us. To that pier only. "Oh, the crew has acted so well at the other places. It would be a nice, different place to visit."

It was two days of liberty afore crew was condemned to the ship. There was a dozen men in the brig and Doc was takin care of a few. Doc got the cuts, bruises, banged heads, and such. He had some he couldn't figure out. Not drunk, not sober, just passed out, of sorts. It was a drug he had a bottle. Too much and ya about die from it. The locals in Cartagena put it in rum and get high. Well, drink like a sailor and about die.

I was there as that grate was rigged. Oh, Bothel had that Cat out of the bag. No, no officer can touch an enlisted and vice versa. It was him to do the service, only. Each got to say his piece. Me and the officers to add. Sutter would have given 6 lashes to each, 'cept, half were Volunteers.

Into his cabin I got his words to me about the words written in their orders by Admiral Stevens. He couldn't flog just half. Oh, was "Admiral Mast," me and my people. He said lots of fancy words to me not fully respectin him. He didn't like me Sirs. Well, ya can't say Capt'n twice in the same sentence. Plus, some other little stuff.

All got bread and water for three days. "To eat, and sleep in the brig when not doin duties." Duties was scrubbing the deck, pretty up the fancy work, cleaning the heads, and little stuff. Doc said, "No, no hard work for bread and water, Captain!" Sutter sniffed at this. A riled up Doc is no one to cross, lest ya want to end up in the privy for most of the day. His medical stuff do that.

The last Frigate was in Barbados for liberty. It is about the end of last round. The last time Doc, Mr. Saltsgiver, Mr. Curry, and Capt'n could make a report to the Brits about this place. No, no general crew liberty. The Petty Officers got to escort small groups off for a few hours. It is an Island so them Marines was all over the place, watchin.

All aboard 06 February, Capt'n comes to the Chart Table and on the Caribbean Chart draws a line from Barbados to Puerto Rico and the Windward Channel. No stop for water in Puerto Rico, with no explanation. Not a big problem. We got water for a month. Ok by me. After the islands we'd miss, it was open Caribbean Sea. He ordered, "Top Gallants, and All the sail for best speed, Mr. Lunger." I thought he wanted to make it to Norfolk early.

It was 08 February, 94, just after noon meal and the lookout said of sails ahind us. No, no top flag. The Spanish have one, like we do, up there. Mr. Curry informed the Capt'n, who come on deck. "Commercial ship. Keep a watch on it." Came it bein hull up the lookout said it be big, like the Spanish Frigate but, still no flags to be seen.

The officers are havin their meal about then and Engle was settin up Sutter's table. Mr. Curry goes to the Capt'n, who gives it a glance and, "Commercial Vessel, Mr. Curry!" The ship is 5 miles off and more sail than a normal ship. So, I have McFeature fetch Gunner, Mr. Mack. Oh, he was mad to be bothered at his meal. He takes one look and down he goes to Capt'n cabin. The skylight showed Mr. Mack about ordered Capt'n on deck for a look. Well, Mr. Mack gave some bad words to his, "Commercial Vessel." On deck, the Capt'n said, "General Quarters. Officers to Taft Rail!"

The Marine range that bell and it was like some on yelled skunk. Up come the crew from below and at stations. The officers to Mr. Sutter at the Taft rail. I caught, 'Unload balls. Bolts. Canister for the 9 pounders at range, Gunner. Mr. Colligan, boarding party assemble. Bos'n, fighting sails. We don't need to light up the lower coursers." 4 one strippers to the ships wheel, Poop set, so I went see Mr. Colligan.

Oh, he was expecting me. I took the Breaktop, loaded it, to left side holster. That sword Colligan had reground went to the right side sheath. He gives me a wink. Them two Gauntlet gloves and vantbrace (steel covered protectors) went on. That guy in Gibraltar gave me them for a small price. Mr. Hood, Chips, put in new leather and such. A big thumb sized cartridge to that carbine and I was up on the Poop.

Sutter turned and had some eyes as I said, 'Boarding Party Ready, Sir! You need your sword, Sir.' I got, "With those iron gloves, you must think you are a Knight, QM1." I said, 'I don't like to get cut on the arm, Sir. Your sword, please!' On with, "With the iron gloves, I doubt you can shoot and hold that, ah, whatever."

I have Mac hold out his hands, broke the pistol, and empty the cartridges to them. I put rounds to that gun from the belt, while watching his eyes. Fine leather is in them Gauntlet gloves. The pistol? Bothel made a lanyard, tied to the gun, to go around me shoulder. I put it to the holster. Left hand Gauntlet, as what it is called, caught the handle of the bird caged sword and out it came from that sheath. Mr. Colligan made the cage from brass and shined it nice. I point it at Capt'n and said, "I'll be on your left, behind, but, You Need Your Sword, Captain!" About that time that ship signaled us with a bow chaser. Woke up all thems, it did. I saw the smoke afore that ball hit well aft and they heard the BOOOM.

Well, it was like that gun never went off. The 9 pounder gun crew was set. Capt'n was at that Taft rail as gunners on deck reloaded them 18 pounders. Gunner had that range finder at the rail and just lookin. The 4 at the wheel were kneelin, in case a ball came over that Taft rail. Me? At the rudder indicator, lookin at Mr. Sutter, and lookin at that ship. Nope, no jinxin in a flat sea.

I saw two puffs of smoke and two shots come either side of our ship. Gunner gets up and I hear, "9 pounders, Captain. At your order."

"Gunner, aft chasers." Well, there was no time to stuff me ears with cotton, not with them gloves on. Them 4 go off, one at a time, and the Aft lookout reported the splashes. The crew adjusts and, I just put leather to me ears. It still hurt me ears, them 4 did.

Capt'n said, "Reduce sail. Prepare to go about East." East wind, through the Eye of The Wind! The Bos'n called, "Ready!" Next came, "Helm to full Starboard! Fire as she bears, Gunner!" The other ship was slow to turn with us. Only the lookout Aft could say what hit.

Our 6 Starboard guns hit it right broadside, as we turned, at not 300 yards. Oh, we got a couple puffs from their guns. The officers will be usin the other quarter head. The bow chasers gave two more puffs above it.

Slug that we are, Bos'n whistle, and the forward 9 pounders lit off two round of canister. Slow, but round we came to the Port guns. Gunner waited, waited, and gave her that full side. The other ship never made it through the wind. Their whole Port side was done in.

We just waddled there, never moved. It was half hour till the lookout said sails on the horizon. From the North came a Spanish Frigate. The East one be ours from Barbados. It turned out we was the bait to entice a Pirate. She could sail faster than all thought.

We hit Nassau, De Bahamas on the 16th of February, 1894, Mr. Sutter called me into his cabin. No, Saltsgiver was not there. Cordially, I got to sit in front of his desk. "Nice weapons, QM1." Eyes and. "So, your duty is to the ship's Captain." I said, 'No, Sir. To the crew.' Oh, that got eyes. 'The ship looks to the Captain to lead them,' and more eyes. 'A good ship, good crew, good officers need a good Captain, Sir. Mr. Mack and Colligan are tired of losing Captains. I set my Boarding Station to protect you, Sir.' Thinkin eyes got me, "Dismissed, QM1."

I about made it to his door and got, "QM1. Are you good with that pistol and rifle?" I said, 'Very good, Captain.' He came with, "And that unusual sword, QM1!" 'I don't know, Captain. I've never had a chance to practice on anyone, Sir.' He said, "With." I said, 'Either way, Captain."

Armoror, Mr. Colligan, liked it with that brass "Bird Cage" he made for the handle. It balanced out the broad, broken off end, bein originally a Calvary saber. The broken off end was why I got it so cheap. No, I never tried it on deck. Some might think I was good at boarding practice.

• • •

It was that Monday afternoon, near the end of June, 1885, after that long trip South, that MaMa and me shot our guns. She had such a smile to hitting sticks. Her eyes also said she was bored, visitin, and said I should go back soon. I did touch up that afternoon lemonade with a pocket bottle, when she went into the house. PaPa and me did it on the porch, that evenin. She came out to our laughin and her bad eyes, then her laugh at us. She knew what we was up to.

• • •

The Gibraltar store keeper mentioned them other pieces he had. I got the knife, marlin spike, and all for a good price. Armoror just gave me glad eyes at that broken sword, and "Oh, what I can do with this, QM1!"

The Packet ship is here in Nassau. Purser is callin for mail. I'll Post this as the 17th of February, 1894, to you.

By Your leave, Miss Judith,

An Old Sea Dog

IN THE YEAR 1894, 28 MAY: SQUADRON

Dear Miss Judith,

Here at Squadron place. The same stuff is goin on. I have me little room, liberty as I want, muster men, and assign work details.

I got your letter, Thank you, and have caught up on Postal Cards and letters from MaMa. I get a letter from her when things happen, else, a card to say Hi! Elmer and Effie expecting another. Harriet and Marlin also. I wonder about Harry and Ruth but the first child comes when it comes.

As for practice with real cutlasses, halberds, or pikes, well, the crew get to hit posts that Mr. Chips puts up. For halberds and pikes, some stand with them cutlasses and the men with them poles are ahind them, like would happen. For cutlass to cutlass training there are, you'd say fences, to keep thems from cutting each other. We call it "Tink-Tink" practice. The fences keep the men apart far enough that only the swords touch. One thrusts forward and the other counters. They "Tink-Tink-Tink swords. It gives them an idea of how to thrust and defend.

Mr. Chips would take it aft, over that line in the deck, so the Middies, yes, we always have a couple, can practice. Mr. Hanna and Curry get to practice with thems. Capt'n Sutter asked if it could be positioned so the Middies could practice with the men. Armoror and Chips didn't like it but did agree. They had to adjust the distance tween the two and add arm padding, just in case. It is still just "Tink-Tink" of the ends of the swords. The men and officers thought this was time to try to hack each other to pieces but, the fences were too far apart.

Well, coming North from Nassau, Capt'n Sutter wanted to get some practice. He has a very nice, straight, dual edged, longer sword. I saw it when he was doing "Tink-Tink" with a Middie. He handled it very well. Come the time for Middie and crew Capt'n Sutter stepped forward for practice! Armoror and Chips was right there, watchin, as BM1 Bothel came to the fence. Sutter kept leaning over the fence to strike and got called for it twice and stopped that practice. Oh, such a look Sutter had. So, I called him out.

No, Armoror wouldn't let me wear me pistol, nor a wooden one. I put on the left gauntlet, forearm piece, belt, sword, came to that fence with a long brass belayin pin to right hand, and wood knife to the belt. Capt'n got to wear me right gauntlet and forearm piece. Each got padding to the offhand. We each reached out to adjust that fence. I allowed it to be moved so his sword could about catch me gauntlet. Not a problem as my saber had the bird cage. He didn't like that belayin pin but Armoror allowed it.

Oh, left hand in the air, French style, for balance, he thrust real well to me "Tink-Tink-Tink." He thrust again to, "Tink-Tink-Tink." The memory of me bein hit in Boot Camp came back. That Master At Arms about beat me to death. Capt'n was using them 'Classic' moves. The third time I came straight on to that fence, Saber and pin forward. He trust and leaned over his fence. The pin caught that sword, which I blocked away from me, and me saber hit his forearm. That is how far over the fence it was. Armoror yelled out, "Once, Capt'n!"

Sutter backed up, cut the air twice with his sword, left hand in the air, and does the same move. I hadn't moved and hit him on the forearm piece, again. Armoror yelled out, "Twice Capt'n!" Well, Sutter says the belayin pin, "is illegal!" So, I handed it to Mr. Colligan and pulled out the wood knife. Colligan said, "Again!"

Capt'n ain't learned and tries the same thing. I catch his sword, push it down, take that wooden knife and throw it right by his ear. Of course, he moves his head. Me saber came up, over, and hit his, me own gauntlet and forearm piece, real good. Armoror says, "Captain. Your arm is damaged. You are done, Sir." Oh, the looks I got from him. No, his saber was still held for a challenge. I thought he'd come over that fence! No, Armoror got tween us and once his sword went to his scabbard throat, as they call it, I did the same.

The log said we pulled into Norfolk on 26 February, pulled by them jackass tugs. The volunteer has thinned out on me list. 4, 1 strippers, and them 2 fore masters signed on. So 30 minus 6 is 24. 6 gunners, thrown off, signed on to Mr. Mack. Now, 18. 4 storekeepers signed on, now 14. Doc sent 6 to the hospital for ailments and bones. Just 8 of them got marched off by Corporal Nichole and Mr. Saltsgiver. Fitzsimons checked them to our list.

I'd already went and gave Mr. Mack, Mr. Colligan, Mr. Hood thanks for a good cruise. Doc Johns and me shared a shot of 'Medicine,' in case of diseases or my return to the ship. I decided I'd done enough time aboard so would find another ship. 'Sides, Susquehanna was headed to Philly for work. I have been there enough, enough times.

On the pier was Warrant Lunger. Oh, I gave him a right good salute and handshake. He leaned close and said, "Captain is checkin the Fore lines," points and, "He'd like a word with you, QM1." Oh, I see you roll yourn eyes at this as is another lie! No, he was at the head of the ship, hands ahind, lookin at that water. I saluted, 'Captain!'

I got not soft nor hard eyes. Just thinkin ones. "You didn't sign on, QM1!" I said, 'Can't till All my volunteers find a ship they like, Sir. Orders, Captain.' Came, "Exceptions can be made, QM1!" I shook me head. 'Time to move on. Good ship, good crew, and, Sir, Good Captain.' Eyes moved at that. 'AND, as I whacked my glove and forearm guard, my Captain was wearing, ah, the crew might think I was good at boarding practice, Captain!' I got a smile at that thought, we both did. "God help the next Captain whose mantel you get to test, QM1"

I still get invites from Regina, through Warrant Silvis, for Friday dinners. Yes, Fitz also, from Zoe. A nice couple. Me? Carrie comes. From last time, Carrie. Your remember Ellis? He was me Clerk 'afore Fitz. Silvis and he are aboard the Admiral ship. He is still heartbroken about that girl who threw him off when Forest set sail for a month, or so.

Anyway, Ellis mentioned Admiral Forest has him watch out for reports with my name in them. It seems Capt'n Sutter mentioned me in lots of dispatches. He didn't say good or bad, Ellis. He didn't need to. Fitz, my and ships clerk, already told me that good and bad news. Mostly bad. Oh, a fine list of, well, it is hard to say Capt'n and Sir in the same sentence, standin in front of his cabin desk. 'Nother reason to leave.

It was after that Pirates of the Caribbean action that men started to sign on. Most liked Lunger, Mack, Mr. Chips, and Colligan actions. All good officers. Oh, BM1 Bothel and Wagner too, with the sails set right to turn and all. All came together for that little action. But!

Uncle Curtis words came to mind after. I asked him why he came home to words of his travels about in ships, places. He gave me that ledger book of courses to places he'd been. I got a wink and, "Come a time the ship's crew come together and can sail on their own." A look and, "Ya train the quartermasters to sail, right proper." A swig of that bottle and, "They want you, but don't need you. Time to get a crew as green as a fresh cut spruce tree and sail to the South 40's, Laddie! East, to Australia." Maybe he got word of one of those. MaMa never said.

J.E. Williams didn't want me. Carney had a good Master. Fran, the next costal luger? NO! Admiral Stevens came up with, "Trading positions with QM1 on Shenandoah. "Same Class, same schedule. The QM1 has too much time aboard and requested a transfer." I didn't like the grin on his face. A trap to get me out of his area. I'd need to talk to this QM1. That got a big grin and, "Oh, Be My Guest, but, Done, QM1!" I never like his grin.

At the end of April that ship came in. The new rule is them jackass tugs be there to tuck ya into that berth. I watched this from that bollard. There was lots of activity aboard and more words shouted than I cared for. This tall guy comes to the Starboard Poop rail and looked about. I yelled out, 'George, where the (dickens) ya been! Been lookin for you all over the place!' I got, "Was shanghaied, placed aboard this tub! Been stuck here since!"

George was the last off the ship. We talked and walked back to squadron. I mentioned Susquehanna, Philly overhaul, and crew. He was goin on leave, home. 'Ya can go right to Philly from there. No need for that extra day on a train and such to here! Good Ship, Good Crew!' He gave me those eyes like I was funning him.

Susquehanna was to off load the hold and be right there. Oh, we had a good time down at Ella and Harold bar. A couple nights of it. Old times seemed better now. Aged, to bring out the flavor. Even the bad days seems less awful. I introduced him to Mr. Curry, Mack, Colligan, Mr. Chips, well, all. Goin back to Squadron he wondered why I was leaving the ship. That was a long story and why we took some nights down Hampton street.

Admiral Stevens was just smiling when George agreed to this 'Swap.' Fitz wrote out them orders real fine. He couldn't put in all them lines from me Service jacket, but, enough. Enough to cover him for most, 'cept killin the Captain! He! He! Me? The Admiral forgot the 'Volunteer' paper he signed. I still had 8 directly under my charge. Till they sign on to a ship, I have to watch over thems.

George stayed here for a week or so. No, not on leave. Liberty. Besides me, he has a woman friend. I didn't ask and he never said. A nice woman. She and I put him on that ferry to Hampton for that train ride home. It was that afternoon Admiral Stevens called me into his room. Oh, no smiles and such there. I got his bad words about, well, a long paragraph of them.

It was Admiral Forest big ear that brought me to that room. His ear is Petty Officer Ellis, me former clerk, his ships clerk, that told him I signed onto Shenandoah. Forest sent note of congratulation to him for his leadership.

Stevens tried to have Fitz write up the orders. Fitz showed him them 'Volunteer' papers, with his name on it, and pointed out that paragraph about, "Until all have signed to a ship, the contract remains unresolved." Almost all had signed on to Susquehanna. The problem was that Bos'n sent some to squadron and they became me charges, again. Some was on that original paper, The Contract, that is, and it is still valid. That is what got me them words. Holben wrote them, Ellis carried them on, to Fitz writin them in the volunteer paper. He! He!

Me work crews have been aboard Shenandoah for cargo hold work and preparing it for the on load of new stuff. It seems George wasn't the only one who wanted transfer. The Captain and Warrant Bos'n got replacements. The 1st Lieutenant went to a Frigate and the Navigator stepped up to his place. Admiral Forest threw in a Lieutenant as Navigator, to round out the Poop.

Bothel and Wagner, yes, still on me list, have been helpin the Bos'n and 1st Lieuy with whistle commands. The new Bos'n, I don't know where he came from, has a real soft voice. Ya can't hear him with a breeze blowin. He sure likes to use that whistle.

Don't ask me about the names of people on the ship. I got mixed up with them officers comin and goin. Sir, Captain, Bos'n, and such is respectful. Oh, Captain, Marine Saltsgiver and Corporal Nichol are assigned to the ship. Don't ask me. The Marines ain't not needed in Philly and that Major wants Saltsgiver off, somewhere, after him and Captain Sutter's words.

Fitz caught me up with the new Captain request to go to the Caribbean. It was 01 June to sail. I added a little note on paper to remind Forest about sailing on Friday. I was shown Forest reply of May 31 or 02 June and, "Tugs Required." It was Ellis that delivered Forest personal reply to me note. "Admiral says he is aware of Friday sails. He might be somethings but not Senile! Warmest regards." Ellis, I figure, add the last part. Forest never says warmest, well, maybe in a letter to MaMa.

To add to me list, Capt'n Sutter dumped some back to squadron as not needed. 4 Older fore masters, 4 mid masters, 4 gunners, and 3 Petty Officers who could lead a gun crew. The surprise was Engle, ships steward. Sutter and him got along like fire and coal oil. I just wonder who is gonna do the cooking? So rounds out me 20 or so.

I got the list of men needed for Shenandoah today. Capt'n McIntire he be. We have not been introduced yet. Nichol has him sign for workers. Good old Fitz mentioned about those I missed comin through Admiral building. Discharges, or time served. Stevens sign them out of service. Some were good men, with a long memory of some bad times aboard ships.

McIntire needs are close to what men are available. It seems he came from D.C. and brought no one with him. It will not be that 'Green Crew' Uncle Curtis talked of. More like most of the cruises I been on. A mixed crew. Good or bad, things are about set.

Carrie and I have taken walks most Saturday and Sunday afternoons. Yes, Carrie, from last here. My escort to Regina suppers. It has been nice weather and only chilly at night. She likes to hear of me 'Ventures,' varied that they are, as you have read about from me letters. We have had too small a time together to think of a future. Oh, I do like to be with her. No, she is no damsel in distress. Very head strong, independent minded, and only like me for the stories I tell. She asked if I might write to her. Oh, there is lots of time to write, there at the Chart Table, or at that smoking lamp lited. I gave no promises of 'High Adventures!'

I'll end this, here in me little room, shush, with a little night cap. No, no one can find me hidy holes. Tomorrow is Monday, 28 May, and who knows what I'll find at Squadron.

By Your Leave, Missy,

An Old Sea Dog,

IN THE YEAR 1894, 10 AUGUST: CARIBBEAN

Dear Miss Judith,

Oh, Shenandoah got under way on 02 June, 1894. The Tide? Them jackass tugs got tied up, aside, and no worry about that. The same pilot was there at the Taft rail, after Admiral Forest, Admiral Stevens, and lots of officer came aboard to say "Fair Sailing." It was Admirals and them officers that inspected me 'Volunteers' and the rest of the crew. Saltsgiver had that podium there so lots of words to us. Captain McIntire signed for our souls, three times. One to Squadron, one to ships logs, and one to me, that got that smacked to me chest by Corporal Nichol.

Come the time, I be at that helm indicator with 3 stripper Bosn's at the helm, Captain was in his chair on the Starboard side and we cast off the mooring lines. Up comes Engle with silver serving tray and gave Capt'n a china cup with coffee and a sweet bread. The Pilot got a mug and a sweet bread. Oh, 'Captain' and 'Sir' to hear. He had on a clean shirt, pants, shined shoes, shaved, combed hair, and towel over his arm. A volunteer as "Ships Captain Cook."

Forest came up with a Captain steward and Stevens provided a 3 stripper clerk. No cook was available. So, I volunteered Engle for the position, to bad eyes from Stiles and Admiral Stevens. I asked and got $20 dollars from the Admiral for Captain provisions. McIntire had no idea he had to provide his own food, or eat with the general officers, which he did for 3 days, till I got wind of it.

So, me and Engle had a long talk. It came to he'd be sitting at Squadron, ah, a long time, or, make McIntire love him. He had to say Sirs and Captain, without grumbling, and cook good meals. I thank Miss Carrie for helpin me with the last part. Two Marines, a wagon, and Engle went to places she thought had the best stuff at lower cost. The silver tray was McIntire's. He had little else. I held her hands and gave her a kiss on both cheeks for the help. Maybe why she asked if I'd write her. I promised no 'High Adventures.'

Engle came back with salt, pepper, some herb bottles, flower, cured hams and beef, and I don't know what all. His pride was 4 china plates, cups, saucers, and crystal wine glasses. Oh, was two dozen bottles of the cheapest, good Madeira wine he could find. Best, Engle can bake some fine sweet bread or cakes, which the Captain gets at every meal.

Ships Bos'n is Warrant Gaston. Bothel and Wagner problem. 1st Lieuy is Lt. Caldwell. He is nice enough. I got to meet the Armoror, Lt. Hardis, real quick. Two Marines hauled that wooden gun crate straight to him as soon as word got out where I was headed. The Admiral signed that paper, stamped 3 times, allowing 'Personal Weapons.' Hardis liked that saber. He couldn't hold it well, bein right handed.

He had to show it to Lt. Campbell, Ships Gunner, and Lt. McGraw, Mr. Chips. That was the day I got to formally stand in front of Capt'n McIntire. They had to be put in the ships log. I had to explain just how I got the Carbine and Break top pistol. Armoror brought along the gauntlet, arm pieces, and that sword. The last items, 'I acquired,' to bad eyes from him. But, Admiral Stevens had allowed them.

The Navigator is Lt. Gaily. So far, so good with him. He has a different form to give the Capt'n for a "Daily Report." Same stuff in different places. No, he never thought to get Gunner nor the other officers to input to it. Each has some paper to give out at the brief.

I asked about an evening "Sailing Report." The Captain only does a morning muster, when the reports are presented. I mentioned "The North Wall." It seems only the ships I was on hit it. It is June, so that cold water was deep and we didn't feel it.

Lt. Gaily had eyes for me speed line and weight. Well, the whole crew did. They had nothin better to watch. When the other, deeper line and weight went into the water, was when I had to explain the difference. I got his eyes when I said I sent reports to DC about the current one. He never heard of such a thing done.

Ship has two 3rd class QMs, Bush and Hood. This be their first trip to the Caribbean. I gave them the Atlantic Chart to figure out our courses. I already had them in a breast pocket tablet. I had to get a feel for how well George had taught them. The first thing to correct was going South, past Cape Hatteras. 'Give it a Wide Berth.' I had them put them courses to paper and hand to Mr. Gailey. He gave me an odd look, so I just nodded me head.

It is still 10 days, or so, to Nassau, De Bahama. The volunteers got distributed to their proper divisions. There was time enough for 1st Lieuy, Warrant Gaston, Fore, and Aft sail handlers to catch on to whistles. Oh, Gaston still shouts loud enough, at times, to about drive the ship forward with his air. He! He! I asked about a Capt'n gig and barge crew, to no good words from 1st Lieuy. So, I had a gig crew in the volunteers and had them ask mess mates about barge crew. Well, word of mouth and I had enough for 2 barges. Just in case. Words of mouth, from me volunteers, was I paid for eats and beverages at the pier. The gig or barge crew I'm with.

No, all is not just glorious aboard. I had to, again, put in writing what Engle was responsible for. The steward provided by Forest is about useless. Engle is to, 'Politely' give him guidance. Capt'n clerk does write nicely. Spelling and math are his bad qualities. Fitz grumbles from morning to night about him. I remind him about, 'Not our ship. Not our Problem!' Oh, such looks he gives me. He! He!

McIntire wanted to go into the inner harbor of Nassau. 1st Lieuy gave him the Chart. He said, as I would have, "Nice Liberty Place, Captain!" The winds weren't bad so anchored not a cable length from that light house. Me and my barge crew put him right on that pier all nice and dry.

Oh, McIntire called me into his cabin for a review of me service record. Saltsgiver was present. No, no words toward him. He said, "Fine record QM1. I wondered why I got a letter from Admiral Forest, with such fine words." I guess Forest left out my bad qualities, he usually says. The only things he didn't mention were in the papers back at the Squadron Blue jacket. No need for me to mention them.

It was a trip down memory lane. QM school, New York, and such. "Oh, you were with Admiral Forest for," this. Admiral Taylor for that. Captain Smith was mentioned. Then the last cruise South. "And, chased by Pirates. Quite a record, QM1. More actions at sea then most Frigates find." That was words from another I'd heard afore.

When he mentioned the letter from that Army Colonial, well, I had to smile. I can now. Lt. Dias only words to us on that open field were, "Move you (butts), Now!"

• • •

On that leave, 1885, I could sure tell some stories at the 'Founding Fathers' meetings. I had the bear claw necklace to prove it. 'course, I had to bring along that carbine and pistol. No shells for them as MaMa said no. I did have a couple empty cases though. Oh, the looks when PaPa and me got home at night. I already learned how to just sip that good whiskey. It was a treat for PaPa.

MaMa got the best of me by draggin me all over the place come morning and afternoon. We could only go so far. PaPa and me went to, "The Hooligan" place, as MaMa called it. We couldn't have come home that night, even with a horse to know the way. Each tellin of me stories, well, that bear got to be as big as a horse, '12 Feet Tall!' The main claw on that neckless was over 9 inches long. Oh, Indians? 'Blood thirsty Devils, just lookin to massacre some Army people.' The better it sounded, better and more whiskey came out. Why we stayed the night.

We went to that place way down South. Them boys were now men, had wives, and toddlers about. Princess about ignored me, which was good. Yes, there was lots of stories on that porch to tell, again. A new audience! Most families left to get home afore sun set. All went to bed at 10PM.

MaMa took me to Ebensburg. No change there. Woman and children on the porch and the men didn't like me stories. I was saved by the pocket bottles fill by the Founders! I remember the calls for the men to come in just after the sun went down. No, I hadn't finished me lemonade. MaMa dragged me in from lookin at the stars.

June 27, 1885, and Philly Navy base hadn't changed much. The staff barracks was still just a barracks. No one knew what to do with me and George. They didn't expect us. Mr. Rainey remembered us. I went and visited "The Master-At-Arms,' Mr. Reynolds. He recognized me when I picked up that play sword in me left hand. Oh, he still whacked me a couple times. I hadn't practiced since I left.

We got caught up in pay and could afford to go on liberty, some. Mr. Rainey had us assigned to his Navigation school staff. He, come to learn, was assigned as "Head Master of Navigation," to the school, from Naval Observatory, Washington, D.C. A civilian. But, all called him Sir. We was his, "Charges," as he said to us, standing in front of his desk. Oh, 'Yes Sir!'

George was lookin for a girlfriend. Them saloons was out. So, he comes up with this plan to attend church, off base, and find a local girl his MaMa would approve of. Sunday morning that trolley took us to one. Like at home, we was15 minutes early. We set in the second row and waited. An old woman, like Grandma, sat next to us. Ok. She elbows me and points to this 'Foot Rest.' When I put me shoe on it, well, I got punched by her and, "To Kneel AT!" Oops.

So, it was a nice service, 'cept in a language I didn't understand. Stand, sit, kneel, to stand, sit, and all. Come the end and I got shoved into a line down that isle. At the end was the Preacher, a glass of drink, and something to each mouth! George and me sorta took to the side door. That was Sunday, 11 July.

Come 18 July, we sure skirted that church and saw a sign sayin Presbyterian. It had a nice greeter, who set us second row, front, and I could keep up with the service. Hands shakes to left, right, and out the church door to, Officer, Navy, and lots of Yes and No Sirs to him. Our names went to his pocket paper. And, come Monday in front of Mr. Rainey for explanation of, "Loud Voices and Singing, In a Church!" It was George who did that. A Big Guy! A Big Voice and terrible at singing. Swear! Mr. Rainey did to our, "Disturbing the Congregation."

Next, George came up with idea of measuring the height of people, well, read that as women, with this contraption Uncle Curtis would have been proud of. It was my design. Just a 2 foot square of wood to stand on. We'd pull this 45 Degree thing with mirror on, to the spot on the 1 inch square stick, attached, so we could see the top of their head. Old principal. Like a sextant.

Up at this park, on a Saturday afternoon, we'd yell out, "Measure your true Height for Free!" For fun, it had two sides to that square stick. The good side measured your true height. Pull a pin, flip it over, and we could measure a gent at 4 foot, rather than 6. A joke.

We measured children, with mothers watchin, and men in hats. I had to say we measured their hats height too. That got some laughs. Ladies? Some had feathers in their hats sooo, another laugh. We got a Philly Policeman there and not good looks. Nope, never took a penny. He still wrote our names on his book. Come Monday morning we was in front of Mr. Rainey. He liked our contraption. "Ingenious. Well thought out." The Police said if we accepted a penny then, well, we was in trouble. Nope, we just did it for the fun of it and added a side to the square stick to make a child measure twice height. That got laughs but not girlfriends.

The next Sunday, 26 July, by me log, we caught that trolley to a Methodist church, up toward center town. Oh, the greeter tried to set us in the first pews. No! We took to the back one, center. The Church filled and we got children, couples either side. Nice, 'How's ya Does,' both ways. It was nice, up to them children fussing. A lady in front of us turned and tried to shush thems. That didn't work. Comes the Sermon, as I remembered, them children got whisked out, for their noise. That woman noticed it and gave us nice words for our patients.

Now, the ladies, and I say that lightly, down close to the base, say George was handsome. I seen him as naked as his mother did. Tall, lanky, skinny, and not handsome. So, this woman, our age, at the end of service, leans over me to thank George for, "Being so nice, with the children." She invites us to an, "Outdoor, afternoon social, at 1 PM." George is lookin in her eyes, silent, so I said, 'Happy to attend.' I got no eyes from her.

Out in alley, ahind the church, George says, "I think she is likes you.' I slapped him twice to wake up his mind and two more times back to base, with his nonsense. Edna, tall, slim, nice voice, nice smile, about doted over him all afternoon. Me? I got me own lemonade, to put some pocket bottle to, and food to me plate. The star Polaris was in his eyes the whole time. She was a nice woman and nice voice to hear. She must have had like the Greek "Serene" enchantin voice to his ears.

It was Monday morning, 27 July, 1885, the Log says, when we got called into Mr. Rainey office afore noon. I was wondering what we was charged with. Here, we found him, a Navy Full Captain,

QM1 in-charge of us, sorta, two QM2 types, and two Marines. We just stood at attention, in front of that desk. I thought maybe that Church Social didn't go well.

Mr. Rainey picked up these papers and read out how, "Under adverse conditions, Independent of Formal Order, Did, Shoot And Kill a Bear, Attacking a Naval Officer." Dias letter. "From Naval Observatory, Washington D.C. Did, under adverse conditions, logged uncharted Islands of Alaska, as directed by their orders." Oh, the Alaska thing. "Under Adverse Conditions, Did, Chart the Missouri River to Head. Which will take some months to decipher." We got some bad look to that. "While on the Missouri River, Did, Shoot, and kill, One Horse, Under a Colonial Army Office, Almost killing Said Officer, But, Did Drive Off a Raiding Party of Indians, Off their reservation, with Intent on Harm to Said Officer and Army Personnel."

We got his stern look, then a smile and, "Strip Off Your Blouses! Out of Uniform." What! Well, them two Marines sure pulled them blouses off of us and next we got a new one about shoved on to break me bones. Neckerchiefs back in place well, "Captain, swear in our new Quartermaster 3rds!" We was handed that paper and had to swear to that Petty Officer oath of Formal words, and signature to paper. Then, hands up to swear, "To protect your ship, protect your shipmates."

The PO1 and them PO2s got to smack us on the arm, "To Tack It In Place, Soes, It Don't Fly OFF." That hurt. This Captain, a 4 stripper, comes up and shakes our hands. I got a whispered, "Your Uncle Curtis would be proud of you." I didn't remember if he was the same one as in Boot Camp. Mr. Rainey said, "And make sure your measurements, of ladies and Gents, is accurate."

Instructing was boring and we had lots of free time tween classes. So, I got asked to help Mr. Reynolds with sword training. He forced me to do it right handed, else I'd train them wrong. No problem there. All but the Senior Boots were not real good.

Me and George traveled all over Philly, sort of, via the Trolley. No, our only duty was as Navigation school stuff. We had lots of free time, all weekends. We had no duty as, "Charges of Mr. Rainey." I could about go home for the weekend. The problem was that stinking train. I just hated that ride. And, Mr. Rainey said no, leave only.

George and Edna was the 'Sort of.' Bein 3rd class we sorta made more money. Edna needed an escort so I got a friend of hers to be my attendee. She had lots of friends. I got to meet most of thems. We attended that church service every Sunday also.

I wrote MaMa about this and got, "Church will do you well." It did, through that summer and fall. The church had regular Sunday Afternoon Socials. Rain? The church had a kitchen and tables in the basement. I got to know all the people there. George and me could entertain them with our 'Adventure to Alaska,' and lots of true stuff to make them laugh.

The Church Socials was no real cost to me and George. Saturdays had cost for the trolley and a bite to eat. Come to find out Edna's father would slip him some money to cover our costs. I wondered why George seemed to always have money for 4. Ah, the fun times we had. It about made up for those months aboard the Brickell.

• • •

This cruise around the Caribbean? I hope ya saved me letter from 'Afore. It was just as boring, 'till real recently. Gunner, Mr. Campbell, has been asking to fire the guns, "Regular, Captain. More than the once a month." Armoror, Mr. Hardis, has asked to train the men in boarding practice, more than once a month. The crew is bored. I asked Mr. Chips if they could make a piece of 2 by 4 round. He! He! He! And, I got more people cleaning the privies, pumping water, and making the Bos'n proud of the 'Pretty Wood Work' than is necessary.

Oh, are the usual stops for water in Dominican Island. We got three days liberty at the Island off the Yucatan. Cozumel. Capt'n set liberty in Cartagena, Colombia. That is where I got the head cleaners and pumpers assigned. They about wore out Marine Captain Saltsgiver and his men. It is just too big a place and more than enough trouble to get into. Doc Stiteler gave some bad words to Capt'n McIntire about the hazards of that town, to no good ears.

It was after Cartagena to Barbados, 13 August, 1894, that Capt'n McIntire thought we should fire the guns at some barrels. The gig crew hauled them off to both sides. We turned through the wind to turn about and "Sides, Fire as they bear, Mr. Campbell." We went about, West, and the sides just shot from fore to aft as we passes thems, to no good shots and no bad ones. Me? "About QM1." I waited for the Bosn's to say ready, to bad looks. Old Slugger that Shenandoah is, made as good a turn as possible and ran down 'tween them barrels, again, with flags on them. Nope. Neither side hit neither one. The lookers in the top mast gave them all misses.

We got to Bridgetown, Barbados, 17th. I be writing from the Cart Table. 8 men in irons in the brig. 4 are mine. The ship has no liberty. It would be more but Saltsgiver and Nichole couldn't identify the rest. I was at that bar I see that woman who has boyfriends, on them Frigates. The Brits, our crew, both drunk, had words I didn't hear, till talked to thems, this morning, the 18th.

Well, drunk sailors and fightin over nothing, as I figured. 'Afore Mr. McIntire, that was not an answer. No one need be there. The whole ship heard his words. "Grate and 12 lashes! All!" He shuffled them papers Fitz gave him and I got words worse than Admiral Forest came up with, for my and their character. I don't recall all of thems. He doesn't have the same flavor as Forest, who knew us real well, so to speak. Yes, us.

I can always say Engle started the next bit of argument about this. I was standing in front of McIntire when he came in and put a mug of coffee afore him. McIntire accepts it and says, 'Engle, how about my sweet bread or cake?"

Now, Engle looked like he ain't slept in two days, foul cloths, hair amess, shoes just a mess, and said, 'Scuse me, Capt'n.' I'd have laughed at this, but was standing. 'Cake or sweet breads be up when I think about it, Sirs, Maybe.' It was that maybe that did it.

Capt'n called in Fitz to get Warrant Gaston, Mr. Saltsgiver to his cabin. Doc Stiteler also. His only words were, "Mast in 15 minutes, Gentlemen!" Nothing gentile in his voice. From the Poop rail he could be easily heard by the Cat hiding in the fore peak space. 'Course, anyone in a mile could too. Oh, he lambasted the bunch of us, "Hooligans! Worthless Warf Rates, dressed as Sailors," and on, and on. Those in irons got 3 days bread and water. Doc had to make sure they could live on that. Engle to make the bread, "Dry, Tasteless, To Chew on, for an Hour!"

Engle became me problem. I am to inspect him each morning, afore Capt'n lunch and supper. He was always up, 'cept this morning, with the Waisters, to start Captain's sweet bread and daily cakes. He was one of thems that got away, got further drunk, afore stumbling back to the ship. I think he slept in the fore peak, with the cat.

It seems a sailors life is caught tween two different worlds. First is the boring days of just sailin. Another is the pure terror of what is goin on around you. Waves as high as a house, the ship healing over so you hang on for dear life. Next, to flat seas from horizon around. Unknown sails on the horizon so General Quarters set and ya wait to see ifn they be friendly. If not, well, the smell of gun powder don't leave the ship for a couple days. It is an awful smell, but, if you are lucky, as I have been, it brings back the moments of action.

One of Edna's friends, George girlfriend, had the scent of the soap MaMa made. It was a special soap that Me and PaPa got to use, out there next to the barn, stripped naked, and washing in that horse trough! Especially after back from, "That Hooligan Place!" He! He!

Time to inspect Engle and Purser is callin for mail to the Post! 10 August, 94.

By Your Leave, Missy,

An Old Sea Dog,

IN THE YEAR 1894, 15 OCTOBER: CARIBBEAN

Dear Miss Judith,

I started and put aside some letters to you. Good as, I got your letter while in Yukatan place, Cozumel Island. A Frigate is here ahead of us. The reason why we got mail from that Packet ship. Else, it would not find us. Squadron is not good at sending mail. Thank you for the letter. This is our 4th turn of the Caribbean.

Oh, the 3rd round of the Caribbean was less like the one I wrote about. Capt'n decided, after that stuff in Cartagena, and all, that liberty parties were supervised. I got two barge crews, 24, assigned to me custody. Nope. Not a word from me mouth. Good crews. Good men. A mixed lot of Waisters, Gunners, and Bosn's that can row dry in but bad weather.

At Yukatan, Cozumel, there was no problems. Down to that place to scrape the sides, do hull work, and get Pollo or Jambo samiches and rum drinks was not a problem. Comes Cartagena, we took our Liberty Parties ashore and back by the assigned times allowed. We, the Petty Officers, lead our "Parties" to places close to the landing. Saltsgiver and Nichole, 'Fanned' out them Marines to no good results. There was no sailors, but to them local, pier side places. No need to go further for thems to find, "Refreshments."

'Tween Cartagena and Barbados, the 3rd round, 10 September, 1894, reading me log here at the Chart Table, I come up for the Afore Mid and mid watch, so thems could catch the last of Smokin Lamp Lited. See your eyes rollin at this. Yes, Captain McIntire strolled up to that Taft rail. QM3 Bush and that Marine trooper just vanish in the darkness.

Ahind me, I heard, "I asked Bobbit," his clerk, that Fritz calls his Hobbit, "if any volunteers had signed on. He said to ask you, QM1." I said, 'No, Captain,' and got, "Well, QM1, why don't you put your name to the list. The men seem to follow your." Back with, 'Orders, Captain.' I got, "You could talk to them, QM1. They listen to you." I said, 'They have to listen to their own hearts, Captain. They follow good officers, a good Captain, Sir.'

Him over the helm barrel and I invite him to take the wheel. No. "With your experience in Battle, what odds do you give this crew." I said, 'You have a 75 percent chance of getting shot right there at the Taft Rail, Sir. A 25 percent chance of seeing the crew massacred in front of you, defending the Starboard ladder to the Poop.' Came, "And You, QM1?" I said, 'Oh, about 50 50 for me, after I knock off as many of them as I got carbine shells for. Close, as they will get close, 3 loads of that pistol before I need that sword, Captain.'

His mouth moved some and, "Just how did your ships Not get boarded. In fact, reports said Admiral Forest closed on the Triremes." I said, 'The Med pirate ship got 3 broadsides. 18 balls or bolts to the Port side. Same for the one here, just up North. But just 12 well placed ones. The other ships missed Stays, Captain. Triremes picked on the wrong captain, a fighting Captain.'

Gunner, Armoror, and Bos'n Gaston got their wishes. Bos'n got Top Gallants and fighting sails to take the ship through the eye of the wind lots of days. Just in case of bad wind, we took to Wear the ship, wind to aft. Think it was the first time them gunners got to load in them 25 pound bolts. I heard them gun crews groanin at supper.

Armoror broke the men into two divisions. They'd attack each other with them wooden pike and swords. Wood pistols were not allowed. The Marines went to platforms Mr. Chips built for them to stand at the Main and Aft Masts main spars. A barrel to each side for them to shoot their rifles.

Me? I got 4 of them young Bos'n to learn to handle the ships wheels when kneeling. Oh, I play SHOT, go down, and Bush or Hood to take me place at the Rudder Indicator. I'd Bang, Bang them and Mr. Gailey would take over. Oh, such lovely days of men yelling, screaming, and tryin to beat each other. That, or the smell of that gun powder lingering for a day. Such laughs and dancing on the fore deck, to be heard, at night.

It was the letter from MaMa, from that Packet ship in Cozumel, that reminded me of her soap. That dang bush, in front the house, blossomed in June, till July, with big, white blossoms. She'd bring some in the house, to the dinner table, in a glass thing. Her and PaPa would get all twinkling of eyes to that smell.

MaMa and Grandma would strip off the flowers, squish them into a gallon glass jug with some alcohol, oil from this big can, and let it sit. Come some time that oil went to little bottles. It was a Gardenia bush. A sweet smell to about to make ya dizzy.

• • •

Much like here in the Caribbean, the sun sets earlier each day. In 1885 George thought the sun, Edna, shone upon his face only when he could see her for Friday evening, Saturday, and Sunday. Mr. Rainey didn't like us, "Gallivanting All Over The Place After Dark." Some places in Philly was real bad after dark. Like, right outside the Gate. He never thought about that as we would go to some of the bars, "Real Close!" He worried about us as much, no more than MaMa. But, she never been to Philly. That is a good thing!

Being his "Charges" was a double edged sword for him, I figure. He liked us, for some reason, and we were like a pain in his butt. Like with the 'Measuring People,' George, and his voice. I may have not mentioned botherin the Base Armoror about shooting the rifles and helping with the cannons, "Can't ya say Guns!"

The Sextants for training about fell apart and the Charts were marked up to the point of not be readable. We asked for this, asked for new of that till, he relented and D.C. sent some 'Old, New Stuff.' Read that as "Stuff" sent back from the fleet as worn out.

Mr. Rainey shifted us between classes all the time. He saw we were bored with the same questions and the results with our instruction. He even brought in a fresh minted 2 strippers to do some of our classes, those that just graduated and awaiting a ship.

George is, was, will always be, tall, slow and a skinny guy, with huge hands. He ain't changed in these years. Mr. Reynolds assigned him to teach the new class for Boarding. Me? I got the next step classes and wore padding. Glancing blows still hurt.

For the, "Boot Introduction Class," me and Mr. Reynolds would have padding on and go at it with blunted steel swords. Once I got back into practice I'd get him some, me left to a right, as I stood me ground on that point. Oh, he got me and I started to get him, some, on the arm. He didn't like that. The Boots, and George, was just with mouths open. He'd change stiles of fighting, some, to hit me. He demonstrated French, Spanish, Italian, and English styles. I "Found" a longer, brass belayin pin to act as a knife. I used it a lot, to keep from getting hit.

Winter, that year in Philly, started the end of October with ice, snow, and cold. No learning to march for the Boot Camps. George and me got to, "Man The Furnace," in the basement. Ya shake that grate, load in coal, and empty the ashes on the walk way. I think, now, Mr. Rainey was getting even for our 'Mischief.' I liked it as it was warm right next to the furnace. Weekends? Boots was assigned to do that and fire watch, which I did, afore assigned a class. Things ya remember, now.

The church had a furnace keeper. The place was just warm enough to take off gloves, for me. I don't know if Edna and George wore them. He. He. Well, they did, outside. I said it was cold, with snow, and ice that winter. Gohner Evens, her father, Minnie, mother, kept us to the 'Parlor' most days. Yes, with one of her friends. The house wasn't a mansion but bigger than most around. The Parlor and formal dining are big enough for 12 people.

Card games were popular. 4 handed games. Virginia, Edna friend, showed up lots as my partner. I always thought Edna and George was playin footsies under that table as, me and partner lost a lot. There was Wrist, which I hated, Pinochle, which Virginia hated, Old Maids, which was something different, and Spades, a new game.

Gohner and Minnie would pair up for Bridge. Each couple, us, would sit out one game. Me and Virginia watched just how this husband and wife whipped our butts every game. Well, they lied! Bold Face, outlandish lied! They jumped all over the 4 suites to come up with their bid. They knew each other real well and how they lied on a bid.

True Footsie's was out. Both of us had tie shoes. Sooo, when getting lemonade we worked out a foot tap for Spades, to start. Just how many and Hi or Low cards. Lost. After some weeks of this we figured out the Liars were using a reverse bid on the second call. We still lost less!

The room was big enough for two tables so, come a time, Gohner brought in a second set of winners. No, they never played each other. Always us young ones to them. I didn't mind. I got to sit at a proper table and enjoy a good supper. Virginia was, probable still is, a good lookin woman with a good smile, laugh, and enjoyable. With the new couple there, me and George got to repeat our 'Adventures in Alaska.' Edna kept correcting us on some of the facts. "You said different last time." Ok, a bad memory.

George and me ate there for Thanksgiving. It was better than that in the galley food. December came, and it was the worst year for snow than I remembered. I put a letter to MaMa that I had two weeks leave, mid to end of December, as, remember, Boot Camp shut down. She said to say there. PaPa only went to the Blacksmith shop as the farms were snowed in. Her only visit was to see to Grandma and Grandpa.

Minnie said George and me was welcome there for Christmas dinner. She pulled us aside and mentioned gifts for the woman. Oh, no ideas from us! So, we got a "Humph, Men," bad eyes to us, and a list of items. She took it back and wrote down the stores to find them in. Whew! Saved, as, we never went to any stores there.

Now, me and George had few things to spend on. Cleaning of uniforms for classes was the biggest. Shush. Fillin pocket bottles had a cost. No, The Sailor and Marine guards knew us and passed us through. The Staff was on leave, 'cept some and us. So, we worked out Navigations class for those who wanted help. Oh, the rest of the time was in 'Boarding Party classes.' Mr. Reynolds took leave so me and George filled up the days with them.

Threw sleet, snow, ice, and cold to make ya freeze, me and George trudged off to purchase them gifts. No, no classes on weekends, so George and me took the trolley up to the stores afore going to Edna home. We showed the list to the woman clerk, to bad eyes, and bad words under breath. We had to stop at three places to pick things out. "Can't be the same color." Minnie had mentioned this to us. Them lists weren't that different!

Christmas day, December 25, 1885, me and George showed up to late lunch, early dinner at 3 PM, with empty hands. We had already been to early church. Edna and Virginia, ya, she kept coming, gave us greetings and such looks! Shush! We had already given them to Minnie to hide. So, comes the time, what do you give a sailor? We got all we need. Was homemade cookies, fudge, and ear muffs. I told Millie what was authorized to wear. And gave hugs and cheek kisses, I did, to Virginia. 'Ears will be finally warm!'

Edna and Virginia each got a card and places to look, like hide and seek indoors. The cards had different rooms, different places, for thems to look. Such squeals from them different rooms as Minnie gave me and George looks. She knew what was were. Each placed their gifts on a different table, in the Parlor, five each. Last was, "Where your partner sits is where you find the last." I was sittin in an overstuffed chair in the parlor. Well!

I got pulled from it and about thrown across the room. Virginia and the cushion parted, to about hit me, and her hands to the sides. I got her Silk stockings, 1, and second pair, 2. 2 handkerchiefs, real fine, 3, and a silk scarf, ah, a black Navy one, like mine, 4, and brown fine gloves, 5. Both were about to tear each chair apart when Minnie says, "And, the last gift might be the partners you have, who gave you the gifts?" I got hands too mine, a kiss on the cheeks, and a peck on the lips. Oh, a nice smile and, "Thank You."

Me log says it snowed and was cold till March, 1886. On March 11th it dumped a foot of it and the next day temps rose. Easter came early that year, the end of March, again, from me log. Oh, woman was in bright colors and such bonnets. It was a nice church service and George still can't carry a song. Edna must have been tone deaf, all this time.

Such a fine dinner in that home. Us men went to the front porch with glasses of good whiskey to sip. Gohner looked at us and we get, "And, what are your intentions, to the ladies?" I could only honestly say I had no idea how long I'd be in Philly. Virginia was a lovely woman. 'I've not got, informal with her, Sir. Until I have word as to my next assignment, I thought that would be best.' He understood that.

I had been to Virginia home, on some occasions. They went to the same Methodist church. I met them at the socials, afore the winter cold, and some after. It was a nice family. James McKaig and Maggie. She said, "Just Maggie." She pulled me aside afore Christmas to this issue. I Said I'd be respectful, waitin to see next assignment. I got her bad looks, but approval, for seeing, only. It was maybe that flick of the butchers knife in the kitchen that caused me to agree! A joke. Not! I sometimes wondered about her, Virginia, and Ida.

It was George that got us in front of Mr. Rainey, again. "No idea of your Intentions! How many months of going to their home, Church, AND, God only know what else. So, Petty Officer Weaver, I have a letter in My Hand, that States, Mr. Guhner, A Fine City council Spokesperson, says, well, neither of you are to see Edna or Virginia." I didn't know how I got dragged into this, "Until Intentions for the Future Are Stated." We went back to measuring people in the park. Nope, we stayed away from that church.

• • •

We got that sweet water in Dominican Republic, like afore. There was no hurry to Nassau. 10 October, 94, the lookout had, "A Nick Of Sails, Ahind." We was tween Isla Beata and Isla Alto Velo, Puerto Rico. It was not my duty. Bush and Hood were bored fixing our position. For fun, I flipped the chart, the ruler made a straight line. I put a mark to every inch and wrote our course. I drew a second line to the left side, as that ship was on our Port side. The lookout said so.

As soon as I could see that nick I gave them the compass reading and they flipped the 28 second glass, an marked the time. 28 seconds later I gave compass reading, they marked the time, and so it went. Well, if we was doing 8 knots then this ship was makin more than 10. I asked Gailey to get the Captain. Oh, "Commercial ship. No worry." Your rollin eyes I see.

I had thems keep up this activity and found Gunner and drug him up to the Poop to look at this ship, aft. "Three master. Hmm." He got Mr. Chips to look, who said, "Three master. Top Gallants set." Thinkin, "That North wind hides any flags it got. It could be a Spanish Frigate." Came his sniff to the air and, "Could be another Pirate, out of Juancho."

Come that ship just hull up, on a wave, Bos'n, and 1st Lieuy was lookin, with eye glasses. Well, come good hull up, we got a signal gun to the North winds, and the Middie said, "Outer Flags, Halt.

We can't see the inner one for the sails." Captain came to the Taft rail.

I caught up Gunner and we had a talk about ships guns and stuff. Over to Mr. Gailey and got, "Wind gauge only, for a fight." So, I go through the motions of each ship, with, "The Wind Gauge." Simpler put, the other ship can decide when to press the action. It depended on how big of guns she wore. No, not good.

There was a counsel on the Poop and the Marine rang the ships bell for General Quarters. I come to the Rudder indicator in full, "Regalia, QM1," from the Captain. Engle about hog tied him to put on his sword and pistol. I had that loaded Carbine, loaded pistol, 36 pistol cartridges on my belt, sword, and a chest bandolier of them 45-70 cartridges. Yes gauntlets and arm protectors.

About then we got that second signal gun to windward. The Middie can only see the halt ones. Gunner said, "3 pounder fore, must be 8, 12 pounders to a side, Captain. Range is 3 miles. Closer and it can about hit us, Captain." About this time our ship caught a wave under the bow, 6 eyes watch me gauntlet raise, and I hit Starboard 15 Degrees. Oh, the butt of the ship skipped over to Port enough to throw most there around.

Oh, the looks I got as I pointed to that ship. All watched as it tried to match us. Me finger back to the indicator, our ship came back to course, and that poor ship about floundered, pressed for sails, just lied over. Mr. Gailey about relieved me. About. 'Next she give a gun to windward, I'll jinx the ship, again, and we go to Port. Yes, Wear the ship and show her our Port guns.' Well, Gunner was there to say yes, with Bos'n and 1st Lieuy givin a nod. McIntire said, "Make ready Gentlemen." We got two signal guns to windward and one of their fore chasers went off.

A nice wave came under the ship, me finger hit 15 degrees to Starboard, and that is when Bos'n blew that whistle. Our speed and weight was enough to carry the ship back on course and the rudder came over to full Port. He called amid ship and we just moved the ship 2 lengths South.

The other ship, ya ask? She went full Starboard, her top gallants masts broke, and their sails was flapping away. Her jib sail blew out of its holes. Her fore main top sail belayin lines was like spider webs in the air. McIntire called for an easy turn to Port, to just close with them.

He give a nod to a gun to windward, our signal flags hauled up to, "Surrender or be fired upon." It was about then that Middie, and lookout yelled out, "Spanish Frigate, Captain." OOPS. But it was his fault for Windward, not Lee signals, and that 3 pounder.

Don, Diego, whatever comes up Starboard side to six marines, whistles and bells like to wake the dead. There was a Lieutenant and another, the interpreter, he gave words to as he looked over our fore deck. The gun crews were set to station and the Boarding Party just so. McIntire escorted them around for an inspection. The skylight showed Engle serving out wine and them sweet cakes. It was a half hour of conversation as it took time, what with that interpreter. They come out, an up to the Poop!

Mr. Caldwell, Warrant Gaston, Mr. Gailey go introduced. Those at ships wheel saluted and get a nod. Oh, I got some fine looks, lots of words to that interpreter. McIntire got, "Captain, you have a Knight aboard!" The Interpreter said the Spanish Captain would like to see my pistol. Out, emptied, to me gauntlet, and I give it to him. I got it back, reload it, into holster, to all eyes.

He pointed to that carbine, which I unload, and give to him. Back, I reload it and put it to its holder. Next, I gave him me Gauntlets to try on. He looks like he is trying to play the piano with thems. Next, me sword comes out, civil, as Mr. Reynolds taught us.

This Spanish Captain had a time with it. I figured he was right handed. He kept sayin words and pointing to the tip, handle, and then that bird cage to cover the hand. Mr. Reynolds taught us this formal thing with swords. I won't bore you. I got it handed back, civil. Gloves come off him, crossed, and to me. I did sword honors, salute him, returned.

This Captain said a length of words, me and him locked in eyes. "Captain," to ours, "in the old ways, when you have a knight aboard, is required to have his origins flag at a mast." I heard, "Sir Knight. And what flag would be flying?" With locked eyes I said, 'The Flag of St. Andrew. Scots clan of McAllister.' The Spanish Captain said, in real good English, "I will put this in my personal Log. I was defeated by a Scottish Knight, A Highlander." Oh, I saluted to that, got one, and off thems went.

Ok, you can roll your eyes, again. It was Friday, 12 October, I be at the ships wheel and McIntire was over the helm barrel. I got, "Don, Diego was trying to halt us, to warn of Pirates in the Bay of Haiti. He liked how you jinxed the ship and asked how I knew to do that." I got his hand up. "He expected us to come about, the second time, to engage him, By the Book, With the Weather gage in our favor."

I heard, "He liked your get up and all. He asked who taught you the sword procedure, QM1." His hand, again. "I said I didn't know. Before leaving, in good English, he asked if you would have shot him. Well, QM1." Freak wave hit the bow just then. I jinxed the ship enough I had to keep him from flyin over, onto me.

• • •

Mr. Rainer had us sit down and write a letter to the parents, Evans and McKraig, an apology, "Fore waisting the women's time, thinking we might have serious intentions toward them." Something likes that. We wrote it out a number of times till he thought we had, "Appropriate words, for your behavior!" Mail? "Gentlemen deliver it to a hand." No, no givin each other words on that paper either.

I put that letter to Mrs. McKraig hand to open and read. She just said, "We discussed this before, but, Thank You," to no hard looks. I don't know what George got. Never asked, never said.

That old log says May, 1, 1886, I was in the park to, 'Measure Your True Height. Free!' No George. Ahind me I get, "Shoes and hat, or not, Sir?" Virginia. 'True height, with heals and hat, Mam! Unless ya want me to only measure to your eyes?'

So, a true measure I did to Mr. Kraig shoes and hat. Minnie, in heals and a hat with a feather. That got laughs for, 'Well, Sir. She is taller than you.' Virginia. "Well, Sailor, to my eyes." To play this out, I had to shuffle that device back and forth some. 'You have to look forward. No Ups or Downs, or sideways, Mam,' to laughs.

It seems Mr. and Mrs. McKraig had taken up Bridge. Missy needed a partner for Saturday evenings and some Sundays. On

Sundays they'd maybe mention Friday, here and there. If no Friday, I could be found in the Park. Come a day I seen her in the park with a young man, arm in arm. Not a bad looking guy. Nicely dressed. It was warm and it must have been July, from Me memory.

• • •

Oh, that Spanish Frigate. We be headed home so had some spare spares. Mr. Chips, BM1 Bothel, and some, went over and got them Top Gallant polls in place. Their sails dropped and got a gun to the other side. Up comes flags that said, "To," and below it was the flag of St. Andrew. We gave two, to the other side and our flags said, "Fair Sail," with a Spanish flag under.

We went through that straight 'tween Cuba and Haiti with nary a sail in sight. It be called, 'The Windward Channel.' I have no answer for that here. We found a Packet here in Nassau, pickin up dispatches and mail. I'll date this as 15 October, 1894.

By Your Leave, Missy,

An Old Sea Dog,

IN THE YEAR 1894, 17 DECEMBER: SQUADRON

Dear Miss Judith,

To catch ya up, "tween Nassau and here, McIntire had lots sign on to Shenandoah. The store keeps like Mr. Hitchcock, the Purser. Bosn's? Some signed to Warrant Gaston. The Aft masters like 1st Lieuy, Mr. Caldwell. The Gunners signed on, most, to Mr. Campbell. A couple wanted to be Carpenter Mates. I like Mr. Chips, Mr. McGraw. Fitz kept up with the list.

Captain McIntire was all happy with that. I hope he doesn't think it was because of that Spanish ship thing. The Signal guns was all that made noise. Round the Smokin Lamp Lited, some remembered, "12 Lashes and all that was said."

4 Oldsters didn't, fearing McIntire might force them to retire. They like the sea and know I'll keep them on me list. At least as long as Doc says they are fit. I keep them to the lower masts. They are the younger ones teachers and tell good Old Stories round the Smokin Lamp. I asked thems about puttin on Petty Officer stripes and be in-charge. I got, as a joke, sorta, "Oh, put me in charge of some of these ships rats and I'll give them orders to jump in the sea, I will! He! He!"

There are 4 gunners who like the liberty at Squadron. Mr. Campbell can be a task master. They would have duty days aboard. 4 Bosn's, ah, are of their mind. There is better food at the galley and no duty, and liberty. They don't mind that Marine tent, when things get full. Well, they might take exception to it, when it gets cold out there.

Engle and McIntire seem to come to some agreement, about Engle. Oh, Sirs or Captain are still required. "Ain't no Marine. Shoes don't need to be Mirrors, Captain." He didn't need to shave but once a week on, "Make and Mend day, Sir. Thursdays." One day of liberty, per port, he was allowed, my words, and some discretion coming back, which meant stinking drunk. "But, I'll say afore and have sweet break or yourn cakes, made night afore, Captain." Fitz made a note of this to his record.

• • •

It is dark out, earlier and gettin colder. Me letter about Philly, from memory, was not good. I check me log and it was a warm spring. It was June that Virginia had that new Bow. Saturday, 06 June, 1886.

On Sunday, 07 June, and I be at that park to, 'Measure Your Height.' A woman came up and said, "To My Eyes, Sailor." I got her on that board, pull that contraption just so, raise that stick to her and come that smell of Gardenia I mentioned afore. They was familiar eyes. "And, you forgot me." I'd measured so many, over time, she could have been any one of them.

She said me name and she needed a favor. A nice lookin woman me age or so. My mind was still figurin out where I seen her when came, "You were my escort, with George and Edna." Oh, me mouth don't work as the brain was goin back in Edna History. Her hand came out and, "Mary. Last we met was last August." Well, no wonder I don't remember. I did remember standing in front of Mr. Rainey, some, since then.

Anyway, her MaMa and PaPa don't like, refuse to allow her to the park, "Without an escort." "I saw you and remembered how nice you were." I asked just how she got there as I didn't see an older couple close. She pointed across the street to two figures on a porch. I smelled a trap, of some kind. She pulled me across that street so quickly I didn't have a chance to pick up me stuff.

I got a hand shake from Albert G. Clark and Martha. They knrw Guhner Evans and Mr. McKaig from the same church. They sat in the porch swing as I kept waiting for a rope to come down and swing me up! Intentions. I said them same words, as I remembered, with that knife flickering. Me eyes flickered 'tween them two. Mary got the nod of approval and I got dragged back across that street.

Me measure device broke down to 3 stick pieces, attached to the board, along with that pull thing, for easy carry. Not two minutes in this 'Walk,' and, oh, I remembered Mary. Edna and her walked ahead of me and George. There was a never ending conversation 'tween the two of thems. It was the same as then, but only her talkin to me.

She had left in September for Valley Forge University and to stay in a Sorority house. She had a, "Marvelous Bow!" He, like her, went home for the summer and why no escort. She asked if I smoked, no, but she found me pocket bottle to further lubricate her words. Oh, she, "Just must have an Italian Ice cone!" This vender shaves ice into a paper cone and puts some flavor to it. She just unloaded about her time at the University.

I got invited to dinner. Albert and me ate, while Mary and Martha just talked on, and on. Done, he and me got shooed to the porch, "To get to know one another." We had a glass of lemonade to sip. Albert looked around, like to catch a robber, and out comes a pocket bottle to add to his glass. I give him a look, he looked around, and I get some. Me pocket bottle? I had just enough left to get me back to base. I always liked poor Albert.

I wrote to MaMa about this and got her words of, "Good you are back to Church, Regular. Mind your manners. Be careful." Me, Albert and thems, sat on the right side of the church. Oh, Edna and Virginia, with Bows, sat in the middle. I got a little wave from thems. The Socials, in the afternoon? Oh, I stayed close to Albert and brought two bottles. Them woman just flitted about like bees to flowers.

You'd ask, so, Albert was in charge of accounting for this law firm. In quiet moments, out back, alone, he'd ask me about my travels. Mary had mentioned them. He'd never traveled so far. Men to men stories need not be so long. I just said of important stuff and not of that stinky train nor the smell of that ship. Oh, I got his eyes to the bears. Me, and George, shot those two. I shot two more, just young ones that come to the smell of burning wood. Oh, how he laughed at the Colonel and all. I could laugh, then.

We, yep all 4, took to strolls in that park after dinner. Yes, the woman ahead and talkin. We tipped hats to woman and gave nods to the men. We stopped some so the women could jabber to the others. Albert would introduce me, to handshakes about. It was just small talk, lookin at the jabberin women. Albert would mention me travels. I had to keep the account short as, the women went off to next bee hive.

Ah, the endless days of summer in Philly. George? He had a girlfriend, somewhere. He didn't say and I didn't ask. Mr. Rainey asked of my activities. Oh, he knew of Albert. Got his bad eyes, I did. He asked of me intentions. I had no better answer to say.

Mr. Reynolds started to take exception to me Belayin pin. Well, after so many class demonstrations, I caught on to his methods. There was something about his wrist movement while demonstratin the French, Spanish, Italian, or so. He had a twist to his wrist, like to get you 'tween the ribs. Inward, not outward. He did it all the time. Did I mention this? Nope. Left hand, I'd twist inward, on his sword side, and use the belayin pin against him. Oh, the eyes I got from him. When he mentioned this I did the opposite. That pin saved me, to his bad eyes.

No, I wasn't at Albert home every night. Mostly on Wednesday, Friday, and the weekends. I think they knew Mary was a wild filly that needed someone to occupy her time, so she didn't go wild. I had no duty, as such.

Mr. Rainey would give us assignments to in the evenings, like, "Set courses from (wherever) to (wherever). We had to set the 'Whey Points.' Those are imaginary spots on the earth to sail to, and then to the next one. The next day he'd review them. Then our "class" got to do the same. I about filled a book with them.

Came mid August and Mary had to have, 'New Attire,' for the start of school. Read that as the women inside a store, jabberin over cloths. Albert and me just took up a bench and waited. Input? Not us. Thems would take half hour to select one blouse. Albert got to pay and we got to carry the packages.

I was thinking of a little gift to give her. Something to remember me by. No, not cloths. I came across this jewelry store and a little silver bear. A broach. Not big, but not small. Ya could put it to a neckless, if you wanted to. Mr. Rainey would think it appropriate.

Come 29 August, 1886, me and Albert stowed her baggage atop, on the back of that Chase and 4, to take them, her to the University. It was two horses for them in that carriage and two for the baggage! He. He. A joke? Maybe.

I got kiss on cheek from Martha and a handshake for Albert. I reached out and put that pin to her blouse, real careful, to a big smile, hands to mine, kiss on both cheeks, and a little peck on the lips. She said, "Be careful, My Sailor." Off she went to waving out the coach window. I went back to, "Measure Your Height."

• • •

27 October, 1894, we tied up to that Northside of South pier, in Norfolk. Admiral Forest, Admiral Stevens, Adjutant Captain Miller, Lt. Stiles, and a pile of officers come aboard. I didn't mind standing there as it was nice weather. We stood for some time.

Out of McIntire cabin thems came to inspect the crew. The volunteers be last, Aft. I saw Saltsgiver come with a podium. McIntire and Stevens sign three times for us. I got whacked by Nichol with my copy of that paper. Such nice came words from Admiral Stevens. "Steller cruise."

Forest come to the podium and me, Bothel, Wagner, and GM2 Burch got called front and center. Forest had these bad eyes to us. We got, oh, his bad words to our poor leadership ability. Not lookin after the crew. Defaulter list he'd never seen in all his time aboard a ship. Men in, "Chains. HIGH crimes." Drunk and fighting. This is supposed to be a welcome, if you please. On, "So, despite this, the ship's crew came together, and On Their Own, Lacking leaders, designed an appropriate Ships Personal Flag to display, So Others Respect Said Ship!" He gave a nod and that Signal Middie popped a flag to the Aft, Port Yard Arm.

All eyes go up to this 4 foot by 5 foot thing made from Old Navy blue blouses. It had 4 different colors of used blue. Three stripper bosn's, not with help from me Oldsters, had to have made this. It had old No. 1 white sail cloth around the edge and lots of Irish pennants. There was stray strings all over. The white crossed stripes were cut by Engle, drunk. I could see a spider web of thread showin. On the inside of the cross was a white officers glove, sown vertical, fingers closed. On the other inside cross was a white glove, like it was over a table top, fingers down. The lower edge of the cross had a red strip that had to come from, once red underwear. I Kid, You, NOT.

Forest looked at it and about swooned. Ya know, fainted. He came back on keel, stood straight, and about yelled out, "And Any Man Who Does Not Give Three Hurzays For This Ships Flag Gets

Flogged!" You are Not supposed to speak while in Quarters, but, the whole ship gives out thems 'Hurzays! Hurzays! Hurzays!' Done! No.

Capt'n McIntire came up and gave me a rolled up a sorta blue thing. It was a small ships flag, as I found out. I have a red one, with white M, from Forest and Monongahela. Another is that yellow one, with snake, from Susquehanna and the red, white, and blue one that replaced it. They are just reminders there in me sea chest.

I know you will be askin about Carrie, here in Norfolk. I see her, more than just some, cordially, and at Regina home. Silvis is in and out with the Admiral and Regina likes company. She was born and raised here. Her father was a sailor, who died long ago. Her mother remarried a store clerk and she now owns the store. Raised here, next to the base, Carrie knows everyone. She worked in the store since she could stand to the counter. Her words.

She, her words, "have no need for a husband." She is a very independent type. "A husband would only be a bother to me." She has a little place over some from the store. I have been there a couple times. A bedroom of bed, chest of drawers, a wardrobe thing, and the usual woman things around. The second room is a kitchen with a table for two, and foyer thing to hang up coats. A comfy place. Nope, she never cooked a meal for me there. There is like a galley, around the corner, to take a meal home. Oh, about no great cost.

I asked her why she keeps coming to Regina home. "I like the woman talk. I put up with men all the time." I asked about me. "Unlike most men, you don't bother me with stupid questions and keep your hands to appropriate places." She likes to take me arm when we walk about. One afternoon she got all cozy and held my hand when we were walking. I think that was mostly to steer me away from where I was headed.

Recently, as a joke, I asked her to marry me. Oh, no, not on a bended knee. I just took both her hands an asked. She got a twinkle in the Wide eyes, a big smile, and said, "So, you made your fortune and never told me. You are giving up the Navy, buy a store here, AND, I'll have a Fancy Surrey and horse to go about in!" She put hands to me cheeks, gave me a little peck on the lips, and, "I like you. But, you tell bad jokes!"

I showed that little flag to her and got Forest Bad Eyes. "And who made this?" I said, 'From the loving hand of the ships company, Dear.' Oh, I got different ones for both sides of the flag. "Well, Dear!" She took a breath, "Mattie and the woman Can Make One Better!" Oh, Forest eyes here. "It is going to cost you, Dear!" It did money wise. As I said, it is the Flag of St. Andrew, with the Gauntlets, and that red strip to the lower edge of the White Crosses.

I paid to have some small ones made, like the one I got, for the ships officers. The crew? "Well, DEAR," and I heard that cost. I figure they made the first ones so they could make more, under thems Oldsters supervision. I had 3 large ones made. It cost me, "Dear!" She is like that.

It was Friday, 16 November, me log says, I got called to the Squadron Admiral office. His clerks act like rats nibbling on cheese, in the corner. Fitzsimons gives me looks and a thumb to the admiral meeting room. No Captain Saltsgiver, nor Nichol was around. I didn't see any Marines outside. I go in to, yep, Admiral Forest, at that dang desk, and a finger to a chair in front of it. No Blue service jacket nor that worn one was there. Just letters at his hand. "Naval Observatory, Washington, D.C. likes your information on observed currents." That letter comes forward, "As you report them, QM1." It is an ongoing project you know about. "They are considering your apparatus, for use as a speed log." His eyes was like your MaMa sayin you got OK grades in school. Not bad, just not good.

The next letter I get was from the Secretary of the Navy. I read the letter head as string of titles, and heard, "Don Diego, of the Spanish Navy, sent his compliments to our Navy. He complimented our seaman skills and all, QM1." His dead eyes and. "Under an Old Admiralty Law, he says Shenandoah has a knight aboard and no Nationality Flag Displayed, QM1." He went on with, "Captain McIntire would have been defeated, as the letter said, to go to Weather gauge." Oh, more eyes. I said that Gunner, Campbell, 'All ships officer determined the action, Admiral.' I hate his cold eyes. No, we didn't need to as, I told you, he had big sail problems.

"The Flag of St. Andrew. Gauntlets. One up to show power and one dropped, for a challenge. A private letter from Don, Diego said he would not care to challenge you to a fight, QM1." Came words of, "He asked if you would have shot him with that big rifle. I replied that I didn't know," Up, about the door and heard, "QM1. Are you good with that carbine?" I said, 'Shot a deer in the neck, and an officer's horse, some 2 hundred yards ahind it, Admiral. An accident. Shot deer at 3 hundred, when I was in practice.' I give him a look and, 'The bandolier has some lead rounds. I can feel them. The last one would have been to him. The rest, buck shot, for theie boarding party, Admiral.' I forgot to mention me pistol.

I be busy sine days as Admiral Stevens has all available sailors come to Squadron for consideration on where to send them. We have to muster 3 times a day. Fitz? He is a tyrant to them 2 clerks at me place and the 2 at Admiral Office. Shush. He is real sweet on his girlfriend, Zoe. He likes to meet her in the evenings. 'Course, he still goes aboard Shenandoah, about daily, to no good words to me.

I still go down to Harold and Ella place. It is close and cold out. Carrie stops in sometimes. Her place ain't that far off. Yes, Ella and her know each other. I think they have a Telly 'tween them places to say when I'm there. She doubles the cost of me evenings. Once, shush, when Carrie didn't come in, for once, I get, all hush, to me ear, "She just might be your soul mate. She likes you." It was a nice thought till I heard, "Harold! Get that food up here afore I deck you." Then came she smile, "Like me and him."

Yes, I got your new letter, Thank you and one from MaMa. I be here in me little room, at Squadron Barracks. It is cold out. It is cold in here. I talked to that BM2 about heat, to no good words. I about need me gloves on to write. Shush. I have a nip in me glass, with Spritzer water. Cheap whiskey to keep off the cold. The spritzer to makes it better.

BM1 Bothel and BM2 Wagner? Both have rooms, other side of this barracks. Little places, like mine. Former closets. BM1 isn't there but as required. More suppers go out the back door of the galley than just for Warrant Silvis and Regina place.

BM1 has a small place down Hampton road for his wife Matilda, Mattie. A nice woman. She has been to Warrant Silvis home, where we met. The Navy wives just get together when the men away. Mattie is a seamstress and works with Carrie. Yes, Miss Carrie from afore, who I did write to. I got one little letter from her at that Yukatan place.

The Shenandoah is to start to load out this next week, 17 December. A little late, as it has but been cold. I'm invited to be to Regina place for supper a lot. Silvis is there, along with Fitz and Zoe. Carrie is a, "Maybe." Always, "Maybe." Christmas, the 25th, she is to be there. I got Regina cold eyes when I mentioned presents to open. Carrie manages the seamstresses where Mattie words. So, I went to do a day visit to Effie, her mother, at the store. Oh, I met Effie afore. She and Carrie are real close in looks. I figure Effie looked, as Carrie does, some years ago. She is a lovely and very nice woman, most of the time, to me.

So, I ask her what Carrie needs, as gifts. Oh, she has that same laugh and said, "A good husband, a nice place to live, AND, a little brat of a girl, like she was, running around her legs!" That was not possible. 'I need some presents, for Christmas.' She said, "Practical ones or ones to joke her?" I said practical and got, "Oh, Poo! You are no fun." I said that friends would be there to see them. That got me odd looks, a smile and, "I'll take care of it." It cost me 5 dollars Gold and two Silver dollars.

The barracks needs a better coal stoker. It is not warm in me room. Shush. It is good I have that cheap whiskey and spritzer water to sip. Oh, it is hot whiskey. The spritzer about puts out the fire. Tomorrow is a Monday, 17 December. I just know Fritz will be in no good humor. He never is on a Monday. He needs to get married! He! He! Have a fine Christmas and Happy New Year!

By Your Leave, Missy,

An Old Sea Dog,

IN THE YEAR 1895, 26 JANUARY:

Dear Miss Judith,

I have lots of time to write. We be underway to the Med. Like I ain't been there before. Yes, we got underway from Norfolk, as we was there! He! He! It seems the officers had a New Year's Eve party's to attend, Monday. Capt'n asked to leave on that Thursday. That was good as the Volunteers did it up proper, for New Year's Eve too. Oh, shush, at Admiral expense. They did it down at Harold and Ella's place. I was not there. Nichol mentioned thems activities.

Washington, D.C. and them in the Navy Department had concerns for the Spanish Captain claiming I was a Knight. It seems that was an old law that was never repealed in Admiralty Law. I, nor officer can use "Titles." Knight is a word, but. It was an accusation, in general, that had to be dealt with. Oh, Ellis, Forest clerk, told Fitz, mine, about all the papers that went round.

Judge Advocate General, read Admiral Lawyer, and his staff got with others Admiralty law types. They found legal terms to cover me. Remember Mr. Reynolds, from Philly? He was a Warrant Gunner. Not a real officer is why he could wack us with them swords. He wore a crossed swords symbol on the right breast pocket of his dress uniform. It designated him as Master-At-Arms.

No, there was no great ceremony to pin that on me. I got called to Admiral Stevens place, a thumb jerk to go into his room, and his bad eyes. Oh, a Captain, legal pin on his collar, had me sign this paper and I got handed that breast pin, silver, as I was enlisted, and a handshake. They said I need to come up with a flag. Admiralty law called for a personal flag. The Laws said it had to be flown, at least in battle. This was before that Christmas dinner at Regina's place.

Fitz, bless his heart, sent letters, signed by Admiral Stevens, Shush, maybe, to Washington about 'Military Protocol' for this "Master-At-Arms" thing, to tell me what to do in, say, Parades, Inspections, all the Navy formal things. That book gave me headaches what with more words of others than Master-At-Arms. I underlined stuff and had Fitz read it also. That boy has a mind for this legal stuff. He underlined more of them words, like I read in that Admiralty law book on that train to Cresson. I gave him wide latitude on liberty, as long as he was there for muster, well, don't ask. He loves Zoe.

The morning of 3 January, oh, it was the usual sendoff ceremony of Admirals, and officers coming aboard Shenandoah. Whistles, bells, them dang Marines stompin and all to them goin into McIntire cabin for wine and what they do. They come out, "Attention." Forest, all, inspect the divisions and back to volunteers. Saltsgiver was at the end of each line, 4, with six, and back to the front. A podium came out and McIntire signed for the volunteers. Forest gives a whisper to Saltsgiver, who gave a whisper back. Oh, to have a Box Camera picture of his face. He had to look up, as I was in full regalia, center on that Poop Rail. I'd have given him a cutesy wave but, I was at attention. That Book said of me place.

Oh, he was red in the face and called me down. I got to that place the book says, in Full Regalia, draw the sword, give him sword honors, and back in the sheath. Me gauntlet glove, with arm piece, give him a proper salute. Forest is more mad than I ever seen. "And Your Personal Flag, QM1?" I turn a quarter to Starboard and yell out, 'Signal Middie! Master-At-Arms Personal Flag.' It was rolled up in light line, Starboard side halyard. He pulled the line and it popped out! Capt'n McIntire, who about spit when I read him this from that book, yelled out, "Salute!" All hands did, warned. Forest about blew up.

Into McIntire cabin he pulled me by me neckerchief. Glorious words came to me ear. The cat in the Fore peak? Well, the Marine Major over the field heard his words. When he had to come up for a breath I pointed to the book on McIntire desk. 'Admiral. Proper protocol is required, performed as prescribed, Sir.' I guess he didn't like that Sir. Ya can't say Admiral twice in the same sentence! Protocol. It was in that book.

Now, that Pilot, yes, the same guy, sure gave me looks, standing at the rudder angle indicator. I hadn't changed. He kept lookin at the gloves, sword, and pistol. No, the Armoror allowed me no cartridges, nor that carbine. Engle came up with china cup coffee for Capt'n and a mug for Pilot, along with sweet breads for both. Ahh, a fine, cold Navy day to sail.

Two days South East, by East, it got warmer. We was headed to Bermuda. We do that in Winter. The North Atlantic, as I've said, is no place to cross. 7 January, 1895, we was standin off the Governors place. The winds was just contrary. North, Nor West, then Nor East. Navigator, Mr. Gailey, mentioned main anchor, in his Daily Report. I mentioned ketch aft, 'Captain.' I got his nod and the Bosn's made it so.

The barge went over the side with Wagner at the helm. Nor Easter gear was under the seats. Lt. Caldwell stayed ahind, in case of bad weather. Capt'n, Nav, Gailey, Gunner Campbell, Mr. Chips, McGraw, and Doc Stiteler came along. I don't know if they had visited here afore. We arrived to that pier at midafternoon. The Governor had a reception committee there. It is hard to miss a ship, right out his winders.

Thems missed looking out the windows during that table talk and invite to dinner. Capt'n forgot the sun sets at a time. Wagner had already gone to look for lodging. He did when the wind came from direct North, being a little shallow of water out there, and the waves growin up. The staff invited us up, in groups, to a fine meal. I see Yourn eyes rollin here.

So, yep, Brit Crowns and down to one place. Edith didn't worn Alfa about us. Wagner, me, and those that stayed here afore, sneak up to the bar, and don't look up. Edith yells out, wrong, "Alfa! Got some here say you owe them good whiskey, a hot bed, and hot woman to sleep with!" Thems at the door just look at her. Edith backed up to block it.

I never see thems look so wild at that knife in her hand. Oh, she just took the other, to their faces, inspecting thems. I heard, "Well, looks like fresh meat to me!" Them sailors sure had big eyes! She turns to the bar, finds me in her eyes and I got, "Do I get to keep them for the night?" I said, "Alfa, is your house. They be in it! Just make sure they are 'UP' by 5:30 AM, please.' Edith don't like Alfa's laugh to this.

I don't know if it was the beer or to bed after bar closing that caused them to look so worn that next morning. Edith, and me went to our bed around 10 PM. I fell asleep listenin to Alfa tellin stories to thems. I could imagine Uncle Curtis down there and carryin on with her. His voice was to me mind as I fell asleep.

The officer didn't look any better, there on that pier. 'Row Dry,' got lots of attention. No, no crew in no mutiny or officers bad words aboard. Bush and Hood had the ships position as the same as yesterday.

The weather to Gibraltar is good, bad, and the usual. I write at the Chart Table, on duty, next to the Smokin Lamp, after dark, and some in the Chart Room, when it is bad. No "Ships Master" is aboard. It is a big table, to look at Charts. It got a lantern over it and a nice, tall chair to sit in, be a quiet place, cept for the ships timbers, and the voices about the ship. The ship ain't but so big so ya can hear thems, below, Smokin lamp lited.

It be rainy out. I be here in the Chart Room. A lantern is tied to the timber above, so it rocks back and forth. I got a Stern window to look out of and see nothing. Just gray water ahind us. I know you will ask about Carrie and Christmas stuff.

Carrie is like that cat at home, well, ago. One minute wanting to be petted and next ya get scratched for doing the same. It came to a call or just sat, or walked off. We was at Regina home that Friday, Saturday, and Sunday, afore Christmas. I walked her to her place to smiles, small talk of the night, and she might well have not been there on that Sunday.

For Christmas dinner me, Fitz, and Bothel carried them pails from the galley to Regina place. Silvis was on that Admiral ship. Oh, Cook 1st Steward, filled thems up, he did. "Shush, they give me extra money for this. Just go to waste. More that needed, for to feed."

Regina likes this one Madeira wine. I gave her 4 bottles on Friday. Tastes nice, but, the men have pocket bottles. The first gift to her, from me, early, was 4 nice wine glasses, for her and the woman to drink from. I got OOOOS. Nice glasses. We had a fine meal and toasts around.

For 'Presents,' each woman got one around, to open. There was scarfs, stockings, and Regina got a personal one from Silvis, to hoots. A wood box comes to Carrie, opened to, two fine crystal wine glasses. That got, Ohhs, and me a cheek kiss. The second round was same woman stuff and Carrie opened a box to two fine china cups.

Oohs, a cheek kiss, and a look. The third round was more little stuff to a box to Carrie hands. It was two fine china plates to LOTS of OOOHS. Me? I got a nice smile, a cheek kiss, and side glance. We said only 4 gifts, with pay and all. 4th round is more little stuff and little box to Carrie. 2 sets of nice flat wear.

They call it flat wear as not silver or gold. It had a pattern on the handles. Regina, probably the rest, had only plain stuff. I got a smile, kiss on the cheek, to OOOHs and all. Her side glance said I was dead meat. Come 8 PM I was walkin back to her place with these 'Gifts' in me arms. Oh, she was Not like Mary up there in Philly. Carrie walked ahead, hands around her waist, and no words to me.

Come her place, well, the boxes got grabbed from me arms, "Night," and up she went. I looked around, adjusted that knife, marlin spike leather, and wondered what happened. Oh, I carry thems out in town, at night. A sailor walkin back alone? Some might take not kindly to that, this part of town.

I made it some steps and heard, ahind, "Effie bought your presents, didn't she!" I turned around to not mad eyes nor good ones. 'You never look in store windows, when we are walkin. Never go in to look! I never knew what you wanted. Effie wanted to joke you, with presents. I said no. What you needed.' She never called her MaMa. I don't know why. Got a nod and, "She forgot to send some along. Come look, please." Oh, a new word to me ears from her.

You can say men are as dumb as dirt to lookin at a room. I took off me coat, to that foyer thing, and her standing there. She turned, so I can see and said, 'So?' I was lookin at her face. It is nice to look at. I got better eyes than I for the last gift. Red cheeks, from the cold, hair mused up from the hat, and her hand went out to the table in the kitchen. Nice hands. I had seen them a lot.

"So," got that hand to her little table set with a silver guiled candle holder, two more sets of flatware, plates, cups and saucers. I got another hand to them two windows in the kitchen. Her hand goes to curtains and those atop. Ok. 'Curtains.' Came her evil eyes and, "New, with lace." Oh, ok. I get pulled, by me neckerchief, to the bedroom. OK, a bedroom. Oh, her hand to a nice flowered bed cover, a nice glass, brass, and fancy lamp on that table. 'So?' I got them Forest eyes and relegated to a kitchen table chair.

Out of the bedroom she came in a nice dress to her feet. I saw wiggly toes. Into that room and out in another, different dress, and same wiggly feet. I figure the Coal Stoker didn't do so good in heating the place up, like at the barracks. She comes back in these, slippers, with a bottle of that Madeira wine, like I bought for Regina. No, she poured it to them two glasses and sat right next to me, at that table. I got better eyes from her than I seen since forever. Tipsy, from the wine, two bottles, Carrie was, ah, another woman. Had a fine night to ourselves, we did. I never knew she could have such a nice smile, to me.

Oh, I caught up with Effie, Carrie not there, about ALL I gave as gifts. I saw what I seen. There was new pillows, cases, sheets, and comforter on the bed. New curtains to them three windows. A dinner set for 4. Those 2 dresses and slippers. Cushions for the chairs, two silver guild candle holders, and other little, 'Personal things?' Effie was, is, quite a character.

I got back, from her, 3, 2 Bit silver pieces. Lookin at that list I asked about, 'No pots or pans?' they were the only thing I didn't see, thinkin back. I got her laugh and snickers to no end. Back on her 'Keel,' I got, "Did you see a stove in her room?"

Somes say I overlook the obvious stuff, but, I noticed the ceramic jewelry box on the mirror dresser. It was not there afore, as much as I saw her room. I saw that new carpet under the table. I noticed her slippers. "It is a boarding house. She eats meals where she lands. Never learned to cook." I got an earful of her growing up here. Her last words were, "I like you. But, you tell bad jokes, like pots and pans," to another burst of laughs. "She likes you. Why, I think, she keeps goin to Regina's home, when you are here." That got her far off eyes and, "About the only one she has seen, regular." Then, bad eyes to, "When you are here!"

Come New Year Eve, Regina invited the usual. Oh, we hauled them pails of food to her place. Cook 1st Steward filled one with, "Me own Plum Duff." That is crushed ships biscuits, plums, if available, apples, cherries, and any fruit in a can to hand. Now, rum, shoosh, or whiskey, Shoosh, is added last, so it don't burn off in the cookin. Ya just let it set to the batch.

Carrie showed up with 2 bottles of that Madeira wine she likes. I noticed the old, warn coat she always wore, and her usual dress and all. She sat right next to me and more smiles than I ever got. Oh, the woman just teased each other to death about the men there. I saw that Fitz and Zoe was about tied at the waist. It must have been that Plum Duff that put thems over the edge. Maybe the wine, we men don't touch.

Come 9 PM Zoe about pulled Fitz from his seat. Carrie was in conversation back to her place, with more words than normal, about the evening and arm to mine. I had to go up, "For a last drink to New Years!"

Well, I got sat at the table and crystal glass, with that wine. Seated next to me, came, "I'd have embarrassed them, to have worn one of the new dressed." That was true. "Same with that coat you got for me." True. I got a nice kiss on the lips and "Next time, ask me! I'll give you a list, Dear!" Next, she was back into her bedroom and changed to new dress Effie got her.

It was a cold night out. Luckily, I didn't have a be back to the base by 10 PM. I didn't need some whiskey and spritzer to feel warm either. 6 AM come early, to me mind, with, BM2 voice to get us up. It was his, 'Happy New Year! Up, and Out!'

Come this last Thursday, 24, January, 1895, we made that offering to Gibraltar. The Lookout yelled down about an Admiral Flag on St. Lawrence. Oh, everyone had to get dressed up for him. McIntire took exception to my full regalia. I had to say, 'First introduction to a Flag Officer, I have to be in Full uniform, Sir,' to his bad looks, but.

We tied up to the pier, after them dang guns went off, real loud, and moored ahead of St. Lawrence. Came whistles, bells, them Marines there as Admiral Taylor came up with his staff. Oh, Capt'n salutes him and into his cabin they go. Over? No.

They came out and had to inspect the crew. Me volunteers were in their divisions. I be at center, Poop deck rail, my place. Coming back from the fore deck Taylor looked up and about stumbled over his own feet. Oh, I got his finger to come down to him. Yep, I gave him Full Sword Honors, saluted with that gauntlet, and arm protector. I turned a quarter turn and yelled out, 'Signal Middie, My Flag, if you please.' The Book says it has to be rolled up, and POPPED, at this moment. I got, "I always said you were a true troublemaker, QM1."

Being cordial, he invited me into the Capt'n cabin. Me, Capt'n, and 1st Lieuy. Engle put 4 crystal wine glasses to the table and some Madeira wine to the glass. I got his toast, "To The Ships Master-At-Arms." Taylor knows his protocol. Salute done, oops, I drank mine down, and Engle puts more to mine. All but me get shooed out of that cabin. Oh, such fine words I got. He'd heard, via Packet Ship that something went on with a Spanish ship. He complimented me flag. Eyes said different.

The flag, ya ask. I gave me idea to Carrie. We made a drawing of it on paper. She said she'd have the seamstresses get to it. Back at her place, after Christmas, and presents, she said I'd have it in a day or so. I saw her Friday, Saturday, and Sunday, afore New Year's Eve party. I got no flag from her.

New Year Eve, as said, we went back at her place. She went to the bedroom, again. Next, she came into the kitchen with this 4 by 5 foot flag, held out stretched, by her open arms. Oh, bright eyes I saw as flag is up to nose, and down to calf and slippers. "Soo?" I said, '2nd best lookin thing in this room.' I heard, "And First?" I said, 'Them curtains ahind ya!' Oh, that sure didn't go over well.

She quickly rolls up that flag and started to beat me with it. Oh, such words a sailor would say I got! It was a good thing there were fire crackers and rockets goin off or the whole house would have been bangin on the door for the noise.

I finally got her arms pinned ahind. With her thrashin around, we ended up in her bed room. In her ear, I said, 'Kidding! Kidding. Perfect Flag, Dear!' That got better eyes. "And, in here, besides the curtains, Dear!" I said, and you'd not like this, 'Oh still 2nd, Dear.' Her big eyes I got. Not as pretty as,' and I got the devil lookin at me when I said, 'That crystal and brass coal oil lantern on the little table, Dear!'

Now, I beat her 2 out of 3 in the wrestling matches we did. Wiry she be. Touch as any man and fights dirty. I got bit three times. No, she won the last match. Cheated, again! But, she ended up laughin to tears. "And, the Flag?" I said, 'Not as pretty as someone here, Dear.' Maybe that kiss is what kept me warm the rest of that night.

The flag? It is the crew version of that St. Andrew, with, ah, better stitchin, and red strip. Yes, the same gauntlets, left and right. For the middle, top and bottom blue, is a sword and carbine crossed. Oh, so pretty I hate to put it to a halyard. I had her make up some small ones. Forest got one and Capt'n McIntire had to get one. Admiral Taylor thanked me for his. Protocol.

I told this to Phoebe, the beer tender here in Gibraltar. She said I was lucky to get out of the room alive. Oh, how she laughed at me jokin Carrie. Carries laugh, after the wrestling, is still in me ears. Effie had paid for half the gifts I saw. I forgot about one, in our carryin on.

The packet is here. I finish this up so you know I made it alive to Gibraltar. I date this as 26 January, 1895.

By Your Leave, Missy,

An Old Sea Dog

IN THE YEAR 1895, 15 APRIL:

Dear Miss Judith,

Yes, I be here in the Mediterranean. The Caribbean would be warmer. Here, it is like Norfolk. We get lots of cold air, down from them Alps mountains. Close to Africa it is a bit warmer. Oh, as is cold on the Poop. I write from smokin lamp, or, in me New Room! Mine and Bothel. The Chart Room is next to the Capt'n cabin.

Admiral Taylor transferred his flag to us. He was in Gibraltar only to greet us. We took him to that Toulon Frigate. Came him, his adjutant, a Lieutenant, and a clerk, with a bunch of baggage, chests, and cloths. That was not me worry. Berthing was. I'm in-charge of assigning it. McIntire got to sleep with Taylor, officers with the gun room, and clerk to hammock. The problem was officers needed more room.

Mr. Chips, McGraw, did some adjustment to the Middie quarters, but, he needed to take down poles we hang hammocks from. The ship don't have full crew, enough, so we shifted places to sleep. It seems me and Bothel was left without a ring to put up our hammocks to. I told the 1st Lieuy we'd hang ours in the, 'Oh, the little Chart Room. Tight, but, OK, Sir.' He gave me bad looks, but and OK!

We left 'The Rock' on Monday, 28 January. Admiral Taylor had visits on Sunday. Oh, yep, guns goin off on us and shore. Bush or Hood man that Rudder Indicator. They have enough time there. Me spot is a stool on the Port side of that table.

The afternoon of 30 January the lookout call down with, "Spanish Frigate, Sails up, Capt'n." They were on the reverse our course and not half hour later we saw that long swallow tail at the main mast Top Gallant. Taylor just said, "War Ship, Captain." Is was a test for McIntire. I seen it in Admiral eyes. "Marine, Strike General Quarters! Boarding Party At The Ready, Tampions off, Gun Ports Closed. 6 Marines Aloft." Capt'n don't like the Admiral eyes. I usually don't either.

Oh, there was regular signal gun salutes back and forth. Captain comes to Admiral and got 6 Marines, whistles, bells, with romp and stomp. Don Estephon, a Lieutenant, and another come aboard. Salutes, handshakes, and to Capt'n Cabin. Yes, a formal ceremony.

The parties came out and start this inspection. Don, spoke to his interpreter, to Admiral, and Captain. Don spoke rapped Spanish. What he said was slow, back to the Admiral. They walked to forepeak, back, and up to the Poop. Mr. Gailey introduced the 4 Bosn's at the helm ram, rod straight. This Don got to me, in Full Regalia, and stopped!

We lock eyes and his words to his interpreter. Yes, I had to unload the rifle, inspected, and reload. The pistol was the same, with the gauntlets on. I pulled out the sword with me right hand, blade to left hand, edge to me, and over. This Don, left handed, went to the Taft rail, does some practice, to the air, with it, and the sword came back, perfectly. I had to salute him.

Our eyes locked I said, 'Bos'n Joseph.' He's was at the helm and came with a rolled up flag to me hand, which I give to Don Estephon. He unrolled me 'Personal Flag.' That was the first time he looked to the Starboard, Aft, outer halyard line.

I got a grin from him, a hearty laugh and, "So, the Highland Knight now has a Personal Flag." He had nice English. "My cousin, in the Caribbean, warned me of one, and not to attack him." A fling of Spanish words went to the interpreter. "So, Knight, you guard the ships Flag. Who guards yours?" I said, 'The ships Navigator and Captain, Sir.' Oh, his eyes and "So, it takes two to guard yours, but, only you to guard the ships?"

Still eyes to eyes I said, 'I have the rifle to shoot those navigating the other ship. Closer, I have the pistol with 36 cartridges for others. They only have their swords, Captain.' I got, "And you are a good shot?" I said, 'I would hope we never find a need to know, Captain.'

Now, I'd already saluted him. He was about to walk off and come back with, "And, your sword? Are you good with it?" Admiral and ships Capt'n are wonderin about me answer. I could see them in the corner of me eye, them leaning to hear. 'Which style do you fight with, Captain? French, Italian, English, or Spanish? I hope you don't turn your Left Wrist, inward, at the last moment, to penetrate the rib cage, Sir,' to his wide eyes.

At the gang plank there was the romp and stomp, whistles, bells, and all, to my bad ears. McIntire hands Don Estephon a small ships flag. Oh, gracious he is for this. His Spanish or English I couldn't hear. I know he saluted the ships flag, Portside, above me. Honors, I returned it, to his eyes to the Starboard flag.

The ships flag? Well, I had Carrie make up two and a couple little ones, as me money allowed. No, the Purser refused to pay me back. I got it back when Admiral Stevens signed on the 'Volunteers.' It was a cost above for the volunteer party at Ella place. Shush, it also paid for a little gift for Zoe, that Fitz gave her. Loves her, he does. She is a nice woman.

'Afore Gibraltar, I approached Capt'n McIntire about the cost for material to make more flags. Little ones to give out and, 'Big ones tear, Captain.' That material shop in Gibraltar set a price for materials. I brought back the material the money allowed.

Oldsters and fore masters took good Number one sail for the outer, white edging. They used the good blue sail cloth I got, for the Main. The material shop had some stiff white piping and narrow red stuff, for that strip. I took them 3 strippers Bosn's and set them to thread. Hearty Thread. No, no Irish pennants. All was sown proper, under oldster eyes. It was one of them that Spanish Capt'n got.

The winds were not good so we skirted the Minorca Islands. No problem there. Just some Tackin and Wearing. We got to Toulon on 2 February. A Frigate was tied up all neat and clean. A pretty thing. It has been there 3 weeks, so shore prices was up, close to them piers. I never go there. I took them 4, 3 strippers Bosn's up to that 2nd story place to have refreshments. The ladies called them, "Cuties!" Me? I got their bad looks and laughs when I said to take care of thems. Which they did. Me helm crew.

O7 February, 1895, we made Gaeta, Italy, for water. It was two days and liberty by watches. Yes, I went to see Monic that first evenin. Me, Wagner, Bothel, Fitz, and Engle. A little whisper to her and, well, Fitz is short, little in stature. He can't hold much to drink. But, Engle is tall, little in stature and can't hold much to drink. Monic girls took good care of thems and come 9 PM they staggered back to the ship. Nichol and the Marines watched after thems. It isn't a far walk. The local pick pockets are.

We was quick to Malta, 10 February. We have to check with the Brits, about activities. Our barge to the pier, Capt'n, 1st Lieuy, and Gailey went to see the Governor. My favorite woman, Nora, the nice daughter of a bar keep, was there. I said no liberty but, the barge crew needed refreshments. Oh, just a bit of beer and sweet bread. That is how I get me crews.

We up anchor afore dark and off we went, South. The next morning we got Frigate barge, as schooner, around us like a baby bird lookin for food. A lieutenant was just waving his hat and South we went in his wake, to him to Port, ahind, Starboard, and all over the place, slugger we be. Not afore sundown there that Frigate be. Tripoli, Libya is not real far off. Not far is sand, to the ships ears.

We made the Consulate in Cyprus, 16 February. It seems none of the officer ever been there. Captain thought crew could also do liberty, one section at a time. Two barges went over the side. One with officers aboard. It had Capt'n, Warrant Bos'n and Mr. Gailey. Yep, Armoror, Mr. Chips, Gunner, and Doc Stiteler got introduced. I did the introductions. The Consulate General and staff remembered seein me.

McIntire brought up about a liberty place, shush, where Engle can get his, "Fill." Mr. Caldwell has been to the Med. He had no good place to his mind. I mention Myrtos, that place in Crete. Water, a hotel for officer entertainment, places close to the landing for the crew. Small enough town the Marines could get some liberty.

Captain got his wish for sweet breads with morning coffee. Engle and Fitz had a fine time of the short time it took to get them well lubricated. Oh, Nichol took them back all nice and easy. Bothel made sure they got aboard, with the help of a line around them. No, I left me helmsmen to their own curse. Me and a couple of volunteers tipped hats to them ladies, up there at that place, up that hill. It was cold. The owner allowed us one table inside. Such nice samiches and wine.

I about forgot that last Frigate. We come around Cyprus, afore Myrtos, and headed South, some West. It was to be 'tween Alexandria and Derrna, Libya, but lookin for us. It had two barges as schooners, one to a side, and headed to Cyprus. They knew we was to supply that Consulate. Ya, with whiskey and not much else.

We got back to Malta, 23 February. It seems a conference was goin on. The Admiral was there. No, no US ship. Just him, Adjutant, Lieutenant, and clerk. He put his flag aboard and off he went to his hotel. Good news, liberty by divisions. Bad news? He rode till we hit that Frigate off Algiers. It was the one that came out of Toulon. We got 1 liberty per. Nora, the bar owner daughter, steered them to low cost places. Too much liberty for too little money.

He was not a bother to me but frustrated the crew by just goin to the fore deck and walkin around. Engle was a tizzy. Two to tend to! Spiel, Capt'n steward, was useless. Both got those sweet breads and coffee each morning, from Engle. We off loaded Taylor to that Frigate on 02 March, 1895. Oh, guns from both to bother me ears. Frigate was off Skikda, North Africa.

05 March we was in Gibraltar. Just us. We picked up some mail for the fleet, and dispatches. We stayed an extra day there as Mr. Hitcock, Purser, asked a Brit Supply Officer to get fish, fruit, and vegetables from Tangier, Morocco. That boat smelled real bad! The crew smelled bad. There barrels of dried fish, baskets of old fruit, and I'll say, stuff. Ships cook, Feterman, about had a fit. He and Hitcock went round about this. I heard, "Paid For! Cook!"

The dried fish was 'Preserved' as they do in Africa. It had an odd smell to it and not to a sailor's taste, after hours soakin. Oh, the crew got me involved, as their spokesman. Purser, me, and Capt'n got to talk of this. It was a one way conversation to me.

07 March we started that 2nd round. The next morning was when, 'Them Rats Ate it ALL! Barrels and crates included.' The Cook said so. I asked the Purser about getting stuff from the local dowl. The last Capt'n thought them was a pest so kept firing the guns, blanks, at them.

With permission, I set the lookout to spot fishing dowls. Bothel and Wagner rigged a barge with fore and mid Lateen sails. Triangles. Arms under the seats, 6 crew, plus Wagner and me snuck up on this fishing boat. Our ship was just a nick on the horizon. US Flag ahind, me St. Andrew was to of mast and a white flag to Foremast. We came up on them pullin a net on the Port side.

That fishin boat crew about jumped into the water when I yelled out. It was that Silver dollar I showed them that caught their attention. No, they don't take Gold. So, in sign language I point to me flag and point to myself. Me crew pointed out the 4 soakin tubs so the fishin crew can see them. I finger each one and hold up a Silver Liberty. 10 cents. Nope, he wanted ten, havin seen me silver dollar.

Ya got to go back and forth in a deal. I showed 5 fingers to his 9. I went to 6, got 9. I counted out 8 Liberties to me hand, pointed to the 4 tubs, and done. That was when I gave him a little ships St. Andrew flag. We shook hands and the crew ate fresh fish for supper.

Goin East, on 09 March, we ran into that Frigate, from Toulon, with Admiral Taylor flag flyin. Yes, cotton in me ears. It was off Algiers. Capt'n went over to Flag and back. Next, two barges over with our Marines and crew arms under the seats. "No, QM1! None of your finery!" We pulled up to that pier in Casbah, unloaded the Marines, to guard Admiral, and sat, waiting. A minor local and the Admiral had a conference. A boy on the pier got some coppers for some fruit, to our crews. The Frigates? No my concern. The next day was the same and the same boy. We got sweet dates, olives, and some local bread. Water? We brought our own. The Frigate crew? Not me concern. I wasn't told what this was about.

I do know there was no goin to Toulon nor Gaeta from water. The North Frigate was in Palermo. We had to stop there anyway, so the Harbor Master could arrange for the water and the Purser had to pay him. I was there, as the new Assistant Purser, and asked about fruit and vegetables, in Aspra, and a local translator. It is a nice little town we been to afore.

The gig landed me and Purser at the pier in Aspra. He went for the water wagons as I walked over to that now older boy, with that sign, and asked if he spoke English. "Some." I never asked him afore. The Harbor master mentioned him. He didn't like the 'Guide' part. "Need bar patrons." I said I'd fill up the place.

Come to find out the area around the town grows the stuff sold in Palermo. They have caverns where it's cool to store stuff. I found that out when we went to a store and I asked about stuff. I pointed to a box of carrots and said I'd want 20. The Store keep and the boy got arms flyin to the words said.

First liberty barge didn't get to the pier till after 6 PM. Feterman made a fine dinner with fresh stuff no one wanted to miss. Oh, I made sure the boys bar was filled. Oh, I got hugs and kisses from his grandma. She was part English and Sicilian. She reminded me of Alfa, in Bermuda. She kept up a good conversation and served out some good food.

Boarding Party practice? Well, I can't fake bein poor with a sword. Bothel, Wagner, and Burch took me place. I get to stand at that fence and play with the Middies. We always have a couple, or the officers. No! All wood stuff. Me sword has a nice edge. Practice puts dents in it. Oh, for weight, Armoror and I came up with lead slugs to places. It gives them a nice feel.

Besides them halberds, swords, and pikes, the crew likes to practice with them revolvers. Colts. They use the same cartridges as me Break Top. The Marines still have some old trap doors, like me rifle, so I got lots of cartridges. Anyway, Gunner put a stick in a barrel, stick to a hole in the bulwark. It is hard to miss from not 10 feet, mostly. I think some close their eyes when they pull the trigger. Just sittin in the water, no wind, a barrel gets thrown over the side so them Marines can shoot. I practiced with them. Rifle and me pistol.

We stopped in Malta for 3 days. There was no Frigate in Toulon so, we was ahead of schedule. Nora took good care of the crew. On to that Consulate in Cyprus. Yes, whiskey only. The crew mostly behaved. Me 4 cuties and them 4 fore masters was to watch. Youngins and Oldsters mixin with youngins and oldsters sure can kick up a fuss. I won't comment more.

We hit that Frigate off Egypt. Purser gave them enough fruit for a meal of plum duff. The crew gave him bad looks when it went over the bulwark. I thought we purchased enough for all three Frigates and us. He does have a habit of holding stuff back.

Oh, stopped in Myrtos, we did. Too much liberty for money in pockets. Purser only gives what is on the books. Me? I don't drink that much and a get nice view up there at that little place. I get a samich and wine. It is a cheap place. It was not as cold so we could sit outside. The women give us, sometimes, a wink. The men give us hard looks. The children give little waves, which got the women winks.

Nora tried to find "Real Cheap" places for the crew. We was three days in Malta and still ahead of schedule. McIntire don't want to hear about, "Possible Bad Weather." I put it in the Daily Sailing Report. No, Gaily gives it, with Bush or Hood ahind. Enterin or leavin Port then it be me, ahind them. We left 7 April.

Two days later the lookout calls out a fishin boat. Barge over, Latine sails set, the same crew, and arms under the seats. This boat just sat there. It was a little bigger than the barge, so we was careful. A silver dollar shown and we parleyed for them 4 soakin tubs of fish. They had no big fish. It was a different Capt'n. I got 4 tubs for 7 silver dimes. Purser gave me a, "Sniff," at the cost. The crew just loved the fresh fish Feterman cooked.

11 April I got to stuff cotton in me ears. Admiral Taylor and that Frigate was off Algiers. Capt'n to Admiral, back, and I got called to his cabin. It seems the Consultant to the Sultan was having a meeting, same place as afore, not far from the pier. Taylor wanted me there to observe. I asked about weapons? Oh, the Marines were to guard him. I was to observe, "Watch, no more."

It was a nice place with low table and everyone sittin on cushions. I couldn't say much for the food. Hand food. Just dip in a hand, or bread, and eat, whatever. I count guards, thems, and all. It seems the Sultan don't like our ships in the area. He don't like us buyin fish or stuff. We, all, must come to him for permission. He had a smiley face with lots of gestures. I figure interpreter left some out.

No, I didn't talk to Taylor. I just wrote out what I saw and gave it to McIntire. I didn't need to ask him if he like the food. Admiral and him dipped lots of bread, but didn't pick up much from the dish. After eating that dried fish of theirs, I could understand.

We made Gibraltar on 15 April, 1895. Phoebe made sure Fitz and Engle got filled up, cheap. I may have helped, some. She has some rum you wonder about. She put it in their beer, ahind their backs. Oh, Engle still slept in, a bit. He makes that sweet bread afore touchin ashore. I got to look after me 'Volunteers.' Nope, not a one has signed on. Nope, McIntire ain't asked. He will, in time.

The Packet is in so I got your letter, Thank You. One from MaMa, also. Me favorite girls. I got one from Carrie. Yes, Norfolk Carrie. I read it through and "Everyone" is "Fine" back there. Her, Effie, and Regina, who she sees, "Not often." There was a, "Thank You for the wonderful Christmas gifts." I read it three times and wondered about something. I can't read more than is wrote. Mail is always welcome.

Purser is callin for mail. I finish this up in me little Chart Room. There is the smell of sweet breads from the Capt'n cabin. Good old Engle at work. There be lots to wonder about. Carrie, Admiral Taylor, and all. 'Nother, Round of the Med.

By Your Leave, Missy,

An Old Sea Dog,

IN THE YEAR 1895, 07JULY: MEDITERRANEAN

Dear Miss Judith,

You say to write when things are goin on. Only news, till not long ago, was Engle found a way to get stinking drunk the first day in each port we hit. No, that is not real news. 'Cept, I didn't help him. He did it right good on his own.

We completed our two more rounds of the Med and it was about a bore. The same ports, 'cept didn't make Toulon nor Gaeta. Nope, not a look at Monic. I made some notes, I be lookin at but, you could read me last letter and would be the same. Even most of the crew was comin back early, from Liberty. Oh, they got lubricated on the local drinks but nothing new to do.

We had the usual Spring storms here. It is warm off Africa and cool North, in European places. Malta was the place the weather changed each time we was there. Cool, warm, then almost cold. Last time it was warm. The seas was glass smooth or, well, as I've said, the place is like a bath tub, after ya put a child in there to worsh. It must have been a giant child that got thrown in a couple times. He! He!

We left Gibraltar for the 3 round on 20 April. No, no African food ship, with a bad smell to it. The crew and fish. Purser decided the cost of fresh fish was worth it. That or the crew would throw him over the side. Also, as I mentioned, we can get fresh stuff from dowls.

22 April we found one of them fishin boats, just sailed up close, and put a barge over the side to it. Purser went along, supposedly, for the ride only. He said 8 Liberty's was too much. He tried to get into the bidding. I paid 9 pieces of Silver as that Capt'n took offense to his words. Well, so did all of us crew!

2 days later I had cotton to me ears as we found the Frigate, Admiral Taylor aboard, off Algiers. Capt'n to him and he stayed a while. Back and new orders. It seems a Frigate, via Packet, decided to stay in Palermo afore off to Toulon. We got some other orders, I'll get to.

The ship ain't been into Toulon, for little repairs, since the first go around. Bos'n and Mr. Chips talked to the Capt'n about the riggin. Don't look to me for what to explain. It was all that stuff up high. Nope, I don't go up no masts. I might, if the ship was sinkin, so I'd be the last to drown. I do know them Top Gallants came on deck and be still there. Something about the iron straps. Bosn's got more names for things than I had to remember when I was in Boot Camp. We have a deal. I navigate to keep us off the rocks. They set the sails, so we don't run into rocks.

No Top Gallants for light breezes to push us along, so, it was a slow go around. We needed them days we didn't sail to Toulon nor Gaeta. I had to be present for the Morning Reports about our position. Capt'n don't like the 6 or so knots we be makin, normally. During one storm I did give him a grin and said, 'Makin 9 knots, Captain.' The wind and current was from ahind. He don't like me jokes.

We found that Frigate anchored in Palermo. Stores went over and Purser off to pay for water, in Aspra. Anchored off Aspra, that was boy right there and off for fresh stuff. The pickins was slim as fall crop was about all sold off. I told Purser Hitcock, 'Beggars can't be choosy!' Oh, There was enough for Plum Duffs for each ship we hit. Shush. We got some dried dates, plums, and stuff that the man said was hard to sell. To a seepin tub, for a day or so, and they tasted good.

Angelo, that boy, liked how I paid for a guide. It was more than that copper, afore. I filled up that bar and two more. Overflow. Florina, grandma, made sure we all got some of her food, to just wonder how she made it taste so good. "Shush. I put in good meat and the Sicilian woman add too much spice, to hide their bad cooking." Oh, we gave her, each of us, hugs and kisses.

Malta was Malta. Nora set the crew to places for refreshments. We was still ahead of schedule. The Consulate got their 'Provision' and the officers got a nice supper. Youngsters and Oldsters got frisky all over the place. Nope! Spring was in the air. It must have been the sweet smell of the flowers. Still not my concern.

A Frigate was down South, close to Africa. Purser made sure they got their share of stuff for plum duff. We went up to Myrtos, Cyprus. It was warmer than last but still cool. Shush. The children put noses to glass in that place we get samiches and wine. The store keep has some hard candy in jars. Few get a piece. The cloths of shoppers say why. In hand language to keeper, two Liberty's to his hand, each child got to choose tween them flavors. Some woman shook their heads. The store keep whispered something, a piece to the child, and we got more nods, from the women. Those men just don't like us!

I can't say much about Malta, again. Nora don't need to show thems where the cheapest places are. Know them by heart. We caught up another fishin boat off Tunisia, headed West. No, no Purser allowed. It seems fish was aplenty. I got 5 tubs for 8 Liberty's. Admiral Taylor and that Frigate be 'On Station,' still off Algiers. The day after we ran into a, I call them Ibex ship. Smaller than the Spanish Frigate, 3 masts. A gun to other side and they wanted to speak. I went in an armed barge, to grins and the fruit shown. Purser sure don't like how much I pay for stuff.

So, the 3rd round ended in Gibraltar, 30 May, 1895, where story starts. Sorta. On that pier was where Gunner, Armoror, and the Marines tried to get a herd of sailors to march, in time, to the beat of that Marine drum. Why? I asked and got, "Because!" Why a boarding Party, ashore, with wood stuff? Me and Bothel watched this, 'Thing.' It was not good.

First, sailors can't march. Second, not in a straight line. Third, some can't hear so well, like me. The ships guns have blown their ears out. They looked like a caterpillar or worm in motion. Last, it was hot, what with thems in wool uniforms. Oh, I heard complaints. They did this the 3 mornings we was there.

03 June, 1895, we left Gibraltar to them guns and our last round, for this cruise. Bush and Hood have done good at the rudder indicator. They know to hold up that finger, a bit longer, when McIntire give an order early. He still gives me the bad eyes. Out of habit, I hold up mine, to more bad eyes. Bush nor Hood can't see me.

Two days out we found a fishin boat and that Ibex together. Oh, no one comes out of Gibraltar not know. I got the fish for 7 Liberty's. They had a full net to the side to on load. That Ibex Capt'n, same as afore, gave the same price for the barrels we filled. Supper was good eats.

The Frigate off Algiers had no Admiral. Junior to Senior and we steered the gig to Frigate. Their Crew said we scraped their ship.

Leaving, our boat hook just happened to scrape some bright work. Came new orders and no Toulon nor Gaeta. Chips protested. Bos'n mentioned Top Gallants and got no good words.

The, ah, 'Ladies,' on the pier at Aspra hooted, whistled, and gave eyes to the 'Boarding Party Practice' of sailors on that pier. I came in the gig, Bothel and Wagner in barges. They had to make a second trip for men and Marines. I will say Florinda made those I brought to that bar a good meal. She'd heard of the, "Practice Parade." That was when Bothel and me gave each other eyes. Oh, hugs and kisses to her. Me brain is sometimes slow. I knew, then, where!

Nora, in Malta, was not pleased with this marching. It took away from the bars. No, no refreshments for me nor Bothel, watching. There was lots of bad words from Saltsgiver, Nichol, Gunner, and Armoror. Admiral Taylor was there to watch. No, no Navy ship, so no cotton to me ears. His flag came aboard the second day.

There was no liberty whilst them was on that pier, in the mornin. Bothel, me, and Wagner watched from the bulwark in the afternoon. No, we was not invited. Ahind, I heard, "Attention on Deck!" Admiral Taylor. I got his finger and he wanted to go up the mast. Oh, he scampered up like a squirrel. Me? I had Bothel get ahind me to, "Watch your feet. Hands to them ropes. DON'T LOOK DOWN!" Which I did, to Bothel bad words and eyes. I guessed Taylor wanted a private word to me.

So, first time in me life I groped meself up to that Main Mast place the Marines stand. I held on to that mast like to crush it. First I seen Taylor grin in a long time. 'Poop is me place. No Top Mast in my blood!' I sat on that platform, leggs, ya both, over the side, and hangin on to the mast braces. One for each hand. Oh, he liked me expression. Scared, I was. We was In-port so the ship didn't rock back and forth.

"How will those sailors act, if they had to fight?" I ask, 'Aboard ship or ashore?' I got eyes. 'They train to fight off a boarding party, aboard.' About that time hear bad words from the pier. Bad marching, to the Marine drum. 'You want to kill some people or just scare them?' I got, "Scare, first, and the last, only if necessary."

I got those eyes he gets when thinkin and, "Word is you are a magician," Admiral Forest words, "And, Actor." I did some acting to each. He looked down, I can, holding onto them big ropes, and got, "I need a show, flags, a display of military ground power, to make a point." I asked, 'Do you have a fighting sword and loaded pistol.' He don't like that.

'Why us and not a Frigate crew?' That got, "The Sultan has heard of a ship with a cross in the sky illegally buying stuff from his ships. I figured your men would run, not fight." I give him a look and said, 'You figure to out run them, as you will lead this parade, Admiral,' to no words.

'Some of the Sultan men had gleaming Scimitars that are for show. Ahind are real ones, Admiral.' Eyes and I said, 'You need this ship to tie up to that pier in Algiers. One morning to walk the men, below, up to that place, unarmed, mostly.' Oh, got eyes. 'I lead them. The officers and Marines are your concern,' to thinking eyes. 'You, Captain, Marine Saltsgiver, and half company, for show. Real fighting swords and loaded arms, Admiral.' I got, "And, the rest of the Marines?" 'Rifles to the bulwark, just in case, Admiral.'

It was Friday, 28 Jun, 1895, that Bos'n Gaston tied Shenandoah to that pier, amid ship, Starboard side, pointed right down that wide street to the Sultan palace. It was just afternoon so street was full of venders and people. The Admiral went off to set up this 'Parade,' with the local Sultan helper.

He returned with 6 Sultan guards and had talked the Sultan into a, "Small party of unarmed men to walk to his Palace and back." I said, 'I need All the men to walk it, Admiral.' Came his, "Tomorrow, 10 AM. Play arms. Wood arms, that the guards will look at."

About 4 PM I took Bothel, Wagner, and Gunner Burch down that street. Oh, just a slow walk up to the palace steps. We waved to the people. The guards didn't like us stopping and looking around. They didn't like us leaning on that wall where the steps went up to the palace. It was high enough you couldn't jump over it, chased by a guard. 'Round that smoking lamp we compared what we seen and talked about this "Parade."

Come that Saturday, at 10 AM, there are 6 guards on the pier. Admiral, to Starboard, Capt'n Mid, and Saltsgiver on the left flank. Ahind is them 6 Marines, three abreast. I had me 4 helmsmen as flag pole bearers. Bothel to me left and Wagner to me right. Oh, them guards inspected each wood sword, halberd, fauchard, and pike for metal. Where metal should be was white paint and some silver to the edges and tips, just for show.

The Marines marched real nice. I told the sailors to just walk along and smile at people, 'Nice, No sneers!' Come that palace and Admiral, Captain, Saltsgiver give some Bla, Bla, words. The ships flag, me Flag, that staff with my ships little flags were presented, and I step forward. I said, 'Bla, Bla, Bla.' Admiral, and so on, turned around, and walked back to the ship, tween them ship's crew on the outside.

Come 9 AM, Sunday, and was Arab 6 guards to the pier. Oh, I rounded up 5 men with wood pikes, halberds, and grab a wooden sword. I lined me men up and motion for these guards to line up across. I come to attention and ships men romp and stomp to attention. I poked the first guard right in the chest. Oh, he don't say ouch. I got this 'Ayeee' from him. Me fist down, closed, and the crew leveled their wood stuff. I poke that guard again and they poke the one across. Well, that got more 'Ayeees' and off they ran. I had me men sharpen the blunt wooden things.

I place Admiral, right, Capt'n, middle, and Saltsgiver left and 2 rows of 3 Marines 'ahind them. Next was the ships, Marine, mine, and Admiral Flag. I couldn't see this as I was behind them 4 flags. On me right is a 6 foot pole with me little flags with Admiral Big M, me flag, crossed arms, the ships St Andrew cross, and that Red, White, Blue, with snake, from Susquehanna.

I heard Bla, Bla from our interpreter and Arab words ahead. Our interpreter said Bla, Bla. Taylor gave words of whatever. This went on for some minutes. Finally, Admiral said something and Capt'n, Saltsgiver, Admiral, Marines, flags move, so I can see ahead to them steps. I saw this table with crafts of stuff and fruit in wooden plates. There was 4 guards, with real swords, as I can tell, and this guy sittin on the steps on a big pillow with a Turban atop.

Me and flag pole bearers come forward. I come to attention and ahind me I heard all them wooden poles smack the ground. I give this turban guy my best sword salute, with slash, and back into the sheath it went. So the men don't suffer, I come to spread legs and them arm guards and gauntlets crossed in front. Taylor introduced me as, "Ships, My Personal Guard, Sultan." Well, that got no good words from him, through that Interpreter.

It seems the Sultan owned the whole world. The land, seas, fish, vegetables, sky, Sun, and all 'atween, by what I heard from the Interpreter. "He Rules the Known World and All Upon it." It might not be exact, but, close. He accused me of buyin stuff, from his ships, "On his Ocean, Without his permission." Something like that.

So, I point to that Big M flag and mention them 3 Triremes, two sunk and the third sent ashore with the survivors. I point to the Susquehanna one and mention the ship that attacked, 'My Ship! Not far from this port! We BLEW it up!' I said our ships protect all ships and trade. 'And the Sultan pays,' and I put up my gauntlet, rubbing the fingers, 'Nothing.'

Oh, that got more fists on table, words in Arab, and English from that guy. Through them words I just kept rubbing me finger together, to more bad words. The words stopped so I said, 'Your Sultan needs to pay us for protection of his trade, OR,' and I point to Taylor and said, 'Sign the Free Trade Agreement.' Sultan laughed, spoke words, and Interpreter say, "What, with painted wooden poles and swords.

I got one of the Halberds and the axe head sliced through one of them Figs, or Dates, on that table, like nothing. The point went through another and with two fingers to down it, the fruit landed in the dirt. I gave it back, got a pike, and did the same. Me sword come out, to a fruit, cut easily, and into the dirt. Oh, silence now. The Sultan gave words to this guy.

Finally came, "Guard, is your pistol powerful?" Out it came, I broke the top, pull out one cartridge, size of your thumb, and placed it on that table. There was some eyes to that cartridge and Arabic words. "Demonstrate its power," and a sultan guard on the left street grabs this poor guy, "by shooting him." The Sultan was pleased.

I pull out that pistol, hide it ahind me back, turn it, and get it by the barrel. Oh, the poor guy is shakin. With me right hand I grab him by his poor shirt, left arm comes over me head, and I put the butt of the pistol right in the middle of the guards head. Oh, he went right down. I picked up his sword, pulled that guy back to where I stood, and placed him 'ahind me.

I come to attention, fist down, and heard that romp and stomp of those poles. I go back to spread legs and point to me personal flag. 'My flag places No Honor in killing a poor servant of the Sultan.' A finger up and, 'No Honor In Killing a Poor Guard, with a dull sword.' I went up to the table and show how the guard sword has no edge, back to me spot.

The Interpreter asked who I, "Can Shoot, with honor?" The pistol came out, I point it around, and come back to, the Interpreter. 'One who lies.' Oh, he went to dirt. That pistol around and I sight on the Sultan. Well, the guards moved so I pulled the trigger, on a dead chamber. The chamber I took the cartridge from.

I walked up to the table, broke the pistol, and put that round back in. Back at me spot I held it in the air and said, 'Come 10 AM, tomorrow, the Sultan will sign this Admiral treaty, at the pier. No more talks.' Oh, that got lots of translation to, "A guard does not understand these negotiations!" No, not a word from the Admiral.

'To demonstrate my pistol power, I will call in bolts of thunder and destruction. One shot, 2 bolts. The second shot brings 4 bolts.' Well, that got laughs. Gave them a chance, counted one, reminded thems, counted two, to more laughs, finger three up and fired that pistol. It got some mixed results. The Guards, Interpreter, and the Sultan flinched. My glove hand went down, clenched fist, the sailors went On-Guard. One finger down, two fingers down, and I got about the third down.

From down that street came the sound of two ships guns, "Ka, Kaboom!" Round balls make a whoosh. Them 25 pound Bolts make a, not whistle, but tearing sound. The first hit the Sultan Palace street wall on the left and took out a top yard of them stones. The second, right, was a bit higher and took out less. It as a sound to hear thems hit that dirt. No, not a boom. A rumble and dirt came over the wall, all over them steps, guards, and the Sultan.

The Sultan got pushed under the table and the Interpreter was the dirt. Oh, me sailors ducked a little. Taylor and McIntire about went to dirt. It took a little time for thems to realize they weren't dead. The Sultan poked his head up from under the table and sure had words. I put that pistol in the air and asked if papers would be signed, '10 ARE, tomorrow, at the pier.'

The words I got were not good. So, I held up me right glove and said, 'Next is 4 Bolts of Thunder and Destruction.' I got words, so I put up 1 finger, to words. 2 fingers got more. Me hands down, I reminded Sultan of 3 fingers, and me hand went to, '1, Sultan.' I waited. '2, Sultan!' Well, when I cocked that pistol hammer I got yells of, "Agreed! Agreed!"

Now, I ain't no fool. They'd not show up. So, I take two steps forward, point the pistol at the Sultan, and shout out, 'You swear on the Koran, By Your God, to be there?' I point that pistol and yell out, 'Swear, to Your God!' I got one shot for him and each of the guards. I got his Arab words and their hand motions.

Came little afore 10 AM, 01 June, 1895, there was drums and trumpets down that street. It took 8 to carry the Sultan. I was ahind Taylor as 4 papers were signed around, across, and the Interpreter signed, points to me, to sign. 'The Sultan signs and swears to His God, to keep the treaty.' The Sultan put something to paper, I sign, roll up the 4th paper, and put it into me gauntlet. Fitz was to make 3. I asked for the 4th, for me record. I gave the Sultan a proper sword salute.

Tween there and here, Gibraltar, I got 5 seepin tubes of fish and that Ibex had fresh vegetables to sell. No, Taylor ain't bothered me. He bothered those on the main deck to no end. I be writin this from the Chart Table, 07 July, 1895.

Botherin me now is the Brits, Mr. Chips, Armoror, and all up there in the mast bangin in them new pieces of iron for the Top Gallants. Taylor, and company, set foot on the pier and them ship wrights came aboard like the local police was after thems.

I did liberty last night, yes, with Phoebe. She says I tell such lies for Sea Stories. I showed her this little flag I got from the Sultan. His personal Flag. I got it after I placed small ships St. Andrew flag and then mine, on that last paper he signed. Oh, she laughed and said I bought it, just for show.

We will have liberty for a couple more days 'afore St. Lawrence is to come in. Mr. Chips say 5 days to get the iron set. I hope you had a good 4th of July. Purser is callin for mail for that Packet to get to Norfolk.

I gave that paper to Fitz to enter into me record. Oh, it has a grand title to it. I saw Fitz write, at the top, 'The Pistol Treaty!' That's what the ship's crew calls it, laughin, around the Smokin Lamp! "A Bang or Two, Of A Time WE Had, Mates!" Gunner served out some extra rum that evening, to the Grog.

By Your Leave, Missy,

An Old Sea Dog,

IN THE YEAR 1895, AUGUST:

Dear Miss Judith,

I start this at the Chart Table, dated 11 July, 1895. We be a day and some 180, or so miles from Gibraltar. It was a nice visit, as always, 'cept for the bangin in the Top Gallants. We be takin the North route to Norfolk. It is summer so the North Atlantic is to be calmer. Uncle Curtis said, mostly.

Tuesday, 09 July, I went lookin at the shops of Gibraltar. About 4 PM I end up at that bar stool, Phoebe on the other side. I decided to get 'Stinkin Drunk,' like Engle. I order whiskey. She give me this cheeky smile, wink, and says, "2 Dollars, Gold." I said, 'One Shot!' I got her smile, wink, and a pint of good whisky to the bar. OH!

I put a 3 dollar gold piece there, push the pint away, and got a bigger bottle, sealed, a wink, and a nod to the back room. No, she picked it up, house rule, and 4 glasses. Me mind can't see 4 people. I can see one, Admiral Taylor.

Open that back room door to, his Adjutant Captain, and McIntire, just grinning. Bottle, glass to table and Phoebe out with a wink. It was Taylor that closed the door, standin ahind it. I didn't look and said, 'And I had to pay for the good whiskey, Admiral?' It was the first time I heard him laugh.

The first shot was to, 'Uncle Curtis, above water and dirt!' McIntire just looked and tipped his shot. The second, from Taylor, "To Your mother. A fine woman to have raised you, QM1!" The Capt'n wondered if the Sultan would honor this treaty. Oh, Taylor reminded him about me actions and them bolts overhead. Got his bad eyes, I did. Oh, such laughter and all, sippin that whiskey, now. Them two sure flinched. I said about hit the dirt. Taylor, "Didn't, I was watchin you, QM1." Well, he did flinch, more than a bit.

Oh, that whiskey did give some lubrication to their mouths. They talk of the cruise and how things went. Come a time, Admiral gave a nod, and we did a toast to that treaty. Done, off they went. That left just me and Tailor. A bad mix, for me, mostly.

It seems Gunner forgot to tell the Admiral, Captain, and Mr. Saltsgiver about the guns part. No, not me place to talk to officers.

They should talk among themselves, I said, to bad eyes. "Would you have sent 4 bolts with the next shot?" I gave him, 'Gunner is a good shot. I did wonder about them lower guns, and the powder.' He said, "Admiral, to you." I said, 'Well, Admiral, I hope there is no next time. But, I have a pass to see the Sultan, Sir!'

From me blouse I pull out the Sultan small flag to table, flat. Taylor looked at it and, "Hump, flag." I point out the Arab swords, scimitars, on three edges. I point to the outside, bottom one. Get had to get out his glasses. It was not Scimitars, but a cutlass and crossed with what looked like me carbine.

The shop owner I go to said it was real Gold, Silver on the emblems, and Minorca pearls for the round things. He just loved it, but couldn't put a price to it. "Priceless, one of a kind." But, I can't roll it up. It bends, a bit, to me back.

Last, Taylor said, "I grant you three wishes, QM1." The first was, 'A safe passage home, for me, Admiral.' I had to think. 'Good health to our families.' I raise that last shot to, 'Next time, on good ground, in good times, Admiral.' We stood, shot down, and he turned to the door.

'Admiral. Would you like me to be your Person Guard when you raise your flag as Atlantic Fleet Admiral? I can use me pistol to signal the gun salute, so you don't flinch, Sir?' He almost had a grin at that. "You must do it from the Main Mast cross member, so as not to hit me, if you can climb that high, and not fall, QM1." Fritz reads all the ship's mail. Pheobe has an ear to the local gossip.

It seems the Admiral had already paid for the whiskey. The pint. She likes to charge double, when she can, and joke me. I got her good meal, at the bar, and she entertained me for the evening. I went back, ah, tipsy, as I still had to be up at 4 AM to clean the deck.

Yesterday, 10 July, Admiral Taylor had to inspect us. It was a show for Taylor. Then, he and McIntire was in a conversation for a long time. The tide turned and we cast off our lines. McIntire in the starboard chains to view St. Lawrence and Admiral Flag. Port chair, chart table, I kept a line, on that Chart, to our position. Capt'n asked for time to bang guns. I said, '28 seconds, Sir.' There was to be two rounds to fire. One for them Brits and the second for Taylor. With about no wind, the current was carryin us out.

Gunner started with the forward chasers and just brought it aft, both sides. Came that acrid smell of smoke and we couldn't see land. The second round must have been a double charge of powder and them cheese wads. I could hardly see the bulwark. That is when I taped Hood, at the rudder indicator, and pointed to Port. Capt'n wasn't watchin, tryin to see through the smoke.

The compass turned and we headed to 270 degrees. I told Capt'n to set fore and Top Gallant sails. I make these hand motions and came, "1st Lieutenant, Fore sails, and Top Gallants." He still was seein nothing but smoke, cause the wind is same as our speed. The ship at 210 degrees, I taped Hood, then the mid rudder indication with me pointer.

The breeze off 'The Rock' blew off the smoke, catches the Fore sails, Gallants, and Capt'n is lookin at Spain, not Gibraltar. He went to that Taft rail and sees that Big M flag on St. Lawrence dip. Our Signal Middie dipped ours. To dip is like sayin Bye. McIntire turned, was about to blow, us turning the ship, and all. He was chewin on words when Engle saved me. He came up with tray of coffee, a sweet bread, and blocked me from his eyes.

Yep, the ship had turned around. I am a magician. I could have always blamed Hood. No. I told thems how it can be done, with the right conditions. Bush was watchin. The Navigator, sometimes, needs to show his skills. Them two just grinned from ear to ear at this, emergin from smoke. Come September and 2nd class stipes for thems.

The Charted Whey points said we'd pass North of the Azores by some miles. Came the Daily Report to McIntire and, "Set points for Ponto Delcado, Azores, Gentlemen." That had to the Bos'n and Navigator. I ain't a gentlemen. One tack or wear was all that was needed. I smelled it, two days out. Sheep!

15 miles out the Top Gallant Look Out called down, "Admiral Flag, Captain!" Closer, "American Frigate, Captain." Next was, "Dress ship. Gunner, Admiral salute!" Oh, he knew of this. I ask if I should be in, 'Full Dress, Captain?' "NO! And No Flag. Barge crew make ready!"

The next Med Fleet Admiral stopped in Azores to introduce his self to the Consulate or Ambassador there. Oh, the flags said he ashore. I still put cotton in me ears for our and their guns. Barge over, Capt'n and 1st Lieuy went over to that Ambassador house to introduce thems to him. I sent one of me 'Cuties' to a place to get two local woman. One to entertain the Middie, one to entertain us and bring some beer. 'No Sheep!' I got other sausages to go with the beer.

It was 3 PM and came this parade of people, down that street. It was just a circle of attention to this guy in the center. We was in the barge when it hit the pier. There was more gold braids then I'd seen in a while. He went into that boat, sittin at the transom, and thought I knew him. There are not many admirals in my minds list.

Back aboard and the barge wasn't hauled aboard. Bos'n Gaston said to re-man at 1600. 4 PM, to you. 'Why.' He said, "Captain to Admiral for talks." 'Return?' I got, "Unknown time." I ask about dinner for the crew. "Captain will talk to the Frigate about that, if necessary." That ain't right. Me brain says so.

I replaced Hood, who was the next QM for a barge. I had him get Wagner and Bothel. Was words to each and off they went. Next, I heard words from Cook Feterman and bangin pots. I saw the ship cat come up that fore hatch and head to the forecastle, like someone stepped on his tail. Came smoke from the ships stove pipe, I heard more words and Wagner give me a nod.

I only asked Bothel to see ifn Feterman could put some bread and samiches in them food buckets. I have bad ears, from them guns, but heard, well, bad words only a cook can say and get away with. Came 4 PM and McIntire and 1st Lieuy were at the bulwark to go into the barge. 'Sorry, Sir. The crew is shippin water, just in case, Sir.' It took 5 minutes and the crew went into the barge with Nor Easter gear and pails over their arms. 'Mind the ships sides, Captain,' and over I went.

We rowed real dry and hooked up to the Frigate chains to whistles, bells, and the romp and stomp of Marines. Capt'n delivered, we tied up to a line from the boom over the Starboard side and waited. Come 5 PM, to you, well, supper for the crew sounded. I waited. Then I sent a 'Cutie' up that line, across the boom, to ask about us. He came back with, "Frigate says they don't serve meals to Supply Ship Scum, QM1." Me feelings weren't wrong. The crew took to spittin tobacco juice over toward that boom. I had the crew put a barge line to their line and drifted off some.

Come 6 PM, well, we opened the meal pales to sausages, some taters, lunch bread, slices of ham, and some sugar dates, or figs. It all tasted the same to me. Oh, we had two hogs head of water and a cup to drink from. We drifted to Lee of that breeze and just waited. Another line to that line and we saw them officer havin a fine time in that Frigate Capt'n cabin. The ships bells sounded and come 9 PM that party broke up.

The Frigate crew, gentle like, helped Capt'n and 1st Lieuy into the barge. Oh, me mind was just jumpin back in time, what with drunk officers. Now, I row when the transom is full of Capt'n and 1st Lieuy. I sit right there watchin thems. Capt'n said, "Portside, Coxswain." I said, 'Sorry Captain. I didn't hear.' I got, "Portside, QM1!"

Ya have to row by the Starboard side and call out who is aboard. That is Boat procedures. I heard, "Boat Ahoy?" The watch asks who is aboard. I said, 'Monongahela, Bothel. 4 lines to Port!' Oh, McIntire gave me real bad looks. 'Captain, I can't say Shenandoah.' I got a nod and round we went to 4 bos'n mates down them lines and about pull them two up the side. Nope. No whistles and bells allowed. The portside is a quite side, for drunk officers.

It was the usual Morning Brief with McIntire. No, Gailey gives it with me ahind. Come the tide and Captain ask about it. Gailey turns to me. 'A cable length from shore, not a Bay, Captain.' "Tide, QM1?" I said, and shouldn't have, 'None Captain, this is the Atlantic Ocean.' He didn't like that, by his eyes. The Frigate and us up anchor at 9 AM. Oh, I had cotton to me ears as them guns goin off.

Came 1 PM, I was down at the Smokin Lamp, talkin. Oh, there came a raucous aft and I got Fritz to me. "Captain Cabin, like NOW!" I got there as two Marines take Engle, in cuffs, and about drag him forward. Not good. I went into McIntire cabin and, OH, he is red and about to blow up.

"This morning Engle served Mr. Caldwell, and I, runny eggs, burnt potatoes, burnt sausages, and little breakfast stakes like leather. Engle said the stove is broken, best he could do. Look." Ok. Came, "Lunch is Oxe tail soup and plum duff, QM1."

Oxe tail soup is made with Oxe tails. There is some meat and a flavor from the marrow, that stuff inside the bones. It is a thin soup, that some cooks add vegetables to it. Some. So, I look and there is a ships biscuit atop. It takes time for that hard thing to absorb liquid. Most, most, snap it in half afore adding it. So, I see two Bargemen atop. Bargemen are ships weevils that get into flower and biscuits, after time at sea.

Plum Duff, as ya should know, is plums, dates, figs, and what fruit is at hand. Ya pound some ships biscuits, to expand, and add rum. So, this bowl looked ok, 'cept for the liquid atop, and two dead Bargemen, (weevils) floating! I take a spoon and tasted figs, apples, crushed biscuits, and Engle sure added more rum than should have. Me spoon moved that biscuit aside and I tasted the soup. I like some vegetables in it. Engle don't. 'And, what Captain?'

"Engle laid it to our table, drunk, and wished us bad weather." There is an Old Navy tail that Oxe tail soup brings on a blow, bad weather. "BARGEMEN, IN MY SOUP! DEAD ONES, IN PLUM DUFF! ENOUGH RUM FOR THREE, QM1!" The Top Gallant men also heard, "THREE DAYS BREAD AND WATER, OR I'D HAVE HIM FLOOGED, QM1!"

I saw Engle in that brig, forward. Oh, drunk. He asked and Gunner gave him a full bottle, "For Captain plum duff, QM1." From Engle I got, "Made a proper, Good Supper, Which I Fed to the Fish, as he Never said he'd be eatin over with the Admiral! Come back Drunk! Drunk! He Never touched me proper ground coffee nor that sweet bread I made. Ingrate! Foul Weather to Him, I say!" I told Bos'n Gaston to put on foul weather sails and Top Gallants to come down. Oh, and got his snicker at Oxe Tail soup, I did.

Still 16 July, come supper for the crew at 5 PM and it was easy sailin, not a cloud in the sky. Was plum duff, with a tad of rum, as I settled into a bench for Smokin Lamp, around the ship stove. I don't know why but the ships cat jumped into me lap, growlin. First ever. Next, the ships head dove down real far. Then a wave smacked the back end of the ship and drove the front down, then up. I couldn't move for that Cat claws to me leggs! Yep, Both!

The tables was just swingin. The bench went out from under me backside. There came bells and whistles ahind. I'm thinkin about havin to climb that mast, last to drown! I was thrown to that deck and that Cat would not let go. Finally, it decided to run to somewhere.

The Poop was awash in water. The Bos'n was under the ships wheel. Hood, on duty, was clingin to the Starboard ladder to Main deck. Them new Top Gallants was broken off and sails flappin in a breeze like a train goin overhead. The Bosn's tripped the belayin pins on the lower Course sails. It was like laundry day back home, sheets flappin in the wind. The Jibs and that Fore Topsail kept us goin forward. The Main Topsail went by the clew holes. I put a stop line to the wheel as the bow buried into a wave, settled, and that big wave just busted the blunt ships back end from ahind. I just hung onto that ships wheel.

The Bosn's cut the line to thems Top Gallants. Only me Old For masters could get up high enough to cut the support lines. Came sundown, well, we looked like a ghost Pirate ship in them dime novel books. Ragged, but goin forward. The forward jib held, a main one, and that fore Top Course. It took four at that helm to hold it from, them waves ahind. They buried us, slapped the ship forward, buried the bow, and up we came. Sleep, ya ask? Well, that cold water sure kept us awake. Ifn ya be excited, well, we on the Poop was. Capt'n, Bos'n, Navigator just clung to that Poop, forward rail. It was a night to remember and I hope to never go through again.

The morning was better, as we could see. Bosn's, at the helm, were relieved each hour, as did me, Hood, and Bush. There were no ships stove to warm up to. We got a small grog 'afore goin back on deck, still wet. So it was through that next day. It would have been OK, 'cept for them waves just beatin the bejesus on the aft end of the ship.

Came 19 July and the sun come up and the wind to not a train overhead. Some slaps to the back of the ship and Feterman served out a noon meal to the crew. It was about a clean crew there. Worshed real good by all the sea water. Come the cloths dryin, well, salt and skivvies don't mix, I'll just say.

Old Davy Jones must have shown upon us as them dark clouds come and like to drown us. He! He! It worshed us right good, standin on that deck. Thursday make and mend day was with salt water. Now, it was a Friday worsh, without make and mend. Come supper it was salt beef and tators. After, sittin on that bench, Old Tom come to visit me. It purred to me stroking it. Usually is with the Oldsters. An odd sign, not in Uncle Curtis books.

Well, Engle got cuffed to a pole, mid ship, as the forward brig took on water. The waves busted the seams of the planks, cause of us smackin them waves. Capt'n cabin, the officer dinin place took the brunt of them waves. They about flooded both of thems and broke out some of the aft winders of each. Oh, McIntire couldn't sleep in his cabin as it was filled, continually, with them waves. Fitz had a fit with Bobbit about getting it straight.

19 July, I got to report to Capt'n it was, 'Over the hump day!' Half way home. He don't look so good at this news. 'Aft waves, wind, under close sails, gave us some good knots to the line, 'cept for the Top Gallants, Captain!' He didn't like this news as his cabin is still a mess. Oh, Engle came in with coffee and a sweet bread, all nice and social. He even begged his leave, "Captain." There was his eyes to both of us and, "Dismissed, QM1."

We got to that pier in Norfolk, 31 July, 1895, with that Pilot aboard. Came them bells, whistles, and the romp and stomp of them Marines. It was hot, standing at Quarters, with all me volunteers. I saw Admiral Stevens, Adjutant Capt'n Miller, and 1st Lieuy, Stiles come aboard. This after Fleet Admiral Forest, first, came aboard. Into cabin them went and out to inspect, "Ships Crew!" Me volunteers always be last.

Oh, just the normal inspection of our ranks. I was in full dress uniform, Master-At-Arms, with arms, but no bullets. I only got his eyes, while inspecting me. No. None had signed aboard. I turned away some of the ship's crew that wanted to be 'Volunteers!' McIntire never asked and I never said not a word.

The podium came out. Saltsgiver, papers, and such to it. We was sweatin in them dress blues. There was awards from the Capt'n to the Oldsters for savin the ship in, "Dark Times. Adverse Conditions. Saving the ship from peril." Fitz and me words, to them in the riggin. Bothel and Wagner got the same. Most of the crew got commendations for that, "While ship was in Throws of Disaster." They liked that.

Stevens forgot to sign our orders. I got smacked by them from Nichol. There was the usual of leave, sick, and such goin ashore. I was last of all to salute the Quarterdeck, to Bothel, Wagner, and Burch on that pier, puttin our bags and sea chests got to that wagon. No, no Bos'n or Captain McIntire around.

Now, only those who have served on a ship, can look each other in the eyes, and give a nod, on the pier, after such a voyage. There was handshakes around and now laughs, at the times. Bothel looked me, Wagner, Burch over and said, 'Mattie will expect you three," and he didn't say them bad words he was thinkin, "to supper, on Friday." We get a wink and, "Bring food and drinks."

I finish this at me little desk, at Squadron Barracks. Yes, me little room. It is not so clean as the last time here. I need to get some of that soap and clean it. Oh, no. Bos'n 2nd don't touch me room. Shush! He might fine me hidy holes of, Shush!

By Your Leave, Missy,

An Old Sea Dog,

IN THE YEAR 1895, 01 OCTOBER: SQUADRON

Dear Miss Judith,

I been back a week and it seems like month. It is 07 August, Wednesday, writin from my clean smelling room. No, I had me charges worsh me, Fitz, Bothel, and Wagner rooms with that soap. Shenandoah is in the ship yard for fore and aft repairs. No other supply ship is in so, not much to do, for them. I got me 24 as I lost two to them doctors, for the hospital to look at. They got bones broke in that storm. The rest were left by the other ships. Fitz about got nothing to do, now, 'cept, shush, liberty with Zoe. The squadron and Admiral clerks are all runnin smooth now. Fitz lubed them up like grease to an axle, real quick. He be a small person and a big voice. Maybe, just maybe, my looks to them put them straight.

It was a fine time with Bothel, Wagner, me, and Gunner Burch with Mattie that Friday. We had her laughin to what went on in the Med. We kept it clean. She gave eyes to Bothel, 'Church aboard and never a drop of drink on Liberty, Swear!' She knew better. But, still gave evil eyes to him, to our laughin.

I went and saw Effie, Carrie mother. I had to say Thank you, for her and Carrie letters, to flickerin eyes. Mattie filled in the story, in a private whisper. Effie, after I mentioned this, said Carrie met a fine man and was engaged. She met him on a fine spring day, in one of my bought dresses, lookin fine, and no more words needed. I passed on my best wishes.

Admiral Stevens didn't sigh for me charges till Friday afternoon, 02 August. Into that room, over with the orders, and he was like to say something, but didn't. The papers to his clerk, money to Corporal Nichol, and so closed that paper. Sort of.

Good old Engle was my volunteer. He left with me group. Come Friday morning I got a note from McIntire. It seems he missed his sweet bread and Engle coffee. Fitz, bless his mother, had a 'Volunteer' paper right there. Engle? He'd found a way to get his usual self on Wednesday and Thursdays night. At musters, ah, ah, he mustered. Nichol had them Marines give him a good worshin, and cloths, and by 10 AM we presented him aboard.

Now, Capt'n McIntire gave him some fine words. Maybe, just maybe, they'd rubbed each other enough to smooth off eaches rough edges. Like a sand stone to granite. Capt'n to Engle. "Temporary. No more," from McIntire and signed them orders.

Regina and Mattie ganged up on us for Saturday night and Sunday meals. Wagner and me, Fitz and Zoe was there. Mabel, for Wagner, and Myrtilla for me. Both are just nice woman. Oh, we still had lots of Sea Stories to tell, so, there was lots of talkin. After Saturday evening talk, well, Myrtilla could ask stuff and I could fill in, from the cruise, while us walked, together, alone, as we was about throw out of the house, together!

Oh, as you always ask. Medium bones. Not big, nor small, like you. Her head up to mine in low heals. Not red, nor brown hair. Don't ask a man about color. Nice eyes and smile. A pleasant voice. Not a giggler, like you be! He! He!

Come an evening down to Ella and Harold bar, Ella gave me a whisper, to me ear, about Carrie. I whispered, 'I heard from Effie,' to her looks. Harold got bad words for, "Food! Up! NOW!" He! He! So much for soul mates.

Such easy weeks it's been, writin on Monday, 26 August. Engle? I ain't seen him. He is still McIntire Cook, as far as I know. I had lots of evening down with Ella, and bar. The weekends was with Bothel, Mattie, Regina, both homes, and Myrtilla. Converses, she does, easily. Lots of me stories to tell. Philly, twice. Alaska. trains, Ptuy. New York, 'No, not the city.' She'd not traveled far. They was nice times talkin to her. Me problem is next ship. Ah, know that answer, and it comes in October. Shenandoah.

Friday afternoon, 30 August, already warned by Fitzsimmons, entered Admiral Stevens room to, Forest, Stiles, Stevens, and officers I don't know. That Fine Blue Jacket, and old worn one to that table, with smiles from all. It be like goin to a lynchin and me head in the Hanging knot. "Well, QM1? Time to sign the papers." Ya, both. Oh, lots of familiar names there. Me finger went down that list. I stopped at one. An old name, with memories. Well, they all do.

I put a "1," and sign me name and put the Caricature to it, like Uncle Curtis signed. I got bad eyes from all. From Forest, "Just 1, QM1?" I said, 'I don't know I want to stay longer, Admiral!' Got his eyes and about a smile. "You'd make a poor farmer, but, have a lovely wife to come home to, QM1." That be an old joke, 'tween us.

One eye from him and the room cleared out. Bad eyes! Just him and me. Oh, such nice words to me last cruise and that treaty. Read that report of, "And, a pistol shot got 2 ships bolts, QM1?" I gave, 'Taylor said I could scare them, Admiral. And, I scared, ah, lots there, Sir.' I didn't say who. "Captain, Admiral, Saltsgiver?" I said, 'Gunner Campbell knew of it, Admiral. You officers should talk among yourselves, Sir!'

Up, attention to him, he get about to the door and I say, 'I asked Admiral Taylor if I, in full uniform, could be his Personal Guard, in his ceremony, as Atlantic Fleet Admiral, Sir.' I got a funny look, like I shouldn't know. 'Please give my regards to Admiral Palmer, former 2nd Squadron Admiral, for advancement to Mediterranean Admiral, like you were, Sir. I recognized him, Azores Islands, introducing himself to the Island Governor, Sir.'

I got no good nor bad words to this. Just his eyes. Fitz, looking at messages, confirmed my eyes in the Azores. Ifn you remember, Palmer was the Admiral who promoted me to 1st Class. He relieved the officer on Susquehanna. That was stories ago. He promoted Silvis, Bothel, Wagner. Lots on me volunteer list.

Monday, 9 September, and they started to load out Shenandoah. Warrant Gaston, Bothel, and Wagner said I was in the way. I got, politely, told to leave. Well, I did have, 'somewhere Better to Be, Thank You!' I already told Mattie I need some small flags, mine. I needed an additional big one. "Oh, just tell me what you want and I get it done." I said I need to stop by where she worked. Yes, I wanted to see Carrie.

It was awkward, for her. She didn't know how to walk or talk. So, I just shook her hand, congratulated her and gave her a hug. At her ear so I said ifn he isn't good to her I get some sailors to Shanghai him and next he woke up would be on a ship the China. I got her laugh and "No. But I'll keep that in mind, Thank You!"

Now, I had me big flag there so just pointed to where I wanted the addition. The small flags to get the same thing. Out came that Sultan flag and I was waitin for her to faint. First was, 'No real gold, silver, or pearls.' OK. Good colored thread, the best she could do. I got there at 10 AM so I took her to lunch at Ella place. She has OK food. "Harold, Up with the food or," and ya don't want to hear the rest. We talked like old times. I complimented her nice ring and told how I got that flag, and stuff from the last cruise.

Carrie and Mattie spent about the afternoon on a pattern for the Sultan flag and all on it. Leave it, Ya ask? I said no three times, 'unless you replace it, as is, if stolen.' That is why it took about all afternoon for that pattern. I paid for the time spent. A hug to Mattie and I walked Carrie down the stairs. At the bottom, oh, I got a hug, kiss on both cheeks for, "It was that dress, coat, and hat you bought me for Christmas that he saw." I forgot the hat. "He said I just 'Looked Like Spring' and had to stop and chat."

Her fiancé' is the son of a local banker. A big bank! A name I never heard, but, I don't get down town to do bankin. Me 'Agent' takes care of most I don't spend. Me Will, some papers, and money things he takes care of when I'm not here. That Navy record says to notify him in case I don't come back. 5 Dollars gold a year he gets. I put that flag in his hands and said ifn it got lost, 'you might wake up on a ship headed for China.' We laughed. He signed a receipt and put down a good figure on value.

Monday, 9 AM, 16 September, I was on Shenandoah, out of the way, workin with Hood and Bush at the Chart Table and Fitz came aboard. His was a red faces, out of breath, and I got, "You and Bothel. Admiral room. NOW!" I ask why and got, "Forest there. All hell broke loose. Something about orders for you and Bothel, NOW!"

We went into Squadron Admiral Conference room to Forest, Stevens, Stiles, Saltsgiver, Nichol, and 6 Marines. I get Forest sneer to, "Arrest these two, Captain!" Marine Captain Saltsgiver. "Take them to your barber for a Proper Hair Cut. Scrub them Pink. They don't need but skivvies to go to the uniform shop for Proper Cloths and Back here by 11 AM, Sharp!"

Three Marines each and they about dragged us to the Marine place, thrown into a chair, and them barbers clipped us good. I got soap on the face and a brush into me mouth, as I protested, to soap in the mouth. Clean shaved and no lookin in a mirror for cuts. We just stripped and about got thrown into two tubs of, 'AHHHH, Hot Water!' Saltsgiver give a look and said, "Admiral Said Pink!"

That tailor in the uniform place had no regard for Private Parts. He measure here, measure this, and that. We might just as well be cloth dummies. The Marines just grabbin arms, legs, and moving to his orders. Done, well, a shirt on, off as too big or small. Pants on, set by them marines to a stool, to cuffs rolled, pins to me leg and off. I know now how a chicken feels, plucked alive. I felt like I was back in Boot Camp, getting outfitted!

I got a new pair of socks and skivvies thrown to me to put on. Oh, no privacy in the Navy and not here. I got black leather shoes to try on, watched by the Marines. This guy come out with officer type coat to arms wrenched ahind me and on, off, another, 'nother! He put this band to me head, to measure. I guess I got a small head, with what this guy says. All this stuff goes into a box, which we get to carry back to Squadron, in just socks, shoes, and new skivvies. The clock said 10:45, in the Admiral Clerk room, as them dang Marines push, pull, and stuff me and Bothel into these cloths. His officer type jacket had a right arm with crossed anchors. Mine, left, had the Ships Wheel. Confussed. Yep, with 2 ss.

That door opened to the conference room and we got about thrown into it by them dang Marines. Front of table, us was, to Forest mean looks. "Raise Your Right Hand and Repeat after Me!" It was the officers Oath, minus a couple words. We be a Polly Parrot and wonder just what this is. Done with words, I had to sign this paper. No, I couldn't read it. "Sign here, Please." That was the first nice words since we got here.

Admiral Forest and Stevens come around and put some devices to our shirt collar ends. Next, ahind, a Marine puts an officer type cover on me head. I don't understand this goins on. Both Admiral are all smiles and shake our hands. 'And, Admirals, what is going on?' That get a laugh from both, Forest said, "the Navy Department has created a new Rank. In spite of both your, ah, varied records, I recommend advancement, which Congress approved, Chief Petty Officers."

We got rowed real dry, front of Forest barge, to Portsmouth Navy yard. We got these whistles and bells comin aboard his Frigate.

There was tables set on the after deck with men dressed as us seated. We got ushered to a table and around was them covers with an anchor. That tie, the Marine about choked me with, was the most bother.

Forest read some words. I just heard, "First Generation of Chief Petty Officers, United States Navy, and Appointed by United States Congress, in Recognition of Superior Leadership." Ok. Last came, "As Chiefs, You are to take care of your men, ship, and officers. You are to guide them all." It was not like I wasn't already doin that!

We got a nice noon meal with servers to give us plates of food and ask, "Another filled of wine?" It was as quiet as church, that deck was. I didn't think any knew more about this than me and Bothel. It was not a bad meal. Officer food, as I seen in the Gun room, reporting stuff. Came the time and Forest stands, we stand, and a toast to us?

Back at squadron I give Fitz that scroll we all got handed, by Forest, after a salute to him on the quarterdeck. He hands me a Navy script chit to go to the uniform shop for, "Your new uniforms, Chief." I spent the afternoon there and stuffed that new stuff into a new seabag. There was different slops, shoes, oh, but the same skivvies.

I hauled it to me room by 4 PM and had Fitz at me door. He handed me that scroll and said, "You are now double protected by this Scroll and Admiralty laws in you enlistment, well, just don't shoot the Captain. They'd need to ship you to Washington, to get enough Admirals to Court-Martial you, Chief." I just had to go show off me new stuff, down at Harold and Ella place. I was all a smile to her, got her looks and, "Harold, come look at this guy. Never saw this uniform!" So, Harold give me a look and, "Charge him double, in case the Shore Patrol comes to drag him off."

20 September, that Friday, oh, Regina, with Silvis, gave a party for the, "New Chiefs!" Ya couldn't wipe the smile off Mattie, lookin at Bothel uniform. Myrtilla was just smiles, but didn't understand. 'Advanced, more money.' Oh, that she understood, sort of. We did Saturday evening and Sunday afternoon there. Her and I kept getting thrown out, to the street, Myrtilla and me. She took me arm for them walks. She has a nice voice, smile, and laugh. Back to barracks, after her hands to mine and nice cheek kisses, I could see them nice eyes, goin to sleep.

The 1st problem was I had to be in jacket and tie. Next, everyone wanted to salute me. Stiles didn't know what to do with us. Bothel go a desk at squadron buildin. Mine is in the Admiral Clerk office. His clerks did their stuff, quiet as Church mice. Burch and Wagner got to supervise the work crews. Bothel and me have a separate, separate table at the Chow Hall. It felt like we had a disease, so separate, separate.

Bothel and me took to walkin around, much a place it is. We watched some of loadout of Shenandoah. He tried to get involved and Warrant threw us both off the ship. I tried to pick up the mail and Tellys. Fitz gave me bad words. His job! So, I'd say I was off, back at a time. That seemed to please thems, Fitz included.

The 25th I did a walk to see about me flags. I got that romp and stomp of the base guards and saluted thems, to be polite. Carrie gave me strange eyes, at the uniform. 'Advanced.' Oh. Out came that Sultan flag they made. I laid that real one next to it. The Gold threads are different. Same with the silver. The mother of pearl is about the same. Well, it was the price for altering the big flag and little ones too!

Come lunch time and she had to decline me lunch. Arm on mine, down them steps, and there was a guy, beside a nice surrey, a nice horse, and he whipped off his hat. Next, his eyes go to her arm on mine. He has a smile and bad eyes to me. I handed her over, to more bad eyes. Oh, the sun shone on him, by her eyes and face. Two hands to his, a little kiss, and his eyes are still on me. Maybe it was the uniform.

I got her nice eyes as she introduced, "The special client I mentioned, Dear. He came to inspect that unique flag. The one I told you about." Oh, he about tried to crush me hand. "Nice to meet you," around. Still bad eyes till her arm went to the crook of his. 'Very nice work, Miss Carrie. Fine stitches. Keep the pattern as I might need a second one.' I whipped off me hat, like he did, gave him a nod, and walked off. His name? Mr. Bad Eyes!

It be an interesting weekend I had. Friday evening, Saturday, Sunday afternoon, and evening at Regina place. It was nice weather so we sat out. All would not fit inside. For evening meals I treated all to that Chinese place. It makes all kinds of stuff. Walkin there, Myra (short for Myrtilla) had to have the crook of me arm.

Come time to go back she took me hands and I got a nice little kiss, "For being a perfect escort." I got handed a Post Card, with her address, and asked if I would mention any, "interesting adventures you might have." Oh, trouble is always me partner.

Yesterday, Monday, 30 September, we had a special muster. Wagner was promoted to 1st Class Bos'n. Burch is now Gunner 1st and lots of others. It be that time of year for, like Certificates of Able Bodied Seaman, or Fore Top Mast designated. Bosn's need those. It was a happy group. Admiral Stevens signed the 'Volunteer' list, so thems could get one last "Well lubricated" nigh ashore. I went along as nothing better to do. I pestered Ella to no end, just to get her ire up. That wasn't hard.

I finish this up at me desk. I have to wait for special orders from the Admiral. McIntire asked for a QM1. He didn't know, maybe, I got promoted. I do know there is no other QM here. It is a legal issue with takin a lower billet. Ya can always step up 1. I don't know about down 1. I just know come Thursday, 3 October, 1895, I might be goin to the Caribbean aboard Shenandoah. I think Stevens wants ride of me. He! He!

By Your Leave, Missy,

An Old Sea Dog,

IN THE YEAR 1895, 24 DECEMBER: CARIBBEAN

Dear Miss Judith,

This advancement to 'Chief Petty Officer' is wearin thin on Bothel and me. It took some days afore the crew knew how to address us. The Oldsters made it worse by givin us a knuckle to their foreheads, like they would an officer. Me 'Cuties,' thems 3 strippers, 'course, had to do the same. I gook thems 8 aside and said the next time they do it, and well, 'you will man the pumps till your arms drop off!' The Oldsters listened, some. Them youngins would do it ahind me back, for kicks. Bothel caught them doin it, and, ah, thems got no pleasure in his kicks!

The crew about went to mutiny over putting up walls next to the Middie quarters, for us two. Mr. Chips had to take down polls used for hammocks. I start this letter from the Chart Table in the Chart Room. Bothel and me livin space. There is more room for each of us than at a hammock pole. And, Bothel don't snore, well, as much as the rest of the crew do down in their bertin space.

We left Norfolk on 03 October, 1895. Admiral Stephens and company did come aboard to send us off. Nope, no Admiral Forest. He was off somewhere. He missed seein me in me new uniform and in full dress. Stephen and McIntire sure gave me dirty looks to me outfit. Armoror said no to cartridges in me leather holster belt. It looked funny without thems. Oh, and me sword now has to have a sash to the handle. No, gold color is for officers. Mine is silver. And, another cost for the new rank. It will take a month of money to me pay book to cover all this new stuff.

Speakin of 3 strippers. Ifn ya remember, the ones on Susquehanna I called me Profits, for their Biblical names. There was Mathew, Mark decided to become a Quartermaster, Luke, and John. Well, I already mentioned Joseph, what with me personal flag to the Spanish Captain. I have James, Peter, and Timothy. Their last names. Thems decided on which rate they wanted to become, after all this time.

Joseph has been around the Chart Table a lot. 'Course, like any young fool, he's been scamperin in the upper yards with them others his age. Is a wonder they didn't fall and break their necks? But, QM2

Hood and QM2 Bush, advanced in September, have been givin him learnin since last cruise. The Capt'n made him a QM. James and Peter took the anchor to their right sleeve. Timothy decided to be a gunner. Burch looks after him, when not a monkey in the lines overhead. I allow Joseph to go along, else he is like a puppy, with sad eyes a lookin at them.

You'd ask about Engle. Oh, McIntire gets his sweet breads and coffee. Now, underway for a couple days, and Gunner gave him a pint of rum to make his plum duff, "For the Capt'n, Gunner!" Plum duff for Capt'n and Caldwell got a shot of it. The rest? I had to tell Engle not to whistle, else, might come bad winds. Spiel, the Capt'n steward, is comin along. He serves the meals real proper. He does lots that Engle refuses to do, like worsh, iron cloths, and polishes shoes. "Ships Capt'n Cook! Ain't no mistress!"

It about caused a spill of the men when I broke out me speed log and current weights. "Oh, No, Sir." I said, 'Chief!' Well, the Oldsters told everyone how to set the lanyards, lines, the wood devices to the bulwark, and all. I couldn't touch a thing, of me own design. "Oh, you just stand back and we'll have it up in no time, Sir!" That Oldster got 4 hours pumpin for that Sir. I came by after half an hour and got, "Can I stop now, Chief?" 'Yes, Able Bodied Seaman.' It is hard to make a man older than you father do that. Especially when you care about them. I got no more knuckles and only, "Yes, Chief," after.

The Smokin Lamp was another thing. Oh, separate, separate to the crew. Like we had leprosy! Some of the men can't write. I know who. I did letters for them in the Med cruise. I write to you, some, from there. It was Kelly, Graty, Lesko, and Blakley. Oldsters and others not much younger. I waited! Come half way to Nassau and I asked Kelly about this. "Oh, don't want to disturb you, ah, Chief!"

Now, afore this, my next name was, "The Scribe," whispered among the crew, 'cause I was always writing to you or MaMa. Oh, I was pissed at this, after all the rest of the, Sirs, and what not. I got up in the middle of thems and said about a deer fawn had spots to hide in the brush. Baby ducks, chickens, just fluff, till full grown. I said I wrote MaMa so she knew I was alive! I changed breeches but, 'Wives, MaMa's, kinfolk should know you think about them!' I always wondered why their shipmates didn't do it for them. "Well,

Chief, don't want thems to know I can't read nor write." It was no secret to anyone!

Fitz will curse me to his dyin breath but, I elected him to be the ships School Marm. Yep. To learn them to write, some. Just half hour, morning or afternoon, dependin on the weather. To do it in the me Cabin. There is a nice table to work at and a lantern to see by. Nothin better to do, I help thems to writin, and readin also. I get them bad eyes from Fitz. He shouldn't complain. He made himself a 2nd Class Ships Clerk. Admiral Stevens weren't payin attention to the letters of advancement he signed. That ink weren't dry and Fitz had on his new rank badge.

We reached Nassau on 11 October. Joseph, with help, set the Whey Points. I gave him a Wheel Book to set them to and told him, 'No sense doing it more than once.' His first try had us about go aground on Cape Hatteras. The Capt'n gig went over the side with Hood there. It seems a Chief can't row. There was no room at the stern for me. I can only go ifn a barge is called for. Hood forgot to take money for crew refreshments. I heard about that, later!

21 October we hit Barbados. Oh, McIntire said we had to round them islands, the Atlantic side, "Just in case a Frigate is out there." It made no difference to me. It is 1600 miles outside or inside the Caribbean. We put a barge over the side to Doc, Capt'n, Mr. Gailey, 1st Lieuy, Armoror, Mr. Chips, and Gunner. I was sittin in the bow, so I told them to row real dry, or else.

Liberty was by divisions. I had one, Bothel the second, and Burch third. It was a mix of rates so all of one division would not be ashore. I took Engle with me. We went to that same bar, as always. Maggie, the beer tender, has a boyfriend on of each Frigate crew. I get lots of gossip as she knows where they be and when they should show up in Barbados. Nope, never two at once, else, you'd hear, all the way up there, that ruckus. I took first evenin so I could watch Engle and had thems carry him back. A Chief don't carry! He! He!

Maggie and that Governor were close on where them Frigates was. They do a counter-clockwise rotation. One is off Caracas and will stop in Barbados for liberty. Why no two are there at one time. McIntire had us follow them islands, first South West, soes not to hit Grenada, then North and Nor West. Sweet water comes from that

Ponce place in Puerto Rico, as you should know. 6 rowers, me, and Wagner at helm, made sure no locals would bother us.

27 October, we made that 1st Frigate South of Haiti. It was watchin shippin comin from Caracas and Cartagena, headed to that windward channel 'tween Haiti and Cuba. Why? Maybe try to sneak up on a wedding, funeral, birthday boat headed to where ever, like that one we met letters ago.

Come the morning of 30 October and the lookout spotted that Spanish Frigate 'tween Jamaica and Cayman Islands. It had on easy sails toward us. We set General Quarters, tampion off and gun doors closed. He dipped his flag and us to him. Our Signal Middie said he wanted to 'Parley,' speak. Oh, we set sails for steerage way, and over the Spanish Captain comes.

Yes, 6 Marines to the side to dang whistles and bells to him up the side. Just him and a Lieutenant. The latter had two bottles of wine in hand. Oh, they had to tour the main deck, then into the Capt'n cabin. Spiel did well with the wine glasses. I saw it though them Skylight winders. Out and up to the Poop deck they came. Mr. Gaston, Mr. Gailey were introduced with me Cuties at attention.

They came around to me, in full uniform, and stopped. That Captain had dark eyes, dark hair, and a mustache. He was taller than me but not bigger. I did the sword salute, just lookin in his eyes, and an arm salute, returned. Just them eyes. It was not the same guy as afore. Don Hernandez, by the log. "My Cousin, Don Diego warned me about this ship,' to just his eyes.

With a small smile and he had to inspect, yep, carbine, unloaded, pistol, unloaded, and me Sword. No, He was right handed, so had a time with it. That bird cage just made it difficult for him to handle it. Back, sword salute, I said, 'Seaman Joseph, Please.' To me hand came me flag, to his hand. Oh, a nice smile he got. "Cousin, Don Diego will be most embarrassed, that I have this." Salutes, to the quarter deck he went and back to his ship. Sort of!

He invited McIntire over for a lunch, and me. Oh, prettied up that ship, they did. All hands to Quarters there. No chickens nor pigs on deck. All hands in their best uniforms. I walked that deck one step ahind them, Fore and Aft. We went into a nice Capt'n cabin and I took up me place ahind McIntire, hands crossed. Protocol says so.

Nope, I just stood there. Capt'n Hernandez would look up, while speakin to McIntire. He didn't offer me a glass nor a plate. Came the Quarter deck and just afore McIntire got saluted off the ship I heard, "May I have a word with your Knight, Capt'n?" Much he cared.

Hard, black eyes he had. I got a little grin and, "Don Diego was correct to say you and your ship is not to be taken lightly. Sir Knight, would you shoot me also, commanding this ship?" I said, 'Only last, Captain. Your helmsmen are more easy targets, Sir.' Well, I got his laugh at that, then that thought hit him. I got his bad eyes, again.

It has been a boring cruise since then. I spend time in the morning, afternoon with readin and writin lessons. I found some small chalk boards in Cozumel. That island off the Yukatan we always stop at. That was 04 November, as ya like dates. No hurry so we had liberty each day there. It is a nice place, with friendly locals, and cheap fruit drinks.

There was ships work to attend to so, yep, Trujillo, Honduras, and them pollo and jambone wraps. Hot peppers in each so both tasted the same. It is just a copper for a samich and fruit drink. No one wanted to take that donkey ride to town. No need. All was right on that beach. Nice, 'cept for Armoror and Mr. Chips hammerin on stuff. The Bosn's was like ants all over the ship. I made sure there was no problems ashore.

12 November we supplied that 2nd Frigate. It was straight 'atween Providencia Island, Nicaragua and Cartagena, Colombia. McIntire went to the war ship Capt'n in his gig, as it was not a hundred yards off. The Purser went to see what they wanted. Word came back that the Port Master, Cartagena, didn't like them and they couldn't buy local vegetables. It was no problem last cruise. There is a long growin season here and aplenty to go around, locals and us.

15 November we anchor not a cable length from that city. Oh, a big place. The gig crew took me and Purser, Mr. Hitcock, to this Harbor Master Place. Seems, he "No Habla Engleses!" I looked at Hitcock and said, 'Sorry, Mr. Hitcock. I guess the Harbor Master in Caracas, Venezuela, will take "A Silver Dollar" to help us out.' I didn't make a turn of me body to that doors when, he Habla "Silver." Purser gave me bad words for this. Oh, he got that 1 dollar silver

coin, after what Mr. Hitcock had ordered was on the pier, goin into our barges. No, I took the gig back.

Third Frigate was just North of Caracas. Seems it had a run in with the local Harbor Master also. Hitcock mentioned this, after comin back with their list. He even repaid me that 1 dollar silver piece. He got that over what the vegetables cost. He charged them that to learn how to, "Properly address the Port Master, Chief!"

21 November, 1895, we made Barbados, again. First round done. I took me group, yes, Engle, to Maggie's place. It is cheap, not far, and she always had the local gossip. As Assistant Purser, I asked about a landin in Caracas. She gave me looks like MaMa did, askin a stupid question. "Your ship Flies?" Nope. "Ya got wheels on the bottom?" No! "Well, Dearie, Caracas is 5 miles inland!"

Maggie 'Habla' some Spanish to the kitchen. The Cook, I know the voice, give a reply. Her elbow to the bar, head to her hand, blinky eyes, and, "Liberty, Please." I said, 'For what! I ain't ordered next drink!' She said, "Cook is from there," and writes on a paper, pushed it over, blinky eyes and, "A liberty for the name to ask for, Dearie!" Outcome that Silver Liberty, (10 cents) finger atop, pushed forward, to her flutterin eyes. 'Paper and your fruit punch, Dearie!'

23 November we had that morning brief to leave Barbados. Mr. Gailey gave the usual sailin report to take us South, past Grenada. McIntire checked his report and, "Sail straight to Windward Channel, Nav. Report in 1 hour!" Ahind Nav, I said, 'Course of West, through straights of St. Vincent and Isle of Elizabeth, Sir. A course West, North West to Puerto Rico for water, McIntire said, "No water. A straight course to there!" I said, 'Fresh water is at half.' So, I got, "Find Another Place, Chief!"

30 November we be 'tween Jamaica and Haiti, North of Jamaica, just doing circles, for two days, when came down a call of sails, from the lookout. That ship took it's time to come hull up. A US Frigate to relieve one of thems. Maybe the East one, which is now probably in Barbados. McIntire went to the war ship Captain and back. Oh, I heard of this one. USS Santee. A Civil War hulk used as trainin ship for the Middies. Oh, those few aboard about had teary eyes to her and then went to the other side and spit.

Like that ship in Philly I did Boot Camp on, she was a sheered hulk, tied to a pier somewhere. They didn't say. Fitz showed me that dispatch of her arrival. That is why I could come up with courses so quick. Congress decided to full man her for Caribbean duty. A big ship with two decks of guns. 64, 18 pounders. 32 to a side! 30 odd years old and I wondered as to her wood. With the full sails, she could bear, they brought her around at, not 7 knots.

There was a new Capt'n and crew on her. Warrant Bos'n, 1st Lieuy, Bos'n Bothel, Wagner, all, about spit over the side as we followed in her wake to Cozumel. We might just as well had tied a cable to her bow and towed her there. At the Smokin Lamp lited I got, "Old Tub!' the Oldsters said she was, well, slow, way back when. I overheard them Middies say, as I did to that ship in Philly, "Old, stank," and, well, bad words.

Cozumel was a disaster. Santee sailors got into fights with each other, drunk, and the town closed the pier to us, also. Mr. Gailey, the Navigator, went over to her, to go over the charts to Trujillo. No! They would set their own course. We followed them all over their idea of South, and bit east. That ship had more leeway than a, nope can't say that. Worse than a drunk sailor, in poor light. I thought maybe, just maybe, they had no keel. That part is under the water that sticks down, to help ya go straight.

They asked about a place to water. I gave their Navigator that place in Puerto Rico. I got his looks, and, "Humph!" Only Mr. Gailey could address him. Thursday, worsh day, was suspended as we was low water. 5 miles from Trujillo, I called out, 'Loss Of Helm, Captain!' Shush, I had the Oldsters loosen the cable clamp on the helm cable. 'Oh, hours to repair, Capt'n. AND, while we are here, Betula is just ashore, and a river, Sir!' Oh, I got bad eyes and, "Warrant, gig over to investigate this river." The crew rowed real dry as I was at that bow.

The barges and water barrels did make that river, such it was. There was shoals on one side, like a sand bar. Around to the East side a barge could navigate. It was not as clean a water as Puerto Rico, but, at low tide it flowed real good. I got eyes from the Capt'n. Someone must have snitched on me. Around the Smokin Lamp Lited, well, it seems the Capt'n knows more about steering gear than I thought. Inspected the fixins, he did, with bad eyes.

The next day we reached Trujillo and saw the beach was deserted, the stove fires was out, and no one about. I didn't ask. Capt'n to Capt'n and back in his gig. "Up anchor. Find the next Frigate!" USS Santee? She anchored too close to shore and no current to get her out. It would take a good Easterly breeze, on them poor sails, to make that offering. I will say our crew blew them kisses and shouts of joy. I got lots to me 'Defaulter' list to pump them holds! He! He! A half hour each, on a dry hold. I had thems make gruntin noises, to make it look good for McIntire.

The 1st found Frigate was off Cartagena. Its ships Doc was hungry for lemons, limes, and greens. Purser Hitcock told me so. We anchored not a cable length from that pier and the Harbor Master greeted us, havin recognized our flag. We on-loaded more than usual stuff, as I could tell. "Mochas Gracias," from the harbor master to that Silver Dollar he got. We sailed back to that Frigate and filled the list Purser had. I got a Silver dollar to me hand and his wink. I figure he made them pay twice the cost for what they ordered.

2nd Frigate was on that South East leg toward Caracas. The barges went back and forth with that beef and pork. There was a special barge for the greens and stuff. Nope, I never passed to the Purser about the harbor master at Maiquetia, Venezuela. Uncle Curtis always said, "Keep that Ace up yourn sleeve. Comes the time, well, better than a 2 dollar Gold piece, it be!"

23 December, 1895, we made Bridgetown, Barbados. Yes, Engle did it up quite right that first night. Even Maggie, the beer tender, wondered about him. 'Course, she was the one to pour out that "Good" stuff to him. Nichol took him back early. I mentioned about the USS Santee commin. Oh, that got her eyes as the third Frigate got to go home. New, ah, boyfriends to have, for her, ifn it ever got here! He! He!

I got caught up with the local gossip. She has more ears on the ground than are rats on the island. Oh, what she don't knows. The Packet crew comes to her place for her good food and her entertaining them. That is why I come to her place! Speakin of which, the Packet crew were there last night. I'll put this to you via that Packet. Have a nice Christmas and a Happy New Year, my Dear!

By Your Leave, Missy,

An Old Sea Dog,

IN THE YEAR 1896, 12 FEBRUARY: CARIBBEAN

Dear Miss Judith,

Oh, I start this just out of Barbados, the evening of 28 December, 1895. The Smokin Lamp Lited there is lots of talk around. Me and Bothel are still segregated to our own table. We got underway this morning for the third, last round of the Caribbean. The crew still in a tizzy about this round. That be why all the conversation goin around.

The officers, minus Warrant Gaston, decided to accept an invite to the Governors place for Christmas dinner. It lasted till, ah, a long time. There was music, dancin, and a late supper, that saved some of thems. Doc and Mr. Chips "helped" each other aboard by 11 PM. I know as I was on Quarterdeck watch. Gunner 1st Burch tried to relieve me at 11:45. I told him to wake up the Marines and, 'No uniform jackets. On the pier, soonest! You also.'

A Church bell sounded at midnight, and then half passed. The Marines on the pier and I could hear them offices comin down the street. As each come to view, two Marines "Helped" each officer aboard. They needed it, else, they might have landed in the water, 'tween the ship and the pier. I ain't sayin they was drunk. Oh, NO! Just well lubricated. Shenandoah was Starboard side too, but, I told the watch, at ships bell, that ifn he struck it for them officer's commin aboard, 'Ya be takin your hammock to the For Top Main to sleep in, till we hit Norfolk!' He understood.

Morning reports, the 26th, didn't start till late in the morning. I got Capt'n coffee and sweet bread, from Engle, at the Chart Table. There was just knowin eyes atween us. No ships bells were sounded all night nor till Engle said McIntire was alive. Then, I had that Marine ring them, 'Real Sharp and LOUD, please.' I put fingers to me ears for thems. Through the skylight I saw Engle serve him his morning coffee and another baked sweet bread. I heard it as Engle must have thought Capt'n was Deaf! Engle got them bad looks, words and, shushed.

Come 10 AM and all the officers assembled in Capt'n cabin for the Morning Brief. Navigator Gaily gave his address and such. The officers around gave theirs and got, "To sail, with the tide, tomorrow, Gentlemen. Dismissed!" I liked that order. Waited for it, expected it, I did.

Bobbit and Fitzsimmons come in that cabin door, around me, and put papers to his desk, fingers to places, and he just signed. It was a shaky hand to that coffee mug. Out they go and he finally looked up. I got his bad eyes and, "Said, DISMITTED, QMC!" That hurt his ears, it did. I gave, 'You said Gentleman, Captain.' I'd have smiled but, I couldn't do that.

I gave him, with Sirs and Captain, about sailin on, 'A Friday, Captain.' I just might have said Capt'n a bit loud! "Old Sailors folk lore, QMC. You believe it?" I said, 'Would you and the officers like some Oxe Tail Soup, for supper, Capt'n?' Oh, that got eyes to me.

I split up Friday liberty so them Marines, me, and Burch got extra liberty. Yes, I went to Maggie place that evening. Fine words she had for the, "Governors Party!" Booze makes for loose lips. It seems Capt'n got a private letter, via that Packet Ship! I gave her a nod and me fingertip sent over an extra Liberty coin to her.

We did that South and bit West to round Grenada, just in case a Frigate be there. Nope. So, we did that North, some West, then West, some North, to Puerto Rico to water. Joseph did most of the figurin. He is comin along. I gave him some books of Navigation to read and had him come into the Chart Room, when Fitz and his students ain't there. I still bad eyes from Fitz on this learnin. The Oldsters are comin along well. They are doin real good with reading and "ritin" on them tablets. Each sent a Post Card from Barbados. There was not much to read, but, they did well.

Out of Puerto Rico, on 02 January, Bothel convert two barges to little sloops. Chips added some keel, fore, and mid masts. He'd done that 'afore. Warrant Gaston agreed as, "Them Middies need training." McIntire asked about them falling overboard. Gaston said, "Oh, Captain, the crew will tie lines to them, in case they fall overboard and see if they can swim! If not, drag them aboard, Captain." He, not me, got bad eyes for that.

The sloop converted barges could expand our range to see the sea. Well, so long as they stayed in sight of the ship. Bothel assigned coxswains, good ones, to steer thems. The Middies were there to learn. The line around them was in case they got 'Persnickety.' Read that as wrong orders, and thrown into the water. Oh, it almost never happens. They sail back to the ship for meals and back afore dark. We don't want to lose a good barge crew!

No to worry about them two boats. They had hogs heads of water aboard. Cook Feterman gave them pails of food from breakfast or lunch, in case! A Middie, crew in the morning, and changed out after lunch. Thems was like a dog on a rabbit chase. Oh, just ahead, ahind, way out to a side or close. Just playin in that wind, they did. It was good leanin for the Middie and crews.

06 January, morning, it was like them two barges, sloop dogs had seen a bear. Oh, just racing each other back to us, tackin to the wind, back and forth. Our lookout had already called it out. Bothel and me, at the bow, was about proud of thems boat crews. No, no Middies got thrown overboard, this time. Them boats ain't back to us and same lookout yells out, "Spanish Frigate. Port Quarter. Starboard side to us." It was sailin slowly on our course.

Oh, we had to go to, "General Quarters. Tampions Off. Gun Ports Closed. Boarding Party Assembled!" We'd greeted her 'afore, so just was in work cloths. Oh, I was in full gear, just in case. Her Capt'n and the Lieuy come over with one bottle in hand. A short visit.

There was a war counsel in Capt'n cabin. Me and Bothel was invited. It seems thems had chased a pirate ship into the night and lost sight of it. Thought it might be headed to the North of Jamaica. Lots of little town are favorable to them. So, he advised us to take the South side of the island. "More friendly to Norte Americano." We put them barge sloops over the side to keep a lookout. They stayed a bit closer than afore.

The next afternoon we come to the West side of Jamaica and the Starboard boat lit off her signal gun. By the time them two got to us, the lookout called sails, and pointed off the side. 'Course, set General Quarters. I had Hood turn over a chart, make a line for our course, and a mark to that ships angle. 28 seconds later I called for another angle, set to the chart. I gave the news to Mr. Gailey.

Come that point forward of us she turned, to get the wind gage. Her stern flag said Spanish. There was no companion to that top mast. At 500 yards she jinxed to Starboard and sent a ball over, to emphasize her flag order to heave to. Gunner said maybe a 6 pounders. Our reply was to jinx the bow toward her and them two forward 9 pounders sent balls to her either side.

That ship Capt'n must have been blind and deaf, as he kept comin. We got another ball from her. Capt'n, in the chains, gave me the nod and we turned Starboard side to her, to Port. His arm came up and our gun ports pop open. Arm down and we sent 6, 18 pound ball to her. Three to her lower sails and 3 to her hull, as I saw. Woke thems up, we did.

She turned to North. We was in a slow turn to Port. Stern to her stern and them 4, 9 pounders went off three times afore she was out of range. We took out the ships stern windows. Na, no sense chasin it. A short action to pump up the crew! Somethin to write home about.

Capt'n in full dress, crew in good uniforms, me in full regalia, we took the gig to that pier in Cozumel and talked to the Harbor Master, who took us to see the Mayor. We apologized for the behavior of Santee persons. Harbor Master understood some English, so he translated this.

Back aboard, Capt'n made it short and clear. "Get drunk, quietly crawl back. Disturb the Piece and the town Mayor will lock you up in his jail. Maybe, I'll get you out, IF we come here again. If not, your name goes to the books for Desertion!" Me, Bothel, and Wagner lead the liberty parties. 'Course, I took Engle with me. There was 6 Marines ashore at a time, to watch.

The town people recognized us, havin been there enough times. We had no real problems. Mess Mates took care of Mess Mates. The Oldsters watched the Cuties. Engle got just drunk enough to stumble back, with a little help. Three days liberty and we left the 12th, of January.

We had to stop at Trujillo. It was time to scrape the hull. No, no tippin the ship over and workin at low tide. Careening the ship is the term. Armoror and Mr. Chips made up this iron angle piece with chains to ropes. The ropes went under the bow sprint, iron piece to the hull, the ropes pull it back and forth to scrape off the stuff from the copper. Three ropes to a side and 10 men to each was why half the crew got liberty in the morning and other afternoon. Just two days to be done and gone. Yes, hot peppers to pollo or jambone samiches and hard liquor fruit stuff.

By now got all the Bosn's were rated to steer the converted barges. Oh, there was more volunteers to man them than seats for. Shush! Feterman sneaks in some plum duff, for lunch. I know as some crews come back late, missed noon meal. "Oh, was too far to get back in time!"

It was 21January, plum duff day, as thems two was not back by noon. We heard thems signal guns go off as one and raced back to say what the lookout already passes on. A Frigate with an Admiral flag at the main. Thems two crews must have been eatin and not lookin! We had time to 'Titivate' the ship. Say clean real quick.

When it was close enough we did that 19 gun salute to this Admiral. Oh, a barge over their side to bring him with his staff aboard. There was 6 Marines to a line, them dang whistles, bells, and into McIntire cabin they went for not 5 minutes. 'Course, he had to inspect the ship's crew. He even addressed some of the Petty Officers by name. The volunteers are in their divisions. Aft, he has to view the Poop people. He got to me side and said words to Capt'n. Oh, I not be there. McIntire got Admiral, now Atlantic Fleet Admiral Taylor, to the center of the Poop rail and pointed up.

I be at the Main sail cross arm, standin in full regalia on the Marine platform. I come to attention, Bothel yelled out, "Attention!" Me closed fist came down to, "Prepare to Salute!" I took out that pistol, with blank cartridge, thank you Armoror, point it in the air, and fired.

Gunner must have double charged the loads in the guns. The forward chasers went off as one. Then down each side, at the same time, upper tier, then lower guns just bellowed that smoke. It would have hurt me ears, 'cept for the cotton. Last was the Starboard signal gun. Oh, the wind was just so, so that gun smoke just hung in the air.

The smoke clears away, some, and I looked up to Admiral Taylor lookin at that Main cross member platform. In the smoke, I climbed down and was right atween the front divisions. At attention, as the crew was, I raise me right gauntlet, close to fist, and yell out, 'Three Hurzays for Atlantic Fleet Admiral Taylor!' No, you are not to yell out, at attention, but. I sure got Taylor bad eyes during all three and the crew back to attention. Well, he had to thank the crew for this welcome. Me? I got his finger to follow him into the Capt'n cabin for, "A Private Talk, QMC!"

I'd talked to Gunner about this afore. Oh, he just loves to shoot them guns, for any reason. Lots of crew members know Taylor. That is why he could name them. Everyone agreed to that crew 'Personal' welcome. McIntire? Protocol book to his hand, book mark to the page, and, well, he chewed on them words.

He asked how I knew he was comin. 'A good Chief hears words on the wind, Captain.' That got his bad eyes but, "OK." The same wind carried that Packet to Nassau and Barbados. A rats ears heard a new admiral was comin to visit in a month.

Taylor chose Shenandoah knowing we hit each ship down here and would to take him to Barbados. He just had to go into Cartagena and see how we got fresh stuff there. The crew got one liberty, by section, for honorin him.

We made that Frigate off of Caracas on 27 January. Gunner was just aglow with that smoke and noise. I had cotton to me ears. Capt'n to Admiral and again with that romp, stomps of them Marines, Bos'n whistles, and bells. Engle cooked a fine meal for thems. They got his plum duff! Oh, He got more than a pint of rum for that. "Oh, Gunner, will be more than two of thems, there will be!" No, Spiel served them. I had to go down and shush Engle. He was whistling!

We made Barbados on the 31st. No, no guns. None ashore. 'Tween that Frigate and Barbados the Admiral about bothered the crew to no end. Bothel, Wagner, and me took turns standing by that aft line in the deck to yell out, "Admiral On Deck!" On the second afternoon we was doing a minor Wear and about missed stays, cause he was on deck. I talked to him and got his OK. He could 'Roam the Deck,' and none would pay attention to him. 'Cept ifn he asked them something, When NOT workin ships sails! He could address them in groups. He likes mixin with the crew. He got this from Forest.

We was in Barbados for three days. Taylor got even with me for that ships greeting. I had to be 'His Personal Escort' for official functions, one step ahind him and Capt'n. 'Ahind him when he sat for 2 meetings and 2 dinners. Oh, I picked up on some stuff. I took liberty, when not 'Engaged' with Taylor. I just went to Maggie's place. My ears picked up some her rats missed. I got me 10 cent Silver back, for a tip on Santee arrival and new Frigate behind it that brought Taylor. She had that "Fresh Meat" look that Alfa gave me crew!

06 February we put in for water in Ponce, Puerto Rico. I was in the Chart Room, workin on me current figures, puttin them to a fine paper to send to D.C. Bothel comes in to says Taylor wanted to see me. Well, we don't keep the place 'Perfect,' as no one is allowed in. I look around and got his smile. Came, "Oh, Chief goes to Admiral." Out the door and I got a point. Yep, Taylor is standin on that Marine platform, Main mast.

Oh, the masts were clear of the crew. Just him and me. No problem for me goin up. I had to practice for the "Admiral Honors!" I sat on that platform, leggs, both, hangin over and a good grip on a Main Chain line. It gave him a grin, watchin me come up, sit, and grip.

He caught me up on squadron and a new Admiral, no name, didn't like this 'Volunteers' thing. OK. McIntire mentioned none had signed on as crew. He offered me a position on his flag ship as "Ship Master." I said, 'To stand behind you, at all meals, in full regalia! I'd die of starvation!' Well, he did laugh at that. Said he'd could have the volunteer papers voided. I said back, he'd have a hard time mannin squadron ships. Oh I did me Sirs and Admiral. He'd say QMC. Chief was a new term to him.

This went on for more time than I ever spent with him. Just roundy, roundy in that talk and back twice to crew. I guess McIntire mentioned it more than once. "The crew look up to you. Talk to them." I said, as afore, 'Captain needs to talk with them,' pointin down, 'On the Main deck, or, take a plum duff with them, Admiral.' Nope, I didn't stand to him leavin. It is a nice view from up there and words to think about. There are times ahead to consider.

I am proud of those Fitz worked with in reading and writing. A first letter to their kinfolk they have been practicing. Each took offence to another looking at what they wrote. "Might Steel Me words, He will!" No, each scratch mark was theirs. I did help with spelling, so those who got it, if they could read, could understand it.

The crew grumbled some about scrubbing down their livin area. They grumbled doing it a second time as they overlooked some corners. With me and Bothel in the Chart Room, they did overlook some things, with their cleaning. Engle grumbled when he didn't get rum for his plum duff. It went to the crews meal. Admiral and McIntire accepted their invite for plum duff.

It is hard not to run into Capt'n and Admiral as I am always about the ship. 'Course, they, yes both, have been badgerin the crew on Main Deck. The crew agreed to this, "So long as whess don't got to salute all the time, Chief!" 'No. they pass that deck line and no salutes!' Then, I got grumbles from McIntire and Taylor. Given me choices, they agreed to this, ah, disrespect, after I mentioned about rope burns, broken bones, and things Doc would need to make an, 'Official report to DC and who was involved, Sirs.' That shushed them two up.

I close this out, 12 February, 1895. Nassau is on the horizon. Purser is callin for mail. I am ordered to man the barge in, "Full Regalia, QMC! Put some ships biscuits in your pocket, in case you get hungry!" A Taylor joke. I got two pocket bottle and biscuits! Shush! Ain't just water in them bottles. The ships water has a taste, by now.

By Your Leave, Missy,

An Old Sea Dog,

IN THE YEAR 1896, 28 APRIL: SQUADRON

Dear Miss Judith,

I be here at me desk at Squadron, the Admiral building. Bothel has his desk with the 1st Lieuy, a stone throw away. No one knows what to do with us, as far as assign us something to do. Wagner and Burch assign work details. Morning and afternoon Bothel and me review the mustered men. Both of us have them little rooms in the barracks. Bothel spends about no time there. No duty, so he has lots of time with his wife, Maggie.

I caught up on mail. Most were letters from me two favorite girls, Thank you and MaMa. Squadron kept the ones received here after the 1st of January. The clerk said the new Lieutenant gave the order. The same thing they do every cruise and no arguing that issue.

We got back from the Caribbean on 21 February. Hood, Bush, and Joseph set all the Whey points. Joseph, mostly, as the others have them in their pocket wheel books from last time down there. Come September I'll recommend him to make 3rd Class.

Two days from here I was organizing the Chart Room, say doin a deep cleanin, when the door opened and closed. I was near the windows and thought it was Bothel. "About time you did something with this place!" Admiral Taylor. I said, not turnin round, 'So you finally fell from the mast and broke both arms, Sir.' I got, "And just Why would you think that, QMC?" 'Private Quarters, Admiral. You should knock first as I might be in a private way, Sir.' Oh, I turn to his small grin.

He took to a high chair next to the Chart Table and handed over a paper. A return to port schedule of events with Squadron Admiral James W. Irwin, Squadron Adjutant Captain L. McMillan, Squadron Lieutenant James Makins and all them others comin aboard. I read down the TBD, time to be determined, items and had to ask about me flag presentation and all.

"Admiral Irwin is not into 'Formalities.' He considers this a normal occurrence. A ship returning to port. No swords, no pistol, no arm protectors, nor gauntlets, QMC." Flag got, "Volunteers will be in division ranks. You stand with your normal Waisters. BMC was with 1st Division Bosn's." I ask about signin for the volunteers. "That paper will be in the group he normally signs." For fun I ask, 'Crew in slops or best dress Blues, Admiral?' Came, "Tomorrow is Make and Mend day. Clean, dress uniforms."

Come that Friday morning, in divisions, up comes this Admiral. An Old Guy. Taylor is my older brother, by comparison. He and his group went into Capt'n cabin with Taylor. They came out to Bothel salute and, "First Division, Admiral." He gave a, 'sniff,' and this parade goes forward. I heard 2nd division from Wagner, Mr. Chips, then Gunner, and the Old Guy comes in-front of me. 'Waisters, Admiral,' and I saluted, got his 'sniff,' and he looked at me uniform.

I was still at salute and he poked the Ships Wheel insignia on me right breast pocket. Capt'n said, "Designated Ships Master, Admiral." I got his bad looks at me Master-At-Arms insignia. His finger comes to the crossed swords, "AND," poke, "WHAT," poke, "IS," poke, "THIS!" McIntire said, "Master-At-Arms, awarded by Navy Department, Admiral." Came another, 'sniff,' and he went to the pier. "Ships Company, Dismissed."

Well, so much for getting them papers signed. Taylor and crew scampered off the ship ahind Irwin. It was like rats desertin a sinkin ship. I rounded up me 12 and Saltsgiver had us form up two lines. That was when Fitzsimmons gave me the bad news. He had McIntire signed them over to me. "Dismissed!"

Yes, now 12, not counting Bothel and Fitz. Bothel, by the paper was, "Temporary, Ships Chief Bos'n." Capt'n signed that other paper releasing me as Ships Master. It seems the plum duff idea was liked by half of the volunteers. Taylor and McIntire just shook their hands and gave them nice smiles. It was not my talkin to them into it.

From me pocket I paid for the volunteers night out. Ella took good care of them. She gave me her discount price as I was a regular. So are most of thems. Monday morning I saw Lieutenant Makins about the papers to sign, by the Admiral. "Busy! Later. Dismissed." Fitz got nowhere trying to get Admiral signature.

Come Wednesday I handed Admiral Mast request paper to Makins. Oh, he just wrote denied on it and handed it back. 'Pardon, Mr. Makins. This is to see Fleet Admiral Taylor.' Taylors adjutant Capt'n had to deny it. Fitz said Irwin denied it, but sent it in mail to Taylor. Friday, after lunch muster, I got a finger from Fitz and, "Admiral to see you, QMC."

Oh, that was a trap to step into. In the Admiral conference room was Irwin. I stepped up to the desk, 'Admiral.' 'Ahind me the door closes to, "Always Trouble, QMC!" Taylor. He likes to catch me off guard.

Irwin signed in his place and then Taylor signed below his. "Now Fleet Admiral Men, QMC." I held out me hand and said, '5 dollars, Gold, Admiral,' handed over Ella receipt, and said, 'Payment for Volunteer Thank You evening we had, Sir.' It seems officer never carry any money. Fitz paid me from Squadron finds and sent a request to Fleet clerk to repay.

The first Saturday evening was with Maggie and Bothel. Wagner got an invite. It took two of us to carry the dinner pales. Cook Stewart took good care of this. They had a new, bigger apartment. It reminded me of Carries place. Chief makes more money. A new woman, Susie, for Wagner and Lena for me. Maggie divided us up on height, Wagner bein shorter. There was just stories of us in the Caribbean. Most was about Santee and getting, "Thrown out of ports!" A nice Saturday evenin, Sunday afternoon, and evenin.

Nothin to do, I take some afternoons in town but most always back for dinner. Cook Steward makes a fine meal. Ella has some good stuff, to munch on. I stopped in to see Effie. Yes, Carrie mother. Well, Mr. Big Eyes, in so many of her words, picked a Rose, which ya know has thorns. I already said she was independent, like a cat. They are engaged but no date is set. Was her words of him settin a round peg to a square hole. Carrie was not one to re-shape. "We will see which gets rounded up or off!" Know that answer, I do.

You would say for spite, I say for business, I went to Carrie shop for two flags. Oh, I had to pass Maggie, at her work place, and her black eyes. I got a cordial greeting, dark eyes from Carrie. Yes, she could make the flags, no time to bein done as, "We are busy." I said, 'No rush. Not underway till end of April.' I got better eyes when said, 'I hear a ship, down in Norfolk, is loading out for China!' Came her thinkin eyes, a smile and, "You have seen Effie." I shook her hand, and give her a bow. I heard, "QMC, you ever been to Shanghai?" 'No, Miss Carrie. The closest was China town in San Francisco.'

Susie is the talker of the two. Lena is a bit shy. She covers her mouth in a snicker, or stifled laugh, like someone I know. Medium height and build. Darkish hair. A nice smile, fine face, and hands. This March has seen some cold weather. 4 handed cards we do. Wagner and Susie sit out, a lot. I'm not familiar enough to Lena to play footsy under the table, for bridge. Sometimes she and I sit out. We talk of where I've been. A new audience. She and Susie be roommates.

Bothel has to put up with Mr. Makins. He is no better, nor worse than Stiles was. An administrator. He says "No" to everything. Adjutant Captain McMillan is a bit better to deal with. He thinks about things, for a moment, then says, "No, Dismissed." Irwin has a back door to his office so I never know when he is in.

Waking around the piers I've seen Irwin out and about. He is about dead slow in walk. I asked Fitz to check his record. He came up with none he could find. I have seen Irwin, with Mr. McMillian, around the piers. The only other places to walk to be the Marine compound, to chow hall, and Navy barracks. That is why I go out to town.

Jessi W. Willaims came in. A costal supply ship. QMSN Mark, now QM3, QM2 Potts, probably QM1 in September, aboard. They are names from letters, afore. Former mates on Susquehanna. Oh, we had stories to tell, from both sides. The Ships Master, yes, they have one assigned, just gave bad words to thems. "Run Us Aground, ifn I didn't watch close. Close to makin Seaman out of both!" He is a Feisty Old sailor. He gave me a wink, ahind their backs. Potts will need to move up to one of the 4 larger cargo ships when he puts on that strip.

Bothel and Maggie were acting odd at our weekend get together. I don't ask me about secrets among couples. It was after loadout of Carney that he came to me. It seems he wanted to be Bos'n of a ship. Local cargo ships come to Norfolk at least each month or not more than 6 weeks gone. I told him it was a good move. 'It needs a BMC to straighten her out!' Which they do. Her 1st Lieuy is why I got 4 more to Squadron list. Good men. Able-Bodied Seaman, Fore masters. Makins signed the request and Irwin added his signature.

Another off that original list. 4 others I can't seem to get rid of. They like the liberty at Squadron.

March has seemed to blow itself out. Out of cold weather. Regina and Silvis gave a little party for Bothel makin his step to "Ships Bos'n." We had Madeira wine for that toast. Yes, all drank it. The pink stuff is just sweet enough for me taste. Saturday afternoon, Sunday afternoon, Lena and me about got thrown out of the house. "Get air, you two!" Wagner and Susie need no prodding.

Unlike Carrie, Lena likes to look in winders and then into the stores. Ooh's and Ahhs at expensive items. Susie and her work in a bank, closed on the weekend. No, not down in town. They make enough for a shared room. "Oh, to have enough for this dress," she said. That put costs of the uniforms I had to buy to me mind. Then them flags and a silver sash to me sword, came to mind. There be not much in her pay check, I figured.

It was 10 April and I got a note from Fitz to see Admiral Irwin. It said, "North Side of North Pier." Hmm. I found Mr. McMillian head of the pier and got his point to Admiral Irwin, some ways down, sittin in one of two chairs. Oh, salutes, of course. "Sit, QMC." Carney is off with Bothel. J.E. Willaims just left. "Impressive Service Jacket, QMC."

From memory, better than mine, he ticked off each time we engaged a ship, shore bombardment, Capt'ns name, and all. "And your Pistol Treaty, written at the top!" He saw Captain Smith was in Washington, assigned to a desk. "I wrote him. A letter from him said you, how did he put it, ah, 'Blead All Over His Good Deck! The last wounded to leave the Poop." True.

He never looked at me. His eyes was to Shenandoah. Next came how he was a Lieutenant under, "Now Fleet Admiral Porter." The name on me enlistment papers. He laughed and said, "Your Uncle Curtis and him sure had words for each other. The only man ever said no to Porter."

Last, he mentioned how he got into a "Naval Match." Firing ship guns in battle. The ship turned too late to engage and, like with Capt'n Smith, got about blown away. "A ball to Starboard rail killed some, put me down. Lieutenant Taylor, 1st Lieuy, took over." I saw far away eyes. "You owe me your flag!" I mentioned Taylor and all.

"That boy looks after me like a mother hen, he does. My legs don't work well enough to kick his ass!"

Been an expensive week for me. I had to see Carrie about flags I ordered, Friday, the 17th. Saturday, the 18th, afternoon, Lena and me, Maggie, Wagner and Susie, "just have to go winder lookin! It is nice out," Susie words. I got Wagner bad looks and a smile from Lena.

The last stop was at Effie Millenary store. They had to try on blouses. Effie and me traded looks. A silver dollar to her got bad eyes. Another one, another, got a nod. We went back to Mattie place with 3 of packages. I paid for our pick up supper at the Chinese place. I walked Lena back home, got two hands to mine, a sweet kiss, and "Thank you."

Fitz? I only see him in the offices. He and Zoe got invites but never showed up. It is not polite to ask. Last weekend, the 24th, Friday, Wagner and Susie ate and left. Saturday, 25th, we did "Lookin," again. No, just looked! I got a sweet kiss Sunday after I walked Lena home. It was three shots of that bottle to sleep. Me mind was wonderin about something.

Monday afternoon, 27 April, I visited Carrie for the flags. Maggie had them laid out to look at. 'Nother cost. I went to Ella and Howard place for the evening. I needed a laugh as I can spin her up to give me a good grin.

It is Tuesday morning, 28 April. Good Old Fitz gave me a list of 'Volunteers,' from all them previous papers. Some names had been crossed off and later added. It comes down to 4, I mentioned, in the original orders, to end that contract. Able-Bodied Seaman and Fore masters, mostly. The 4 that grabbed and dragged them Oldsters back to that Muster line. It seems like ages ago, two pay grades ago. A good thing, for the money I spent at Effie place. Mr. Bish gets me good interest on what he holds for me.

I did a walk to them piers and laughed till I cried. Times and places to remember. Uncle Curtis warned me about this. "A Sailor takes them Fine Sailin days and thanks Davy for thems, he does." He took a sip of bottle and I get bad eyes to, "Times to 'member when them Top Gallants get blown off and Top Mains go by them Clew Holes, Me laddie!" Only in me minds bad eyes, no memory, I see that rail explode and nothing more. Sometimes still feel them wood shards, at odd times, like at the pier, right then.

Carrie, Lina be there. Oh, woman from afore there to. The sweet smell of gardenia and the awful on of Talig kayak! Last was that tan glove waving from the platform of Lincoln, Nebraska. Ida. Then comes Uncle Curtis words. "Water 'ahind, is 'ahind! Mind your helm here and now, to take Ya to Where Ye be goin, Laddie!"

I finish this at me desk, afore noon meal. This afternoon, I am to be in full regalia of sword, pistol, no cartridges, get to do 'Honors' to Admiral Irvin. He is to inspect what 'Volunteers' I have for Shenandoah. J.E. Williams took some. Some followed Bothel to Carney. First asks, First gets!

By Your Leave, Missy,

An Old Sea Dog,

IN THE YEAR 1896, 27 MAY: ATLANTIC CROSSING

Dear Miss Judith,

We are underway to the Med. The Chart Room lamp is on a nice Starboard lean. High seat to this table, I be. It is the first time aboard a ship, alone, in a ships room. I am designated, again, Ships Master. Yes, of Shenandoah. Compass says South East, and some East. The Barometer is, has been, concave, convex, but steady. It is warmer out as we be headed to Bermuda. The North Atlantic is still rough. The room has a smell of old paper and new tar to the planks. We have been out of Norfolk for the last two days.

Yesterday I got called into McIntire cabin. It seems he went over the list of volunteers he signed, and mentioned somes names and why not assigned. Bothel took a couple good ones with him to Carney. Williams requested some. 'I assigned what was not spoken for, Captain. Some didn't think you could name them, Captain.' That was why Bothel got some of the best.

To go back some, after that 'Pier Introduction,' Admiral Irwin had me do some walks to the piers. He put more flesh on Uncle Curtis and Porter too. A jovial person Admiral was right there. He laughed at some of Curtis and Porter stuff. A Ships Master and Captain arguing about wind, speed, a course to take, and all. "Hard headed they both were."

Come the afternoon of 28 April, me in full regalia, Irwin came to that podium to me 6, 4 from Carney, 2 from J.E. Williams, and 4 new boots. Shush. I had Fitz put them new ones to me list. In our walks, I encourage him to use, ah, 'Sailor words to their true character, Admiral,' which he did. I warned the Boots to this.

Comes the time and I go to attention. All do. We practiced this just once, at morning muster. Me gauntlet up and one finger. Hawk ups a 6 foot flag pole with that white flag and big M on it, around, and into that wooden plate, right of Irwin. At the second finger, Stoops came forward with the Red, White, Blue flag with that snake on it, to another plate. Third finger and Oldster Carney come to that wood pole with that modified St. Andrew flag to a wood plate. 4th finger and Craig up me personal flag.

Craig stopped just shy of that wood plate. I give that sword salute, slash, to sword hilt, did a gauntlet salute and, 'Three Hurzays to Admiral Irwin!' Done, me flag to a wood plate. The Pole and flag bearers were them 4 that are on the original list. Oh, Irwin thanked us. Gauntlet up, 'Salute. Two!' That ended the ceremony. Plates and poles went to Admiral Irwin conference room, ahind that desk. I figure Taylor will spit when he sees thems.

No. the Gold, silver, pearl flag is mine. I didn't have Carrie make that yellow, swallow tailed one, from Susquehanna. It is in me sea chest as it is bad luck to show a flag, dishonored by them Brits. I don't have one for St. Lawrence.

1st Lieuy, Caldwell, now the Navigator, is a pain in Hood, Bush, and poor Joseph butt. Ya, both. He switched with Mr. Gailey. I gave him a book to read on navigation and it was like he never heard of such stuff. It took 'tween Norfolk and Bermuda 'afore he learned the earth was round.

'Afore, we set a course and he just set best sails for that Whey Point. He had no idea of goin to Bermuda. I would ask to have him demoted to Seaman, but can't. Capt'n, and us, shoot the noon sun, when visible. It took some time afore I'd set his "Mark" to the Chart. It says the Latitude and longitude or our last position. No, gave him a good sextant to use. I wanted to make one like Uncle Curtis did, back when, at home, for him to use. I would even set it close to the mark!

Fitz has started up his School Marm classes, again. He must be bored stiff. He still checks Bobbit spelling and math. Me "Gents" come with them slates and each has his own place to sit. Lord help the one who, "My Place! Yourn is OVER THERE!" I put their places to a paper because of this.

Hawk, Stoops, Carney, and Craig have a Boot Camper assigned to each. They can only go to the first mast cross member. I had to have a talk with them three stripers about teasing them. 'You will be cleanin the heads, three times a day, come another word!' Thems three stripers got assigned a Boot, to help them learn the ship.

It was 4 easy days sailin and we made Bermuda. 5 May. We took a barge over as them officers like the place. Mr. Gaily stayed ahind to watch the ship. Yes, forward, Main anchor, and that ketch aft. The winds just don't mind our wishes. At 4 PM we hit that pier to the Governor and a reception group.

McIntire said they was not to stay long. There be no watches to their pocket that I've seen. They are always invited to supper, drinks, talks, and no rowin back at night. I sent Wagner to find quarters for the night. He came back in a huff and handed me a paper to read. A note from Edith. I put a note to me Wheel Book paper and gave it to the most junior person in that barge and said, 'My compliments to the Captain.' He Polly Parroted, 'Family honors are required. Request to stay the night, with selected crew members, Captain!'

Bos'n 3rd, Marshal, went off and back. Across my request was, "Denied!" A paper from me Wheel book, signed, to Wagner, and the barge went back to the ship. I was there as it and another tied up. Wagner assigned watches. I wrote a note on Wheel Book paper and gave it to the barge watch. 'Give to the Capt'n, when he arrives!'

Sun down was ago when got Marshal gave a poke to me back. I went out the boardin house door, salute Capt'n, the ships officers and welcomed them, 'To the wake of Alfa.' Respect in me words, I evoked, said, them words from that 'Protocol Book.' Well, it seems Capt'n and thems know to be 'Respectable, Honorable Gents!' They did one shot salute to Alfa, gave regrets to Edith, and left.

I don't know where from, but, Edith found a cook that was like her mother. Oh, sharp voice, bad temper, tasty fixins, knife to hand, and sharp of eyes. Etta. She harassed me crew members to no end. She gave winks, cutie smiles, and bad eyes to complaints. Don't ask me her age. Maybe MaMa age. The same frame and height. Kind, then fire eyes, and stories to make you smile. She used bad words sailors like! It was a fine wake.

Edith laughed, smiled, and snickered at the words the crew gave about Alfa and stayin here. Sad eyes, at times. Heavy of heart. I'd pick on a crew member, about Alfa, and set the place to cheer again. Alfa had cutesy names for each one. The color of eyes, curly hair, what she could pick out to tease. Me? It was like Grandpa, MaMa side, always called me, "Skipper!" I never knew why. Maybe Alfa did it for that ships wheel on me shoulder.

Edith went to her bed just after 10 PM. She was noddin off, sittin at the bar. Oh, all had to give her a hug and cheek kiss. She thanked me for bringin those Alfa knew, with a cheek kiss. I think the evenin of the men's thanks and talk of Alfa wore her out.

In me bed, not much after, Alfa and Uncle Curtis voices to me mind. Grandpa, Grandma and, "Them Hooligans," as Mama called them, now also gone. I should have had two more shots. I would have but, MaMa voice said to watch after Edith during the Wake.

I was hopin to get extra bit of sleep, goin to bed after Edith. I wanted to be well rested, standin front of McIntire. She woke me at 5 AM and about dragged me to the kitchen naked! She gave me a moment to dress. I got a knife and shown how to cut up taters and onions. She never stopped talkin for the next hour on Uncle Curtis and Alfa. He was her third husband, "Yes, married here!" Don't ask me about wives of Curtis. He never said. I only know I found her name in that book of ports that he left ahind in that sea chest.

The note said, "A sweet kiss, good whiskey, and soft bed to sleep in." Ok, I didn't remember them exact words the first time. I said I was, 'Owed a kiss, good whiskey, and comfy bed.' I reminded Edith of what I said. Two hands to me cheeks and Edith gave me a nice kiss. I got a twinkle in her eyes, a slap on me butt, and a wink to, "Cut tators and onions for breakfast!"

It seems only Brits can own property in Bermuda. What property they bought was in her name. She never changed it. Edith said he, "Loved her dearly, but loved the sea more. A few years here, she told him to go back to that life." No, Edith was to second one. I got more flesh to him. It ended with, "He had kind, gentle eyes, always looking toward the sea."

Oh, Edith wouldn't take them Brit Crowns. "My pleasure to have you all come." I watched, last in line, and gave Etta 3, 5 dollar gold pieces. Edith smiled as each crew member gave her hugs and cheek kisses. I got a hug, cheek kisses, and she pulled out this envelope, to me hand. "Twice a year, we received one of these from your Uncles agent, in Norfolk. A check was enclosed, which has always carried us over, when boarders were few."

Two barges rowed back real dry and quiet. The officers said not a word. Barges aboard and Capt'n said, "Up Anchors, Mr. Gailey," to whistles, romp and stomp round the anchor windless. "Mr. Caldwell, set course for Gibraltar." I has been two days and not a peep from the Capt'n. Oh, I be getting thrown out of me room by "The School Marm!"

Caldwell gives Capt'n morning reports. Hood, Bush ahind him. Joseph is a bit green for that. No, no words from Capt'n after Bermuda. He didn't avoid me. There was no reason to talk. He gave orders to Caldwell. He has taken to walk the deck. The rule is he steps over that line, on the deck, and no disturbin crew members at work. Mr. Gailey said that to him second day out of Norfolk. No, no injuries. Like with Forest, Taylor, and now him, the crew don't salute, give nod, "Capt'n," and he can talk with them.

Around Smokin Lamp I heard words about him. Good ones, mostly. Oldsters and some, grumble some. "Like he be lookin over me shoulder, to complain!" Wagner passed on about the 3 strippers and Boots turnin from their work and saluting him. I had to take thems aside and mentioned cleaning the heads. "Yes, Chief!" I took them Oldsters and such aside. 'Capt'n is tryin to be personable and know what you do.' "Why!" 'Cause!'

17 May and I got sheep smell in the wind. The Azores Islands. No, we are not to stop, as I heard. Fitz comes up to the Poop Chart table and said McIntire wanted me in his cabin. Hmm. Attention at his desk and got, "I'd like to congratulate the men, in your Chart Room, for their reading and writing ability, QMC." I said, 'No, Captain. Comes that time, they will invite you to view their progress, Captain.' You are not to say that word to a ships Capt'n. 'It would embarrass them, you thinking they can't read or write, Captain.'

"Dismissed, Chief." Not to that door and, "A word, Chief." Oh, not official now. Back to his desk, and he put three books on his table. Ships books I recognized. They was, Principals of Navigation, Old Sailors Tales, Naval Observatory North Wall, and Navy Protocol. I put a finger to each, which is not to do without permission. "I denied your request for liberty, out of hand, as I didn't think it was warranted, Chief." With better eyes, "The note you left, with Bos'n Marshal, ah, brought things to mind, QMC."

That note was simple. 'Respectful Request Captain, and ashore officers, of USS Shenandoah, attend the Wake of Alfa, wife of Retired QM1 Thompson, Ship Master, Sir.' Marshal escorted them. 'Edith greatly appreciated you, and the ships officers attending, Captain.' I got, "And you, QMC?" I said, 'I expected no less from the officers and you, Captain.' Eyes to eyes and Engle came in with coffee and sweet breads.

25 May, 1896, we made the outer harbor of Gibraltar. Wind to Nor Nor West was enough to get us over that Chart Line, into that bay. An Admiral flag to St. Lawrence mast and we banged them guns. The barge went over the side, to that pier. Nope, I just stood with the barge crew. It was midmorning. I don't go to a pier without a hogs head of water and breakfast stuff to food pales. We can put up a sail, ifn one needs a privy. I learned that afore times. BM3 Marshal went to St. Lawrence and came back with, ah, 'Shove Off Mate,' to his requests.

We didn't get favorable winds till McIntire came aboard, afternoon, and the wind came from some South and just West. Just enough to get sails up and tie up ahead of St. Lawrence. We had a barge take over that Fore line to put our headlines at that pier. Monkey fists on light line went over, and pulled the hawsers to the bollards. Liberty was by divisions, divided up. I took the first eve watch on the Quarterdeck. It was the worst I seen men dragged back from shore leave. Doc Stiteler got to take care of thems. Saltsgiver, Nichol dragged back some injured or not, "For their protection, Chief."

26th, May, I was in front of McIntire for the Daily Brief. The Brit Police and St. Lawrence Captain had charges for our crew. "A long Defaulter List, QMC!" Me pocket wheel book came to hand. Saltsgiver and Nichol answered to each name I gave and what they knew. I got McIntire bad eyes. I mentioned BM3 Marshal and his goin to St. Lawrence for, 'barge conveniences, Captain.' "Dismissed, but QMC."

From me jacket pocket, I had to wear jacket, but no tie, I put a paper to his desk, 'Request Admiral Mast for myself and charged crew members, Captain.' Oh, he wrote, "Denied." I said, 'Admiral Palmer Adjutant Captain is next, Captain.'

Ya have to laugh at this as, it would be me first meeting with Admiral Palmer. McIntire about bit his tongue when I mentioned this. 'Protocol says, Captain, I must preset flag and all, Sir.'

This afternoon, St. Lawrence got underway to Norfolk, with the tide, much it is, was. I told the crew to not joke them, nor show their, ah, back sides. 'No, No Crow Calls!' That gives bad luck to the other ship. The Admiral Flag shifted to us. Admiral, plus staff, were already ashore. I took my assigned group ashore after that good dinner Cook makes. Pheobe entertained me for that evening.

I close this out to you, 27 May, hear at the Poop Chart Table. The Packet ship arrived just after St. Lawrence left. Nope, no word of Palmer and company. Yes, I have a letter to MaMa about Alfa and Edith. I enclosed that Church notice. She puts them in that family Bible she keeps up with. Me? I got me logs to remind me of things.

By Your Leave, Missy,

An Old Sea Dog,

IN THE YEAR 1896, 07 AUGUST: MEDITERRANEAN

Dear Miss Judith,

We got underway for that first round of the Med, 31 May, 1896. I be here in 'Me Hidy Hole,' as I call it. I sorted out them Charts we be needin for the next days. Oh, now you'll be askin about Admiral Palmer. He, and his flag, are on that Frigate not more than a cable length ahead. Ya, both of them.

I am here as there are more officers on that Poop deck than about space for. The hands be crows to them masts, adjustin sails to that Frigate speed. I told Mr. Caldwell, Nav, to have Capt'n send a flag request for, 'Our Best Speed, Sir!' The third time was when I came here. I hear them whistles less. Yes, I wrote afore about tryin to keep up with one of thems. They are not potbellied, like we are.

After I finished that letter of the 27th, I decided to do a turn of Gibraltar. I visit places to look for stuff. I was up one side of that road and took lunch at a place. That was when I heard them heavy guns of a Frigate salute the Admiral flag at our mast. I wasn't told about that. Not me concern. I be on Liberty!

I had Doc Stiteler with me. He likes to pick up them amethyst chips to use for fine cutting. I laughed as he ordered tea, to me other stuff. The Waiter, with a heavy Brit accent, said something he don't understand. 'Doc, he wants to know if you want milk, in your tea.' He never heard of this, but tried it. I put a hand over me drink and said, 'No thank you.'

Now, Doc went back to tend his patients with a broken bone and some with cuts. I, sorta, meandered down the other, the sea side of that road. A town bell sounded out the time. There was no time set for me to get back to the ship. There was a couple of pawn shops to look in on.

I was about to Pheobe place and got about accosted by the Admiral Lieutenant. I recognized him. He escorted me to the back door of her place. In to Palmer and his Adjutant Captain at a table. OK, I took a seat. Pheobe come in and sets down small bottle of whiskey and 4 glasses. I caught up her hand to mine, push her bottle aside, put a 3 dollar gold piece on the table and, 'Good Whiskey.

Bigger bottle.' She about sucked the air out of the room, leaving, and brought it back in, with a better, bigger bottle, and poured it to them 4 glasses.

'A toast, to Admiral Palmer.' Second, 'A toast, to my mother.' The third was, 'To Uncle Curtis and wife Alfa, Gentlemen.' Oh, I got looks around, 'A toast, Gentleman!' Admiral and me snapped them glasses to that table. The other two, did some sippin, 'afore to the table. He twitched a finger and thems left. Eyes to me, me request paper came to the table. He wrote, "Denied," across it. "Someone might think you are a favorite, QM2."

Well, I had to looked at me Chief badge on that left sleeve. I felt for them fowled anchors on collar tips. Yep, still there. "It was the sorriest day of my life that I had to promote you." At least I got a small smile. It seems he had some watch for me name in ships reports. "I saw Captain Smith, in D.C. His is doing well. And, You?" I said, 'Why, Thank you, Admiral Palmer. Still above dirt and water, Sir.'

With no list to paper, he went over the noted items he heard of. Pheobe looked so I ordered some crackers and beer. There was no sense getting him drunk, talkin about times, ahind. "And when do I get this Salute and Flag I heard of, QMC, Master-At-Arms?" I got his finger poke to me jacket. 'You need to tell Captain McIntire of the time, Admiral.'

He mentioned about getting underway, "Sharp, Friday, QMC! Give the Frigate crew a day of Liberty!" I said would be nice, 'But, never on a Friday, Admiral. Give the full Frigate crew some time ashore, Sir.' No is not a word Admirals like. "Friday, 29 May, I expect your ship to be to my inspections standards and all, Chief!" The last salute was, 'To a peaceful cruise.'

The Marine struck that hour on the ships bell as Palmer came aboard to whistles, more bells, salutes, and his inspection began. Oh, he inspected below deck, the stove, and rattled them pots. Up Starboard side of the Poop, the Signal Middie popped the ships flag and an Oldster gave him a small copy. One that Carrie made.

He came around to me, Portside. The other Middie popped mine and I did that ritual salute. Seaman Joseph stepped forward, unrolled a small one of mine, for Palmer to inspect. He looked real close to that lover corner crossed stuff and had to look up at the me big flag. I got his eyes and, "Sultan Treaty?" 'The scimitars to mine are a sign of respect, Admiral.'

Monday, 1 June, that Frigate dipped her flag and sent us on our way. She went South, toward Algiers. Warrant Gaston and Mr. Gailey whistles for normal sails. We settled on course, sails just set, them Fore'masters hit the deck and heard, "Spanish Frigate, Due North," from the lookout.

"General Quarters, Mr. Gailey." Oh, them Fore'masters went back up to set fightin sails, set Top Gallants, up come the Fore, Mid, and Aft courses, lower sails. That is like a woman uppin her skirt for a mud puddle. We do this so them guns don't set them afire!

Oh, a dipped flag and the hoist said he just wanted to talk. The crew stayed at stations. The boarding party was formed forward, with formal lines of men. They at the Fore deck had full wears of pistols and cutlasses on them front ones. There was Pikes and Halberds ahind. The same Spanish Capt'n and Lieuy went into to McIntire cabin and thru the skylight I saw Spiel serve out the Spanish wine.

Out they came for a normal inspection of the crew. The Spanish Capt'n and his Lieuy jabbered away. He give a nod to each division. Respectful he always is. Up the Starboard Poop and he came around to me. I had to do that salute, bein in Formal arms, and all. Just his eyes to mine. To McIntire was, "May I have a private talk with your Knight?"

I motion to the Port gangway area, as it was the only place not occupied. Get his dead eyes, no smile. "Our Nations are in some disagreement. Should I not dip my flag, I am ordered to engage you." He said it like in normal conversation. I nodded, pointed to me personal flag flyin and said, 'I'll dip mine to half mast, as a Challenge, Captain. I'll only shot you, last, if necessary, Sir.' That got wide eyes and he was gone.

They was them same eyes Mr. Reynolds had, back in Philly, when I defeated him in our last match. He twisted the tip of his sword, to hit 'tween the ribs. OUCH! Me fake knife blocked it, I went to left knee, cut him under his liver, up, and put that wood sword to his back. After that, I'd mostly guard to his thrusts, for demonstration. Young, quick, I was. Yep, them eyes. Memories that stick to your mind. Palmer put another to join it. "QM2."

I had to dig into me old logs to remember it, correctly, as you like names and dates. Me old mind knew, just about, what and when. QM2 was not the problem. The smells in this room didn't help out, at all. No, no smell of gardenia. That was a Mary smell.

• • •

She went off to that Valley Forge University at the end of August, 1886. I went back to, 'Measure Your Height!' George was with his girlfriend, Edna. It was mid-September, Reynolds and I doing exercises that I did that trick. It was a 'flinch,' as he'd got me afore, a couple times. Maybe a reflex.

Monday, 20 September, 86, we got called into Mr. Rainey office. Me and George. I figured we was, he was, in trouble for some weekend activity. There was Rainey, Command Capt'n, Reynolds, and the QM1 instructors. Mr. Rainey read that paper and we got congratulated. Then came, "Strip off the Blouses. Out Of Uniform." The QM1 instructors about broke our arms getting them new blouses to our bodies, with a Quartermaster 2nd badge on each.

George and me had been sittin in on that light house mechanism class. There was nothin better to do. It graduated Friday, the 24th. The students got certificates. Me and George got orders. His said a Frigate, Portsmouth, Virginia. Mine was to Service Squadron 2, Norfolk. We got three weeks leave. We took the last two nights on a little liberty. Little as, the new pay raise was when we got to our destination. Yes, they came with train tickets on Sunday morning. The cheap rate. Oh, we got 'Navy Script' to use.

By now you should know how I got home. There was eyes to script for the tickets to Cresson in that Stinky, first car. Ptuy! MaMa met me at that station. Oh, I got hugs and kisses from her. She gave a bad look to that sailor mustering new boots. I hurried her off to that train to Ebensburg.

At Ebensburg station, George and me shook hands and a smile atween us for all the stuff we'd been through together. "Fair winds.' He was going on to Ohio, somewhere. I never saw him again, till aboard Shenandoah.

MaMa sniffed me twice. First at Cresson. At Ebensburg I had to take a bath. I said it was that 'Stinkin Train.' The second sniff was at the cloths in me seabag. Me 'Best' uniform got handed to me. I got a wrinkled nose from her, about others in that bag. They wasn't up to her standards. I got extra money while was in Philly, for cleanin cloths. I guessed that cheapest place was not me best choice. He! He! Shush. An extra coppers meant another beer.

It was September, not hot nor cold. Ebensburg was the same as 'afore, with women, children, more of them, on that porch, and the gents to lawn. 'Course I had them pocket bottles. It gave some taste to that lemonade! Oh, the gents don't want a splash. Their eyes flicked to that porch at me offer.

Tuesday, 28 September, 86, MaMa and me made it home. Cloths to the wash tubs was her first order. We had a family meal with all there. You should know them. Elmer, wife Effie, and their 2 children. Grown some. Harriet and husband, Marlin, and child. Harry and Ruth, his wife, child. At least them children could be civil. The women all gooey over them and men to the porch.

• • •

You'll be askin about this, first Med Roundy. That Frigate came out of Toulon to picked up Palmer. I guess he don't like sleepin with our Capt'n. The Frigate must have better 'accommodations.' That said, we headed straight to Palermo and Aspra for water and green stuff. Yes, Assistant Purser, me, hired Angelo to do the talkin. The evening down in town and Florina, his grandma, entertained us tween two of them bars. Oh, the crew just loves her and her food.

9 June we made Malta. Nora was there. No, no liberty. Capt'n and Mr. Caldwell had to check on stuff. The 11th we found the first Frigate off Lydia, watchin traffic tween Egypt and Tunisia, Tunisia. The 15th we was at that Consulate in Cyprus. Flowers were in bloom and so was them Oldsters and Me Profits. Liberty by watches.

I had to watch thems, some. The first 6 hour liberty they got flirty. The second one was, ah, their concerns. I only worried about drunk sailors. Saltsgiver and Nichol, yes, aboard, kept defaulters to a minimum. Engle? Spiel warmed up that sweet bread and made coffee. Capt'n, as I saw, choked it down during morning report.

19 June we met that Frigate off Alexandria. Oh, it went back and forth to Libya too. Next we would see it was in Toulon. The dry African air and sand play on the wood and rubbin iron. The rotation of thems said where she be headed. They appreciated the green stuff we had.

Stopped in Myrtos, that place in Crete, for water, and liberty for each watch. Me? I take it as I want. The crew know where to go. The Marines know where to hang out and the officers have that one hotel to dine at. Yes, I gave that samich and wine guy a Liberty for children candy. He poured me a bit more per glass. The women gave me a wink and the husbands gave bad looks.

We stopped in Malta for an overnight. Nora was in better humor. She gets back hand money for sailors to a bar, from the bar. No, she guides them to not expensive places. I give her a liberty, or two, dependin on numbers ashore. The bars, ah, 'Guide Back' some the Marines don't see. Engle was first one back to the barge.

29 June, had Admiral Flag to a main mast South of us, near Galite Island. Oh, McIntire just had to go say, 'Hi!' The Frigate was shifting to next station off Libya. I guess we was to guard that area. We did! Fish from two dowls, green stuff from two more, and sweet melons for supper.

We made Gibraltar on 01 July. We was to stay just enough to give each division liberty. Me? I take what I wanted. Yes, I had to harass Pheobe. The Packet arrived with news that the Frigate didn't go to Toulon. It is sittin off Algiers with Palmer aboard.

Thursday, 02 July, morning brief and McIntire wanted to leave, "Tomorrow, on the tide! Dismissed!" the room cleared, to me standin there. Fitz and Bobbit handed him papers to sign. He never looked up with, "Old Sailor Tale, QMC. Dismissed." 'Course, the crew heard this. Around the Smokin Lamp lited, after lunch, I got words from about all! I stood amongst thems and said, 'And, No Whistling Nor Scratching Back Stays, Ya hear! No Worry Beads askin for a South Wind, Neither.' The Papists do that.

It was an early tide, just after breakfast and Morning Reports. I watched the ships flag at the Top Main Mast. The tail had flown

North since afore breakfast. We singled up the fore and aft lines, Capt'n said, "Cast off! Underway!" The pier crew run up that accommodation ladder, as, the wind pushed the ship forward on that pier. Oh, the eyes I get from him. "1st Lieutenant, secure the ship to the pier!" We was stuck. The next tide was the next morning, unless the winds shifted. Come noon, McIntire set 4 hours liberty to divisions.

I bothered Pheobe to no end. No, I was just tippy, comin aboard. I had to quiet me Mind. Didn't. Dreams, smell, times afore, and Uncle Curtis words were in me mind. That Starboard rail exploding, and the sound of 2, 18 pounder, 25 pounders bolts overhead. Came Engle at me ear of, "QMC. Sweet breads and coffee on your table. Been talkin in your sleep, ya has! Bush and Hood thought you should sleep in, a bit."

4 July, well, the tide went out afore breakfast. The shore guns were not going to salute us at that time. Luckily, we caught a nice breeze off Gibraltar Rock and stared the next round of the Med.

5 July, Almeria, Spain, to the North, the lookout calls down about that Spanish frigate. "Gonna cross our bow, what with that press of sails he has." I flipped over the desk chart and had Hood mark our course. The lookout set the Frigate angular position. Not 28 seconds later I compass shot her top flag. We set General Quarter real quick.

I heard that gun of hers to leeward and the Signal Middie says, "I see the Flag of St. Andrew and above it is Kilo, Captain. He must want to talk." The lower sails got bloused up, some, our speed came off, but the Top Gallants remained set. They give us headway, just in case.

That Spanish Captain came up our side like a true sailor. His interpreter got a hand, carrying two wine bottles. Yes, them Marines did a romp and stomp all proper. Formal greetings over, well, he come up that Port ladder, to the Poop, and dead eyes to mine. Don Diego, from the Caribbean Frigate, some time ago. "And, where is My Flag, like my cousin received from you?"

In Captain Cabin, Diego and McIntire got seated. Me? Officially ahind McIntire. They just talk a while, the Interpreter not required. Diego speaks English. Spiel brought out two crystal glasses and Diego asked for another. He stood, put wine to the glasses, and hands me one. I had to remove the gloves and arm protectors. It is protocol thing. Like me not allowed to sit at the Captain table.

We went to the Captain bay window and chatted seaman talk of weather and seas, through that bottle and into the next. The last poured out to glasses and he said, "I have warned fellow Captains about these ships. Cousin warned you about our countries, ah, differences. I told my Admiral he should attend to your country Frigates." He gave me a wink, raised glass, and said, "I told him a Highlander may be aboard one of this class and they kept the Romans out of Scotland." Stoop gave him the ships small flag, while Seaman Joseph gave him one of mine, there at the Quarterdeck.

We met Palmer and Frigate off of Algiers and then to Palermo, to tend the Frigate there. Yes, liberty in Aspra and such good food from Florina. Angelo and Purser got the vegetables taken care of. I left the youngin and oldster to their own demise at the Cyprus Consulate. We forum the Frigate in the East and we went to Myrtos. We got two days liberty in Malta, so two Silver Liberty's to Nora, her nice smile, and a cheek kiss.

Comin West, well, the Frigate in Palermo relieved the other off, yep, Algiers. Captain to Palmer, back, and not a word to me said. The fishin boats go to droppin their nets and sailin off. I had Mr. Chips rig up a barge to look like one of thems. Yep, we snuck up on one, then the other. Oh, they couldn't run off. I paid out a Silver dollar for 6 tubs of fish. They saw that coin and the deal was done.

Now, one Ibexes', as I call them two masters, had no problem comin alongside. Oh, Purser and that Captain are like two thieves toward each other. Each was just shoutin and hands in the air. Purser just likes to haggle about stuff. They did come to an agreement and we had sweet melons for supper.

Nope, Captain McIntire and me ain't said but some words 'atween us. He ain't been over the ships wheel barrel neither. I figured I'd hear some words from the crew about signing on. Around the Smokin lamp be normal conversations. I be awaiting for lightning to strike the ship to shake up thems. Old Tom, the cat, about ignores me, Thank You. I still feel his claws in me leggs, yes, both of thems, I do. The Oldsters took care of him for the flees he gets off Africa.

Other than Don Diego, well, it has been about a boring cruise of the Mediterranean. Yes, we had normal weather for a summer. Some storms came off Africa and then Europe gives its reply to thems. Add in the waves from the Atlantic that hit Palestine and they just churns up the water.

7th August, 1896, we tied up in Gibraltar, just us at the pier, this morning. The wind, not the tide, carried us in. Bos'n Gaston just chirped on his whistle to no end to get us all snug and tidy. I be here at the Chart Table awaiting noon meal. Feterman has some nice smells comin from below. I took the afternoon watch on the Quarterdeck to be ashore tonight. I just have to bother Pheobe. He! He!

By Your Leave, Missy,

An Old Sea Dog,

IN THE YEAR 1896, 29 SEPTEMBER: MEDITERRANEAN

Dear Miss Judith,

Gibraltar is ahind a day as I start this. No, no major problems with liberty there. No other ship was in, like St. Lawrence, to give us problems. Just the usual minor defaulters list. Engle don't count. Captain McIntire already knows, that second morning there that Spiel will give him sweet bread and coffee to choke on at morning brief. I noticed it, at the back, next to the cabin door. Him and me are still not talking, much.

Capt'n has started to be on deck, again, to talk to the crew. He stopped that after the St. Lawrence stuff as, he didn't want to be familiar with some he might rig the grate for. I remember the charges from St. Lawrence Capt'n. The grate would have been rigged, had there been a Capt'n Mast.

You should remember from me letter that I put in a writ for Admiral Mast for thems, which Admiral Palmer denied. No, not to me hand. It had to go to the ship via normal, "Official," packet. Fitz found it. Admiral Palmer said about "Normal Seaman Punishment," and all. Fitz wrote it up and gave to Bobbit, McIntire clerk, to give to him. Bobbit put it to his desk and Capt'n signed it, among others.

That first liberty, after, in Sicily, well, McIntire wanted to cancel shore liberty for thems, "Defaulters!" I had to mention to him, in a formal conversation, that punishment had been given, 'According to Admiral Palmer's Denial of Admiral Mast, Captain.' Oh, such word to hear from him, I got. I thought he'd burst at a seam, as red as he got. Bobbit and Fitz got dismissed and Old Tom, up in the forepeak, heard his words to me. But, that was 'afore times.

We found that first Frigate just off Skikda, Africa, 14 August. The Admiral was aboard. Tween Gibraltar and her we did pick up some green and fish from them locals. Bos'n Warrant Gaston keeps tellin me of thems proper names of their ships. The same fishin boat has three names and them Ibexes has more. Say, 'Bos'n, as long as they have stuff, I don't care.' He just gave me bad looks.

We was too far East to go to Toulon. The Admiral said so. So we went off to Palermo, Sicily, and next Frigate, on 17 August.

Yes, we watered down in that little town, East, and oh, good liberty. Florina's food is to just taste. Purser and Angelo be like father and son. The food dealers provide as they have, this time of year.

• • •

Now, MaMa and me, by the log, says we arrived home on 27 September, 1886. It has been a year or so since I was gone. We had a big family dinner with me siblings, wives, and children. After was to the porch, for us men. The women was cooin and encouraging them little ones. PaPa gave me a wink on that pocket bottle.

It was just local visits MaMa wanted to do in the day. Horse, Old George, was still the character. MaMa never liked him. She is always with her hanky to her nose. Some evenings I was with PaPa and the 'Founding Fathers' meetings. It seems they met more when I am there. I only had old stories of the bears and stuff to tell. PaPa and I went to visit, 'Them Hooligans.' They lived close to the earth and served out some fine stuff to drink. Such laughter on that porch I remember to this day. And, we dipped in the horse trough when we got home. PaPa, older, was still wiry. He about drowned me in it. I'll never forget MaMa bad looks as we put on them britches. I guess she didn't like our laughter.

Made that long haul down South, we did. Just MaMa, PaPa, and me. It was a good visit as Princess ignored me. Her father was just as nice as ever, helpin with Horse. No, no swimmin in the pond. The boys, now men, had wives and more children around then I cared for. Princess and women kept them kids company and the men could pass around that jug, on the porch. MaMa stayed mostly with the woman, so PaPa and me could catch up a swig. No, we always went home the next day.

I just remember MaMa hard eyes at PaPa and me on that porch. I guess we, all the men, were just laughin too much for her. Some men even stayed up to 10. PaPa got bad her bad eyes and went in. Me? I had just filled the lemonade glass. It was them stars overhead that I looked at, wondered what me future would hold.

The 1886 log don't say we came by your place, exactly. You'd have been 10 or so then. Your MaMa would have tucked you into bed afore we men got to tellin stories and such. I didn't say MaMa was rollin her eyes at us, but she probably did. The women would take to the kitchen while we men was story tellin in on that porch. It was nice September weather. The porch is best for passin that pocket bottle.

MaMa wore herself out with visiting and Old George was just finding his prime corrals to visit. 15 and 16 October was family supper nights. MaMa served out some fine meals. Siblings and them children got scooted home right after. Me ears just don't take to them carryin on. I already checked with the Train Station Master and we set me time to leave and trains to Norfolk. He asked about the night's sleep I'd have and offered third high on a berth. I said no and payed him that Navy script and for meals only.

She talked me into takin that sea chest with me. No, the carbine and pistol had to stay there. Me orders were stamped for thems. With an unknown future, I left them ahind. I carried that seabag and PaPa took to the other end of the chest. It was about empty, 'cept for them old books of Uncle Curtis. 25 cents was charged to transport it to Newport News, Virginia. That is where the train stopped.

Oh, it was after Sunday Church that we took that train to Cresson. I guessed I needed some scripture afore going. That and a proud MaMa makin sure the whole congregation wished me luck, commin out the door. Yes, MaMa was in second best dress, gloves, umbrella, and that big purse, for her pistol. One odd clunk from it said so.

I had 4 pocket bottles on that train to Ebensburg. I passed on 2 more from the 'Founding Fathers' men. Me fore sigh was bad. We got a nice reception there and a quick walk up to that house. Yep, men to the lawn and woman, say children, on the porch and all.

MaMa sent me off to Cresson with a cheek kiss at 9 AM, 18 October, 1886. Cresson Station Master didn't kiss that Navy Script. I got a point to South Track that said D.C. It should have said lots of towns to get there. I logged them in as train stopped, to get out of that smelly first car. There was Newry, East Freedom, Claysburg, Greenfield, and the big town of Bedford. I stopped loggin stops till Cumberland, Maryland. There was nothin Merry there.

Eats was eats. I got the last servin from the dining car. I gave the porter a Silver Liberty, 10 cents, and got promoted to first eats. A bit better. Say Warm food. We got into D.C. at 9 PM. Oh, they had to add them sleeper cars and another dining car. Such a hustle and bustle on that first car. It seemed most traveled cheap, like me. I found a couple sailors to talk with. Another 10 cents got me three egg and bacon samiches. I gave one to me two new companions. One was a Seaman of 2 years. The other was a 3rd Class Bos'n. Thems was good samiches.

I put me seabag to the end seat, next to that window and curled up to it, like I did going to Frisco. Seabag, Seaman, Seabag, and 3rd took up that seat. I woke to them stops, every one of thems. It was a long night.

• • •

19 August, 1896, and an East wind sent us West, around Sicily. We did a quick stop in Malta. Just one night there, as, shush, Capt'n had to entertain someone, one evening ashore. It was just 4 hours liberty for the crew. Spiel still warmed up them sweet breads and coffee for the Morning Report. Capt'n tries hard to swallow the coffee.

We found the last Frigate on 27 August. It was 'tween Crete and Alexandria. It sent out two barges, rigged, to find us. Purser gave it what was needed and off to the Consulate in Cyprus we went and got there 30 August, 1896.

It seems the Consulate want a ride to, "Athens, Greece, QMC." I asked Mr. Gailey, the Navigator, if the ship had wheels to get us there. It was a joke. No, he was earnest in, "Capt'n says Athens, QMC!" I sent QM3 Hood to me room to fetch that chart and spread it out on the Poop Chart table for him to see.

The skylight over the Capt'n cabin was a nice to view the argument goin on. I got called into this. My warning of winds, currents, and all I gave made no mind to him. 'No South wind can get us out of there.' Well, 1st Lieuy and Bos'n agreed. We would be stuck there for some time!

It weren't just the Consulate that come aboard. He and three others came with such dunnage to believe. I thought they was leaving for good. The 1st day out, 01 September, well, Baby was in the bath tub called the Med. Dr. Stiteler gave them something to sleep. They couldn't get out of their hammocks anyway.

We anchored of Piraeus, Greece, 04 September. A barge with me, Capt'n, and Mr. Consulate did a more than mile pull up to that Port Masters place. We had to check in with him and arrange for transportation to the local Consulate place. No, Mr. Consulate spoke fair Greek. Don't ask me about that language. Me ears are about gone from them guns blastin away. I had to escort thems to the place. I gave Oldster, Kelly, enough for a bit to eat for the crew and warned him of the local Uzo. 'I smell it on any, you'll all sleep in the forward horse chains!' It smells like sweet candy. The samich guy in Myrtos gave us some.

It was two days of pullin him in again to get things set. Another barge crew, with dunnage, put them 4 on that pier to a carriage. Shush. We had to have a snack for the long pull back. Each crew member got a sip on that Uzo stuff. It sure put a sweat to them rowin back to the ship. It was an outgoing tide, luckily. He! He! It is mean stuff!

We made Malta on 12 September. One day liberty and off to Toulon to see Admiral Palmer. There was so and so winds but we made it there on 19 September. I got two days liberty and two days of Bos'n and Chips bangin on wood and iron all over the ship. The Opera house and two streets over was me place.

Out of there on Wednesday, the 23rd and Capt'n set shortest course for Gibraltar. Yep, the Balearic Sea, 'tween Spain and Minorca Islands. He didn't like my flag hoisted up the Aft, Starboard halyard. He came to the Poop and looked up, gave me bad eyes, but said not a word. There was two reports from the lookouts, yep, more than one, of Spanish ships hull up on the horizon, "Sailing Large, Captain. Not toward us, Sir!" He gave a sniff to me. Shush! It could have been the Red M one I snuck to the Main Mast top.

Made it to Gibraltar on the 28th. We sprung something in the top riggin so Chips, Bos'n, and them Brits made noise for two days.

I did me rounds and bothered Pheobe in the evenings. Well, her and a new girl, Lydia. My age, I guess.

The Packet ship came in this morning, 29 September. Thank you for the letter. Oh, got one from MaMa also, wonderin about my enlistment extension. It could be my last letter to her got lost. It happens. So, I just finished a post card to her about that. Capt'n sure hates I had Mr. Caldwell, Mr. Campbell, and Nav, Mr. Gaily sign ahead of him. Names to remember in the future.

A boring cruise, knock on wood. The best thing is a new girl to bother. Oh, Pheobe just rolls her eyes when I spin up Lydia. She is a fiery, red headed, Irish woman. I sign this to you afore I go off to bother her again. We are not to leave till Thursday.

By Your Leave, Missy,

An Old Sea Dog,

IN THE YEAR 1896, 21 NOVEMBER: MEDITERRANEAN

Dear Miss Judith,

I assigned Helm Indicator position to 3 stripper Joseph when we left Gibraltar on 1 October. He is doin well with QM stuff. Hood and Bush are about bored there, leavin "The Rock." There was some little wind so we couldn't hide the ship, which they like to do. I took his helm position, so no need to look at the Capt'n eyes. That boy just grinned from ear to ear, moving his finger. He was quick with it, so I slowed up the helm, a touch.

The outgoing packet said Admiral Palmer was off Bizarte, Africa. I told Joseph to keep us off Africa. Hood and Bush showed me his 'Whey' points to there. I had to ask him if he liked Feterman fish supper. Oh, he did. I said thems fish dowls didn't tend to be in Spanish waters. Oh, October winds and stuff, well, we just might need to go North to make some East.

06 October, 96 and found that Frigate and Admiral right there. Anchored in 10 fathoms of water, our boats took across them fresh greens. Oh, we caught up two boats of fish and greens not two days out of Gibraltar. Hitcock and Captains was shouting and waving hands like a bunch of Italians. Not my concern.

Me current devices over the side to Port and hydrometers over the Starboard and I paid no attention to them romp, stomp, and whistles. I came out of the Port place of leisure, noting that current, entered Me Chart Room to, Palmer and McIntire at me Chart Table. Oh, I backed out, read 'Chart Room' over the door, and went in. We don't salute inside, so took the forward seat of the table. 'Capt'n, Admiral,' I had to say.

Ifn ya 'member, we bombarded Tunis on a previous time. 'Course, you 'member the 'Pistol Treaty' with Algeres. It seems this Bey in Skikda was botherin shippin and overland traffic to both places. The merchants took to addin "Signal Guns to their sides" loaded in iron balls and grape shot to fend off this Bey boats. 'So? Go into the port and put guns to his place!'

I got words as it seems this Bey was a nephew, cousin, or some relative to someone. The Sultan wanted us to deal with him. I got reminded of times afore and Algiers. Ships boat would go to the Harbor Master and denied Frigate entrance. Frigate entered and got surrounded by dung boats, yes animal matter, and pelted. The ships crews don't like that. Four eyes to me and I asked, 'Kill him, negotiate with him, or make him a friend?' I hate when they just nod their heads.

Palmer said, "I hear you are a 'Magician!' You can hide a ship in gun smoke, turn the ship around, and emerge going the other way." McIntire had witness to that. "Up in the Main Mast to signal an Admiral gun salutes and then appears on the aft deck, unnoticed." Tailor in the Caribbean. "And, I heard you were an 'Actor,' to rival a stage performance in Toulon, QMC." That must have heard of me 'Gaul Fever' thing. Left hand to the table and that ring finger still, never will open to a flat hand. 4 eyes went to it.

Palmer mentioned how I, "Negotiated piece with the Sultan of Algiers." Two 18 inch bolts tore up his wall and dirt ahind, it did. "The Sultan said the ships Iron Guard is a hard negotiator, but honorable. Think about it, on the way back to here." Joseph set that course Nor, Nor East to Gaeta. McIntire said so.

• • •

October 19, 1886, we arrived at Richmond, Va., at 4AM. 100 miles at 35 miles an hour. 5 hours, it was, for the stops in every place the could train stop at. I didn't log them in as I didn't care to. Richmond and Pittsburg was about the same. I got off to stretch legs and not smell that engine. We put a lock to our seabass bags on that bench seat so Seaman Myers, Bos'n 3rd Robertson and me could take some air. It was just better than in that train seat. We returned and gave bad looks to some sittin there. Back to me, Seaman, and Bos'n 3rd sleepin.

It was 75 miles from Richmond to Newport News, Va. and 5 more hours. We caught breakfast at 6 AM, the first serving. I gave 'nother Liberty for that. Myers and Robertson got to sit with me. Yep, 9 AM we hit that stop to, "All Off." The Steward said to follow the crowd to the ferry. 'Cause of the samiches and all, Seaman Myers, and BM3 Robertson helped me with that sea chest. It was extra money for that sea chest on that ferry to Norfolk.

The ferry landed us at Claremont Ave. at Noon, 20th of October. I remember the place, now, from trips down to Norfolk. It is the only place to catch a ferry to Hampton. Not that I go there much. I asked someone about a traveling to the Naval Base. I got a jerk of a hand pointed down a street. Three streets East and we hit Hampton Blvd. I'll just say it was like outside of the base in Philly. It was 10 cents to the base. I showed that sea chest and it cost another.

The horse drawn trolley sure took a time to get to the naval base. I could have walked faster, but for the sea chest, and knowin where to go. There was lots to see and nothing to see but acres of nothing. An hour of that ride and it stopped at the gate. The Marines at the gate sure looked us over and pointed left. "Squadron HQ down the road." Not much to see of this place.

Orders to this clerk, orders stamped, assigned to the barracks, got meal chits, and sent off. I was assigned to top bunk, "You bein a 2nd Class." 2nd Class Bos'n, the barracks leader, gave us words of the regulations. Me chest went to this room off the stairs. I strapped the seabag to me bunk. Meal times was said and other stuff. 2nd Class, so I didn't need to do sweepers and cleanin the barracks. I found a bench ahind that place and put the last of me pocket bottle to some water.

• • •

08 October, 96. Capt'n McIntire liked that water from Gaeta more than from Aspra, Sicily. I ain't sayin but, he liked more than the water. Monic sure gave me the voice for not comin around in a while. Hell and damnation was in me ears till I put silver on the counter for her. She took care of me mates I brought along. No, no overnight there. Bush said the Capt'n came up the Port side just after the afore Mid-Watch was relieved.

14 October we made Palermo and then down to Aspra. The crew was sad, hated to leave there. Besides the, ah, usual entertainment for the crew, Florina, Angelo's grandma, arranged for the town square to provide evening entertainment. The weather was nice so outside tables were set up. For a low cost them two bars served drinks and the food came from all over the place. It was like a street get together.

Me, Florinda, and lots of husbands kept an eye out for improper things. All got back by hammocks to poles. Mates had to help some of them.

Came a Nor West wind so we did the Straits of Messina, turned, and the wind just got us to anchor there. ABS Stoop took me and a bunch up that long street to MaMa's place. Words to his face, bad hand pointin, and come time I told him to stay overnight. It was enough for us to get back to the ship. All us couldn't carry him down safe in our hands! He! He!

21 October, 96, and found a Frigate off Syracuse, Sicily. It couldn't get no North goin wind. Thems sure didn't seem to worry about that. After a month off Africa, was a nice liberty place!

It was two days in Malta. 23 to 25 October. Nora, at the pier, liked me Liberty coins to guide some to places. Capt'n likes this woman at the embassy. Why two days liberty for us. I ain't sayin. I look after the ship crew only, on land.

Joseph, with looks from Bush and Hood, set our course to Athens. McIntire wanted to, "Just go straight their!" At the cabin door I just watched as Mr. Gaily showed the chart. "Some Islands are between us and there, Sir." Twice a day I checked our position and went over the charts. 4 times a day I checked the current meter over the Port side and made notes. Twice a day McIntire was lookin over me shoulder at the Chart Table as to where we was. It is the Mirtoo Pelagos Sea with some islands about.

We anchored out of Piraeus on 29 October, did that long pull into the Harbor Master place, and send a message to the Embassy about the Cyprus Consulate. We pulled in on the 30th to his note to be there on the 31st. I gave the crew a rest and a shot of that Ozo/Uso/OOzo stuff. It varied on the bottles I saw. It was cool, what with a wind from the North. The crew sure sweated out that stuff on that pull. It wasn't till half way back that they got their rhythm to row and BM1 Wagner could steer the barge proper.

It took two barges to get Ambassador and his staff back to the ship. He was at that pier so no shots for the crews. I didn't need them to row wet. We set him and all to dirt on Cyprus on 03 November.

They had to have an arrival dinner with the Capt'n and officers. We arrived in the morning so the crew got 4 hours of divided liberty.

It is a small place so even the Marines go time ashore. Those that had been there 'afore, like youngins and oldsters, well, the weather was mild but it could have been cold and not minded it, what with former familiarities! Wagner and me sat on the veranda and got catered to that good food and fine local wine. Came that time, Capt'n, and he could be heard to the ship with, "Ships Crew, Up!" Capt'n took to the Port side of the ship. He and them officers.

05 November and Frigate boats, with sails, was there to steer us to it. It was a Nimble little craft that just sailin around us. Lines across to the Frigate and they got what they wanted. November, so pickins was slim. Purser held back some for us. Even us was on small pickins. Barreled cabbage was on our menu. It was well seasoned by now.

We stopped in Myrtos for water and liberty on 6 November. The samich guy, up that hill, had words to me like Stoop got in Massena. I didn't understand a word. He must have been he expected us there sooner. I did a turned hand and made like the ship sailin all over the place. North, East, West, East, South, and so one. I put hands to the air, pointed to bread, sausage, cheese, and put a dollar Silver to the counter, to pay for all. We got wine and samiches to our liking. I put a Liberty to his hand and got his wink. The children gave a wave, women a wink, and the men, well, gave bad looks. Nothing changed there.

We anchored at Malta on 12 November. We had good winds. Capt'n had to entertain someone, so we didn't leave till the 14th. I gave Nora one Liberty as I went ashore. I figured the bar owners would make up that difference. I met up with her second evenin ashore. She showed me a nice place to eat. A fine meal and conversation we had. Mostly about ships coming. She knew more of when they would come than the harbor master.

She has blackish hair, hazel eyes, and a darker complexion, what with the sun. Younger than me and a nice smile, when not joked, like I do to her. I thought you would wonder. Too many men had tried to, "Court me with hollow words." A kiss on the cheek, slap on the butt and, "See you next time, QMC." She be like that.

16 November, Shenandoah and A Frigate put anchors down 2 cable lengths from shore off Skikda, so as not to get dung boats. We

put a ketch anchor to aft to keep the ships Starboard sides to shore. This 'Bey' place was on a rise, with brush and not tall trees under. We took in a barge, me standing at the bow, 4 Marines and 8 sailors to row. BM1 Wagner at the transom with Marine Capt'n Saltsgiver on one side and the Admiral translator on the other.

This Harbor Master place was just a dirty mud hut with three doors. The inside smelled just like the outside, bad. One guy was at a desk and another seated in the corner. The translator and this guy talked for 5 minutes and 'No' was all he said. His head shake told me so. That guy ignored Saltsgiver as I was in full regalia. He kept flicking his eyes to me with each no.

Comes that time and I unbutton me coat and put a small copy of me personal flag on his desk. That got more words 'atween thems, 'No.' I reach ahind me and put that Sultan flag atop. This guy stuck out his hand as I pulled out that sword and flashed it above them flags. I almost got his fingers. Oh, a change of words from this guy and the second guy goes out the door like something bit his butt. The Translator said he was to see the Visor about Admiral meeting with this Bey.

The translator, me, Saltsgiver sittin on hog head barrels, at the pier, when this kid of sorts comes and makes a jester for a drink. BM1 filled a cup, I took a sip, and handed it to him. He downed that cup and asked for another. BM filled it, kid took it, and I asked BM1 for ships biscuits. We always have them at hand. I bit one and handed it to the kid. Well, they are hard. The kid sounded like a squirrel chewing a hickory nut. I gave him the rest in me hand. 'Atween drinks and biscuits the kid, Akabar, as I heard, the words just flowed from him. The translator gave us a running account. I just nodded to Saltsgiver the whole time.

The Harbor Master finally came over and said the Visor would see us. He offered his other guy to guide us. I declined him, pulled a large copper coin from me pocket, and handed it to Akabar. I might have gave him Gold, from his smile. Translator, me, Saltsgiver, and two Marines set out to this Visor.

The boy gave a continual talk up that street to the palace on that hill. He tried to get us to walk through the trees, but I said no. Translator left off some of what Akabar said as this boy pointed to shops, people, side streets, and all. I mean words and finger points. He only shushed up when we got to a side door of the palace that had two guards with scimitars.

That Visor was real civil once I put me flag on his desk and the Sultan one atop. The Translator handed over the Admiral request for a meeting. That got set to noon the next day. I asked to go around this "Grand Palace" and take in its sights. The Visor said he'd have a palace guard escort us. I guess he wanted to make sure we didn't steal anything or get to close to something.

Akabar gave us a running account of the iron doors at each end of the place the Bey greeted quests and number of guards present. Around the North side I asked about the beach and guards. In a whisper he told the Translator how he and local children played in the small trees and brush area but never was set upon by palace guards. I let him take us down a wooded path to the beach. At the pier I gave him another large copper coin and a bag of ship biscuits, to his grin. Translator told him what I said to a node of his head.

17 November and our barge brought me, full regalia, and McIntire to the pier. The Admiral and the Frigate Capt'n in another. Admiral, Frigate Capt'n, and Interpreter was escorted by 4 Marines. Ahind them McIntire was me, one step ahind, and two Marines. We went up them stone steps and the two outside guards opened the 2, oh, 4 foot wide by 8 feet tall iron doors. The Frigate Marines stayed outside as my two followed me.

The room was 16 feet by 30 long with a glass dome in the middle to lite up a neither long, nor wide table, normal height, and chairs to our side. The other side of the table was pushed again them stone steps and 3 big pillows was set there. Two guards closed the doors at each end and a Guard at each corner. There was two guards to the door to where the Bey lived. Came a time and was horns, symbols sounded, the guards opened them doors, and out comes a guy to look at. All the doors closed and the guards put a 4 by 4 long board over iron angles. We was trapped inside.

This Bey had on a turban twice his head in size. Well, its color did match the flowing gown, 4 sizes too big. Down them stones steps and he plopped his butt on the large center pillow. I ain't no good judge of age, but, a Signal Middie looked older. Visor was on his right and his interpreter on his left, who jabbered away at Admiral Interpreter. Me and them two Marines moved the chairs so Admiral and Capt'ns could sit at the table. I was close enough to his ear to say, 'Smile. Don't move unless I tell you to duck down.' No, no sir there.

I forgot to mention the three guards that came in with the Bey and this guy with a huge fan. A long stick with long feathers atop. The room had an odd smell to it. Each it dipped, well, that smell got worse, and the flies were driven my way. 10 long minutes of interpreters words flowed by to no end. This Visor claps his hands and the door to me right opened to two guys haulin in a big silver tray with some animal and stuff on it. They brought more flies with thems, all over that tray. The flies in the room joined thems already upon it.

I have been in a Sultan room for a meal. The Bey raised his hands and his interpreter told our side of the table to, "Dig In." Admiral and Capt'n arms reached out. 'Ahind, I bumped his chair and said, 'The Host samples the meal afore quests, to see if it is to his taste!' Well, that started the first round of words.

That Interpreter said, "Bey just ate. Food is for his most honored guests." Plates, but no silverware, was afore Admiral and Capt'ns. I snatched up a plate, went over to this silver tray, and moved it close to me. With gauntlets, I opened me coat and pulled out that knife and marlin spike. Such looks I got from both table sides.

This, ah, animal, maybe a goat, had not been gutted. They had piled some rice on its back side. The dates were green, the olives yellow. I stabbed that thing with the spike to get a good hold and stuff to imagine came out of it. The knife to the hind quarter and I cut off a chunk to that plate. The marlin and knife added some olives and dates. With me gauntlet I pushed that plate to the Interpreter and got bad eyes from both sides of that table.

Well, it seems, being left handed, 'Their Dirty Hand,' I'd ruined the entire meal! So, came claps, the right door opened to the same two comin in and the flies left with that rotten animal. That Bey started the final act of this play by asking, through his Interpreter, if the Admiral felt safe, "with just three guards."

I thought I was being civil by explainin me flag and then that Sultan one. Maybe he took offence when he reached for that Sultan flag and me sword flashed above it. "Clap!" His guards came to attention. Oh, the Marines drew their swords. The Visor and Bey just smiled at this. Me coat was already open so the Sultan flag went to me back and sword in the scabbard. A Colt pistol came to me right hand as I pulled that break top from the holster with me left one. I warned him, I did, of 'thunder and destruction,' like with that Sultan. I only fired a shot at each exit door to get the Bey to agree to the Admiral terms for free trade and stop harassing our ships.

The Bey and his guards escorted Admiral, Capt'ns, me, and 36 boarding party members to that pier. Oh, he gave fine words to us, through our Interpreter. The last boat, ours, pulled off that pier to Akabar, his two other guides, and a sack with 5 pound of biscuit they held up. The coppers must have been in their pockets.

Oh, I'm just going on about nothing. 21 November and here at Gibraltar. The Packet is in to take mail to Norfolk. Admiral Palmer is ashore to go aboard our relief ship. It should be the Monongahela. Maybe I'll see George Weave. I will have time, till then, to go ashore to bother Pheobe and Lydia. Pheobe likes when I bother Lydia. The people in the bar drink and buy more drinks when laughin!

At that pier, the first time, Akabar had no good words for that Bey. The guards come once a day to collect tribute. Town was very poor because of this. He had on a dirty bit of turban and his, ah, real long shirt was no better. I'd have put a put them 18 pounder bolts to his palace and slept well after.

'Tween that Bey place and here I have been workin on the "After Action Report," as much of an action it was. Oh, most of them guards, especially ahind that Bey, had scimitars for show. I noticed that right away. No, most on our side of the table had real ones. I'd go on with this but the Purser is callin for mail. I'll send this to and ya catch up the rest in me next letter.

By Your Leave, Missy,

An Old Sea Dog,

IN THE YEAR 1896, 15 DECEMBER: ATLANTIC CROSSIN

Dear Miss Judith,

I start this letter on 22 November, 1896. I spent morning, afternoon in Gibraltar and took lunch at this hole in the wall place up King Street. It makes a muscle boil, like Talig did in Alaska. Different roots, add some pepper and it is real good to the tongue. I am here in me hidey hole as the crew is sprucin up the ship for the Admiral visit, tomorrow.

I know you will ask, so, 'tween Skikda and here Palmer wanted Saltsgiver to write an, "After Action Report." He and Nichol got me involved for times and paper. The first word to paper was "Boarding Party Practice-Ashore." Goin round that palace we came to the sea side view. We could see our ship. Saltsgiver moved a finger from the ship to this place Akabar said had a sand beach. I took two fingers to that spot. He nodded his head.

On the East side, afore goin down into the brush and trees, Akabar pointed out the only two story house I could see. The Bey threw the people out for looking at his steps. I only needed to nod me head. Back aboard I went to the officers about, 'Boarding Practice-Ashore.' All thought it was a good idea, something different for the crew. It was listed in that Daily Report Capt'n McIntire signed, along with lots of papers.

Boats and people went over at 11:30. Packed them boats, we did. After the crew went ashore there was 4 and coxswain left over to man the boats. They hit the beach, Saltsgiver said, about the time the Capt'n gig took me and Capt'n ashore. He found Akabar and two more boys there. Coppers, biscuits to hands, and one lead Nichol up that gully to the West side of the palace.

Nichol said he raised his head over this bank and saw two guards at the doors and two standin by the wall, with a silver plate atop. Horns and cymbals sound. He was bored till the doors opened and them other two took that silver thing in, came right back out, and the doors closed. Not much later them doors open and same two guys go in, come out, and took that plate around to his right. Time later, he don't have a pocket watch, and come, "This pop sound and the iron door rang. Well, the guards just looked at that door. I knew it was you, QMC. We put two of them 45-70 lead bullets to the doors, above them."

He gave chuckle and, "They pulled on the door handles to no end. About then me and the Party hit the steps and they just was banging on the doors to get in. Next I know the doors open inward, the two guards go inside, and I find my Private standing there!"

Saltsgiver said he sent the sailors with the other boy and had Akabar lead him and two Marines to that house. "Oh, it was empty below and the same with the upper part. The East palace door right there, out that window. Akabar found us some stools to sit on. I sent him below for the noise he made chewing the biscuits. My sailors were down in the trees, through the bushes."

Said he saw us go up the steps and go into the palace. "The first problem was the Frigate Marines standing on the upper part. I didn't want to shoot them. So, I wrote a note on my pocket tablet and had Akabar deliver it. That kid pulled their coats till one took the note. Well, they sure ran down the steps and over to the wall on my left."

He got bored sitting on the stool. "I wondered if all this landing was required." He gave me a smile and, "We heard that pop and the iron door ring out. The guards looked lost. As you asked, put two rounds of 45-70 to them doors. Oh, the guards didn't like that." He looked at Nichol and said, "Guards didn't notice us till I hit that top step. Oh, they just started banging on that door to get in. The door opened, they went in, and, is one of my Privates right there! I entered to you, QMC, standing behind the Admiral with two pistols drawn, looking to shoot a bunch of people!"

I only fired two shots. One at each iron door. Oh, they sure made a noise. Them lead bullets just splattered and rang those doors. The Bey ducked down but came back up with a smile. Me Gauntlet glove fingers ticked off about to 4 when both doors got rung from the outside. The Bey didn't like that, nor me pistols. His guards didn't like me aimin those pistols at them and abandoned them doors.

After that muscle boil I meandered up the street and down. There was nothin new in the trade shops. A church bell sounded 2:30 so I went for some drinks afore goin back. Yes, I was goin to see Pheobe and Lydia. I needed a good laugh.

I was down to that bar and got thems with elbows upon it, head to hands. Lydia put a tray on the bar, 4 glasses to it, and a small bottle of whiskey. I hated their smiles and battin of eyes. I took off bottle and hands said a bigger one. No, I made sure that seal wasn't broken. A new bottle, not Old refilled one.

Lydia went into that back room, tray to table, and I got McIntire, Admiral seated, and his lieutenant ahind. Officers carry no money, so I put 3 dollar gold piece to her hand. She poured 4 shots and was gone. My first toast was to, 'Uncle Curtis and Alfa, God Rest.' I poured the second to, 'My Mother and Father, who saved you.' I got their eyes, but downed. Admiral and McIntire had eyes 'atween thems, they did. 'The Interpreter should have told you to not touch that dead animal tray afore the Bey. If you had, then I wonder what ransom the ships would have paid.'

Palmer asked if I really had to unload my pistols and reload with only 5 of the 6 cartridges. I nodded and, 'As I told the Bey, I only shoot people with real fighting arms. Three ahind that Bey had toy scimitars. 15, in three pistols, to take out 12 guards, was only fair.' "Fair," said Palmer! 'Yep, as the two Marines had a pistol each, Sir! That got me a look.

"When he reached for the Sultan flag, were you going to run him through with that sword?" I said, 'No. He held out his left hand, his dirty hand. I was just gonna stab it and put the sword point into the table, Sir.'

"You never mentioned a 'Landing Party,' QMC." I said, 'Boats don't go over the side without the Bos'n. Armoror had to issue weapons. Mr. Chips made me a two pistol rig. BM1 and GM1 was assigned by respective officers.' I looked at them 4 eyes and saw that Admiral Lieutenant smirk. 'Ships officer acted under the signed Daily Report, Admiral.' I thought McIntire would get sick. 'It seems you officers never speak amongst yourselves.

I poured out them 4 shots. 'Akabar told me and Captain Saltsgiver all about the Bey and his men, the beach, and abandoned house. The Bey was to take you hostages at the first sleight to him. Why we were locked inside. The Guards behind him, in the palace, have play scimitars. He's afraid someone behind him will kill him, Sirs,' to eyes around.

Palmer came back on keel and, "At the pier, you gave him your personal flag." Yep. "You said some words to him and he gave you his personal knife and sheath." Yep. "What did you say to him, QMC?" 'Oh, Admiral, nothing special. I just reminded him of his words to honor open trade, kindness to his people, and all.' Got his looks, I did. On with, 'If I heard him catchin up tribute from his people or troubled the merchants again, well, him, and his guards might just want to sleep, if they did, with both eyes open, Sirs.' It is a nice knife. Has rhinos horn for a sheath. It has a nice iron blade, ivory handle, and glass thing atop.

Admiral handed over his report to D.C. I read it, thanked him, said to scratch most off. 'I just did my job as Master At Arms, designated, Admiral,' to looks atween thems. 'If I killed the Bey the Sultan would have established another, maybe a worse one.'

He took out another paper for me to read. Oh, flowery words of, "Commendation Letter, QMC!" I looked it over and put it in me jacket. 'Tomorrow, Captain Saltsgiver, Corporal Nichol, the Boarding party members, and everyone who helped them get into the barges and shore safely must be congratulated.' Maybe not the ships cat. It milled about our feet, like we was fishin, and was lookin for a meal. 'I held the situation at hand, only. The Bey, seein 16 to his left and 16 to his right, well, he only had 12 more guards in the palace, Sirs.'

Dinner is sounded. Feterman always serves out a good meal. The last toast, ya ask? To Akabar. He told Saltsgiver and me all the good stuff. Oh, the Admiral nor Capt'n would have authorized the landing party. 'Without them, there would have been a blood bath in that room. The Marines and I would have shot about all the Bey guards. Without me, your ransom may have taken some time to get there, Sirs.'

23 November, 1896. Fitsimmons and Bobbit are still mad about me makin them write out the letters to the crew for the Admiral to present. No, just one per group, like the boat crews and names under. They will be squeakin paper to get one into the service jacket of all the men. The ships officers got called up front, first, by seniority. 1st Lieuy, Bos'n, and so on. Saltsgiver and Nichol got about the same words on them papers. I was mid Nav Deck, full regalia, as all come

forward. Yep, Cook and Purser came forward to Admiral words. The last men got his words, McIntire stepped forward and said, "And any man jack that doesn't give three Hurzays, 1st Lieutenant, take their name, and we'll rig that grate." He took down no names.

24 November, 1896. Monongahela came in this afternoon and tied up to the pier ahead of us. Palmer flag shifted to them when he went aboard. A QM1 came off her and I asked about George. They had switched billets. This QM1 was goin to sea from QM school. Mr. Rainey agreed to it. No great details but it seem George got in with a woman and wanted time ashore with her. Yep, George and women. He didn't say ifn it was the same woman I saw in Norfolk.

QM3 Joseph, QM2 Bush, and QM2 Hood set the Whey points to Norfolk. Yep, Admiral promotion. It be winter, so we be on the Southern route. I was shufflin them charts in me room and turned to McIntire in that far Chart Table seat. I need to put some salt water to the hinges so thems squeaks! Yep, two of thems. He asked if I could conger up a, "Levanter wind and current to carry the ship quickly to Bermuda? You being a Magician, QMC."

Oh, I searched around the room, High and Low. I pulled out this drawer and that one. Searched real good, I did. I put an old cigar box on that Chart table. From it took 3 empty 45's and put them on the table. I took out a 4th, a loaded one. 'There is magic,' pointin to the loaded 45, 'in it, I left the Magic out of these,' pointing to the empties. 'The smoke from 1 brought 2, 25 pounder bolts to the Sultan in Algiers.' To the other ones, 'Two brought forth a Boarding Party of 32.' I got his looks when I pointed to the loaded on. 'If I send this magic into the water and disturb Davy Jones, well, I can't predict what he might give you, Captain.'

Well, he chewed on some words right there. "The crew has done well, on the cruise. I thought they should get a time ashore, in Bermuda. Some, your choice, could stay overnight and, ah, see Edith, QMC. She being your cousin, daughter of Curtis Thompson, and all." I had to thank him but said she was Alfas daughter, not by Uncle Curtis. He gave me a queer look and, "You could have not mentioned that and I would not have been the wiser, QMC." I said, 'As you should stop by, I wouldn't want you to say something to be embarrassed for, Captain.'

26 November, 1896. Now a day out of Gibraltar, headed to Bermuda. Me Speed and Current line weights be over the side at 7 and 12 fathoms apiece. I learned the depth on the cruise. The speed line matches that Log board, mostly, as long as the ship ain't like a child rocking horse!

30 November, I got that sheep smell on the Starboard Side. The winds be from the North, why I smell thems. The current line be acting funny. I just log it in to them islands 60 leagues to Starboard. We don't need them closer. There be a kind wind and makin some good speed.

Mr. Gaily and poor Joseph get to give the Navigation report to McIntire each morning. Me? Ahind thems, near the door. I get Capt'n eyes on our position, bein ahead of projections. 3 boards higher and the ship in stay sails says, by me Speed and Current Log, we be doin about 11 knots. Navigator, Gailey, reported, "9 by the Log, Captain."

December 9, 1896 and Bermuda Governors place is just South of us, two cables length away. Is a nice East wind, some North in it, but we have the main anchor, forward ketch, and aft one laid out. No tellin for wind. The Liberty barge crews are assigned, yep, three of thems. Overnights are assigned and to row the first group ashore. I sign this off as goin to Capt'n gig, first over, with me in it. Purser and me are to see about a money exchange.

December 11th. Last leg to Norfolk. Oh, all had a good time in Bermuda. That Packet was there afore us to say we was to stop over. The Governors Secretary and Purser set up at an exchange desk. The men got half a Crown to spend. That is enough for 10 large beers or 10 shots. It is just enough to have thems in 'Fine' spirit, being rowed back to the ship, come 4 PM. I was there watchin them.

2 barges held all the overnighters. Something like 30 of them. They hit that pier just as the sun set. Governor was nice enough to invite them to a meal. It was real good food. McIntire and the officers was invited to an evening social with the Governor, to stay all night also.

Oh, I sent QM3 Joseph right off in the morning to see about overnight stay at Edith place. He was gone half an hour. He came back in a sweat, a blush, and looked like the devil was ahind him. I couldn't make out what had happened. It ain't but a short distance to Edith place.

It seems Etta got hold of him as he came in the door. She gave him lots of hugs and kisses. 'Course, Edith heard the noise, came down the stairs, and just was joyed to see him. Hugs, kisses, he being slight in height and weight, well, they just bowled him over. Each said they may have over joyed him, "Just a bit. But, he is so cute!"

BM1 Wagner and GM1 Birch set up the boat watches. Edith had room for 16 only. 4 rooms with 4 beds. Wagner took the rest to the house Edith said. All came to Edith place for the evening of free beer, words to be heard to the pier, just like last time here. Those who stayed paid the 1 Crown to Etta. Oh, the people from all around that street came to enjoy this occasion. It was a rousing time. Etta called out her common names of the crew to make a red faces of thems. It was a laughin evenin. Even Edith was less frowned, from afore.

Come 10:15 PM or so and Edith was nodding off. I led her up to her room and went into this little place with a cot, as 'afore. I was worshin up when that door opened to Edith in her night cap and stuff. I had to go to her room. She shows me the property papers, marriage to Uncle Curtis, and what not. All Brit and legal. I just said, 'I'll take note of them tomorrow.'

Next I know a Bos'n was strippin off the blanket and orderin me, "On Deck, You," bad words. No. It was Edith getting me up at 5 AM to help her with breakfast. A splash of water, dressed, and to her words in that kitchen. She filled me ears with more of Alfa, Uncle Curtis, and, "Can't you cut tators proper?" It seemed not.

Barges and Gig crew pulled back to the ship at 8 AM. They took on the next shore leave people. Oh, I was there as Fitz and Bobbit stepped ashore and took thems two to visit Edith and her papers. Thems scratched on paper for an hour, they did, copied all them words, and noted the seals and such. Edith didn't know what was a foot. I just mentioned the Capt'n would sign and seal the papers as official documents, 'Just in case.' All us got her hugs and kisses. I paid for Fitz and Bobbit drinks at the bar.

The first evening ashore, McIntire and ashore office did come to Edith place for a drink and. cordially, offered their best to her. Edith was just a swim with their words. Gracious they were to her. I expected no less of them. They are good officers. No, no money for the salute drinks to Edith. I gave Etta 3 gold 5 dollar coins. She gave me a look! I nodded to Joseph and said, 'Maybe you can make him blush some more.' The sign in book said the Governor send few to Edith place as not many stayed there. Ships do come by Bermuda in the winter.

The run up to Norfolk was to fair winds. 11 December and I took the afore mid helm to the Nor East wind and staysails set. The ship likes this wind. I shot Polaris, true North, minus 1 degree. A 25 knot wind, healed over to Larboard, and I put a stop to the wheel. It was just short of white caps on the waves. Next was McIntire over the barrel and his eyes.

"Good cruise, QMC. Defaulters, about none." He be lookin for words. "None in Gibraltar nor Bermuda that I head of." He had tasted old sweet breads and bad coffee, from his steward. Engle got drunk each day, he went ashore.

"Admiral Palmer Action Report left a lot out of it, from what you did." I put the helm a bit to larboard to throw him off, to grab onto the ships wheel. 'Akabar pointed out the situation, Captain,' and on with, 'Duty says ship, crew, and you, Capt'n.'

A stop, again, to the wheel, I leaned over the barrel and said, 'Fitz students would like to send you a personal letter, maybe thank you for a good cruise. Their words I can't predict. And, to show their reading ability, they'd like to be called forward at Sunday morning Church, to read a passage each, from the Bible.' "Have Fitz present the letters, after reading them, QMC."

So, come 13 December, 1896, sober, shaved, best uniforms, toes to the line, in divisions, Church was rigged. There was the usual song sung, and Capt'n read some words. No, no collection plate was passed, He, He! He did the Old Testament reading of Hell and Damnation. A song was sung and he called up Kelly to give his reading. Up came Graty for the second, Lesko was the third, and Blakley for the last one.

Well, they must have practices some hours on each passage. They did real well. Oh, finger to the Bible and to each word. Just short passages, they did, till Blakley stepped up. Old guy, big voice. He turned the page marker and said, "Ya, Though I walk through the Valley Of Death, I shall fear no evil. The Lord is with me." At that he stopped, looked at Mr. McIntire, and said, "And you, Capt'n." Yes, he finished the Psalm, with no extra words.

15 December and here in me room in the Squadron barracks. The jackass tugs put us all snug in the South side of that North birth. Oh, the crew was inspected by Admiral Taylor and Squadron Admiral Irwin. Each sent me an eye, there Mid Poop. McIntire said no to full regalia. Me flag had to be on the Starboard, Aft yardarm. There was Capt'ns aplenty to be piped aboard. It took a full hour to get thems off the ship.

Fitz and squadron Petty Officers took care of getting all ashore settled. I just stood around to thems activity. I took this evening down on Hampton road. Yes, to see Ella and Harold. Nothing changes there. I caught up me mail from me two favorite girls. Letters to hand, to re-read.

I am not goin up to see family at this time of year. MaMa said there is lots of snow and cold. I made an appointment to see me 'Charge de Affairs,' Mr. Bish about me holdings and those of Edith. I will see what I can find to entertain me over Christmas. Merry Christmas and a Happy New Year!

By Your Leave, Missy,

An Old Sea Dog,

IN THE YEAR 1897, 18 JANUARY: SQUADRON

Dear Miss Judith,

Here at me desk at Squadron. Saturday, 19 December, 1896. Mr. Makins, Squadron Lieuy, don't know what to do with me. I haven't heard from Admiral Irwin. BM1 Wagner and GM1 Burch handle most of the morning and afternoon musters. I just stand ahind thems.

The Boots, from the start of the cruise, signed on with Mr. McIntire. So did QM3 Joseph and some of the others. Fitz gave me the official count this morning. 4 Oldsters, now with reading and writtin, followed Fitz ashore, more than for me. Engle, ya ask? I signed him into Squadron roster. On Admiral money he made it back to the ship on the 16th, to tend to Mr. McIntire needs by afternoon. He volunteered to be Capt'n cook, as, well, Spiel can only serve the food, and do domestic stuff Engle refuses to do.

I went to me agent, Mr. Bish. His sign says, "Ships Chandler/ Husbandry Services." He gave me a receipt for that Sultan flag. I gave him that letter Edith gave me from someone here in Norfolk. "A Lawyer. I'll look into this for you," he said. I gave him all the papers Fitz and Bobbit copied and Capt'n notarized.

I saw Effie, Carrie mother. Wanted to test that water, I did. Oh, she was as kind as ever. Carrie married that banker and, "Oh, she is a handful to him!" She still runs that seamstress place. Regina place was next. "Friday evening I expect you and them rascals to bring dinner."

Up that second story stairs to the same place I was afore, to sowin machines workin cloth. I gave a wave to Mattie, wife of Bothel. Her jaw opened and that machine stopped. Carrie has a little enclosed space with desk. I opened that door to, another with open jaw! Well, I did get a smile and kiss to a cheek. Oh, she was so surprised. I handed her two tubes of big and little flags.

I needed that rhino knife on a corner and showed that knife. Mattie had to be present for the design. I needed new big one and a couple extra little ones. Oh, it was to cost me. Come 4 PM I got to escort Carrie down the stairs, arm on me arm, to a carriage and 2 in the street. Mr. Big Eyes was there, not happy to see me. Her kiss to his lips and I still got his black eyes.

Fitz and Zoe had been in correspondence through the cruise. At my insistence they had to be at Regina place for Friday night dinner. He had to carry food pails, along with Wagner and Burch.

Reginal place ain't but so big. Food pales to the kitchen and not much room to sit. She introduced Wagner to Cora, me to Viola, and Burch was to Margaret. Reginal has good taste in women. The kitchen table sat only 4 so I had a plate in me lap and Viola next was next to me on the little couch.

After eats, Reginal asked about our cruise. I started out with how boring it was. All the same places Silvis had visited. Wagner who started it off with, "Stormed the beach of this Sultan. Cutlass in hand! QMC loaded down with pistols and sword, inside. He took on that Turban head and all his guards, himself! The door opened to him ahind the Admiral, pistols in hand, blood all over the place!" I thought the woman would faint for his words, what with their mouths open. He gave me a smile.

Well, I had to explain what actually went on. Wagner and Burch, 'Risked life and peril in them overloaded boats. The waves about sunk thems with all the men in them. Twice the men a boat can hold!" I had to say this, to get eyes from them. 'Oh, I was just barley holding me own, what with the Sultan Cut throats and them scimitars around me!" Yes, I went on, in bloody fashion, 'Till the doors burst open and here is Wagner and Burch to save me from peril!' I got ooohs and ahhhs. The women were holding their hands and all. Regina just gave us looks.

I walked, "Just Vie, please," back to her room house. No, not the same as Carrie. She is a secretary to some ships chandler. She has a nice smile, voice and asked about, "The Sultan thing?" I had to laugh at me story, which she did also, as 'added some, for the story.'

Tuesday, 22 December, and Mr. Makins said to see Admiral Irwin at the piers, "North side of North Pier." I found Adjutant Captain Lloyd at the head and Irwin some distance down, sittin. I Salute and, like PaPa, said, "Sit." He was looking at Susquehanna.

"McIntire had some sign on, from your Squadron Volunteers, just some." I said, 'Good Captain, Admiral. Some just like the liberty granted at Squadron, Sir,' to no good look. "They follow you, QMC. The Marine Major, Admiral Taylor, and I read the report sent of the Bey action. I have read better Fairy Tales, QMC."

"Captain Saltsgiver gave a better report of the landing to Major Dixon. A full report, QMC. He is in D.C. for a full brief to their General. The first Marine landing since the Barbary Coast fiasco, I might add. Private Waltermire and Kenwood will make Corporal from this. Nichol, Sargent." His voice was straight forward, like your grandfather 'a talkin. "Saltsgiver will make Major when his time comes."

"Palmer, too quiet for his good, mentioned you not much, like you was about not there." I finally get his look and, "Palmer could advance you as Forest mentioned you with the Triremes report. You got Chief for that bloody action with Captain Smith. He mentioned you highly. If Palmer had said such words I, the Navy, would have made you a Warrant or commissioned you, QMC. Palmer would return as Atlantic Fleet Admiral. Admiral Forest would have taken over as Chief in Charge Pacific, rather that Admiral Dewy, who is to be assigned."

No eyes to me I got, "Screw your (butt) into your desk and I want your words to everything you did from leaving that ship, to see the Port Master, till you came back aboard, after you gave your flag to that Bey. I want to know what, ah, the boy said, and where he said them, precisely, QMC." I got his bad look and, "The number of flies on that dead carcass, QMC."

Regina had already mentioned Christmas on that first Friday evening and, "Presents for your ladies is expected." It was a nice Sunday afternoon so we all did a look into the local stores. Wagner and Burch kept giving me looks. We had to stop an Effie place. No, I was not to spend the same on Vie. Effie knew where she lived. "Such a Poo," and gave me a wink. I said no! She would pick out the presents and get them to Regina place. I mentioned Madeira wine for Regina and something for Mattie. She gave me a wink, asked for, "7 dollars, for all". I gave her an eye and handed it over. No arguing with her. Wagner and Burch pleaded poverty.

Thursday, 24 December, Admiral Irwin called me to his office at 1 PM. Oh, I handed over that report. His lips moved as he was reading, like I do. He did hand gestures, asides turning the pages. I got a chuckle, frown, smiles, and a shake of his head. "Palmer never knew he was walking into a trap." I shook me head. "McIntire authorized the Landing party for an exercise of the crew, in your morning, Daily Report." Another head shake. "Ships officers and crew had only some clue as to your intent, QMC." It was all there in me words. I got, "Dismissed."

Squadron misfits, as I call thems, got dismissed after 11 AM muster, 25 December, till the next morning muster. Fitz, Wagner, Burch, and me hauled them pails to Regina place for the afternoon Christmas meal. Food for a bunch and plum duff for all. Turkey, stuffin, tators, gravy around. Oh, so good eats. Silvis, BMC Bothel and Mattie were there. It was a full house.

The first present was crystal wine glasses, to Regina, so everyone had one. The second was 6 bottles of her favorite Madeira wine, for the toast. It was to be only three presents around. Regina handed out the presents, one at a time, to each woman there.

Fitz had not forgotten Zoe. Effie had remembered what each woman looked at. Gloves, a shawl, stylish winter hats. I saw me 7 dollars wasted. Well, Regina had a 4th round. Mattie, Zoe, Cora, Margaret, and Vie got handed a wrapped box. Inside? A blouse each had looked at, at Effie place. Ooos and ahhs around. I got a cheek kiss from Vie, as did all the men, from the woman.

Come 9 PM I walked Vie back to her place, arm on me arm, to a nice kiss to me cheek, smile, and into this boarding place she went. I even noticed her lamp light came on, first story window. I made it about 10 feet back to base and heard me name called. Vie, in hat, shawl, comes up to me with a bit of her red hair out from that hat, green eyes I can't see, as it was dark out, and her right hand glove to me face. Smack! "How dare you!" Bigger eyes I get with another right hand glove and "How dare you intrude on my room!"

In the walk back I have to think about this. Oh, you be quick MJ. As quick as Vie and her right hand. I be slow in mind, what with the Madeira wine and pocket bottle to glass this evening. I didn't think I was drunk.

26 December, I was at me desk, late muster, when Wagner and Burch came in to mention muster. "All clean and sober, well most."

They had nice, joyful voices, and mentioned the night afore. When I looked up, well, thems sure shut up. Sowed glove seams just make a mark. I noticed them when I was shavin.

After lunch, I went out the gate to Effie place and finally got her attention. The glove marks was still there. It seems Vie had come by and wanted someone to remove the items. Effie told her I was head over heels in love with her. "First sight and just smitten. He wanted to surprise you. Your landlord let me in. I set them up." She knows of her situation. Paid just enough to have good cloths for work. "You show up at Regina place for lunch tomorrow and," I got a pat on me cheek, "learn to duck, quick."

27 December, Sunday morning, Fitz begged off goin to Regina place. He was goin to Zoe place. Only 3 with 6 pails of food and in to Cora and Margaret. Regina and them sorted it out to dishes. I got a glass, spritzer water to it, and added some from pocket bottle. It was cool, the sun was out, so I sat on the porch swing, thinkin and sippin.

The door opened, I saw two feet from under a coat, and a glass with fizzy water to me eyes. "Can I get a shot, QMC?" Vie. I poured in a bit, got her glove hand to tip a bit more in, and she sat aside me. "Thank you, for the extra presents. I am late as I was tryin to decide if I should wear the new blouse."

I was at me desk, Monday, 28 December, after I just inspected me motley bunch of Squadron people. I passed down each line, 4 by 8 people. Nichol had the Marines line thems up as they couldn't do it by themselves. Engle was there. It was my error in givin thems liberty. Lt. Makins decided to join me in this inspection. I got his eyes, till I heard from him later.

I took the afternoon to see me agent, Mr. Bish. Uncle Curtis agent died some year afore. A lawyer was assigned to watch over the account. There was no death certificate for Uncle so the Navy kept sending his pay to lawyer. His management fees ate most of the interest to the account. For a fee, Bish got the account sent to him. In all, with what I assigned, Edith will get a better check each quarter. My biggest expense is at Ella bar and to Effie, for Christmas stuff.

Thursday, 31 December, to Regina place, for the evening meal. Wagner, Burch, and me. Vie, Cora, Margaret were there. I got some foldin tables from Effie. They are big enough for two so I shared one with Vie. After eats Cora and Wagner took to the porch swing. Burch and Margaret went for a stroll. Me and Silvis entertained with lies from past sailings, to laughs around.

Come after 8 PM, arm to mine I walked her back to her place. She had to show me what Effie had sneaked in to her place. It was smaller than Carrie place with a table for two, and worsh sink in that kitchen. She got 4 crystal glasses, 2 bottles of pink Madeira wine, 4 place silver, and fine china settings.

Oh, we just chit chatted on each other bein here. Vie from Portsmouth, across the river. You know me story by now. I like that pink Madeira wine. It is about sweet. I got a pat to me face and a little kiss to carry me back to base by 10 PM. Both of us had to work New Year's Day.

01 January, 1897, Happy New year, MJ. Of 32, 4 fell dead on their faces at morning muster. Engle was one. Yesterday, the Paymaster paid out wages. The officers had a party so no Mr. Makins. I had shipmates drag them off to Marine tent. The cold might sober thems up. I am waiting to hear from McIntire.

Monday, 18 January, 1897. I hate Mondays. I am stuck at me desk, waitin for the next surprise. I still seein Vie. I'll get to that. Bothel left in Fran on the 8th. I traded scoundrels with him. He threw some off and I gave him no better in return, He, He! Willaims was in so saw QM3 Mark and QM2 Potts. That ship lost some for whatever and can't be choosy. The same with Carney. Burch and Wagner went over their lists and tried to fit. The problems was somes had already been thrown off them. Come volunteein and there was lots of Backeruppers. 32 now to 14, sorta. I don't count those at hospital.

Admiral Taylor is busy so Silvis is in and out with him. Wagner and Burch have been skippin meals and weekends at Regina. The same with Fitz. Women. We did cards for 4 the last 2 Fridays, and Saturdays. Regina gave me a hint about Sundays. "Do something with Vie on Sunday, alone, together!"

First Sunday we stopped at Ella and Harold place. Sailor only knows bars. But, just for refreshments of spritzer and a shot of whiskey. It keeps the chill off the body. Effie place is open 7 days a week. Regretted that, I did. She showed Vie, "Oh, New prints," and about everything in that store. I got off cheap. Vie only needed some candle sticks, "for the table!"

Last Friday, the 15th, was a busy day. A note said, "Admiral Inspection at 10," to you. All, me included, had put on dress uniforms and all. Saltsgiver would only give me the sword. 'Pistol?' "No." Gauntlets and arm protectors? "No, QMC!" The 6 Marines line up them 14.

Precise at 10, out Admiral Building come, Admiral Taylor, his Capt'n and Lieuy. Next was Irwin, his Capt'n Lloyd, and Lt. Makin. There was Major Dixon and Saltsgiver also. Yes, to the romp and stomp of them Marines. And they were allowed guns! A podium set so Taylor spoke first. Nichol, Waltermire, and Kenwood get kinds words for their action, dealing with that Bey. The Marine Major and Saltsgiver pined on their Sargent, Corporal pins. The Major stepped up and Saltsgiver gets fine remarks in a, "Letter of Commendation, from," some Marine General.

Taylor comes up, asked Irwin to step forward. He had been sittin in that chair, along with Capt'n and Lieuy's. I heard, "From the President of The United States, as read in Full Congress, Recognition for Superior Leadership of 2nd Squadron," and lots of words. It was odd as he kept lookin at me, ahind Irwin, as he read those words. The End, right? No.

I got a bow seat in the barge with, ahind, Capt'ns, Lieuy, and Saltsgiver. The Admiral gig had Taylor, Irwin, and the Major. The crew rowed real dry, in perfect timin. Not 10 minutes and comes the high side of a steel ship and a steel gangway right there. I followed them officers. I know enough to salute the Flag aft and the Capt'n in full uniform right there. I got pushed to a spot. The ship's crew was in full gear and at quarters.

There was whistles and bells to Major, Taylor, and Irwin to 12 Marine line and romps and stops! A greetin from ships officers and Taylor stepped to a podium, Irwin in front. Bad ears, off to the side, and only cached, "From the President of The United States, Authorized by Congress," and Taylor was readin a paper to Irwin. Next I looked up to people at the flag position and they popped a Vice Admiral flag at the Main Top! Swords flash, so I pull mine, and heard that boom of 15 gun salute to, "Vice Admiral Irwin."

The salute over, I get grabbed and pulled into the ships ward room, that officer place, to stand 'ahind this chair. The officers come in and Irwin is at that chair. I knew enough, from Algiers, to push it forward, for him to set in. No, the stewards serve the wine and food. I look over at Taylor, head of the table, not feet away. He gave me a smile and wink. I wish I'd have brought some ships biscuit and a pocket bottle. Regina, Vie, and Mattie just laugh as I told them this.

A Capt'n gig brought us back to that pier to a Carriage for Irwin and all. I never knew a pier to be so long. The galley was closed. I kept me sword. The gate guards gave me looks, but no guff. I caught up a samich at Ella place. "Harold, come look what's come in!" Harold opened his mouth and put me hand on that sword. He fixed that samich real quick. Regina, Vie, and Mattie had to look at that sword. No, I bought the meals from that Chinese place.

I found that Vie does has a sense of humor. She laughed and snickered the whole way back to her place. Taylor got me good. I had to tell about standing there with a growlin stomach. I had to laugh with her. She had to light up them candle holders so we could see to take up them crystal glass of Madeira wine. I did get a little kiss, besides the snickers.

Yesterday, Sunday, sunny, but cool, we walked over to Lamberts Point, so I could show her that iron ship. USS Texas. It was just commissioned, so Admiral Taylor got to inspect her. I told her of the boomin guns and all. I pointed out the, 'Ward Room, just aft of that torrent.' I said how wood ships, like mine, had the Gun Room. I got a strange feelin, lookin at it.

She about walked me leggs off. Yes, both. The place she works at is just off Hampton street. A Ships Husbandry service. They provided what ships comin' and goin' need. We had to go by Effie Mercantile as, "Such fun to look!" She needed, "Napkins for the table." We had Chinese food, just her and me. I got a nice, little kiss. One shot, shush, in me room, didn't calm me mind about Vie, nor that ship. Nor did the second one.

This morning? New Boot Camps and some from the Fleet, transferred here. Problems. A couple shore billets returnin' to sea. Fitz and Zoe must have had a fight. He is short to all, in temper. Makins called me in for the drunks reported by the Marine guards.

McIntire is lookin for a new cook to be assigned. There is none on me list to give him. Only Irwin was jovial. He asked if I could put his Admiral pennant in a wood box, "To hang on my wall, QMC." 'Yes, Vice Admiral Irwin.' He liked that.

I finish this in me little room. I needed a laugh so be just back from Ella place. She gave me, "Ah, love, like me and Harold has." Next was, "Harold, I ain't got all night for that order!" Back to me with nice eyes and, "Vie would make you a good wife!"

I did another two shots while writin this. Edith words come to me mind. "A good, loving man. But, one eye always on the sea."

By Your Leave, Missy,

An Old Sea Dog,

IN THE YEAR 1897, 15 FEBRUARY:

Dear Miss Judith,

It is Tuesday, 26th of January, 1897, at Squadron desk. Thank you for the letter. MaMa wrote about a virus goin' around. You heard about those gone. It is cold here also. Not like MaMa says it is up there.

Ya say to write when things are goin' on. Sometimes I could write a card about each day or so. Last Tuesday, the 19th, I got things settled here so went to check on me flags. Mattie was in a sweat and said Carrie would be back at 3:30 to show thems. I saw Mr. Bish, me agent. He had a, "Curator look at your knife."

I had to visit Ella place, for a refreshment. She badgered me about Viola to no end. 3:30, I went up them stairs to Mattie, Carrie, and Mr. Big Eyes lookin' at me Flags pined to two 5 by 5 foot boards. That original ships flag and mine.

Carrie introduced me to, "My husband, Robert." I got his card to me hand, nice eyes, a handshake, and "Carrie mentioned all it tells of you, QMC." I give short story of the sword and carbine, scimitars, and the rendition of that knife. "Interesting history, QMC. Carrie should invite you to an evening party, to tell your stories."

Carrie, 'ahind him, shook her head no. I didn't say yes or no and gave him, 'I like small, social gatherings, Sir. It is hard to talk at formal suppers.' Carrie caught up his arm with, "We must go, Dear."

I rolled up the little flags to tubes, unpinned me flag, turned, and Carrie hit me with a tube. She got in another swipe 'afore I rolled her up in that big flag. There came lots of wigglin and good sailor words from her. It took a second for her to settle down. I unwrapped her and got a tube to me face. Oh, she was hot.

"You should have just thanked him and said no, QMC. Now, he'll be looking over every initiation I send out for your name." I said, 'Oh, there will be a fight 'atween a couple bar maids for that invite!' She put that tube to both hands, holdin that flag. Quick, she be.

It was hard to manage the big tubes and little ones. Carrie took a little one and held out her arm. As we walked to the stairs I got, "Effie mentioned you are seeing Miss Williams. A nice woman." I gave her a nod, a cutsie smile, and she Whacked across me chest with that tube to, "You be very kind to her."

I got a spritzer and shot at Ella place. The card said, "Robert B. Miller," and his work titles. Ella took it and I got, "Oh, You be in high social standin to get this, QMC."

The 20th, Wednesday, I got called into Admiral Irwin conference room. I opened that door to him, Capt'n Lloyd, and three officers. A trap, I figured. I stood to his desk and was sociably introduced to, "Commander Walbeck, Lt. Clark, and Ensign Donahey, QMC." Irwin pointed his pen ahind to thems and me to the chair.

A stack of paper to him and he put most to me. First was the original Admiral Palmer action report. I knew it. The same with Capt'n McIntire report. Came Saltsgiver report that I helped write. Next, Saltsgiver report to General in DC. I already read it. Palmer letter of commendation to me, "It fell out of your formal Blue service jacket."

A folded sheet of paper come to me. "Fleet Admiral Forest has recalled Captain McIntire, 1st Lieutenant, and your Navigator. He needs good officers. Admiral Forest says you are quite a Magician, professional actor, and quite the play director, QMC." He tapped them papers. "Friday, this one, the 22nd, you will direct this change of command. Be in full regalia, QMC." The pen to ahind, "Any words, Gentlemen."

This Commander Walbeck asked permission to take Shenandoah out, after the change of command, directly, for a day or so. Irwin eyes was only to me. "Perhaps I should consult the ships Master, before I submit my sailing report, Sir." Pen to me and, "Well, Ships Master, QMC? Your thoughts on this?"

'Admiral, never on a Friday.' Walbeck comes back with, "Old folk lore. I've sailed on many a Friday and no harm came, Sir." I said, 'I would recommend a Pilot, jackass tugs, Sir.' Walbeck mentioned it was no different than a Frigate. "I'll take her out under my orders. No pilot required, Sir." Pen to ahind, "Have your sailing report to me soonest, Commander. Dismissed."

"Palmer send the original report, in case the first never got to Forest. His revision stands. It came with a letter. You wish to read it, QMC?" No. It came to me handed and another letter over. I got his thin smile and, "Forest words to you, personal, QMC."

Irwin directed, "Fully manned crew for this evolution, QMC. His chances of making it to sea, QMC?" I said, 'Bos'n is going to be real mad, scraping his good ginger bread work, Admiral.' I got, "Your sailing report for Friday and Saturday, soonest."

I found BM1, GM1, and the squadron people in that warm Marine tent. 'Change of command, Friday.' I gave a version of thoughts and, again, to Saltsgiver, in his warm office. I needed to talk to Gunner, Armoror, Mr. Chips, and Engle. Yep, still cooks for McIntire. Steward, the Squadron Galley cook, just gave me eyes when I asked to trade him for someone.

I caught up Joseph, Bush, and Hood for the sailin report. McMillen, the officers cook, served out coffee. GM1, me, and BM1 gave out ideas as Fitz and Rishell, his assistant, took notes. Came an agreement with all, on this change of command, Fitz and Rishell was to make it formal. I had to catch up a small ships flag at Carrie place.

I told Mattie what I needed as Carrie was not there, "No!" I put 5 silver liberties to the table and that nice red ribbon came to that flag, folded, with needles to the cloth. Her machine put thread and stuff to that flag and I was out the door. She asked about Friday supper. 'Formal gathering to attend to Friday and my social calendar is full for the weekend.' I held up that flag.

Thursday morning Wagner and Burch caught up their divisions to our plan. I talked with the Gunner, Armoror, Mr. Chips, and the Signal Middies in the Ward room. Rishell handed out papers for each to look over. I gave words to Engle about sweet breads and coffee.

Come that afternoon, easiest was set general quarters. There is no question of who was to be where. Saltsgiver knew to receive and send off officers. I was center Poop rail, Saltsgiver at end of Marine line, we went through me hand signals, start to end, and dismissed.

I was outside Vie office place at 5 PM and about missed her. She was bundled, huddled, and movin fast. I mentioned dinner and got her and friend to eat at the Chinese place. Ya take a bowl, scoop of rice to it, and pick out what you want in it. Take a wood fork or spoon and set at the bench. No, no napkins. I had to watch your dribble. Vie said nary word till, "That is Rose." She was one size smaller than Vie.

I introduced meself, proper, got her smile, and words to no end, about me and the uniform. I paid for her bowl heaped bowl. Seat saved, she sat, and I caught Rose works at the same company, at the dock. She talked with food to mouth and in. Brown hair, eyes, and more smiles than Vie had, and questions to me. She chuckles and laughed to me responses.

We went into store for evening wine. Two of pink stuff and a spritzer bottle for me. Rose brought a chair to Vie room. She lives across the hall. I felt like a third wheel on a dog cart. Only Rose would give me questions and words. Me vest watch said 8 PM, so excused meself. 'I need to catch up men on liberty. I'm sleepin aboard for formal change of command, tomorrow, and,'

Rose come back, with a wink to Vie, "And your formal thing, Friday night, QMC? That costly flag for Mr. Miller, Carries husband and all." Maggie! 'A personal flag to Ships Captain McIntire, Rose, tomorrow, and to sea, at 11 AM. I caught you up for dinner, Vie, to tell you I'd be away all weekend,' to no words. 'So, Vie, you think me such a scrub of a sailor I'd not be proud to have your arm, to any social event I was invited to?'

In the hallway, me pea coat over that jacket, fingers to buttons, and I got pulled around. It was Vie. Two hands to me cheeks, a kiss, and, "Don't move." That was the first good smile and green eyes all evening.

A street from Ella place I heard me crew. Oh, thems havin a good time. Vie loved their attention. Each had to give her some words. Came time, Nichol, Marines herded me volunteers off to the ship. I took Vie back to a nice kiss and, "Monday, Chinese, my sailor."

At 9:30 AM, Friday, the crew was at General Quarters. The new Ensign and 1st Lieuy came aboard with that Commander following them through the Marine line and McIntire greetins. After, thems stood like turkeys on a scratch. More salutes, handshakes around, till I wanted to shoot them. Saltsgiver tried to herd thems to Capt'n cabin. Admiral Irwin comes aboard and the turkeys was scratchin, hand shaken, and more saluting around.

Came the time, I put a pointer stick to deck above Engle and he rousted them to the door. Them officers went to chairs, aft, with blankets over, as it was cold out. Navigator, Gaily, then 1st Lieuy,

Caldwell, gave short words to the crew. Ensign Donahey and Lt. Clark relieved them. As each stood at the Marine line, me arm came down and they got three "Hurzays" from ship's crew. At gangway, an Oldster gives them a little ships flag. I fire me pistol and both thems got a 2 fore and 4 aft chasers salute.

Capt'n McIntire said some nice words to the crew. That Bey action came to his words, "and," lookin around, "a much better bunch of misfits I never served with." He made it to Saltsgiver and me hand went down. Oh, the crew "Hurzays" him three times. The Armoror stopped him as an Oldster showed him the new ships flag, with the Bey's knife on it. He rolled up, it hit McIntire hand and I put a pistol shot to air.

It started with Port, forward chaser and just followed aft, through 18 pounder upper guns, signal guns, to 4 aft chasers. No, not timed. A following, continuous boom. Gunner was just grinning the whole time. The breeze, above the ware houses, showed a nice East to North breeze. On deck there was a little breeze.

I saw McIntire tryin to fan the smoke off his face. Another oldster showed his personal flag with a big red "M" on it. McIntire bein a highlander, Scottish Clan name, it was a St. Andrew flag, the crew red to white stripes with a scimitars and horn knife other each end.

At me signal, Engle released Irvin from his chair. At head of Marine line me arm came down. Yep, three, "Hurzays!" At the gangway, me Oldster pulled out the new ships flag with scimitars and horn knife. Admiral accepted it real good. A pistol shot to the air and 14 ships guns went off to Gunners watch. Me pistol shot counted as first of 15.

Gunner must have double charged the guns, what with the smoke over the ship. When it cleared another Oldster gave Irwin me new flag. I gave him that sword salute, returned, and gone. Done?

The ships bell sounded 11 AM. From the Quarterdeck, Walbeck started shoutin' out orders. He pushed me from Mid Poop rail, to more orders. He gave cuss words when no one moved. Me right, gauntlet hand showed him the formal ceremony paper. Me left gauntlet finger went to the last line. "Oh!" I repeated his orders, 'Dismissed."

In 1st class uniforms, the crew moved slow, so as not to get thems dirty. Walbeck was sure mad about that, cursin' to himself. The line was cast off and ship didn't move. The outgoing tide held ship to pier. Walbeck wanted Warrant Bos'n to us the spare spars to push us down the pier. Bos'n Gaston, I thought as a joke, told him the ship had a better chance, "Sailing her out of here, Capt'n!"

Walbeck ordered up fore and main mast top sails, to Gaston, "That is my order, Bos'n." So, Twirly, Twirly on his whistle and the crew to them masts. Sails was sheeted in, lines belayed down, to a puff of West wind, and the ship went forward, buried that bow in the muck and mud of the bank at the shore end of pier. The keel creaked, aft sank and the ship leaned a bit to Starboard. We was stuck good. It was not comin' off till high time, 10 PM, by my sailin report.

We didn't sail so the volunteers went back to squadron. I had to see the Port Master about a Pilot and tugs for Saturday. Irwin, in his coach, saw what went on. The Commander was his problem.

Friday evenin, the same day, I was in that seat, at the end of Ella bar. The Admiral volunteers was havin a good time it. Got a hand to me shoulder, turn to Vie, and a dirty look. "So, why am I not on your arm for this social event?" Ella came over and said, "I sent a runner to fetch her. You need someone to keep you out of trouble, QMC."

That social broke up at 9:30 PM for me motley crew to go back to the ship. I took Vie home and said what went on. I mentioned the ship should be off the mud, 'About the time them scoundrels are aboard.'

The Pilot came aboard, Saturday, and straight to Gaston with a handshake. Walbeck sat in his chair, tended to by Engle. The jackass tugs cast us off to fair winds through the channel. Walbeck did good with callin for sails. Well, Gaston only gave him a couple bad eyes. We fired the guns, did Tack and Wear exercises and all he wanted to do. The jackass tugs tucked us all nice to the South side of North pier, yesterday, Monday, 25 January.

That evenin I escorted Vie to that Chinese place, arm to mine. I saw Rose come in and got her thanks for payin. She had sullen looks, nary a word. I tried to joke her, some, to bad looks. Vie kept lookin at me. I finally ask Vie if she knew of a plumber to 4 eyes to me. 'Rose voice tube seems clogged. She needs a plumber or some sailor to give her a lip lock to open it up!' Rose went red and looked to explode. Vie clasped a hand to her mouth but I still heard her laughter. There was no hand to mine. Rose gave no smile and said, "He better be a good kisser." The people in the place thought we was crazy, just laughin.

01, February, here at squadron desk and I pick this up to continue. Rishell is me new clerk. Fitz found him stuck at Judge Advocate place. He is quiet, efficient. Irwin signed off on the transfer, don't ask. We go aboard Shenandoah most days to keep papers straight. Bobbit doin good.

27 January, last Wednesday, Rishell and me carried a food pail to Vie place, for a dinner introduction. Galley cook, Edwards, gave Rishell looks. 'New clerk.' Vie place a bit tight for two tables and 4 chairs. The Good food was major talk. Came the second bottle and Rishell mentioned his work, ships reports. Rose and him was just an open scuttle with word pumps goin. Vie gave me a smile.

Friday night, Saturday night, lunch on Sunday, he and I carried two each to Regina place. Silvis and Bothel was out. I needed to entertain her and Mattie. Friday and Saturday was cards. Rose and Rishell sat out, mostly talkin. Mattie, Regina, Rose and Rishell, begged of Sunday dinner.

3 PM, the sun out, cool, we walked to the base, much it is. Shenandoah was the only one there. I salute the deck officer and show her around the main deck. Vie was in awe. The more we walked the deck, the more crew come above to answer her questions. I open me Ships Master door and get hand to her nose. It needed airing out, I figure. By the time we reach the gangway, even Old Tom, ship cat, was there. There was like a formal reception line, as each tipped their hats to her. Vie smiled, nodded, and gave a hand to each.

Monday, 15 February, I'm about tied to Squadron desk. Shenandoah started load out last week. No need for me to be there. I assigned Rishell to count wagons, in me stead.

Night of the 3rd, we took food pails to Vie place. I get, "QMC, how about we visit my family, in Portsmouth. We can go Friday after work and back on Sunday?" I give a cutsie smile and raised eye brows. "Oh, there is a guest room or my brothers, who lives in Baltimore." I did it again, got bad eyes and, "PaPa would shoot you!" Those were words from long ago that came to mind. That long road south and Princess words. I laugh real good and said, 'I don't know if I can put with you that long.' Rishell and Rose laughed real good. I got her bad eyes. I agreed to Saturday, 8 AM. Yes, I saw her that Friday evening. Just us.

Rishell got me leave orders signed, shush, so I could collect me regalia. I got looks on trolley and Vie. So we took trolley to Norfolk and caught ferry to Portsmouth. No. I stepped off the trolley, to greet her, she turned me round, and into a warehouse we went. She talked to a woman there and we was escorted onto a tug. "PaPa owned the warehouse and this tug."

It was a short walk us High Street to a wide building, three stories high. The left door sign was, "Tobacco," and the right, "Spirits." There was a side door to the upstairs place and a shout of "PaPa!" I found an older gent, my height, wider, in a work business suit, and thinin hair. "Frank, please." 'Most call me QMC, when polite.' That got a laugh. He turn out of the way and "Elizabeth, QMC." I was starin at Vie, some years in the future. A lovely woman, well, both are.

Me pea coat came to the holstered 45 and me sword. 'I heard this is a wild town, Frank.' From me canvas bag comes thems gauntlets and arm protectors I put, on. I pull a small ships flag from the bag and hand it to him. Into bag, me flag to his hand, unrolled. Both got handed around. Vie hadn't see them. Oh, the words just flowed from them.

Frank walked me shoes off showin' me his big warehouse on the river. It was a busy place. There was barrels of wine, whiskey, tobacco, cases of all he said goin and comin'. "Men smoke and drink. It goes hand in hand." He exports, imports tobacco, spirits, and all you could ask for. Lunch and dinner was at places that served out good food. Frank seemed to know everyone, everywhere. It was an evenin' after of me stories. The Flags helped tell the tales. It was a fun evening of talk. His good bar kept me whistle wetted.

Sunday mornin' was church day. I got last bath. I dried off, skivvies on, and the door opened to Elizabeth. "I thought you might need a, Tow!" Her eyes went to them 3 big red, purple spots on me leg, a smaller row up me arm, and the scares to the hair line. I got her big eyes only.

It is a big gray stone church. I 'membered all the songs, from Philly. Flashes of that time, places, and people, women, were there. George. Lunch was at. another place. Frank went to tables, handshakes to men, and cordial to the woman. Elizabeth only gave big eyes to me.

Hugs, kisses around to Vie. From Frank, "Good stories, QMC." I got a hug from Elizabeth, to ear, "Does your mother know all what you have been through?" I said, 'No. She is such a worry wart and might think I was in danger, at times.' I smiled and kissed her cheek.

Oh, Mondays at the Chinese place with Rose and Rishell. They go to her room after. The same with pails to Vie room on Wednesdays. I guess he is a good kisser. We did a social on Friday and Saturday night with Regina and Mattie. All begged off Sunday dinner, yesterday. I get a nice kisses from Vie, when her eyes twinkle, like last night. At times she has a question not asked. Is like her mother's eyes, after seein' them scars.

I gave Walbeck me recommendation to sail to the Caribbean on the 25th or 27th. Thursday or Saturday. Joseph, Burch, and Hood have been learnin' Ensign Donahey navigation. Me Ships Masters room got cleaned out. That borax stuff makes it smell better. Me helpers done it.

Them letters, ya asked. Forest had no interest in goin to the Pacific. Taylor had been there, and declined the orders. The rest was about me, most to Irwin. No good words 'cept, "his mantel has been tested. A more capable office I could not find. But," with bad words a sailor is proud of.

To me, ya ask? Forest resaid how he should have allowed Taylor to put the cat o' nine tails to me. Doubted I'd have been a good farmer, married an ugly woman, and had ugly children. Words from long ago. "I give you a new Ensign, to your boat, in that pond, QMC. Maybe he can help you find shore." Another Old joke, 'atween us. In his other words was armored costal cruisers. USS Texas, came to mind. "The future, QMC."

I put this to the Post, Monday,15 February, 1897.

By Your Leave, Missy,

An Old Sea Dog,

IN THE YEAR 1897, 21 MARCH: CARIBBEAN

Dear Miss Judith,

I start this one on Monday, 22 Feb, still at Squadron, to sail on Saturday, the 27th. Walbeck made up his mind. He and them officers to have a social on Friday. Me volunteers be at a social at Ella place.

Now, last Tuesday, the 16th, I got called to Irwin office just after 9 AM and his formal pen to seat. Came a time and Capt'n Saltsgiver comes in at a sweat, to pen. There was a paper to me to read. 15 February, Mr. Robert B. Miller, Sr., Dear James. A personal letter. Frank and Elizabeth was mentioned. Daughter Viola there. That weekend visit and all you know, from me letter. Robert, Jr. and Carrie was on that paper.

Thick, 4 by 5 inch cards come to us. I open to formal invite to, dinner and social after, 19th, Friday. "Ships Master, QMC, and Miss Viola Williams. I request QMC in full regalia." Well, it was them words with an RSVP card included. Robert Jr. card fell off the corner. I turned it to, "QMC, See Effie immediately!" It was Carrie writing. Saltsgiver was about white, still sweatin, and out with, "Admiral, Eva and I live a modest life!" That is his wife.

I bumped him, turned the card, pointed out that word, and said, 'We accept, Admiral.' Saltsgiver turned more white. 'Rishell will write formal orders for us. I heard they have good eats and whiskey, Captain.' Bad eyes from Irwin and Marine Captain whiter. I signed the RSVP and his clerk took them away.

That evenin' I caught up Vie after work and straight to Effie. I already had been to her this afternoon. Effie caught Vie up like ships cat to a mouse and into this back area. Eva, Vie size, with Saltsgiver, well, got snatched to same place. Hour later thems come out, regular cloths, good eyes, and smiles. I took all to the Chinese place to eat. I took pails to her place Wednesday and even Rose wouldn't give out any information. Just smiles 'atween thems.

Effie arranged a Chase and 4 to pick me up at main gate. Marine Capt'n and wife, Vie were at Effie Place. White gloves to hands and to seats. The women was all smiles and gabberin'. Saltsgiver looked like to a hangin. Me sword gave me trouble to settle. The woman didn't like me canvas bag. It was a ride to that brownstone house on Colley Street.

I gave Pea coat to lady at the entrance and kept canvas bag. Vie, reluctantly, handed over the cape Effie gave her. Vie to me arm we went down the line of Robert, Jr., Carrie, Robert, Sr. and wife, 'nother, wife, 'nother, wife. I gave a handshake to all and, 'Just QMC, please.'

You'd ask so, Vie was in a stylish, simple hat. Violet jacket over white blouse with some frill. Violet skirt, stylish, to ankles. Simple pearl neckless and earrings. Eva hat was with a feather, stylish, skirt and jacket to match Saltsgiver red strip, white blouse, with simple lace to neck. A neckless to match earrings. The men were eyes to them. Thought Carrie would faint.

Saltsgiver gave Robert Jr. a ships flag. I gave him me personal one. He liked both. There was good food and wine around. Robert Sr. kept up the conversation. Eva, Saltsgiver, and Vie was the mice in the corner to this. They must have had a bit of cheese in their mouths.

These sliding doors open and all to seats in this other room. Guests of honor, Vie, Eva, Saltsgiver, me to the front. Robert Sr. started it with, "A story, QMC!" From somewhere, a chalkboard comes in. Shush, I put it on that RSVP. Chalk to board, gauntlets on, did a simple drawin of the Sultan place with the ship, streets, and the palace. I handed it to Saltsgiver to say how he marched up there. I needed to loosen him up.

He bored the people, me to death. I took the chalk and gave them, 'A Roman formation, and square. Pikes, axes on poles to center. At the front was cutlasses and pistols.' Ohhs, ahhs. '6 Marines in the front to blunt thems Arabs attack!' Ohhs, ahhs. I gave the words of sultan interpreter wanting me to shoot someone and show the power of the pistol.

I did the pistol trick to thems. Yes, the only real cartridge to Carrie. Pistol out, I cocked it and pointed it round the room. Thems was a bunch of scared people. 'Who should I shoot!' I pointed up and pulled the trigger, no sound, and some laughs. I told the ladies to cover their ears. Most did. I cocked the gun and, 'I'll call in thunder and destruction,' raised the pistol, pulled the trigger on a blank cartridge. I got claps. "QMC, weren't you worried about the big gun shells hitting you?" 'I trust the Gunner, Mam.'

Robert Sr. asked about, "The Bey and your knife." I wiped off that chalk board and left it to Saltsgiver. He drew to no end. He did better, sayin how the boats landed, Akabar, his friends, and how he divided up the men.

'Oh, locked inside. Guards to them doors.' I gave a wink to Vie. Pistol out, I showed how I reloaded, after unloading. I gave Vie a real cartridge. I said those words I gave the Bey. 'So, who do I shoot?' I waved it around to none duckin. Pistol to the air, women hands to ears, and, clicked on and empty chamber. 'Remember the Sultan story? Now, cover your ears.' Oh, it was just a blank. I got claps around. I let Saltsgiver explain about shootin the door and chargin up to save me. We got claps around.

The women got to ask us questions first. Oohs, ahhs, smiles, and cheek kisses. We had to show our swords. Me brass handle got lots of words. Each, even Carrie, Vie, and Eva got to try on the gauntlets. Carrie kept closing them and lookin at me, direct. Arm protectors? Only Mrs. Miller, Sr., about got them on.

Us men got directed to another room to fine cigars and lots of brandy. We had to show our swords. Saltsgiver has a Marine Mameluke. It is a straight one with white false ivory grips. Mine got the attention, along with the break top. Saltsgiver showed a nice Colt 45. Me gauntlets and arm protectors got lots of try on and words. Yes, the chase dropped us off accordingly.

Saturday, the 20th, to Effie as I had their jewels. Both was afraid of getting robbed. It was like a mother and daughters talkin', returning the cloths. Vie lookin' at stuff, as Effie charged a dollar usage, each woman, and one for the carriage. Admiral orders got charged 5. Flags cost. Saltsgiver invited us to his place for the evening. I said I'd bring food.

It was a small place of 4 rooms, including a privy. Eva had an office job, like Vie. They just chit chatted. The night afore got lots of talk of ladies about ladies. It was Eva that asked about me face scar. The Captain Smith battle where the rail exploded, wood splinters, me at the wheel indicator, and then down. I didn't remember much. Saltsgiver gave his view from tween number 1 and 5 guns. He gave an account that got eyes from both of thems. Eva had big eyes. Maybe she just saw how dangerous a ships battle is.

It was Vie that said her mother had peaked in on me, in the bath. She blushed. I had to tell how I pulled them wood pieces from me leg and arm, a silk neckerchief to leg and wound around. I pointed to me scar and said, 'Doc did this first. I screamed as he used a dull needle for the rest.' Oh, such eyes. I said, with a wink, 'Give ya a private showin in the privy.' Came blushes, noos!

Just me and Vie Sunday afternoon and evening. We meandered around. Oh, had to stop at Effie place, and Ella bar. We took Chinese back to her place, "to use the china." That question came, round about. "So, QMC, how do you know Effie and get the invitation?" That was easy. Mother of Carrie. Well, Regina did introduce us. Mattie worked for her and, 'Makes me flags!' I told her how Effie liked to joke Carrie. I mentioned Christmas presents, to the china at hand. 'You and Eva were better dressed than her that night. She likes to do that, at me expense.' I did get a kiss for that. 'You have a need, see Effie,' which got a look.

26 February, she had to take me hand on that bar stool, as the volunteers were doin' it up right. None missed sayin' hello. Scoundrels all, but polite. In her room, she handed me a card, her address, and asked if I'd write. "Your address, QMC, should I want to?" 'Front of the envelope invite I gave you.' Into her other room, some time, I heard strange things. She came out dressed in white lace night cap, white light, long sleeve gown, lace to neck, down the front some. Lace around the bottom to ankles. Up like a ballerina on toes and she did a full turn. A little Princess all grown up. Another Effie gift. I had to smile at the 'membrance.

27th, Ensign Donahey was to be Officer Of the Deck for fore noon watch. I relieved him. An enclosed chaise and two come down the pier at 8AM. It stopped short of the ships brow. Walbeck came out, lookin around. The ships officers there to greet him and directed into his cabin. He was to review volunteers, Saltsgiver in front, with his salute.

The quarter hour bell ain't rung and I get called into his cabin. Ahind his desk, officers to places, me in front, and just words to me, "Who authorized the ship to be moved, AFT, and what are the underway orders." I mentioned the ship was shifted per, The 'Sailin Report, yesterday, for getting the ship underway, today.'

The Admiral clerk caught me up, at squadron, sayin he didn't get a, 'Sailin report to the Admiral, authorizing ship leaving port, QMC.' That was the afternoon afore. 'I come to the ship, Sir, and you ashore.' Shouldn't a done it, but, I pointed out all the ships offices initial on that paper. I signed in his stead, as 'Ship Master, Sir.' "Officers dismissed."

A paper to his hand, from Irwin, designated, "Ships Master." I could sign the report. The volunteer list to desk, last page, addendum to it, was me name. 'Ship's Captain must review the volunteers, for his approval, Sir.' I get bad looks. 'The Sailin Report will make you look good, either way,' to his eyes. 'I take the ship out, run into something, I get the Court Martial. The ship makes it into the channel, you get the credit, Sir.' Next paper to him was, 'I put up a finger and you give the order, Sir. You have the deck. I control the rudder, Sir.'

I met the Pilot at the end of the pier. Oh, the same guy. I give him where I want the jackass tugs to tie up, 'Propellers with thrust, to keep up a head of steam,' and their rudder position. I got bad eyes, me arm around him, and smile. We talked to the tug masters. I offered him places to sit. He wanted to be me shadow. A chair to the quarter deck, for him, and Engle gave him coffee and sweet breads. No, not me.

Irwin came aboard with lots of officers into Capt'n cabin. At me signal, Bush dropped the pointer above Engle. The officers came out of the Capt'n cabin like turkeys at a scratch. I about had to shoo thems off. Irwin at the brow, I give Walbeck a "1" finger. "Prepare to get underway." He dismiss all hands. I give "Two" fingers to, "Brest lines in, single up fore and aft lines."

The Pilot went to a chair, Starboard side, on the poop deck. I put Walbeck to center of the Taft rail. Bush, Hood, two new boots to helm and Joseph on the rudder indicator, me back to him, facin aft. I was watchin that channel buoy. Engle brought coffee and sweet breads for Capt'n and Pilot. That buoy stopped goin south and started headed North. The out goin tide. I give Walbeck three fingers to, "Cast off all lines, gangway aboard." It took a couple minutes afore the ship comes off the pier. Shush, I could scratch a spot and Joseph would call for rudder changes. Oh, he knew what to do. I just touched them up, some. Ship, pretty as ya please, got out into that channel.

I turned forward as Ensign Donahey said the ships heading. We was goin backards though. I heard Walbeck say something so, 'Ensign, call every 5 degrees of ships head change!' I just kept nodding to Joseph and rudder calls. We came nice around, clockwise in that South, West wind. The bow sprint came through that wind, I held up 4 fingers. "Gib, Fore Top, Main Top sails!" Bos'n and 1st Lieuy did their tweerly, tweerly, to the foretop men already there. Well, it was a sight to see and hear, "Belay, Belay." Ol Shenandoah just smartly went up that channel.

Now, that Pilot gave Walbeck a good hand shake. "Nicely done, Captain. I'll note it in my report of getting this ship underway, to the Admiral." I got a slap in the back from him and in me ear, "Why don't I have you as a pilot, QMC." He gave words to ships wheel men and Joseph. Handshakes to 1st Lieuy and Bos'n and down the ladder to tug. I only got eyes from Walbeck.

Left later in the day, we headed to that North Wall straight out, to make it 'afore pippin hands to hammocks. It was dark out but I saw Engle gather up glasses and such. Told Walbeck three time of this, I did. He was grumpy, at that Taft rail. The hands to station, time, and, wall gave a small push to the ship. I got grumbles from the crew and, "Humph," from Walbeck.

There is that line painted to the deck again. Walbeck wants to go on-deck and get to know the crew. I assigned an Oldster to stand there and give him a knuckle to his head. The last salute Walbeck get till back to this side of the line. He wanted to argue about this. I said of me 'Ships Master Report' and who all I sent it to. I mentioned Doc also made a report of sick, injured, and why it happened. Yes, he got to review them, but! That shushed him up.

It was the 3rd of March, I in me Chart Room, and a little bell on the door said someone came in. I heard a stool legs squeak but didn't look up from that paper and said, 'How can I help you, Ships Captain?' "Drop the Ships part, Ships Master." Oh, he don't like Commander and me 'Sirs' was wearin' thin on him. I looked up to him and asked the names of the 4 oldest and 2 youngest mates aboard. I got no answer. That is why they painted that line, again.

1st Lieuy, Clark, and Ensign Donahey had been visitin' the fore deck since Norfolk. I assigned oldsters to each one so we don't have thems getting' a line around their hands and pulled aloft. I learned that afore. If I'm on the Poop, I watch thems from the fore rail. I watch for crew monkey shinin', like a false salute, 'ahind officer backs. That gets a turn scrubbin' the fore privy or pumpin' the wet bilge. If GM1 or BM1 catches thems, well, I don't ask. Their men to look after.

No, we are not goin to Bahama, directly. Walbeck wanted, "to skirt Cape Hatteras, straight to Key West." We was on that larboard tack, South, South East, when we left Norfolk, in a nice North wind. I set Whey Point to night orders and got woke at the change of that watch. Ensign thought to wear, "closer to land, QMC." In me cabin I showed him, 'Us, here. See that light house, come an East wind and just might find dry land, Sir.'

We got to skirt the Grand Bahama, Alice Town, and the Guy Cay islands. The look outs in the very top could only see thems or the Florida mainland. I ordered South, a little West, and the lookout would say land or not. Come time and West was ordered. 08 March, 1897, and that ugly beast of USS Maine was at anchor off the little navy base of Key West. An Armored Costal Cruiser, of iron. Texas looked better. I wondered who put the design for it to paper. Oh, Gunner, Mr. Campbell, was just lookin at a pretty woman, his eyes to her. Joseph got 12th pull on the barge to take in Walbeck, 1st Lieuy, and the purser to her. There was special loads to her, mostly pulled by barges. Our yard arms might tangle in her, ugly stuff, topside.

I warned Walbeck about the winds and all, in this season. We made Nassau, de Bahamas, on 11 March. We was lucky and had to tack into that wind about to Miami, Florida, to get some South. Bos'n and 1st Lieuy given me bad looks each day. It about wore out the men at the sails. Then, Walbeck wanted to enter that little channel, "Closer to the Governors Fort." I said, 'Sure, Ships Captain. The men need liberty for two or three days, when the wind will get us out of there.' No one likes me jokes. The ships officers gave looks.

It is 1600 miles around the Atlantic side of them islands, down to Barbados. "The ship did it before, in case a Frigate was out there," said Walbeck. Ensign and 1st Lieuy agreed. A nice North, some West and East winds around, so the crew wasn't like crows in the trees.

21 March, 1897, we anchored off Barbados. That Brit place. 2 days liberty, by divisions. Maggie, at the bar, was about heart broke. USS Santee went back to Annapolis. She had a boyfriend in the different divisions. It got sent ship back as she couldn't catch a row boat. She caught me up to frigates movements. Still has a boyfriend on each, who write letters, delivered by packet ships.

Somes of that Packet crew were there last night. I caught up some other things. I ain't sayin they read the mail. The hear things from their start of sailin, till here. I close this out to you as Purser Hitcock says last post out. I need to sort out charts for this first round of the Caribbean.

By Your Leave, Missy,

An Old Sea Dog,

IN THE YEAR 1897, 09 JUNE: CARIBBEAN

Dear Miss Judith,

We left Barbados on the 23rd, March. Commander Walbeck said, "On the Tide, QMC." I quit tryin to say this is the Atlantic Ocean and not in a bay. I told Joseph to put down 10 AM. Walbeck was determined to follow the previous 'Roundy's' of the Caribbean. So we did a course South, some West, to go around Grenada.

On the way North, past Martinique, Gaston, Doc Stiteler, and Cook Feterman asked about takin on water. Warrant and Doc were worried about health of the crew. Mr. McGraw mate reported water aboard. When it is below half the crew don't do so good on Thursday worshin. A low water and none for the scuttlebutts on deck. Is hot down here. Feterman has to put that salt meat to fresh water or the crew complain of the taste. I get earful from both sides.

26 March we run smack into this Frigate off them British Virgin Islands. Commander to Captain was the signal. Oh, I got caught up in this as, "Inform their Navigator of our intended cruise." I took Donahey with me.

Quarter deck, introductions around, and a Petty Office took us to the chart room. Just like us, it was on the port side, next to Captain cabin. A knock and the door opened to an older gent, white shirt, no tie, and just a head nod. I introduce meself and Donahey. "Ships Master, Bracken." The jacket on the hanger had Warrant officer stripes. I pull out a full Caribbean Chart and got his hand to same type of chart table.

Per Commander request I went over our circle of this place. I said where the other 3 Frigates should be. 4 weeks or so round for us to get back to Barbados. I mention water in Ponce and near Trujillo, where the Frigates stop for minor repairs. It was like talkin to Horse, back home. I got dead eyes, a shake of the head, and no words. I mentioned if they were chasin a ship to put a flag to barrel and over the side with a waxed envelope to course and where they were headed.

I thanked him for his time. Oh, Donahey got his handshake, polite and all. Come to mine, I got dead eyes and, "Very informative.

Nothing is different." The Packet ship crew in Barbados mentioned a "New" Frigate added to the Squadron here. They didn't know where it would be found. We do now.

13 April, in Trujillo, I was sittin on a bench, drinkin, ah, fruit punch. I was there as Mr. McGraw, Gaston, and Hardis are bangin around the ship. Chips with the wood, Gaston crew are putting line and tar to them boards. Armoror is bangin on that ships stove. Purser Hitcock gave us coppers to get meals ashore. The stove broke.

'Tween that new Frigate and here was a bore. We watered in Ponce. The men smell better and Feterman has water to seep the salt meat. We stopped in Cozumel for liberty. Commander, 1st Lieuy Clark, me in full regalia, went to see that Harbor Master. Oh, he recognized me. We had to see the town Mayor. He was gracious to us for stoppin. It seems a Frigate stopped by and, well, I know the meanin of two spits to the side and bad words, even in Spanish.

Engle, ya ask? He and Clerk Rishell handle drinks the same. In Barbados, Maggie gave thems some good stuff. They was back aboard 'afore hammocks put to rings, to sleep in. In them hammocks, shush, 'afore time, and thems was all comfy cozy. The same in Cozumel. Engle was sober enough come 5:30 to make Commander coffee! Less words to me ears.

If ya ask about Spanish Frigates, I can't say I seen any. Oh, nick of sails here and there. The barges was rigged with sails, over the side, since Ponce. The Middies and barge crew just love bein, "Dogs on a chase!" Shush. Feterman still gives thems some plum duff in those pails.

03 May, 1897, writin at the Chart Table. The officers are ashore to see the Governor of Barbados. We arrived this mornin. I will go ashore in evenin. Still a borin cruise. The wind be wind with some fair and some not. I just set the course and them Bos'n mates do the rest. The first Frigate, the one known, was off Honduras. It asked for some stuff. The Purser went over and caught up what they was up to.

The next was 'tween Providenia Island and Cartagena. It looked like they was fishin over the side. Purser and me, his assistant, went to the Harbor Master in Cartagena with list. No Habla Engleses, or what me bad ears heard. A silver dollar in Mm hand got better eyes.

He found someone who could Habla better than him. A 10 cent Liberty, silver, to this guy and, "No Problemo!"

Third was off Caracas, or so. I figure it was just waitin for that time to come to Barbados for liberty. They got little from us. Just maybe he knows how to get stuff from in the ports.

Left Barbados for the 2nd round on 6 May and caught up Ponce and water on the 10th. We have seen some sails. None of our, nor Spanish Frigates. Mostly commercial ships from South America goin North. Our barges, with sails, out both sides, have found no barrels. Jamaica was on the Starboard side on the 14th. The Caiman Island past to Starboard on the 15th. Next is Cozumel for liberty.

Commander and me still be at Logger Heads to what I call him. A logger head be and iron rod and big iron fist at the end. Ya heat thems on ships stove, dip in a bucket of tar, to melt the tar, to fill spaces in the ships planks. It is an Old English term. Bos'n talk, like all them animals in the fore of the ship. Bosn's, for fun, will slam thems together to make a loud sound. Ours be quiet, bad looks, no words, but, I do have to give Sirs and all.

Now, about 9 AM, 18 May, 1897, me and Mr. Donahey, in gig, landed at that pier in Cozumel. Just dress uniforms. 'Mr. Hernandez, Mr. Donahey, our Navigation Officer.' I got nothing but a bad look. I gave a, 'Hello,' to his assistant, Mr. Garcia. Polite, I ask if the ship crew can have, '3 Days Liberty, Senior?' I stuck out me hand for a shake and got a line of Spanish. I understood the two spits to the dirt and the name of that new Frigate.

Last here, we had to dress up and see the Mayor, Mr. Mendoza, about liberty. I said, 'Pore Favor, Habla Mr. Mendoza?' It must have been a joke. I got laughs, and, well, more Spanish than me ears could translate. Their gestures, ah, I understood.

With poor gestures with hands, I ask if he, point to him, knows, point to me head, someone, gestures around the place, 'Who Habla Ingleses, Pore Favor?' Next was my gestures of, you know me, you know the ship, and I point out the door, 'Pore Favor?' Garcia must have joked him on this as he starts laughin to no end. Hernandez is about to blow up. Again, 'Pore Favor?' I got his hand up and, "Si."

Out that back door, down South, where I've never been, down the street, around a corner, and to a church. I saw lots of children around 3 nuns. Another was sittin on a stool and leadin a group of children, sittin on a low bench, in a song from back in me past. A French song. Song over, hats off, up ahind her, he said, "Hermana Catherine." Came some words and she turned to us. I said me name and introduce, 'Mr. Donahey, Shenandoah Navigator, Mam,' to a face as lovely as Elizabeth, Vie mother. Oh, a hand to each of us and, "How may I help you?"

Hernandez came off with a long bunch of words to her. Her hand to his arm shut him up. We get to sit on that low bench as she took to her stool. I just said we was asking for liberty. That got his sentence of words, hand to his arm, and I asked what had happened for this refusal. She listened, attentive, hand to his arm a couple times, and nodded her head.

What she translated was worse than I thought. I said I'd need to report this to our Captain and to see the damage, and a translator, with me, if I had questions. She had children to attend. I said, 'Any one I can understand, Mam.' She stood, we stood, and, "Pietro, come here!" Roll yourn eyes at this as a boy 'tween Akabar and Angelo, come over. Words from her to him, I asked 4 questions.

Yes, Hernandez was Port Master, or close enough for me to understand. I asked if he was an honorable person. 'He a good person?' "Si!" Pietro words, with gestures, told me he didn't beat children with a stick, or something like that. He could count to 9. 10 was, "Dias." Close enough. Last was, 'What do you think of Sister Catherine?' Boy was in love, "Angelica."

That boy was like a feral cat lookin for a meal. Up that street, turned right, left, down to street, left, right, and we found the market street. Spanish, French, English words to all around. His hand passed over a fruit stand and an older lady about hit him with her long stick. Pietro talked as I put a copper to her hand. She picked out the 4 smallest ones to our hands. I couldn't shut him up, even eatin. 'Pietro, damage.'

Now, the 'Refreshment' places were 'tween the road and the water. Four that I remembered. The first one, closest to the pier, was burned posts in the air and charred wood around. I recognized the iron grill, toward the back, and some barrel hoops. We went to the second. Half of the 8 feet by 8 feet place was burned. The roof fell and smashed the tables flat. The third place looked like someone tried to pry it apart. Oh, posts broken, roof tilted to the floor boards in the front.

That 4th place looked funny. No, fire damage. The roof was there. From the front, saw place was tilted, some degrees. Pietro translated the words me mind had to think about. “Seniors, bla, bla, Casa, Finito, Centavos, Buenos Noaches, no, no mass.” That was about what I understood. It owner tried to close up the place but the sailors wanted to drink more.

Further up, round the corner, and some, was that quiet place I go to. We sat at table, a Liberty to table, and I order, ‘Fruitos Wine.’ I point to Pietro and, ‘Fruitos.’ It is 1 centavo per wood mugs. I put me pocket tablet, pencil to Hernandez, and said, ‘Damage, cost.’ I point to where we came from with, ‘Uno, Dos, Tress, Quattro.’ Pietro gave me a look and, ‘Cinco, Siete, Ocho, Nueva, ten,’ and I got his smile.

Hernandez wrote real nice. Total, 2000 centavos. Drinks done, I ordered another round. I asked Pietro about the, ‘Hand carts.’ He did hand motions. “Si! Two!” Another 100 centavos. I asked about, and had to grab a pole, right there, and boards, with hands to table. I pointed to the nails. Pietro and him jabbered to no end. Poles and boards, “Si! No iron, Why no fix.”

The next jabber was thumb to fingers. Ah, money. Came jabber and, “Centavos now, workers manyana.” That meant tomorrow. I went to the privy, back and opened me hand to a 5 dollar gold piece, 2, two dollar ones, and a Silver dollar to Hernandez. That got looks.

‘Pietro, can the wood be delivered by,’ hand motion, ‘2 today?’ Words around and, ‘1100 centavos to Mr. Hernandez hand by 2, today,’ to words. ‘I bring men. I bring iron. I need the owner there to watch the work.’ I stood and put out my hand, to looks. I got a hand shake from both. Word ‘tween them and Pietro says, “He says you are bravado or estupido to carry such centavos, Senior.” I open me jacket and put the 4 inch knife to the table with me left. Came that marlin spike from the right one. Pietro crossed himself. ‘2, by the church clock, Senior.’

From my jacket I gave Pietro a large copper coin. ‘Tell your Angel I need you at the pier by 2. I’ll talk to her this afternoon.’ The coin and Angel, both, got his smile and gone.

Walbeck was in a hurry to get to that pier 'afore 2, in his gig, with Purser Hitcock. We tied up on the South side as 2 barges had Chips, Armoror, Bos'n Gaston and men to look like shore boarding party. There was mallets, saws, axes, and stuff Chips said to bring. Wagner and Burch already knew where to go. Pietro was in that place to see Mr. Hitcock count out that 1100. He handed over 7 Silver dollars, and some in Liberty's, 10 cents coins. The rest was in large copper coins. Done, I sent Pietro to supervise and translate.

Walbeck and me walked down that street to that church and hats off to, 'Sister Catherine, Captain Walbeck.' They walked, talked, and came back. I got her hand in me left one the right over hers. I closed her hand and thanked her for Pietro.

Back to the Establishments we found burned place was cleared off, and stakes where the poles were to go. The Merchant sat to hogs head of nails. The next place was stripped of planks with poles goin up. The third had planks off, some, and Mr. McGraw, ah, givin instructions with Pietro aside him. The last place, the tilted place, Bos'n Gaston had, "found a horse, Captain." Their ropes was rigged to tug chains and they was just leanin forward. There was no need for us to be there so I took him down the street to me quiet place.

The waiter got a Liberty to table and came wood mugs of wine and fruitos. 'What did you and Sister Catherine talk of, Captain.' Oh, that got eyes to me. He gave kind words of her. Then, hard, "$30 to repair shacks, QMC! $30!" I said, 'A good will gesture to the venders and town, Captain.' He didn't like me grin. "And, Now why Captain, QMC?" 'Seems you now care about your crew, Captain.'

It was about 3 PM and the 4th establishment was square with smoke from the grill. The Owner was at the bar of boards over two barrels. Oh, handshakes around and words to Walbeck. The crew was off, workin on the other places. The next place was in order by 4 or so. The Owner was pleased with the place. Like the other, there was benches to sit at, roof over, and a bar on barrels. He offered a drink. Me fingers said small one. They serve out some strong stuff.

Third place was OK. There was more ships hands that space for. Mr. Chip's mates were directing activity. Pietro had learned a lot of bad English by now. I just hoped he never said it to Sister Catherine. I told some to return to the ship for the next phase.

The last place was a work in progress. Chips, Armoror, and was Bos'n directin work. Again, more hands than space. I sorted out those required and sent them back to ship. I set Walbeck to a barrel across the road.

5:15, by me watch, come a line of sailors with pails down the street. The benches on the last place was up and pails to thems. More pails and sailors go by, up to next place, and next. The ship's crew not workin took up a wood plate, and woofed down some food, drink from a hogs head of water, and back to Mr. Chips, Armoror, Bos'n orders. I ain't sayin of the water quality.

Next I know I we got Mr. Hernandez aside us. The Church bell quarter hour strike of 5:45. I took him and Walbeck on a tour of the work. The burned place had 4 men poundin nails to each side. The roof was comin along. Next place, half burned, had some finishin up to do. The third had a fire in the grill. We sat and the owner give a little cup of drank, and so to the next. Mr. Hernandez says some words we got little cup. He said some words I could make out. But, he was sure smilin, along with that owner.

The hammerin stopped and we get Pietro, excited, to take us to that first place. Mr. Chips, Bos'n Gaston, and Armoror were in front of it. The Owner gave words to Hernandez and he shakes hands around, with words to Pietro. It translated, "Liberty, good!" The Captain just sent the crew to ship to stow the equipment. They needed to wash up. "Bos'n, a round of ship grog, when done. Another round at 9PM."

The next morning, 19 May, a boat alongside with Mr. Hernandez and into Captain cabin with them ships officers. Out, salutes, gone, From Gaston came, "Dignitaries at 10." Most crew had worshed last night. There was still had uniforms to brush, shoes to shine, and such.

A boat pulled off that pier and I told Gaston to rig a chair, 'For a Lady!' Ya couldn't miss that white outfit. It was sure a scamper of bodies, lines to halyards, and a proper seat. Mr. Hernandez come up the side real good, usin the man ropes, with seaman in gloves to attend. The Mayor, Mr. Mendoza got the same. Three seamen went into to that boat to get her seated proper and up come Sister Catherine. It was three hands to bring her aboard and set her feet, proper. The dignitaries, and her, our officers, went into Captain cabin. The crew was at General Quarters.

I was in full regalia at mid Poop rail. The guests was ushered up the ladder to me place. I called the crew aft, right below, to hear his words. Well, the Mayor gave words, which Sister Catherine interpreted. That woman had a voice, probably from heardin children around that church. The Mayor said some nice long words, she may have added some to or not.

Speech over, I got to take her arm, to help her down the ladder, to the chair. She lifted that gauntlet and whispered, "I thought you were more than a common sailor, gentile, concerned for your men, gracious in your gift. Are you a Knight?" I point to me flag, Starboard side, aft. "My blood is from a Scottish Highlander, Norman, from Mary Stuart, Queen of Scots.'

20 May, we skipped make and mend day as crew was ashore. I went ashore in the afternoon and after supper for the crew as I had to remind the venders to only give out 1 free drink. I reminded all to pay for drinks. I was the only Shore Patrol ashore. Shush. I inspect each place, and then stopped at me quiet place, for just a short drink, and back to inspect. No, there were no problems there.

23 May and found that New Frigate in Trujillo Bay. It was anchored a bit far in, for me. The beach benches are deserted and no smoke from the grills. I could think what happened. Walbeck and Hitcock went over and back quick. Our holds come open to flower, peas, beef, and pork barrels over the side to her barges. Then came beans and pickled cabbage. It hadn't stopped in Cartagena as yet. Barges aboard and left them there. Walbeck was real sharp with his orders.

29 May we was in Cartagena. Me and Hitcock to the Port Master and Silver dollar. The 'Hablas' guy a Liberty. I took a day to on load that stuff. No liberty. Into the Caribbean and there is that next Frigate. Captain and Hitcock must have cooled down as it got some of those greens from Cartagena, along with barrels of cabbage.

01 June and was the 3rd Frigate off Caracas. Well, the harbor town 5 miles south of it. Walbeck warned Engle he might have supper aboard that ship. Good, as he took to the Port side to, ah, return. No mind to me. I was in the Chart Room for that thing.

Made it here, Barbados, 08 June, 1897. You like dates. The Frigate just left, ago. Brits only want one ship in at a time as it is a small town. I saw Maggie for news, last night. The Packet is in so, Thank you and MaMa for the letters. I got one from Carrie, Vie, and Effie. I did a quick read and need to reread thems. I need to talk to Saltsgiver. Eva, his wife, was mentioned. You women seem to talk and write in circles. No dates was given. There was some afternoon socials mentioned and some evening event or stuff. Vie mentioned Rose. Effie? "See money spent."

Oh, the Captain and $30. That was Bobbit fault. He can't add. Hernandez put figures to me tablet and lined up the 50 centavos wrong. Looked like 500. Bobbit added up the cost to 3100. The paper said ship had to pay 1100, which Hitcock gave Hernandez. I got what I paid Hernandez and, Bobbit math, what Walbeck signed for. I put 1, 3 dollar gold, and 3, 2 dollar gold coins to Sister Catharine hand, closed. There was 2 dollar left over for me expenses.

Now, Hitcock gave me bad looks at them figures and asked how I came up with "10 Dollars" to give the Harbor Master, originally. Shush. He can't add neither. It was 8 dollars. I have that secret funds place. Right there, from my secret place, I placed 3, 2 dollar gold pieces on that table. Me Gold coins came back and what he paid out went to that same hidin place.

Oh, Sister Catherine about made her water when she opened her hand. 'This is money, above that I gave, to start the repairs. I thought, just maybe, you could put it to a good cause, Sister Catherine.' I gave her a bow and went to see about me Captain and crew. Uncle Curtis was there in me thoughts. "Be gracious to those in need. A copper to Davy Jones log might come in handy, in case ya can't get into Heaven by the front door." His wink and, "Go around them Pearly Gates to his door. He just might let a good sailor in, Laddie."

One more roundy and to Norfolk. I'm supposed to take leave when we return. I know how that goes. 4000 miles, days, and someone changes thems minds.

By Your Leave, Missy,

An Old Sea Dog,

IN THE YEAR 1897, 12 JULY: CARIBBEAN

Dear Miss Judith,

We left Barbados, "One the Tide," as Walbeck requested, the morning of 10 June. Our last round and maybe leave home to see you and MaMa. I left it to Joseph and Donahey to decide the time. The officer had a night of it with the Governor and the crew did it up right at Maggie place. The Packet crew left with me letter to you. Nice guys. I bought them a round.

14 June, we had to stop in Ponce for water as the crew was getting to smell. Walbeck noticed, on his tours of the deck. He can call names to men real good. The 17th came a call from the lookout. "Frigate on the horizon. It looks not good!" General Quarters, "Boarding Party, Guns OUT!" It was just afore that Windward Channel off Haiti. Hull up I saw boats over the side. Closer and men was workin on the fore, mid, aft main chains. That is the ropes that hold the masts in place. Commander, 1st Lieuy, Clark, and Bos'n Gaston to Captain.

Gunner and me at the bulwark, he goes over the damage. "Not Spanish. 9 pounders, real close. It meant to take out the masts and board, but forgot them 4 foot thick hemlock masts can stand on their own." Round that Smokin lamp Engle passed on what he heard, from Walbeck desk.

It seemed a "Spanish" ship put up signal for assistance of some kind. The Frigate Captain slowed, to see what they needed. "Proper signals, and all, so it didn't go to Quarters. It come along side, tarps off guns, the deck ports opened, and shot its 6 balls." The Frigate turned to Starboard, the Pirate to Port. Its aft chasers shot out the Captain winders. The Pirate Larboard side shot six more balls down the Starboard side and ran off. I guess thems thought it was us! That Frigate went to Trujillo for repairs.

Gunner and me went over this action in me room, on that Chart Table. No General Quarters was not set was not good. We replayed this and give eyes to each other. I told him why I always kept the Spanker Sail, the one over me head at the wheel, neutral to the wind, not pushin either way. I said, 'They should have been at Quarters and turned broadside at 500 yards.'

'Tween there and Cozumel, Gunner sure had a grin, what with the smoke from them guns. The men like the noise, smoke, and hearin if they hit close to the barrels. Boarding Party practice, after, is more personal. We have rules and not don't tryin to hack each other to pieces.

Mornin of 20 Jun, gig, with me and Mr. Donahey, went to that pier in Cozumel. We was in dress uniforms, into Harbor Mast place to only Mr. Garcia. No, he couldn't say about liberty and just no to any words I said. Mr. Hernandez arm motions said, "Around." I told Mr. Donahey to stay and wait for him. I asked about Sister Catherine to a hand up, 'Gracious.'

I went to the Church. The little benches to the left was deserted. Over to the right, under a tree, is a bench with 3 nuns seated and one standin, with a book, head down. I walk a ways, her head come up, I stop, and 6 eyes to her. Head down, 6 eyes to me walkin. I stopped, their eyes went to her. I got to about 10 feet from her and the book closed, words to thems, and Sister Catherine turned to me.

'A teacher has eyes in the back of her head.' Came, "I can see eyes moving, to behind me." Me hand out, her name and get, "Sir Knight." Oh, I had to point to me shoulder badge, explained it and, 'Just QMC, Mam.' I said I had 10 men, 'who would like to do Confession and Communion, Sister.' I got, "And you, QMC?" 'We are here only for 3 days. Your Priest may not want to sit for that time.' Came good eyes and a laugh. "No bread or wine unless you confess first, ah, QMC."

She put out a hand and, "Perhaps you would like to view the Church, inside?" I point to the crossed swords, said its meaning and, 'I wouldn't like to disturb the quiet and holiness of you church. God may shake,' givin a movin hand, 'it, being displeased with my presents.' From somewhere she pulled out a vile and askes for me hands. Cork off, dipped a finger, she crossed both me palms. Well, I looked at her and said, 'So, now my hands are cleansed of sins?' I got a nice laugh and, "No, palm oil. Your hands are rough and dry. Please rub them together, QMC."

"Come." She must use that palm oil a lot as she has soft hands. Into the church, she kneeled, did her hand cross, stood, finger to water and onto me forehead also, a smile, "Temporary blessing, so God does not disturb us."

I got the grand tour. Father Ricardo was out visitin the sick and injured. It is not a big place nor a small one. Sunday it was and the noon service mentioned. This was well afore that time. I mentioned crew lunch time. "Father Ricardo has a small service at 4 for workers."

It was like leadin men to be hanged. They asked for it. Sister Catherine led them in the door. They knew the ritual of kneel and water. She crossed to me forehead. No need to tempt fate. 10 sat at a bench, her hand to each, to this booth. Each went in, come out and quietly to that bench. I never seen their hands so quick to cross themselves!

The sailor were 10 times better dressed than the workers. A poor lot in life they had, I figured. A small biscuit to mouth, sip of the cup, down the aisle, and water to crossin themselves. Sister got me hand, I got more water across me forehead and out the door we went.

Them sailors ran off like the devil was ahind them. That or they were goin for refreshments. I caught up her hand in me left, put right across it, and closed hers. She didn't open it and I got, "You do know you can't buy your way into heaven, QMC." She didn't like me laughin at that. I set her to that bench, under that tree, still snickerin, and told her that tale Uncle Curtis said about a back gate to heaven. Davy Jones, "Checkin your log book, Laddie! Good dead, a copper entered, in case you need entry fee."

Well, she had to laugh at that. 'His Sailor Tales, Sister.' I mentioned MaMa and her starchin his shorts, maybe, cause of some of his stories. I mentioned Oxe Tail soup and some of my own ventures. I got her finger to that scar, eyes, a soft hand to mine and, "The Sisters and I will offer a prayer for your safe journey, Sir Knight."

No trouble there in Cozumel. Mates took mates back. They was their hand built places. I did rounds and to me hidey hole, now occupied by them 4 readers, and some quiet others. I did a walk through the market place. For 5 coppers I got a big bag of this fruit.

Not peach, not plum. It has a sweet, odd taste. I gave it to them out to those at the hidy hole.

We left there on the 23rd of June, goin South. There was a nice wind but that current 'tween Mexico and the island about kept us back. Oh, I had me speed and current lines over to measuring it. Past the island, both back to normal. The 24th was make and mend day as it rained all day. Cloths got worshed in that nice water. It was warm, sailors no pride, ah, well, I just had to laugh at thems. They got a body worsh and cloths at the same time.

25 June we found that Frigate in Trujillo, fires to grills, and sailors around. Commander, Purser to Captain. Barges over the side, lines to halyards, and as requested went over. I noticed the Frigate Captain winders were being worked on. His Armoror set up a forge thing on the beach with an iron table there. When I went to get a samich and drink I saw his iron barrel to forge and sand loaded to it. He was tryin to make glass. The Blacksmith I worked for, back when, could make some glass stuff. I helped him some. Not me nose to get into this.

1 July and we anchored off Cartagena. Hitcock and me, his assistant, as ya know, went in with his list to the same Harbor Master and Habla guy. I be about learnin this Spanish, for each port. It differs in each place. It took time to on load it all. No, no liberty. The barge crew could get some refreshment, there at the pier. A new crew to each barge. We left on 2 July.

Two days out, 4th of July, we met that Bad Frigate. The one that tore up Cozumel. They got lots of beans, them barrels of cabbage, and normal stuff. That Captain was all over the deck with bad words. Even I could hear his stuff. The officers scampered to places and the crew was mostly in the masts. No, not me place to comment on this.

We anchored off Barbados, 8 July, 1897. I took them letters over for Mattie to read. Bein a woman, I needed her as translator. She read thrice and still had no clear idea of what went on. I gave her a Silver liberty for drinks and one for her readin.

I had to explain how Regina introduced me to Carrie. She was not lookin for a husband, her words, and me a sailor. Understood. Effie, her mother, was the mercantile owner. OK. She met Mr. Miller and they married. Regina introduced me to Vie and Rose a friend.

Vie, me went overnight to her home in Portsmouth. We, all got to Colley Street for that evenin with Carrie, as you know. 'So, translate.'

There was no good news from her. Carrie invited Vie to her, "Social. Eva," Saltsgiver wife, "was her companion." Effie provided the cloths. "Another evening social and Rose was her escort. Effie provided the cloths." My money. "Carrie likes her and convinced Vie to accept a male escort, of no name, or names, QMC." Me mind said she could do much better than me. I told Effie to take care of her needs. It might get some coppers to me log, if I need to see Davy Jones at that back gate.

12 July, on Mr. Walbeck tide, we left there for home. Time and tide were no matter to me. Fair East winds took us through them islands of Lucia and St. Vincent. Ya could hardly see thems from the top masts.

We on loaded water in Ponce, 16 July. Fine water to seep that salt meat in and the crew to worsh in. I suggested we take the channel 'tween there and Dominican Republic. The Packet crew give words to me ears. Walbeck wanted to take the, "Wind Ward Channel."

It was the 14th and the lookout said of a Spanish Frigate ahind us. No pennant to the Main mast. I heard that and be at the Poop Chart table. It gave a gun to us as the signal Middie said, "Request Assistance." Well, Walbeck come to that Taft rail and lookin. Hull up, the next gun was toward us. I send Hood and Burch to find the Gunner and Bos'n. I ain't gonna have no "Parley" on me poop! I jinx the ship to wakes them up. I got Walbeck eyes and just pointed to Gunner. Walbeck called for, "General Quarters, Boarding Party, Tampions off, Guns out on my order."

That ship come to 500 yards and another gun. Even the lookout yelled, "Ain't Spanish, Captain." Walbeck looks at 1st Lieuy and I heard, "Guns out! Port Helm!" I threw Hood from the helm indicator. Left gauntlet to indicator and right one in the air.

Me and Walbeck had been through this times past. Spanker was to Starboard, for East, some North wind. I close that fist and point to Starboard!

The stupid ship fired their forward 4 pounders about then. Walbeck privy got that Starboard hit. The other missed. Walbeck jumped when our two Aft 9 pounder went off. They jumped his order to fire. Eyes to him and, "Hard to Starboard. Fire as she bears!"

Two stakes higher, rudder and spanker sure pushed Shenandoah around quick. Number 9 and 11 spoke. 5 and 7 fired. 1, 3, and, 9 and 11 again. The other ship was slow to her Port. There was more to their guns than to sail. We got two shots wide from her Starboard Side. Our forward chasers sure put canister to her mid. I saw the puffs of smoke.

Our Port guns only spoke once as we was turnin fast. The Aft chasers got in the last word of this. They fired three more times at that ship till it was out of good range. There were only shots to its hull, as I saw. Her sails not harmed, 'cept for the canisters, so we couldn't catch it. "Helm to mid, resume course, QMC."

Gunner Campbell came into me room and we talked of this. We had to laugh as aft 9 pounders took offence at the other ship firin at thems. He, nor I, saw any wild shots. The crew got a bit, a bit of extra rum to grog after evenin meal. He gave me a wink with it to me mug. Action time? Not 10 minutes, by the ships log.

The Pirate was just slow in that turn to Port. 1st Lieuy and Bos'n whistle let fly the sails. It? The crew was at their guns. The wind about didn't help it come around. It lost time and speed. That is why them balls or bolts sure smacked its side. It was good we started that fight at its maximum range.

I sat at that table and remembered Campbell settin up the ships gun, back at the Sultan place. He had that Range thing to us waving from that wall. There was some uphill to there. I saw his calculations to that. He was like Uncle Curtis and the sun. Gunner, he gave me a wink and, "It should be over your heads, QM1." I gave him eyes then. The next he said was, "Else, you and Admiral will only hear the boom!" There was no need for me to duck. I stood to that fire. Campbell was always good at his work. 500 yards and the guns was dead on.

Morning of 18 July and the lookout shouts down of, "Two masts, no sails on the horizon!" Oh, we set General Quarters to this. Come a time and we see smoke from it. Fire! Comes the time and I recognize this thing. An iron ship. The smoke was from the funnels and boilers under. It was just as ugly as that Maine. USS Brooklyn,

Armored Cruiser. Only Gunner Campbell saw a lovely thing there. I saw a Commodore pennant aft. Through a glass and there was a little Big M flag forward. Strange, it was.

A gun to lee and the flags said Captain and officers to this thing. I request to go over and give this Commodore me personal flag, our first meeting and all. I was allowed only me sword. I took QM3 Joseph as 'Aide de Camp.' Him to carry the ships and me little flag. A protocol thing. We took a barge, 12 to row, to this ship, and iron gang way, up some steps to the Main Deck. We went forward, with not much room to walk, to that reception line. I gave a nice salute to that Lieutenant at the end.

We got ushered into officers dining room. The new term for Gunner Mess is Wardroom, as I learned. Walbeck introduced himself and his officers to this guy in white uniform sittin at a table. Last, I step up and Walbeck said who I am. That got bad eyes from this Commodore Cook. He gave words to Captain and the Commanders aside him. Walbeck mentions me being "Appointed Master at Arms," and got no further. This guy just spit out bad words and, "Armed, Enlisted in Officer Quarters. I Never Heard Of Such Actions!" His next words was, "Out, and take your," whispers to his left guy, "What the," bad words, "does he need with Aide de Camp? Is this a joke on me? I'll not have it! Out, I say. I have enough here for a Court Martial, I do!"

Out, I took Joseph and set him to a pair of short bollards. They use them to put lines to a shore pier. The boy was green, red, white, and not breathin real good. My foot to the other, I leaned down and said, 'Ol Uncle Curtis once told me, it was best to walk into a new situation like ya was naked.' I got his eyes. 'Be proud of what you got to show.' He didn't know to laugh or cry, but breathed better.

'Ahind me was real bad words to Joseph butt to that bright work. My shoe, on the other, was criminal offence. Have me to a grate, "Oh, I will." I had the sword turned so to be comfortable, which he couldn't see. Around, right hand to hilt, left to that bird cage and say, 'Chief, first and last from your mouth, BM1!' Now he looked like Joseph did.

I took a person card from me jacket, 'nother required expense, put Pencil and words on its back, and handed it over with, 'If you have a Chief aboard, to his hand. If not, to Admiral Forest, BM1.' I grab up Joseph and we saluted this guy at the gang way. He said I had to, "Ask My Permission!" I said, 'Not a ship ya be thrown off, Ensign!' I told Wagner, at the helm, to shove off. I got his eyes and, "Captain?" I gave him a finger and to ship and sent him back to that iron thing for them officers.

I went up the Main Mast chains to first landin. It gives ya a good view. It was like someone hit a hornet nest on that ship. Men runnin all around that iron deck. A gig hit the water, men to it, to that gangway, and down come, not an officer. I yell to the deck to receive that boat. No, no Marine line. He came up the side like born to it and came up the chains the same way. I just stood there, lookin around. "First QM I seen up a mast." A Chief Bos'n mate.

His talk did a nice dance around the Commodore and BM1. "BM1 likes his bright work clean, QMC." I asked, 'Who sent you?' He danced around with his words till "Commodore sends has regards and would be, ah, will receive you proper, QMC." Down the mast, I went to our Armoror. BMC gave words to him. No, I was not allowed arm protectors nor gauntlets. Sword and pistol, but no cartridges. Joseph only went cause I said I'd have him stripped naked, cuffed, and taken with me.

We took his gig to that iron thing and BMC went up the gang way first. Someone must have starched that Ensign skivvies, for how straight he saluted us. Down that narrow side to 6 Marines to a side and just whistles, romp and stomp, to Commander returnin me salute, and his hand motion to this place. Commodore in front, Walbeck and ships officers ahind him, as I seen. Joseph give this guy a ships flag first, to our salutes. Joseph pull out me flag, unrolls it, and rolls it to his hand. 'Course, I have to do that sword salute and all. Them officers all went away, somewhere. BMC caught up me and Joseph to a hatch, ladder down, to the crew mess, I figure, by the looks. We got set at table.

A Steward in white come and placed plates, napkins, and silverware to us. A voice from Davy Jones locker come to me ears. I put a hand to Joseph arm, so he don't run off. Oh, words from long ago, not good, was toward me character. Joseph was about to stand when I gave him a finger to stay seated. Him stood at the table and gave, "You should stand, in the presents of an officer. Both of you." I said, 'We would, Mr. Forest, but, you aren't here.' I looked at Joseph and said, 'Only a little,' and did fingers thing to him, 'flag to the foremast.' Yes, we stood then.

Joseph stifled a laugh. Forest took that seat and gave bad eyes to me and his finger to, "Sit!" His hand went up and came a Steward with Plum Duff. Next, he set a wood mug to table. It was good duff and, oh, good grog. Forest gave a hand to Joseph, but I said, 'Aide de Camp, Admiral. Speak freely, Sir.'

He asked about MaMa. I mentioned Alfa, Curtis wife, has passed. It was just old sailor talk, to Joseph wide eyes. Smith would make Admiral, but, like Irwin, shore only. A sad thought. I mentioned this cruise and Cozumel. 'Captain Walbeck is comin along, Admiral.' I said of the short action with the Pirate that shot up, 'Your Frigate, Admiral.' I gave a small action report, 'Second hand, Admiral.' Came, "And yours, QMC?" there was not much to say, 'We were ready for them and gave it two sides of guns.' We had just some small talk and he mentioned iron ships, twice.

No, no Pirate ships in that big bay of Haiti. 'Afore mid watch, at the helm, a nice wind to Nassau, and got Walbeck over that barrel. A larboard lean, stop to the ships wheel and, "Just who are you, QMC, to know Admiral Forest, personal?" I said, 'Former, Monongahela Captain, Commander. You should read my personal file.' Came, "Not Captain, Ships Master?" I said, 'You hesitated, with that ship. Then, you didn't look to the spanker sail for you call.' His mouth moved I said, 'But you did well, Captain.'

I end this to you, 22 July, from Nassau. The Packet is here to get this to you quicker. Hope to see you soon.

By Your Leave, Missy,

An Old Sea Dog,

IN THE YEAR 1897, 06 SEPTEMBER: SQUADRON

Dear Miss Judith,

30 August, 1897, here at me desk in Admiral Office. I've been back a week. Rishell uses the one in the Lieutenant building. I just got done signin up for 1 year and fingered down those 15 lines, 'memberin times past. I need to catch ya up on stuff here. There was not enough time to tell this to ya 'afore.

We arrived in Norfolk the morning of 30 July, 1897. The jackass tugs put us to that South pier. Aside me volunteers, I saw new Commodore, Adjutant Captain, and Lieutenant come aboard. Forest warned me of this. Irwin retired. Into Walbeck cabin they went for some time, out, and to that pier. Saltsgiver gave Nichol the list, to me. Walbeck gave good words to us. The Squadron Lieutenant office was a mess and the two clerks overwhelmed by the volunteers. I finger shooed them away and set Rishell to that desk. Medicals logged in and papers for me. I signed as Ships Master, so they could catch the barge to the hospital. There was still words from the men. That new Lieutenant came out and gave them some bad words. Saltsgiver snatched him up and into that room they went.

The Clerks didn't know if there was room in the barracks. I signed a paper to get meals for 14 Marines and me 16 volunteers and had Nichol take them to the Marine tent I saw was still up. Me, Burch, and Wagner went to the barracks to see about men and rooms for us. The BM2 had turned them back into storage areas. His log said he had plenty of bunks. Burch gathered up the volunteers. I needed one room for Rishell also and gave orders for things to take care of.

Out the gate and I set an appointment to see Mr. Bish, Me agent. Effie gave words to me ears and another circle talk. Hand Up, 'Money owed?' It was 10 dollars, above the 5 I gave her afore. Regina was not home so went to see Ella about tonight crew visit. I got a quick drink to hand. "Sailors always welcome, QMC." I was gonna ask about Vie, but figured I'd another circle of words.

I got back to squadron office and order had been restored, by Rishell. The clerks was two Church mice at desks. We went to the barracks and he got ushered by BM2 to his room, the same as he left it. It had a clean smell. Oh, I saw me room and had to go down to me crew and thank thems for the effort and said about Ella place, 'After you had a nice meal.' Agreed!

Sargent Nichol, Corporal Waltermire and Kenwood, 6 Marines to front and back, lead me motley crew to Ella place. Yes, Engle amongst thems. Rishell went to see Rose. Oh, they did it up right, they did. It cost me a pretty penny. Money? Shush. Chief pay is good. I get a little extra for that Master at Arms pin. Designated Ships Master is another extra. If I show that paper a lot of commercial ships would offer me more money. Nope, no Vie. The Marines got some drinks also. They are about me crew.

Saturday, all days, BM1, GM1, Rishell run squadron. Commodore clerks came up with a little table and chair for me to set in. Lt. Olson, Adjutant Captain Serger, and the Commodore was not around. Mr. Bish went over his books. There was nice figures in me and Edith accounts. A collector said he'd pay me $50 for the knife. No! I didn't need flags, but stopped by Carrie place anyway. The local ship, Fran, wasn't in so I knew Bothel was out. I got a hug and cheek kiss from Mattie. Carrie was not there. She said to bring food for supper, "And, bring them two scoundrels with you."

Cora was there for Wagner and Margaret for Burch. Mattie saw thems some while we was in the Caribbean. It was a nice chatty evening. They liked my stories of Sister Catherine. BM1 and GM1 could do best at that Pirate ship shoot.

Monday, 2 August, yep, the day afore I took leave, I got called into Lt. Olson office. He had two papers to desk and a pen atween. Re-enlist and leave granted. "or, no leave, QMC. Commodore order." I asked for a, 'moment. I need Rishell as a witness, Lt.' that boy caught up me two service jackets, that legal brief from afore, and to his side. Rishell speaks those legal terms. It was some time for him to go page by page through that Blue jacket. Olson checkin off them items to that legal brief.

Oh, I got to see Commodore Griffith and Adjutant Captain Serger. He was seated at that table. Rishell gave them same words to him, me affront. The Adjutant just give whispers to Commodore ear.

Rishell pointed out the, "Coercion, threats, denial," words and read, "The Giver, his mother, presents is required, Sir."

I may have set him off, next, by presenting the volunteer list and receipt for our welcome home at Ella place. He never heard of this. "Denied." Rishell gave them legal terms and, "Admiralty laws. Signed by Admiral Irwin." His hand shooed us out, leave papers signed, in me jacket, and Rishell paid me Ella bill. I was back to flush with cash. A dollar a head, shush, plus the Marines.

I remembered that stinking train ride home and back. Day, night, and next day, both ways. I sent a Telly to MaMa to just meet me at that station at home. Ya can't tell MaMa nothing. She met me at Ebensburg. She sent me off, back here, from the same place. I had a full dress uniform to change into, after worshin up there.

The first night, 4 August, was family supper night. It about wore me out watchin the young ones run around. Even me bad hears didn't save me. The little girls are the apple of PaPa eyes. MaMa spoils the boys. All went quiet by sundown. They left! I had a chance to tell some stories. Oh, funny ones. I skipped over the rough stuff, like MaMa did, tellin PaPa about that Lieutenant at Cresson, long ago.

You, my dear, were my surprise worth goin home for. You are lookin just lovely and all grown up. You seemed to have glossed over having a bow! A quiet one he was. A bit stiff, or maybe because I was there in my full regalia. He kept lookin at the arm guards and them gauntlets. I thought he was gonna run off when I pull out that sword. It does make a sharp sound commin out. Now you, he had big eyes to as you flashed it around. It would be a bit heavy for you to use. The blade has been reduced some and Armoror made the bird cage handle to balance it out.

Saturday afternoon, 7 August, PaPa and me went to visit 'The Hooligans,' as MaMa calls them. The men were busy in the fields and only two women were there that remembered Uncle Curtis. While cookin, worshin cloths, doin house stuff, they were polite, but had no time for me stories. The men came in for supper, ate, polite with a jug, and off to them fields. MaMa was surprised we were home afore dark. We had to dip in the trough anyway. Surprise! Church on Sunday. "You need to cleanse you soul," from MaMa.

We went early soes I could stand at the door to greet the members comin in. I shook hands to thems leavin, also. Yes, in dress uniform. No, no gauntlets or sword. The service ain't changed. That was about the only thing the same. I went with PaPa to the Blacksmith shop. He had lots of work, and a full time helper, besides PaPa. It was harvest time so PaPa went off to fix broken stuff.

I had to say Hi to the tanner. He had a helper. I wondered if I looked that young, back then. Oh, leather shop was a good smell to remember. He was tannin hides twice a week. I didn't mind that smell, back then. MaMa did. He asked about, "your Possible Bag?" I have it right here at this little desk, that has no drawers. I carry it daily, with writin stuff and the papers I need. Your letter is included.

As I shook everyone hands at church, MaMa took me visitin less than last here. She was also helpin Grandma next door with stuff. Grandma still makes them good sweet rolls. Worshin, cloths to line, ah, she be getting slow. Grandpa, as you know, is gone. With my Uncles in the fields, she needs some help. One of them Uncles need to marry one of them 'Sweet Hearts,' they visit on Sundays.

When PaPa came back afore noon, Saturday, 14 August, I loaded up that wagon with what MaMa said and we headed to that place down South. I needed pillow to the seat of the back bench. We got there about 3 to just Maggie, Nora, and a bunch of children around. The men were still in the fields. Horse, wagon, to barn, I took to a bench on the side porch. Nora brought a glass of lemonade. Shush. A pocket bottle from jacket wade it tasted better.

From around the corner come a line of youngins, strip to skivvies, who grabbed a towel from the basket and head to that pond. Them boys and girls was not 10, I suppose, and the dog was runnin around them. I am not good with ages. I was watchin me, years ago, Princess, and them boys headed to swim in the pond.

Came a time, Nora came out, yelled, and broke up the youngins tryin to drown each other. Oh, out, the littlest to oldest girl to tub, soap, and about drowned again to a towel over, to such laughter. Boys the same. It was memories of years gone by.

The wagons come from around about 5. There came saw horses and boards across for tables and benches set. Food came from wagons and the house to table. The men come from the fields and I saw

Princess father, Benjamin John. They called him Ben, BJ, Jay, and Jack around. He is as nice as ever to me hand shake. He had aged more than the 4 years, last I seen him. He loves them children. I saw sad eyes to him, from Nora.

After eats, the tables and benches got moved as the porch was full, like high seats in a theater. In full regalia, I took center of this and got to tell of me ventures. The sword and pistol got passed around to all, but youngins, to inspect. I did that Sultan trick to thems. Shush, I borrowed some blanks from Mr. Hardis. The youngins found some 3 foot, good size sticks, and I had some of the boys attack me. I had two sticks to their 1. Swift little bugger them was and lots of, "OOOh, AHHH," plus the some shrieks. Mostly, I tapped them on the head or gave a swat to butts. It was good practice, for me. They were unpredictable.

Afore sun down, all was packed up, and wagons to home. There was lots of waves till out of sight. Oh, I just sat on that porch rail and told my stories to BJ, Nora, MaMa and PaPa, drinkin that, Shush, lemonade. Oh, I had lots of stories. I mentioned Sister Catherine and crossed palms. The crew after confession. The vender places they fixed up.

Benjamin brought up sea battles. With me hands, I spoke of some of the short ones, like the last one, in the Caribbean. I mentioned a good crew, good officers, good training, and other ship get the most damage. They were a good audience, 'cept for MaMa. Oh, she laughed, snickered, and all. Her eyes had question, not asked. The sun went down and thems to bed. A pitcher of that lemonade not empty so, well, times afore to came to mind!

MaMa helpin Grandma, I did like Uncle Curtis and just did a walk about. The town was growin. No, I had to be back for lunch with Grandma, her, and the uncles. Supper was at home. It seems the 'Founding Fathers' met each night with me there. They liked me stories. I got MaMa eyes on leaving and especially returnin.

The 18th, Wednesday, MaMa and I shot her pistol to dirt that afternoon. My 45 was a bit much for her. A number 3 in 38 would do her good. A 3 inch barrel, I figured. I got a nice no. I dug out the lead and to pot over fire. Just her and me. When I was worshin in the trough, ah, she peaked.

Was high words to me ears from her. It went back to that enlistment contract and, luckily, her pistol was empty. "Scars!" It is hard to miss that those on me face and head, she didn't mention afore. She did now! Oh, the letter from the officers came up. Not to worry, I was fine. Vented, she did. She sat and mumbled till I said, 'Wuves ya.' I got better eyes and, "Best you write, true, to what is going on!"

She mention to PaPa about goin to Ebensburg, "on the 20th, to visit." She later told me, "No sense you being bored here." PaPa and me did it up right at the Founding Fathers meetings. No, watched him like one of me own and made it back home on his own. MaMa didn't like the sparkle in his eyes, either night. Got squinty eyes, I did.

Yes, 2nd best dress, umbrella, big purse, with pistol, and all, we took the afternoon train to Ebensburg. It was 2 hours of me mentionin places like Trujillo, Barbados, Bermuda, and Alfa antics. That got a tear to her, but also laughs. Gibraltar places, Toulon, that place in Cyprus we go to. Oldsters and youngins, movin bushes got good laughs.

I might just as well have dropped her off and headed to Cresson. There was children fussin on the porch and women tongues a waggin. No 'regalia' for the men. They sat under that tree like statues. Come morning of the 21st, MaMa kissed me on that scar and gave me bad eyes. I said, 'Wuves ya." I got a hard look and, "It is nice of them officers to say you are alive and well," with a kiss to me cheek. I hate that train ride.

Last week was quiet enough. Wagner said we was invited to Regina place, Wednesday, 25 August. Cora was there. Spritzer to glass, I went to the back porch swing and tipped a bottle to it. You can roll yourn eyes here. The door opened, closed, and shoes to me eyes. "I need a shot, QMC!" Yes, Vie. The whiskey must have straightened out her mind. She talked straight, in time. 'Course Carrie was in them. So was Robert Jr., Senior, and them wives I met.

I said Vie is a good lookin woman. They probably bet to see which of thems got a proper Bow for her. Eva, on the first invite as her escort to a social. Rose, Rose, again Eva, till she accepted to be taken by one of the men, now her Bow. I walked her home to a cheek kiss and, "Thank you, QMC."

Regina hasn't given up on me. Friday supper I was introduced to, "Nellie, but call me B, please." I gave my given name and, 'Everyone calls me QMC, if not bad words, B.' Brown hair, bad light for eyes, and about to me eyes in 2 inch heels. A nice smile and laugh. We got relegated to porch swing, "to get to know each other." She only took a small bit to spritzer.

She is a secretary to a warehouse manager. There are lots of ware houses around Lambert Point. It is a rail head place with lots of trains in and out. A small apartment, 2 trolley stops down, at a place called Wards Corner. I passed it to catch the ferry, to go home.

We did all day Saturday together. After Sunday lunch we got thrown out the door. The trolley down some, over, down Granby Street. B led the way. The place reminded me of that Park up in Philly. I never knew they had an animal zoo here. She had to have that shaved ice and syrup atop. It was a nice day and all. A cheek kiss at her building and I caught the trolley back.

Pick this up Monday, 6 September. Last week was a zoo. Carney, Fran and Bothel, Williams, with QM3 Mark, QM2 Potts came in Tuesday. 'Course, they threw off some and gave a list of needed men. I got back some, "Old Volunteers!" Rishell got to figure out if they counted to that first list. Bothel, Wagner, and Burch to figure out distribution. Lt. Olson just gave me looks.

2 September, Wednesday, into Griffith office, to a chair to sit at. He pushed over a thick envelope. A letter from Retired Admiral Irwin to, "Charles." A personal letter. He mentioned to pass this to me for, "Early Friday evening dinner." The invite said, "QMC and Mrs. Nellie B. Dips." I couldn't accept for her. I got his grin and a point to the bottom of the letter, I didn't read. She accepted, carriage to pick me up at the gate, and then her.

She led me up them stairs to, not a mansion, not a brown stone, like Robert Sr., but good sized. She went first to that line with lots of smiles and, "B, good to see you." She knew Irwin, wife, a hand to Robert Sr., wife, Robert Jr., and Carrie. A trap.

I was the Church mouse at that table of good food and wine. B was the center of it all. Blue gray eyes. I said a nice smile and laugh.

Into this other room, there was chairs for all but me. Irwin said, "Stories, QMC." Shush. I took a little bottle of olive oil and some glass crystals from the flower base, on the table. I was a thinkin mouse.

I told of walkin up to Sister Catherine so I brought up B for the hands out, open, close, head up, down. I had to speak both sides. The oil to her palms got her eyes and laughs. That water cross, 'Just in case.' Next was her hand in mine and them crystals from pocket to hers. I said them words, put her to seat, and told Uncle Curtis tale of gettin in heaven, to some groans.

I had to tell of first seein Alfa, Uncle Curtis wife. I brought up B for that also. Me hand to her head, squinty eyes, pretended to have that knife, and gave her words. I said about next there, men backin to the door, and what words I could remember, to laughs around.

This broke up to men on the back porch with good whiskey and cigars around. Irwin asked about USS Brooklyn and Commodore Cook. Oh, he laughed at that. I mentioned we didn't immediately stand to Forest as, 'just his little flag at the foremast.' I got, "One day, QMC, he'll hang you, for all the things you did or didn't do proper." I mentioned the wood plate and them flags to it, in that room. "You gave them to me, QMC."

I saw B Saturday and Sunday. She showed me around that Wards corner place. We ate at an Italian ristorante. Florina, in Sicily, cooked better. Room, shush, little nip. Mail this to you tomorrow, 6 September, 1897.

By Your Leave, Missy,

An Old Sea Dog,

IN THE YEAR 1897, 04 OCTOBER: SQUADRON

Dear Miss Judith,

Tuesday, 14 September, 1897, here at the table they say is me desk. A Packet came in from the Med with messages for Griffith. Shenandoah was to leave on the 30th. It seems the ship we were to relieve has a problem and stayed in Toulon extra time. Problems with the masts and hull as it ran into a storm. I weren't there.

Monday, 6 September, after your letter to mail, I got called into Lt. Olson about assignin men to Carry and Williams. 'Working on it, Sir.' I said I need to talk to the men and ship officers. The men was easy. Those thrown off I just told to pack sea bags and leave. I'd sent paperwork to DC like they'd never served. That got eyes.

One mentioned he was Able Bodied Seaman, catch up any commercial ship he wanted. I mentioned a civilian Master would have him throw overboard, 'First you light off your mouth, like you did to be there. That or the Captain. Come 4 PM muster, be hear, one last chance. Next time is Admiral Mast, Brig, out.' I scratched two from me list.

The ships Captains and officers got me words. I took exception to hands, sticks, or what not to men. I went in Dress uniform, Masters badge and crossed swords. I touched that silver pin and mentioned Lt. Lovelace. One officer said it took Admiral permission. 'I have a 3 star on that would love to see me perform, Sir. You choose what wood thing you want. I'll bring Belayin pins.' I got no takers.

Tuesday, the 7th, I was watchin the men workin at a pier, to just to walk around. Up comes a Surry with Irwin in it. I sat on a bollard so we be eyes to eyes. B was in his words. Her husband passed. He offered, accepted, for her to stay at his home, for a short time. She is an independent woman. He got her the job and apartment. He heard I was to come in, talked to Regina, to get B out, socialize. "Forest words about you might be true, but, I know you are an honorable man, QMC." I said I'd only be here a short time. That got a grin and, "That is the best part." He never said how or when the husband passed. I didn't ask.

Wednesday, the 8th, I got an invite to a Saturday afternoon social from Robert Sr. the weather here is nice, so to be an outside thing. It seems Vie and Bow decided to their make intentions know. No, to show they were a couple and could now hold hands and kiss, in public. I saw B that night, so had to ask about a dress. To Effie we went, as a "Semi-Formal" thing. Dress uniform for me, but, I needed to show her off. Irwin order. It about said so in that invite. But he couldn't sign orders to cover costs.

The reception line was Robert Sr. and wife, Clara, as hosts. Next was Frank and Elizabeth, Vie parents. Robert Jr. and Carrie and came Vie and Bow, Stewart S. Hamilton. It was on the card he gave me. He is a friend of Robert Jr. Oh, she was sure radiant standing next to him. He be my height, younger, and a bit stiff the occasion. Her dress? Stylish, light in color. Not as bright as her smile, holding his hand. There was delight in her eyes. Irwin and Agnes, his wife, were there as informal guests, like me.

B, ya ask. White frill blouse, Tan jacket, and matching skirt. Pearl necklace and earrings. A brimmed hat and a colored ribbon to match the skirt. I told Effie we weren't to make her above Vie. Bad manners. But, make B smile and that was a far as the men went. She turned many a young man head, bein just a charmer. Me? Oh, love havin B on me arm, the nice eyes I got, and her smile.

This started about 1 PM and out on the back yard. Hand food tables around so groups could nibble and get drinks. Me? Irwin, Agnes, and B just had to show me off to all the women. Names, handshakes, questions to answer, and it were like a Merry Go Round. The women took over the Go Round so Irwin and I got to sit at a bar. We watched as Agnes, Carrie, and Elizabeth introduced B to every young man there.

The lawn social broke up around 5 PM. No, we had to stay for early supper. The women "Freshened Up" and as men went to the porch for cigars, some good spirits, and pesterin me with questions. Come dinner, B and Agnes were in conversation. I sat next to each other women at the table. Vie and Steward sat across from me. He was a church mouse to this table. Vie and Elizabeth was like B and Agnes. Both groups kept pullin me into their talk.

Well, me and B got front seats to the other room. Irwin started it and B pipped in with, "Tell about Sister Catherine again." She played Sister. Next was, "Pietro," 'bravado or estupido.' That got me jacket open with knife and marlin spike passed around. Oh, some eyes I saw. Last Wednesday I was in a hurry and that 'Possible Bag' got B attention when I carried in the supper pails. 'Nother story. There was some new people so I told of Alfa and Edith. That lead to the boating officer and crew, about drowned, tryin to get to the ship. The officers was green, white, and throwin up. It was a good audience. I liked the good whiskey and cigars after.

In walks around B asked lots of me background. I got eyes when I mentioned MaMa putting that pistol to that Lt. desk. 'She was a bit mad at him.' A question finally came to her mouth as to why I never ask about her. 'Well, Uncle Curtis said,' and got hand to me mouth. Oh! I said Irwin had stopped by, at the pier, and mentioned stuff I already knew of her intelligent, independent, educated, and so on. 'Course, I had to mention nice voice, smile, eyes, and stuff. 'I am only here for a short while and enjoy every moment with you.' Oh, that got me good eyes.

20 September, 1897, I was at the Admiral table. The ship loadout started last week, on schedule, though we won't leave for some time. I got told to stay away. Good. It was wet and rainy outside. Oh, I have a rain coat. Those on the pier have Nor Easter gear to put on. The wagon drivers suffer the worst. Not paid well. Rishell begged off 'Counting Wagons,' as he was busy with papers. He shuffles thems to bins, took thems out, to another one. Watched him, I did. He don't like the rain. He likes that Liberty card come 5 PM, as he loves Rose.

B likes the Chinese place. I took her there after seein Effie. We tried to take it back to her place and it was cold by the time we got there. No, stove there. Her room is twice what Vie and Rose live in. A corner place with a sink and privy. Across the hall is the tub room. She tried to stuff lots into that place. Even a table for 4. A comfy place. Enough room for 2, hammocks to poles and I'd fill the place!

We have become the couple to invite to evening dinner and social. I got invite from Robert Jr. and Carrie for Friday. All were my age or so. A new group, so I got to tell old stories. I used B for Alfa and Sister Catherine, again. It seemed odd that the 4 couples was like brother and sister. Oh, I can take a hint. B loved the attention she got. Effie dressed her real good.

Saturday, the 18th, was an afternoon social, hosted by Irwin and Agnes. Hand food and a circle of women talkin. I thought B would get dizzy from roundy's and introduced to all. Robert Jr., Carrie, and I noted two couples, brother and sister, from Friday night, and more. It turned into an evenin social also, with a different group. B and me got caught up in the reception line. I gave up on 'memberin names. Irwin wanted to hear of some sea battles. I used B as the other ship. She was the "Show," so I showed her off. I'd whisper in her ear what do. I did hands and 'Boom' for guns. Irwin understood what was goin on. Most just watched B turn as I banger her.

Yesterday, Sunday, the 19th, it was formal at Robert Sr. place with 16 couples. Commodore Griffith signed them orders so I could get me pistol and got back the spent money. Me best uniform was showin wear from usage so got a brand new one. The stuff for B needed to be covered. A carriage costs some. Oh, told Effie 'B' was the 'Show,' for the evenin. Arm to mine from Effie place and I still had trouble with that sword and canvas bag. B looked at that pole and stand I had 'tween us. It was a 5 PM reception time.

Up them stairs we went to Robert Sr. and Clara gave eyes to us, B was in a stylish hat, ribbon for color, cape, and skirt to match me uniform. Pearl color of blouse, lace to neck, sapphire neckless, and earrings, like her eyes, when I rile her up. Carrie just opened her mouthed. B and me got to be next in greetin line. I ain't a woman or gent we greeted didn't say, "You look so lovely, B." I just loved her smile and eyes to me. I just stood there, greetin thems.

I seated B to Agnes so they could talk and watched. B got the eyes from the table people. I kept leanin back so they could see her. Oh, I just smiled through the dinner. B would glance at me smile. The men had only eyes to her.

Come show time and we be at the seats of honor, front. The Driver brought in the pole and stand, to the front. Robert Sr. said, "Story, QMC." From the canvas bag I dug out that bear claws neckless and gave it to B to hand around. I had B be Talig. She had to have her stoop down some, for his height, make a scowling face. Everyone laughed. I mentioned that first bear and us runnin off. Oh, the 6 foot crabs we ate got looks. I had to say how bad Talig kayak smelled and him in general.

I said about the beauty of the country, Talig boil, and how the smoke from the fire attracted deer and bears. That one bear just lookin at us, afore we shot it. When it came to me shootin that one with me pistol, a cartridge to went to B and passed around. I said about Dias, thinkin I was shootin him, and the shots. A 45-70 cartridge to B and hand around. I told of Talig tellin his family about, "Ruined the hide. Not good for gloves!" I got nice laughs. Male eyes was to B.

Into that canvas bag and I dug out the small Big M flag, to B, handed around. I explained Admiral Forest flag, and the Monongahela. Back, snapped to pole, came the Susquehanna red, white, blue with the snake. No, the yellow one is only for me to see. That Imitation Sultan flag got lots of words and looks. Then came the Shenandoah, modified St. Andrew, to B hands, back, snapped to place on the pole.

I pulled out me flag, to B. As she held it I explained the challenge gloves, like on the Shenandoah one, the crossed sword and carbine, used to shoot the bear. The scimitar on the bottom, ah, was a short story. I dug into that bag and brought out the Bey knife, to B hand. I opened me jacket and said if it got lost in the room, 'I'll use this one to find who has it!' It was a joke. They wanted to see both knives.

I got the arm protectors and gauntlet out and put them on B. Well, with her arms out straight, I got them on. She has shorter arms then mine. She gave me bad looks, but, all eyes were to her. The social over and the women got to try on the arm pieces and gauntlets. B got to swish me sword around. All the women did the same. I got a good nod from Robert Sr. Carrie still had to open and close those gauntlets, to me eyes. She ain't never gonna forgive me for not say no, to her husband. Maybe. You have our history in me letters.

28 September. Last week I talked to Griffith about shiftin QMS. Potts made 1st and needs a big ship assignment. Susquehanna was best choice. He be sittin over in Squadron office. Lt. Olson gets to bother him. 'Tween Bush and Hood, Bush liked the J.E. Williams crew and QM3 Mark. Bothel, on Fran, Hood took her. Shush. I didn't say squadron got a QM fresh from Philly.

I told BM1 Wagner and GM1 Burch they needed to apply for warrant. Good leaders. Oh, they will make Chief, like me, come spring advancement. But was, is to a Frigate or new armored Cruiser. The Squadron Warrant Bosn's like where they are. I sent a note to Admiral Taylor about this, signed by Griffith. He showed them his reply. He remembered thems, gave nice words, and recommendations.

I saw B last Wednesday, the 22nd. She wanted to try the real food place near her apartment. We ordered fish and rice with gravy. One taste and I reached for the pepper, to her bad looks. It didn't need salt. The Cook needs lessons from Feterman on these eats. I got two bottles of a medium Madeira wine to take to her place.

A tipsy B is a hoot. Oh, she just talked of her growin up in Baltimore, where Irwin was from. Friday I caught her up comin out of her office place as she wanted to do Chinese. After, I had to stop in a say high to Ella and Harold. She laughed about their antics the whole wat back to her place. She had, "Social obligations at Admirals home all weekend."

This afternoon, walkin around the piers, I got Irwin in me ears. Yes, both! It seems I did a good job of showin off B. "Too Good, QMC!" Oh, she has 3 suiters. He had each over for formal introductions over the weekend. "Very nice gentlemen. Good, established families, professionals." So, the problem. "Stiff as boards. They could hardly carry on a decent conversation with B. She likes you, QMC." With me leavin, that problem would be solved.

He asked if I could dance. Yes, around a subject. It seems Saturday 2 October, there was an afternoon dance, at Robert Sr. place. B wanted me to escort her. It would be Vie and Stewart first dance. I'd get first dance and last dance with B. 'Tween, she would test these suiters. Her card was already filled out. I got to dance with the suiters escort. Suites, ties, but not formal. I asked how to dress B. "Stylish, like that tan outfit." I ask and got $5 to hand.

No place to go so I start this at my table. I took B to that Italian place last Wednesday and got 2 bottles of Madeira wine she likes. We cleared out an area in her place and she showed me dance steps. I was like a drunk sailor with them feet movements. I finally figured out is like on a ship in rough weather. That learned, me feet got stepped on less. I even learned to swirl her, without hittin furniture.

We practiced on Thursday evenin, as Irwin had a suiter to Friday evenin meal.

Yesterday, Saturday, 2 October, I had to shoo her back into her apartment as she could hardly walk in the shoes she probably forced her feet in. I said to put on comfortable ones or not goin. She groaned the whole way to Effie of, "Shoes are old."

As Effie got her dressed up I took the shoes over to shoe department of the store. A liberty and George, leather guy, put some shine to the shoes. The place has slip on velvet covers. The lady helper picked out covers, on, and back to the back. I said to fix her up good, but, not too good. Out she stepped and I hoped Vie has sense enough to dress up as well.

Out she came, just lovely, in a light blue jacket over pearl frilly blouse and skirt to match the jacket. There was three rubies on a single gold chain and earrings to match. The hat, stylish, had a small blue, white, and red ribbon to it. She kept lookin, turnin in front of this full length mirror, and kept liftin the skirt to stickin out each shoe.

She came to me sittin there and did the same thing. I grabbed both sides of that skirt, me hands to her chest, and let go. That got her bad eyes. 'Your skinny legs stockings and skivvies don't match your nice shoes!' It is a woman joke she knows from Regina Dinner. They made this up about semi and "Formal wear."

It was like an afternoon social, but to dance. The same tables of hand food, bars for refreshments, and a small band on the veranda. Robert Sr. has a big flat stone area for dancing, with tables around. Irwin caught me up about first dance, then sit, talk. Her lead suiter took her next, as I got his escort. It was a mixed group of older and younger people. Elizabeth did dress Vie nice. Vie couldn't stop smillin and no one couldn't pry her hand from Steward. They didn't change partners. It was a short playin from the band. They wanted lots to dance and talk.

Durin talk time I got to meet the next suiter and escort. I hardly got a drink down and up I was. It was hard to keep mind off feet and answer questions from partner. Nice ladies, all. I kept a distance so shoes didn't get trod on. The third time around I saw them suiters were still stiff. One rest period I got ahind each and said to compliment B on hat, dress, neckless, enough to get her smile dancing, sittin, or, 'Admiral Will cross you off his list.' I danced and sat out a couple with different women. I watched B and the suiters. Just one may do her well. At least they made B smile, some.

Last dance over, with B, I went around and thanked the ladies for not steppin on me feet. No, not invited to dinner. Well, next I know there was 3 women catchin up Irwin on this. He gave me BAD eyes, he did. I got to sit one lady and had two across at the far end of table. B? One suiter each side and other across, middle of the table.

Admiral and B gave us bad looks, for the snickers and laughs from our end. Come after that was social time and he got me for that. I tried to hid, in the back. Snickers from the woman gave me away! "QMC, front for a story."

I called up Stewart and Vie, the honor guests, and tried to pull their hands apart, gently. Couldn't. 'See, joined already,' to claps and laughs. I needed Vie for the story and whispered what she needed to do. I asked B about me Possible bag. There were no good words from her about it.

I told of the Founding Fathers pretending to attack. Me and Vie shuffled feet, pretended to shoot goin ahead and ahind. I said of the Militia. Vie got to stand up for tree or bend over for rock as I Pow Powed on either side of her. I said how the Buckskin shooters scattered like chickens in a yard chasin bugs. Vie movin around the room, me behind her. I gave the content of a Possible bag and no woman would put a hand to it. We did that first time to Cresson, with MaMa, and props of a big purse, cane for umbrella, and such. We got laughter and claps through it all.

Robert Jr. and Carrie took us to B place. She liked my stories. Into B apartment and she disappeared into her bedroom and out in her to floor robe. Sat, her feet, with brown fuzzy slippers went to me knee. She pulls up the hem to, brown long johns. The same color as the slipper. Matchin Regina wear. I like tipsy B. She had bought some bottles of her favorite Madeira wine. A time to enjoy, we had. A nice smile and twinkling eyes, she has. I gave her that invite to have. Women keep thems. I got her card, with address, "to write, of any adventures, QMC." She asked for Chinese dinner on Wednesday. I have no set time be to the base.

04 October, 1897, and another Monday. The mornin was a time of it. Potts, Burch, Wagner are takin care of problems. Squadron and Commodore clerks are like bees around a hive. Rishell is scratchin out orders for me volunteers. We be underway on Thursday to the Med. I am designated Ships Master of Shenandoah. Walbeck hasn't decided on North or Southern whey points. I like the Southern one and to Bermuda!

Here in me room, to finish this up. For laughs went to Ella and Harold place. I had to see about my scoundrels there on Wednesday. Tomorrow is to see Mr. Bish and Effie. Money to each. My extra cash to him and pay for Vie and B stuff, in the future, at Admiral request, informal order. He mentioned Frank and Elizabeth concerns. Both are trying to be independent woman. Yes, me Damsels, not too distressed. Maybe another copper to me chest and a Davy Jones entry to me log. I'll drop this in the mail, 'amorrow, goin to another day of it.

By Your Leave, Missy,

An Old Sea Dog,

IN THE YEAR 1897, 01 NOVEMBER: ATLANTIC CROSSING

Dear Miss Judith,

The Shenandoah be three days out of Norfolk, headed to the Med. A big pond to a small one. In me Cart Room, to stool, and a paper to the Chart Table. Oh, there is a nice Starboard lean of the ship and it is like a proper writin desk. Ifn ya be askin our course, the same these last days of, East, Due East. Commander Walbeck couldn't decide North or South whey points. Well, that is better than the North route and a bit shorter than the South one.

I dropped your letter in the Post, Monday, 02 October, and to me table. Potts, Wagner, and Burch got to take care of problems. I only get involved when they can't agree, like men assigned by Lt. or me. Rishell, right there, 'To my list.' It was about 2 unrated seaman, fresh from Boot Camp, and QMSA Nupp. I'll get to that.

Problems solved, I went see Mr. Bish, me agent, at 4 PM. He logged in me extra cash and we reviewed Edith and me accounts. No, he can't go back and collect money from that last lawyer, Court appointed, and all. He was a Thief, with a license. I hoped to see Edith. It was a nice thought. Not after this 3rd day and goin Due East. Walbeck ain't gonna turn South to visit.

After him I went to visit Effie. At first she pretended to be busy with the store and walkin around. Followed her, I did. I pestered her with little words. She finally came to her register and stopped, when I put that paper to the counter for her to read. It was from Mr. Bish. She gave me a hard look and put it in that drawer of hers. She is still a lovely, an older version of Carrie, as I said afore. 'This voyage I'll make me fortune! Back to here and I'll ask for your hand in marriage, Effie!' Oh, that put a smile back on her face. I got hands to me face, a nice kiss to both cheeks and, "Not after you pay their bill, QMC." Came bright eyes from her and a laugh heard by all around.

There was no time for back to base and a good supper from 1st Cook Edwards. I went to the Chinese place. They make a boil like Talig. I got bumped from ahind, in line, and turn to Vie, Rose, and Rishell, with grins from thems. I paid. I paid for four bottles of Madeira wine and spritzer for me pocket bottle. Inside the apartment place, Rishell, Rose take a bottle each and into her room. Vie gave a look, the rest to her room and, "Why don't we walk and talk, QMC?"

We walked and talked to Ella place. She gave bad looks at servin what Vie wanted. By second tall mint julip, Vie was well lubed up. She can't handle 'good' whiskey very well. I used me dance steps to get her back to her place. Her leggs and feets, both, was like she was dancing!

A glass with spritzer and pocket bottle, Vie with wine in her glass, we sat at her table. I asked about Stewart. Oh, she loves him dearly but, "A Fuddy-duddy, at times. Not as humorous as you, QMC." She wanted to hear more of me stories. There was Pheobe and Lydia in Gibraltar. Next came the flirty women in Toulon. "Monic, in Gaeta, fixed up the men with what they want.' I hedged a questions about meself, I did. No, I blabbed on what the men wanted, to a blush. I mentioned Myrtos and up that hill for samiches and wine with the children waving, women noddin, and the men givin us the evil eye. You know of the Consulate in Crete and them oldsters and youngin sneakin off. 'Nope, I nor you want to know!' But, I whispered some of what I didn't see. Vie just laughed.

I told of me last leave. MaMa squintin at us afore and after Founding Fathers meetin's. Vie die a good imitation. I had to mention South, and other old memories. I mentioned leavin to Vie up, into her room and out with her robe on backwards. Rose and her tie each other into them Corsets, from the back. "She will be busy, for a bit." I did that dang cord from the front and me arms around. Rose must have Bos'n in her blood. Vie was never a "Fuddy-duddy," after some whiskey or wine. I could only leave, "After we act out one last story, My Sailor." Vie played her part well, 'cept for stifled laughs and giggles. It was a two part story. Well, she said Stewart was a fuddy-duddy. I got a nice kiss to, "Take care, QMC."

Wednesday mornin, the 6th, me and Rishell went into Griffith office. I got to sit. Over comes a letter in Elizabeth Williams hand writin. Next was from, Carrie. Another from Mr. & Mrs. Miller, Sr. and one from Irwin. Last across was from Admiral Forest. "It seems you know a lot of important people, QMC." Rishell got to hand over the "Volunteer list, Commodore." I got Griffith bad eyes as he signed them two copies. One was mine.

Front of me men, I said to pack sea chests, bags, and decide to go aboard tonight or here at 8 AM. Nichol said that marine tent was available, "For those not fit to stand straight, tonight!" There was the usual wagons at the barracks at 1 PM and they had the afternoon to settle aboard. Oh, the sailin orders was signed with jackass tugs. Pot belied Shenandoah is loaded out.

At 5 PM I got B hand to mine and onto a trolley, North. She asked for Chinese and wanted to meet, "your motley crew." She must have not had lunch as heaped that bowl of hers. I was not worried of Rishell and Rose. He was to take a pail to her room. Vie? Wednesday is when Stewart and her have an evenin at his home.

At 6 PM I had her settled at the corner of the bar, the easiest place to greet the scoundrels. We heard them long way off, singin a Marine song. In came Nichol, Corporal Waltermire and Kenwood, straight to her and hand. Ahind was 18 more with knuckle to heads and, "Mam," from each. From her hand they went to a table and jugs of beer to mugs. I got her eyes. 'As formal as they get B.' She gave nice words for them. 'Course, I know thems well. Last was them 12 Marines in uniform and 12 more "Mam," to her. Ella gave her a stuff drink to sip. She was still overwhelmed at them all. She had such a smile, watchin their antics.

Come 7 PM, after two stiff drinks, I caught up her hand, to stand. We caught up a shot glass of beer for her and me and I said, 'To my motley crew and a good voyage, Salute!' They started the line to wish her well, all of thems. It about embarrassed her, but B gave a, "Thank you," to each.

It was a trap, her apartment. The glasses set and wine was there. I had to take of me jacket and put the leathers of knife and marlin spike aside. B said, "Tell me about your scoundrels." I said, 'Only have this evenin, B.' Well, there was me readers, the oldsters, the youngins, which brought up the Consulate. The change of flags, 'As the Brits mention Yellow.' The Cozumel work she knew of. It was a short story why the lead Marines got advanced.

Prepared, she was. The first bottle gone, she came back to the table in that to floor robe with another. Her feet to me knee with the same fluffy shoes and her hem up to show them brown stockins. "Family, QMC." You be rollin yourn eyes here. Now, in conversation I'd mentioned some of them. The 'Hooligan Family' always got her laughs, especially me and PaPa after. B stood, "Strip, Soak, Soap, Scrub." She was like MaMa said the words with a scowl on her face. Close enough.

I already mention Benjamin, Princess father. I told her of the last time, in full regalia. I brought up first time, with Uncle Curtis. MaMa eyes to that jug around and Uncle Curtis stories. B can do MaMa eyes. She had a nice laugh to me stories.

Came that time, mid 3rd bottle, I mention leavin. B said we needed to act out, together, "a last one, to remember." The story got her bad, good and some cute looks. She did it very well and got carried away, in her way, to some parts. It was a comedy, serious, light hearted, and got her smile, only after, and such laughs still in me ears. I got a nice kiss and, "May you find your Princess, QMC."

I was smiling about that thought when ship warped to Port. Me mind, in thought, missed them whistles or I'd have been on deck. Gaston was to Port poop, BM1 Wagner to center, Lt. Clark to Starboard, and the ship stalled in the turn. Donahey called it early, to no whistles. The crew was like a herd of sheep, all over the place. Walbeck plates of supper went over the table, to Engle bad words. I made it to the poop just afore Walbeck and his bad words. "Oh," says Donahey, "it was the time on the Daily Report." QM3 Joseph was in the Privy and QMSA Nupp didn't know any better, "He called it, QMC."

Nupp is me, long ago that be. I have him assigned to a lower hammock and the new seaman above. Wagner and Burch have one each and an Oldster assigned to each. They need seaman learnin. I needed to do some learnin to Ensign Donahey too. Like, make sure all are there for changing course. 'Ship turns only with me on deck, Sir! Day or night, Sir!' Oh, Walbeck caught him up, there in his cabin. I got words and Ships Master was among thems.

Rishell has 4 readers to the Chart room in the, morning and afternoon, dependin on sails. It seems others want to learn more readin and writin. The Chart Table is full but I have those black slates, from afore, for use. He be a good school Marm. At his request,

I'll sit at that little aft winder and help with one. 12 to 16 days to Gibraltar, so there is lots of time to spend toward thems.

18 October, 'Nother starboard lean to Chart Table, not to warp, them old letters come to hand. Elizabeth, Vie mother, thankin me for supportin her. She is of an independent head and her love for Stewart was in them words. Carrie, ah, asked for, "Arm protectors and gauntlets, to fit, so we could square off, proper." I guess she is still not pleased with how I had Effie dress Vie and B. Robert Sr., Clara hand, was thanks for presentin Vie and B. The stories were entertainin and the escort woman were favorable in their comment toward me.

Irwin letter was in his hand writin. Thanks for lookin after B and presentin her at socials. I am an entertain actor and a magician to get B to smile. A skilled producer of stories, "to include B, and Vie, QMC" There was also some mention of some bein undisciplined at dinner table with snickers and uncontrolled laughter, at me end. The women liked the slightly, salty talk.

Forest letter started, as always, with past deeds. Like about insulting him for not standin at that table, quickly. His small flag to the forward mast meant he was a guest, and not there, official like. He was not present at me flag presentation to the Commodore was for the same reason. That is in that protocol book. Wagner and Burch got good words toward them. "I am looking for Leaders, QMC." The "Volunteers" was about a spit word from him. "Dedicated to your men, QMC. Admiral Irwin thinks highly of you. Thank you for takin care of Mrs. Nellie B. Drips." Irwin must have sent him a letter.

Yesterday, the 18th, was Plum Duff day, half way across. The Waisters got to sleep in till 5 AM call. There was no sense worshin a deck bein rained on. We had those canvas enclosures to the fore and aft hatches so we could get about the ship. Less water went below.

I forgot to mention the ship got new 6 pounder breach loadin guns. Just 2 fore and aft. Gunner Campbell can't keep his hands off them. Is like a new lady, to him. 4 different rounds, cartridges, to shoot. He gave a talk of them to the officers, handed some around, and they treated them like new born children, afraid to drop them. The gig put barrels out some distance for crews to shoot at. Walbeck took exception to them goin off next to him. They have a sharp sound and are accurate. The canister is lead balls and shrapnel, squares of iron, that sure sink a barrel quick. More cotton to ears.

Nupp and the two seamen can go to second yard arm. I still have Able Bodied Seaman watch thems. Young and foolish, at times. I only saw the oldsters swat them once or twice, as I was watchin. That is the easiest way to learn what not to do. Burch and Wagner have sent a couple I sign on to have a talk with. One, with mouth, a sea lawyer type, got told he'd be me practice dummy come boarding practice.

23 October, Nor, Nor West winds about. I caught that smell of sheep this morning. The Azores Islands are some 50 miles to North. I knew it two days ago when that Current line got some South to it. An odd current I just put to that log. People in DC can try to figure it out.

Oh, me sea lawyer. Armoror Hardis formed up parties and put the old ship crew against new members. He kept correctin the new ones to attack and defense. 'Mouth,' as I call him, didn't listen. He tried to hack his way in and his defense was poor. I had Hardis dress him in padded body, arms, and head. He chose wood cutlass and I got two longer belayin pins from the rack. Doc Stiteler got to see the 3 poke marks front, 4 to the back, and his foot. Somehow, he whacked his foot on Number 1 gun. Wagner says he is quieter. It could be me Orlop visit remark of that Packet Ship in Gibraltar.

Sun up, the 28th, and I set us closer to Africa than Spain. The wind has been followin the sun. Some from West and North. I be at helm indicator when lookout calls 2 Spanish Frigates closing. Nick of sails, I saw. Came hull up the mast pennant said Spanish. I had Nupp fetch gunner and his range finder. No dip in either flag. Walbeck was there, Taft rail, just watchin. Come Gunner call of, "In their range, Captain."

I call the starboard Signal Middie for me flag to halyard with 'Alpha flag, Uniform (Danger) atop.' He winds them in light cord and up they went. I went into Chart Table, found a small flag, gave it to him said, 'To Aft mast, Sir.' Wound, hoisted, and I gave eyes to Walbeck. Gunner, older than him, wiser, in me opinion, got Walbeck ear with a whisper and I saw his eyes. "General Quarters. Tampion off, guns out on my order. Susquehanna flag to Port."

It took only a minute and the crew was at gun stations. The Boardin Party takes some longer to get weapons. I always be last, to get set and inspect boardin party. Carbine to spot loaded, loaded pistol, set arm stuff and gauntlets, adjusted the sword belt and, 'Boarding party ready, Captain.' I heard, "Flags!"

Walbeck sure didn't like this situation. His eyes said so. I was watchin the 5 guys, each side, set them breach loadin 6 pounders. "Ready, Captain," from thems and I loudly said, 'Spanish territory or neutral Morocco, Captain.' I gave him a choice, I did. He did well with, "Guns Out! Starboard rudder!' Wagner aft mast hands snapped the pusher over perfect.

We was broadside to these two Frigates, caught off guard. I figured we'd go North. Turned North, they did. Both dipped that Spanish topmast flag and kept goin. We yacked back through that good wind, we did. I said wind was following the sun. We anchored just over that bay line, Gibraltar harbor.

St. Lawrence carried Admiral Palmer flag. Our barge, me at bow, pulled Walbeck to that pier just after 1 PM. St. Lawrence is not me favorite ship to visit. They have been a problem afore. We had hogs head of water, a bag of ships biscuits, and sail for a Privy. We needed all three as them officers must have been in a big conference. Come 4 PM was me concern.

Boat Bos'n sent one to that quarterdeck to ask for "conveniences," my words, like a meal. Oh, I heard the words he got. Just like last time with that ship. I went up that gangway to a Lt., and bad words. I took off the Ship Master badge with, 'Give this to Admiral Palmer, Sir,' and said to pass on to Captain Walbeck that his boat was returning to ship, 'Fore Conveniences, Sir.'

I waited 15 minutes, all proper. The boat oars up, aft seat, I called for, 'Lines off, push off. Row Dry.' We made it some distance and there was a bee hive on St. Lawrence. With me bad ears, I couldn't hear their words. I went up the ships side, boat settled to boom, when other boat, rowin wet, got to us. Seems that Lt. was slow in passin on me words. He didn't want to interrupt that meeting. Walbeck recognized that Master badge. That Lt. didn't like me answer to his words and rowed back wet.

The boat crew got first eats, 'afore 5 PM. No, no grog, as they had to rowed that barge back to that pier. Oh, we got a greetin party with and officer and aygulet over his shoulder. No, thems to watch the barge. They lead crew up the gangway to a BM1 takin thems below. I was ushered into the gunner mess and Admiral Palmer, seated. "So, QMC, you are now my problem, again," to his fake smile. I got a nice glass of wine served. We talked of 'Old Times,' and the Spanish ships that greeted us.

At the bow of barge I got bad looks from Walbeck. The same look in his cabin. The walls have Engle and Bobbit ears so, "Crew, ship, and then me, QMC?" I said, 'A Good Captain minds his crew, Sir.' I still got his looks with, 'One hand for the ship and one for the mate, Sir.' He'd have said more, but for the two ships rats ears.

30 October, early morning and just enough West wind we tie up head of St. Lawrence. 10 AM, she rang her ships bell and went off, with that tide of Gibraltar. Palmer flag up on our mast, she saluted us, returned, shore salute, and gone. Palmer was ashore with the ships officers.

Ships liberty is by division and I go ashore as I want. Joseph has his places to visit. I took Nupp with me, that first day. I showed him all the sights and the place for cheap eats, drinks, and all. He had young eyes, like I had, the first time there. He would have just wondered around.

I went to that one dealer about smaller arm pieces, gauntlets, and short practice swords. No hurry. I'd be back here sometimes. I got Talig boil at that place and had to see Pheobe and Lydia. I got bad words from Pheobe as, "Wheres ya been." I got a cute smile from Lydia. She be a fiery, Irish red head, when riled up. I don't do that, much!

01 November, here in me room, sortin charts. Palmer had meetin's, greetins, socials, all weekend. We are to leave Wednesday, 03 November. Purser Hitcock callin for mail. I guess I've bent yourn ear enough, for now, Me Lady.

By Your Leave, Missy,

An Old Sea Dog,

IN THE YEAR 1897, 25 DECEMBER: MEDITERRANEAN

Dear Miss Judith,

We left Gibraltar on 3 November with BM2 Marshal at ships wheel, along with Nupp, and them two boots. Joseph was at helm indicator. I was at the port side chair to Chart Table and Mr. Donahey to starboard. Walbeck to Taft rail, Palmer stepped to the aft mast chains. The wind was such, blowin of Rock of Gibraltar, we couldn't do no fancy stuff. Came bow around, counter the clock, and got them two Spanish Frigates watchin us. The bay be a neutral place but gun crews to stations and our boarding party was there. Course 180 set, and, well, somes I seen, up in the top gallants, gave them butt kisses. Shush. Ya drop a side of yourn pants and pat a cheek. They are not supposed to do it. No comments from any, so, I didn't either.

Walbeck and me are back to what to call him. The crew, Palmer there, I give 'Captain.' Otherwise, 'Sir.' I ain't seen Palmer, 'cept on the fore deck, minglin with the crew. That white line is painted and I have an oldster there for last knuckle to head. I hoped to get rid of him on the first Frigate. Oh, no. The whey points was set, closer to Morocco, to set him at Toulon. He wants to go 'tween Spain and Minorca Islands. Joseph and Donahey presented this and gave three whey points, for winds.

First day out of Gibraltar I had Bos'n rig a barge with triangle sails fore and amid. Me small flag to forward and that imitation Bey flag to mid. We caught up a fishin boat, Shenandoah hull up, and got 8 seepin tubs of fish for 8 Liberties. Back, I took two little ones and gave them to Engle for Palmer and Walbeck, to his grin. I gave him another for him and Bobbit.

The next morning, just 'afore that whey point, come a leeward signal from a, and Bos'n argue this, an Ibex or Zibex, I don't care. It had fresh melons and fruit. Hitcock negotiated this buyin stuff. We just stopped, put out bow and aft ketch, so theys could come along side. Thems two argued back and forth to no end. Hitcock don't speak Arab and he don't speak English but Liberties and tubs got agreed to. So, we had fresh stuff for meals.

04 November, morning, I came up on the poop after login in the Speed and Current lines. 6 knots. I told Bos'n Gaston he needed Top Gallants. Palmer Admiral flag was flyin nice. We had just a breeze on deck. He asked what I knew of sails. I said I could turn the ship quicker, 'Should we get into a fight with a Spanish Frigate.'

I mentioned the time 'tween Spain and Minorca Island, 'Be over 10 hours at 6 knots or less with 8 at 10, Bos'n.' He went to Walbeck, who kept lookin at Palmer so I yelled out, 'Nice Top Breeze, Captain,' to his bad looks. We got gallants put up

That Spanish Frigate must have come out of Alicante. I had Joseph show Knupp how to turn a chart, make a line, marks every inch, and turn the 28 second clock. I took the angle to the Frigate mast. Time, I call out angle, and so on. We was trackin that ship movements, doin over 10. I mentioned this to Mr. Donahey, to Walbeck.

That ship came hull up and lots of sail on it. I was about to send for Gunner Campbell when Walbeck did. By the time we got right 'tween Spain and Minorca Island it be in our range. We have a standin order on this. The whole crew knows it. I saw them meanderin to positions. The wounds on me arm and leg started itchin and Walbeck calls for, "Quite to Quarters. Boarding party, guns to ready."

By the time I got full regalia, to the Poop, it seems the Spanish Frigate decided to match our speed. Campbell kept that range finder on her. "Max range, Captain, for chasers." Palmer said not a word. He was judgin crew and Captain.

Time for that whey point turn, off Valencia, another Spanish Frigate was about ahead, and broadside. She had just enough sail for steerage way. I had BM1 Wagner up the Pusher sail, neutral to the wind, from the West. Walbeck called for ships flag and mine to, "Main mast spar, outer halyard, full up. Gunner, guns out, transverse Port and Starboard forward. Mr. Donahey. We will go East, till the last gun fires, then, West to engage both. Gunner, all to hull." I took rudder indicator to have Joseph mark the time. BM2 Marshal, Knapp, two boots get me finger to sit on the deck.

At our gun range, Campbell went below deck, up, and had words to Saltsgiver at Number 1 and 3. The forward Frigate didn't respond to our flags. I saw Captain countin on his fingers. At the last one his two hands closed and, "Flags to half! Signal gun to Port. Gun ports open. Fire on my order," still countin on his fingers to hands closed. "Helm to Full Starboard. After the last guns fires, hard to Port!"

Frigate saw us go East, open gun ports, and dipped her main mast flag. "Helm full Port!" Around we came, Starboard guns was to that ship and round to guns at that one to South. Oh, her sails went a flappin and dipped that flag of hers. I guess she saw them Larboard gun ports open and guns run out. "Steady to course for Toulon, Mr. Donahey."

This Afternoon, 05 November, the readers left me Cart Room, me back to the door, and that lower hinge squeaked. I turn to, 'Captain Walbeck. To what do I owe your presents?' Came his bad eyes and, "Again, now Captain?" I just mentioned his actions, with them Frigates, 'Ship and crew, you, Captain.' He didn't like that nor me sayin he, 'Did well!' The log said it was a 5 minute battle, that didn't happen. Oh, potbellied and all, spanker set, she surprised me, the ship did. It was 'cause of the crew actions.

Late evening, Sunday, 07 November, Toulon, France, we arrived and I showed Nupp the town. No sense him runnin with thems and havin to see Doc Stiteler for sailor stuff. A bar maid caught him up as, "A Cutie." Good, as next I know I got hooded men around me. Oh, it was Admiral Lt., Commander, and him, in Monk dress. Shush. They didn't want to be noticed. "Last here, QM2," his joke, "I didn't get that bottle you promised!" I said, 'Drank it, with a lady. You didn't show, Sir.'

We had good whiskey in shots to Uncle Curtis and Alfa, and MaMa. He mentioned Walbeck and our problems. Sirs and stuff. I said we kissed and made up, to his looks. Well, we did, in me Chart Room. I mentioned ship procedures on meetin ships. 'The crew were ready afore him. He kept his eyes on you. He could be a fightin Captain. Hesitated, as you were there. I needed Gunner to catch up his ear.' I got, "And you, QMC?"

I still get that tinglin in me arm and notices from the marks in that leg at odd times, like now. My poor hands and bruises, from Mr. Reynolds back in Boot Camp, came to mind. 'You tell the Spanish

Admiral, if he takes us to battle, he will have a butcher's bill on his hands, and loose some ships Captains, to my hands, Sir.' Palmer transferred his flag to that Frigate there. I took Nupp back to that place and the ladies. I have to look after me men, well somes of them. I can't keep an eye on but so many.

I pick this up much later. Nothin goin on. We left Toulon 09 November. Sailors don't need but 4 hour liberty to catch up on what they need and all. Came some nice winds so Donahey said we could run that channel 'tween Corsica and Sardinia. Ahind him, I nodded to that. Water and vegetables in Aspra was mentioned. "Gaeta!"

We got there just afore supper on the 11th. Walbeck was off the ship like it was a fire! Hitcock ordered the water, not be at the pier till next afternoon. The workin party to load the water got first liberty. I took Nupp and boots to see Monic. I got me ears chewed for, "And, just where have you been?" A Liberty to the bar, I got drink and explained, 'All over the place.' Engle needn't have made sweet breads for Captain. He didn't come aboard till noon next day!

I found a new young boy there at the pier in Aspra and gave him two coppers. The second was to lead us to Angelo. It ain't a big town but no sense runnin around, lookin. He and Hitcock went for ship's needs. I went to get hugs and kisses from Florina. The best part was she was cookin. I got to taste her evenin meal. The ships men filled two bars and the tables laid in the street. No, it wasn't cold outside.

We left on the 15th. Walbeck wanted to go East and through Messina straight. I didn't say yes or no to this. The Dailey Report mentioned the wind, come later in the day. It would be from the north. I couldn't say East or West. Bos'n Gaston gave no words.

16th, evening, ABS Stoop took a bunch of us up that long road to MaMa place. The wind changed to East and so we moored in Messina bay. It was a good thing he took a bunch. It took 4 around him to get him back to the ship. MaMa does make some good meals, cheap.

We did a day and a half in Malta. A Frigate was there. It came from the East and goin to Toulon. It couldn't make North through Messina straights. I asked Nora to take me shoppin. I got her lovely smile till I said what for. I paid for the evenin meal to get less bad looks.

Morning of the 20th we caught that Frigate from Tripoli and sand in the ships ears. The 25th and we found the last one East, Nor West of Alexandria and made the Delegation at Girne, Cyprus on the 27th. A new Captain and officers so they had an evenin party. Me barge crew got some good eats from that kitchen. I was the boat captain, just to make sure officers got aboard dry. It took hand ropes and two crew to each for that. I ain't sayin nothing here.

It was just a short stay in Myrtos, Crete, and the usual happenens. We got water, some got drunk and hauled back to the ship. The officers went to that one, only hotel, for their stuff. 03 December and back to Malta. It would have been nice but Palmer was there. We had to hoist his flag, him in a hotel, as we found out. His Lt., on the pier, said so.

We only did just over a day in Malta. Nora was not happy, so I took her to a more expensive place that had better wine, which she liked. Palmer came aboard after noon, the 4th. Thems had an Admiral meetin in Capt'n cabin I had to attend. It seems we was not to touch in Gibraltar without his direct permission. He to be aboard till we met Frigate 'tween Algiers and Oran. I just might had measured the distance 'tween and put a pin on the chart. Best was we got some fresh fish and stuff from that one Ibex. Palmer gave looks to this. Engle said Palmer liked the fresh fruit. No, I couldn't keep it from him. He! He!

Just re-read last parts of this letter as we stopped in Aspra for water and vegetables. No, no straights of Messina. There was an East wind and got some West to get to Malta. Walbeck must be sweet on a woman there as, shush, he stayed overnight, somewhere. We hit the two Frigates off Africa, gave whiskey and cabbage to that Consulate. We got some cold wind so I only took a few to the samich place in Myrtos. Oh, all seem to have places to their likin.

25 December, 1897, and here in me Chart Room. The wind is just nice from the East and some North. It be followin the sun. There is a nice lean to Larboard and Purser Hitcock says there be a packet in Malta, so he asked for mail. The Chart Room was filled with Readers, Oldsters, and some writin home. Oh, "No Steelin Me words," around. I had to laugh at that. Slates on laps, it is a writin desk, for most. We had a good supper of the youngest pork, peas

and cabbage on the side. Feterman did good with the plum duff. Gunner, wink, wink, gave a bit extra rum to the grog. Just enough for the tongue.

I hope you and Bow had a Merry Christmas. Have a good New Year, My Lady.

By Your Leave, Missy,

An Old Sea Dog,

IN THE YEAR 1898, 28 FEBRUARY: MEDITERRANEAN

Dear Miss Judith,

If ya say I ain't wrote in a while,' ya be rite! Nothing was goin on, here in the Mediterranean. It is winter here, so the baby was playin in this pond bath tub! Walbeck asked for and got mostly good winds. No, he don't like the Straights of Messina. We missed out on nice meals from ABS Stoops MaMa place.

This is the 3rd round of the Med. We left Malta 30 December, 1897. I gave Walbeck a choice of that or January 1, 1898. I don't sail on a Friday. It was three days of liberty, so Nora was pleased. She took me to her place, for her mother's cookin. Like Nora, she is a mix of Brit and Malta. It was a mixed meal of Brit, Malta, and spicy, but not hot.

Our yard arm split 'tween there and the first Frigate off Oran, 4 January. Mr. McGraw and Armoror Hardis tried to put an iron strap around it. Chips told Walbeck it would, "just hold till Toulon." We had to go quick, by the Balearic Sea. Yes, 'tween Spain and Minorca Islands. I got some looks for that. We made Toulon on the 8th, with two Spanish Frigates ahind us. The ship and me flag was at half-mast to that broken, ironed yard arm.

The first day in Toulon, there was 4 hours liberty went to the men who would shift that long piece of wood. It took a day for Mr. Chips and the French carpenters to make it. Up it went, sails hung, and we left on, "The quickest course to Gaeta, for water." The winds were such we shot the straights of Sardinia and Corsica. Walbeck left the ship as the brow went down and didn't come back till the next morning. Engle and him have this agreement. He says ifn he will miss meals. That makes me life easier.

The crew got 4 hours, each division, at Aspra. Oh, just enough time for what they wanted. Hitcock and Angelo took care of ship's needs. That evenin the crew filled up two bars. Florina cooked a meal for us all. Good eats. Just read me last letter for our stops. Yes, provisions to the Frigates, Consulate, and two days in Myrtos. Shush. The officer partied till late. We got back to Malta in good time, Sunday, January 30th.

Walbeck said it was to be a short stay. 4 hours by divisions, three that they be. I went in the first barge, to make sure Nora was there. After gettin thems to bar seats, she said me stuff was ready. Next door was a dress shop I got pulled into it. Effie place is huge, by size. A blouse didn't cost but what I'd give her to help the crew. I got her kiss to cheeks, her MaMa cheek kiss, and best, MaMa meal.

For the 4th round of this Pond we went straight to Gaeta and Walbeck down the brow. He didn't come back till afore the water was comin aboard. Monic made sure the crew had a good time. I always do, 'cause of her. At Aspra, Florinda gave us a good meal and kisses around. It would be the last time there, for a long while.

The Consulate gave Walbeck and the officers a fair well party. It was about cold out. I guess the oldsters and young'uns found places to keep warm, in their doins. There was lots of hankies from the pier and smiles on the crew faces. The gents in Myrtos gave nods to us at that samich place. It was cold, so we was inside to see the children noses to the candy counter. They got two pieces each, by me money. The mothers and ladies got to choose also. I liked their smiles.

We made Malta again, for the last time, 25 February, 1898. The lookout called down about our Frigate, "Admiral Flag, Captain." No much later came, "Spanish Frigate, Admiral Flag." Oh, Gunner Campbell was aside himself for glee. 15 guns to fire for each. Oh, the words he gave to make things ready. I thought GM1 Burch would be startin some with a stick, so in a frenzy he be.

Oh, Gunner knew how to take care of this situation. Fire both sides, timed, together, and let thems argue with who got Port or Starboard salute. The Signal Middie read the flags words to Walbeck, and we dropped the main anchor and a ketch aft. No turnin with the tide, nor broadside to thems. The anchors ain't set and a gig sets off from our Frigate, rowin like bein chased by someone. Up the side comes that Admiral Lt. I remember and into Walbeck cabin.

I got called into this all officers meetin. I mean even Saltsgiver was there. He had dragged Nichol with him. That Admiral Lt. held the floor 'afore Walbeck desk. It seems the Spanish Admiral heard of us, "displaying battle flags and guns to the side as a challenge, gentlemen." All eyes came to me. Especially after this Admiral said, "Starboard one appeared to be a Knights flag he has not been presented!"

The short story is he can't go aboard an American Frigate. We can't go aboard his ship. We might see his dirty skivvies, I guess. He can't come aboard us as he might see out new guns and our dirty skivvies. I mentioned I'd have Saltsgiver, Marines, march me up to the steps of the Governor place and present my flag to him. After, the Admirals and Captains could have a meeting. Agreed.

1 PM, 26th of February, I watched the Spanish Admiral barge row ashore with him, two Captains, and two Lieutenants. Palmer went in his gig with the Frigate Captain. Walbeck and Saltsgiver went over in his gig. I, the Marines, took the barge. Nichol to lead Corporal Waltermire, Corporal Kenwood, with two more Marines ahind. I took BM2 Marshal for my full flag and Knupp to bear the ships full flag. Joseph had my flag pole. The one with all me flags on it. Just a small procession so I told me sailors to just walk along, 'Don't trip. Hold the flags up.'

Saltsgiver marched them Marines sure good. It wasn't but a short distance to the Governor steps. Me and Joseph can't see much, what with ship and me flag ahead. At the Governor place, the Marines turned left and right, Nupp and BM2 move to the side, and me and Joseph step up to this Spanish Admiral. We practiced this for not 5 minutes. Me gauntlet moves said what the flag bearers to do. Glove hand closed, forward, they dip the flags poles. It looks nice. Glove up, up came them flags.

I stepped forward and salute the Spanish Admiral. To left gauntlet come me small flag from Joseph, I open it on me right gauntlet, and told him about all the symbols on it. I roll it up in the right gauntlet, to his hand, backed up three steps, and did that sword salute.

This Admiral called me forward and mentioned, through interpreter, that I should be at his left side as, "Military consultant." I said I had to stand behind Palmer and give him bad looks, crossed arms, to distract his thinking. He gave me eyes. I said would be best if, hands around, he and our officers had open talks, no extra eyes and ears, to speak frankly to each other. 'A warm sun to my face, I could sit quietly, and have some refreshments. I see dark days ahead for us, Admiral. It might be the last peaceful day, Sir.' Agreed!

Saltsgiver marched his people off. I set me three flag bearers to an empty table and sat at the next empty one, to watch them, and Governors door. I told them two beers and sausages only. Waiter to me, I asked for the house red wine and sausage. They call them Bangers. They are a nice breakfast link. Them two Spanish Lieutenants was like lost sheep and didn't know what to do. Finally, they walk over to me table. I stood, saluted, and offered chairs to sit at.

The waiter comes with a wine bottle with no label, sausage on this plate, and three glasses. I got a little pour to glass and it was a very poor house wine. On me left, Don Juan got a pour and across from me Don Alexandro pushed his glass away. Havin tasted the wine, I reached in me jacket, and outcome that pocket bottle, and I poured some in the glass. I offer it to Don Juan, who accepted a small pour.

I pulled out me knife and cut that sausage into bit size pieces. I stabbed a center piece and offered it to Don Juan, accepted. Another stab and a piece to Don Alex. He didn't take it so to me mouth. Alex and Juan had some low words I didn't catch, with me bad ears. Another piece of banger, I downed the wine and poured in more pocket bottle. Juan declined it. They talked and I don't say I know much Spanish. I picked up some in Cozumel, Cartagena, and places. Enough that their eyes said I was in them words.

I caught up BM2, gauntlet off, hand into coat, coins to his hand, and whisper what I need. Off he goes, gauntlet on, and eyes to me. The piers ain't far, so in not much time BM2, thumb ahind, and up steps Nora. Up them two jump, me up and hand to ever lovely Nora, and introduce thems. Her smile is all they looked at, gabberin away. I poured some wine in that unused glass. She took a sip, called out a name, said some words in Maltese, and the waiter appeared. Bottle, glasses gone, he came back with labeled bottle, 4 glasses around. Alex still pushed his glass off.

I let thems talk for a bit and asked Nora to translate. 'Don Juan, may I see your sword.' I ain't sayin he refused as Nora said not a word. Me left gauntlet took the napkin from the table and to my mouth. The other hand got a Colt pistol out, cocked, which they heard, cover it with the napkin, as they watched me place it on the table. Oh, the eyes I got. Nora didn't see the pistol.

With me left gauntlet I pulled out my sword, turned the blade from Juan, and set it on the table in front of him. My hand, open, I asked him to look at it, to Juan and Alex said low words. Me hand gestured to give it to Alex. He had a time with it, bein right handed. He did, politely, give it back proper. Back into the scabbard, hand to hanky, the Colt went back to me jacket. Nora translated it was a nice sword. "Unusual, QMC," from Nora.

I asked Nora, again, if I could see Juan sword. It was a battle of eyes to me. Juan did, politely, hand his over. It was a nice sword with a silver handle, and engraved with maybe a family coat of arms. I ran it across my palm glove. No edge and the point was dull. But, I told Nora it was a very nice piece. Nora translated my questions on the engravin. I asked and got Alex sword. Another very nice thing. No edge and no point. Again, I complimented it. It was two month pay for just one of thems. Business over, it seems each was on one of the Frigates we challenged, goin to Toulon. They recognized the flags. Nora just translated their words.

Alex didn't like us lowerin the flags, gun to windward, and all. Juan was more civil and asked about the symbols on them. I had BM2 hold out the flag, for them to see. Easiest was my Gauntlets. A closed left gauntlet and I tapped Juan on the shoulder. He got the idea. For the other, I reach across and pretended to slap Nora cheeks, took it off, and threw it on the table. 'A challenge, Gentlemen.' They understood that.

My flag held out to see, I said about the sword edge out. Without the sword, I held a pretend sword edge to Juan. He understood. A hand to say the gun lock toward edge is ready for action. Nora didn't understand and just repeated my words.

Juan said it looked like the Navy ship alphabet flag, Michael, M. I pointed out the red strip, 'For ship crew, bloodshed in battle.' I mentioned it was based on the, 'Flag of St. Andrew, Scottish national flag.' That got those two jabberin so even Nora couldn't make out what they said. Next I know thems stood and their hands to the fake swords. I stood, hand into jacket for pistol, left hand to sword. I got both half way out and Nora screamed out, "They are apologizing for not recognizing you, Your Highness!" They bowed, Nora bowed and curtsied real nice. Me grain was slow, wonderin which to shoot first.

Ahind Juan and Alex was the pole bearers with them sharp pikes toward them. Once I got me whit's about me, I gave hand signal to hold. I told Nora to have them turn around. Alex face turned white. I gave them PaPa finger to, 'Sit!' 'Apology accepted, Gentlemen. Please sit.' That got three church mice at the table. I reached over and took Nora hand and said, 'As a Scottish Knights wife I can have you tottered for a better understanding of Spanish, my dear.'

I said to translate that for Juan and Alex. That got laughs around. She thought, interpreted, "Highlander," as Highness. I had to tell how I got the arm guards, gauntlets, and sword, now modified. The name Captain Don Estephon got eyes. Same with Don Garcia and Don Hernandez. There was lots of chatter from them and Nora couldn't keep. It seems each was now a Squadron Commander under the Admiral I gave the flag to. It was a nice social afternoon.

BM2 alerted me to Admiral conference bein over. Hand to me right arm I introduced Nora to the Spanish guy first. He looked to be the oldest. There was smiles around as he introduced his Captains. I introduced Palmer and she had to have hand to Frigate Capt'n and Walbeck. It was like a circle of men with her caught in the middle. I was afraid she'd get dizzy and fall. So, I reached in and caught her hand. I thanked the Spanish Admiral for a quiet afternoon, translated, I hoped.

Walbeck tucked into gig, I gave the barge crew got my look and point to the ship. It was just out of ear range and Nora lit off like a broadside with words I didn't understand. She started in Spanish, switched to French, Italian maybe, oh, Maltese came out, and it ended in English. She came in work cloths, "not dressy enough for officers, QMC," and kept pokin me chest with her long finger. I kept backin up and comes her fist to me pocket. The problem was me pocket bottle. She dented it. Oh, her howls of pain. Broken bones! Crippled for life! No man would want to marry her. She'd sue me, make me marry her. I took her poor hand, kissed it, and said, 'Will you marry me?' That stopped her words.

I said I could get ships doctor to look at it, to her eyes. 'I guess you can't shop for a skirt to go with that blouse.' Her eyes went to that store and used that hand to pick out 5 'afore she made up her mind. I carried that paper and string package back to Emma place. In the door, more languages to Emma, into back room, and to more words. I got Emma eyes. Out, she showed the new blouse and skirt, back to that room. Out, in work cloths, come words, and Emma caught me up with, "A simple dinner at 6:30, if you are still alive."

Nora was busy with 3 ships crews so I just found a spot to watch her work. She was a busy bee on flowers. I was approached, twice, by gents askin ifn the flags they saw, "in your Parade are registered with the Ministry?" I was in plain uniform so I got no highness stuff from them.

The next day, after morning muster of, 'All present and sober, Captain,' I called Rishell into the chart room as I need his fancy words on paper. I did the drawings of the flags. The gents gave some words to go on the paper for the Ministry. I went to the Ministry building afore 3 PM and I'll get that. Yes, a story. Anyway I went and sat in the sun at that same place, just down the street. That waiter brought the better wine. Come a bit after 4, Emma and Amelia come to me table. No introduction was required so they sat and get wine to glasses that came to thems. Emma asked, "How did your visit to the Ministry go, Your Highness?" She already knew how things went. Amelia started that frenzy.

I entered the "Assistant Secretary" office in normal uniform, but with pistol and sword. Semi-official attire. This room had 8 desks and people scratchin paper to no end. The guy at head table just tells me to sit, a couple chairs were there for that, and he'd get to me in a moment. No, he never looked up. With the sword, I just stood. A good lookin woman got up, papers to hand, readin, and puts them in a pile next to this guy. She takes papers from another box, looked at them, head up to me eyes and I got, "Your Highness!" Well, chairs legs screeched, heads bowin, and the head guy about fell out of his chair, as Amelia did a full curtsy.

Malta, the town of Valetta, ain't large. It seems Nora, "Highness," our little parade, got flashed around quicker than a brush fire. Amelia was right there, just getting off work, to hear, "Highness." She would have not said a word but for the scar on my head, plus the uniform. She recognized me.

In that room, I had to catch up her hand, to get her standing. Loudly I said, 'Please, don't mind me.' To her and this gent I said I was here un-officially, for minor papers to the Ministry. I asked if she could make up the papers to say I had presented my documents. Amelia thought it funny I had to kneel next to her desk to make sure the words were to me likin. She did this first in pencil and plain paper till said what Rishell might think were best. Done, I told her of Nora mistake.

I invited Emma and Amelia to an evenin dinner at a place Nora would see us at and catch a meal. I got to tell me stories and heard of the local gossip. A bit of that was our parade and, "Oh, we got to see a Royal Highness!" Even I laughed at that. Nora flittered in and out the whole evenin. She gave me a nice good by kiss at the pier. I turned, got her kick to me rear and, "Take care, Highlander." The barge crew thought that was funny.

We left Malta this morning, 28 February. Palmer is aboard. He wants to meet the incoming supply ship. It should be Monongahela. I'll see about a load of fish and fresh stuff from them ships off Africa, sailin south of this imaginary Spanish line. 'Cept for last Malta stop, it has been boring cruise. I expect same to Gibraltar. Sign this out to you, My Lady.

By Your Leave, Missy,

An Old Sea Dog,

IN THE YEAR 1898, 29 MARCH: ATLANTIC CROSSING

Dear Miss Judith,

Gibraltar is a day ahind now. We left yesterday, 07 March, 1998. Oh, the usual stuff goin on there. I had Pheobe, Lydia to bother, and got some Talig boil from that little place. But, I be getting ahead myself.

'Tween Malta and Gibraltar we caught up a Frigate wantin provisions. We got salutes from them, returned and all. Palmer went over for talks. He just looked at the seepin tubs of fish I brought back to the ship the next day. Oh, he gave eyes as this Ibex, Zibex, came along side. Hitcock and that Captain rattled on for a time about price for stuff. A boom over and we on loaded lots of fresh stuff for Feterman to make good meals for the crossin.

We made Gibraltar on 03 March, in the morning. Two Spanish Frigates dipped a flag and we returned it. The gang way down and I thought the rats were chasin Palmer off the ship. I guess he didn't like sleepin with Walbeck. Maybe Engle bothered him to no end.

I took the afternoon to look over things to buy. That pawn shop guy had what I asked for and asked where I'd been. Well, not in Gibraltar, thanks to Palmer. He tried to cheat me on the price. "Holding Charge." I said he could hold thems some more! It was not a good or bad price, to me thinkin. The things need some work, to look good.

04 March, Palmer came aboard at 10 AM to start this inspection. It should have been at 11 but, we knew it would take longer. He had to inspect each division, getting salutes, and namin a lot he recognized. Done, back to Quarterdeck area, and Saltsgiver, to read words, had the podium there, and papers to it. Me? Center Poop deck.

His first words were to, "Old Tom, Ships cat," for words to laugh at. Reader, Kelly, had it in his arms. After Saltsgiver words Engle set a plate with a little fish upon it. Kelly set Old Tom to that dish on deck, twitchin of tail, a growl, Old Tom puts teeth to it, and off to the forecastle!

The boots got promoted to Seaman 2nd, Nupp to Quartermaster SN, and Rishell to Ships Clerk 2nd. Proud of that, they was. There were words for Marines parade in Malta, gun positions, and Gunner Campbell for that Balearic Sea display. Chips, Mr. McGraw, Armoror Hardis for us makin Toulon. Donahey got called up to Walbeck and Palmer pined on them Lieutenant bars. I fired blank to air, and he got the lower three guns fired, to port side. It sure sounded as one and the smoke to blow from you face. Campbell must have double loaded thems.

Last called up was Commander Walbeck to Palmer and his Captain aide aside. Saltsgiver read the orders from D.C. They took off his silver leaves and put on those silver eagles. Na, he knew it was comin. He didn't know, when he turned to face the crew, that Seaman 2nd, was to give him a ships flag. He saluted him and Lesko comes forward and give him me personal flag. He had to turn to me sword honor and salute.

He turns to the crew and oldest oldster, Craig, come forward and holds out a flag to him with, "Captain. The crew made up this personal flag for you to fly, from the aft mast." No, they made it from material I got from Malta, before Nora got her blouse. A blue field to red, vertical and horizontal strips. The white was a 'V' and 'V,' which looked like the German, W, for Walbeck. The oldsters had the boots make it, under their eyes. It took three tries afore I thought it OK.

Sword out, I did that salute, crossed it to him, and pistol out. He looked at me funny. I pulled that trigger, on a blank, and all Port guns, forward, mid upper, mid lower, and aft went off. A rollin bang. The Middie popped that flag from the aft mast. Surprised thems, we did. Palmer and now Captain about reached for their fake swords. I called out, 'Any man who doesn't give three Hurzays for our Captain gets three days head duty!' I got bad eyes from Walbeck and Palmer. The crew did them 3 Hurzays!

That evenin I went out for a walk afore goin to my not so 'Hidy Hole.' The pawn shop owner said he might have something of interest. I didn't make it there. That Admiral Lt. caught me up, escorted me to the Governor residence, and about shoved into a room with Palmer, him, and others I don't know. It seems them Spanish

Lieutenants had snitched on me. I pulled a gun on them! Asked for their swords! I about caused a ruckus in Valletta!

Gave them me orders as Master at Arms, I did! 'Full regalia was required, Gentlemen.' They didn't like my personal list for that. Just maybe I didn't need that second Colt, right side of jacket. Palmer just smiled. Then I mentioned the "Protocol" book.

They left, to just Palmer and me. He poured out some fine whiskey, I had to taste it, handed back that empty shot glass, and asked for another. I to sit and we chatted a while. Walbeck flag, and the borin cruise was there. I said how ship was able to get fish and green stuff off Africa. 'Be nice to the local merchants and be respectful, Sir.'

We did a shot to Uncle Curtis and Alfa. He said his relief was comin on the next Frigate. Four to be in the Med, what with the Spanish tensions and all. It was a name I heard of but, out of DC. A shot to MaMa. No, no need to write her. He never was a talker so stood to last shot. 'In good times, on good ground, Admiral.'

We did catch up on mail, thank you. Engaged. Congratulations. I'll miss your wedding, bein in the Caribbean from June to end of October. I got one from B. She hasn't made a final choice of bows. It seems, "None are as entertaining as you, QMC." I guess I over did my job. Vie said she had been invited to some socials and thanks for Effie helpin her with dresses. I ain't spent much this cruise and might need all I have to deal with Effie.

Monongahela came in the 5th of March. Palmer shifter is flag to her. After the meeting at the Governor place, I didn't see him again. We left Monday, the 7th, to about no tide. A little breeze off the Rock helped us turn. Gunner Campbell and Burch were in a frenzy for all them salutes to Palmer and shore. The two Spanish ships dipped their flags to us. We did dip our ship and me flag to them, with a signal gun to Port. Walbeck flag acknowledged them with our port guns.

Walbeck hasn't bothered me, so I went to see him about Bermuda. He didn't like the ideas I brought up. I said he should talk to the officers, as they might want to see Edith, as they had afore. They talked, the wind and weather permittin, things were agreed to.

For this 'Crossing,' Donahey and Clark have switched positions. Donahey makes calls for the aft mast. I had to touch him up on a neutral Spanker sail. I got Wagner to have BM2 Marshal assigned to watch the wind and sail. BM1 Wagner has the Main, and Bos'n Fore and bow sprint.

Clark didn't do much for navigation. The whey points were set, nothing for him to do. I assigned him chapters of "Methods of Navigation" to read. Now I was his, "School Marm." Good weather, for a sailor, nice sailin, so Rishell has me Chart Room most mornins and afternoons. Some have borrowed them slates and paper to work on their words around the Smokin Lamp.

We arrived Bermuda mid mornin, 21 March. I told Walbeck to anchor out, cause of the wind. I showed him the chart to, "Anchor in. A short row to the pier, QMC." I mentioned a loose ketch anchors fore and aft. Denied. I caught up Bos'n Gaston after. BM1 Wagner got me words also. Both had been to Bermuda afore. I told both to take first liberty, after noon. The crew had already been divided up to time ashore. Only a third ashore at a time.

The gig over with BM2 Marshall aft and me forward, with Captain, Clark, Donahey, and Doc Stiteler. Doc was to say we ain't scurvy and such. I talked to the administer about changing our money for Brit as I said some crew would be doin, 'Over night at Miss Edith place.' I got, "You mean Mrs. Edith Cassidy Hostel." He'd, "arrange to have the exchange, outside."

The officers went off to see the Governor as I sent BM2 down to see about boardin at Edith place. He come back in a huff and a thumb over his shoulder. I could find the place about drunk, till now.

That house had a front porch added and it was just big enough for two little tables. There was paint to the outside and a new door. Knocked, I did. I waited some, knock again. Edith answered it. I only recognized them eyes as I got about bowled over by her throwin herself to me arms. There was words to me ears, more words, and I got pulled into this place.

I hardly recognize the dinin room with the nice tables, and lamps around. The walls was painted, new stools, and nice bar top. Oh, I got more hugs, kisses and, "Etta, we need good whiskey, a comfy bed, and come give QMC a kiss." BM2 got as good on hugs and kisses.

From the kitchen come Etta in nice dress, hair made up, no knives in hand and, "About time you two came to visit. Got any for me to take care of, QMC?" We got her hugs, kisses, and to ears, bad words to our character, BM2 and me to bar, and thems across.

Mr. Bish, "Bless his Soul," sent better money to her, on Uncle Curtis investments. Enough to fix up the place and get attention from, "Oh, we had the Lt. Governor look it over." Eyes to Etta, "She cooks him meals he loves," to laughs around. I mentioned about 20 had a silver dollar, required, for overnight. Her place was now a, "Hostel, not boarding place." She'd put us up, "around. But, here for the evenin, and a comfy bed for you, QMC." I got a wink for that. Etta gave a wink to BM2.

Captain and Governor, officers, took some time to talk. BM2 and me took up a position to see the ship. That aft ketch was out on a long line. BM2 took Walbeck and officers back to the ship. A barge, liberty crew, unloaded Bos'n and BM1. I warned them of the changes at Edith place. Come time, 4 PM, BM2 came back in Captain gig with Walbeck, Chips, Armoror, and Donahey. I got tea and crumpets from the staff, watchin the ship. I saw Bos'n and BM1 take the barge back to the ship, with first liberty party.

The Governor staff brought me bit to eat at 5 PM. The barge came off the ship at 5:30, lee of wind, so, not a wet row. It was me 20, with silver dollar, to exchange to a Brit Crown. The exchange guy grumbled at the time. I said they could sleep with him. NO!

BM3 James, newly minted, got them to that pier. I caught him up to conditions and, "The gig can't go back, QMC. Wind and surf be up a bit." BM2 and him divided up watches to gig and barge. I waited for officers to come out, long after 6 PM. "Sun is down, QMC!" I mentioned it happened every day, "Captain." The Governor asked them to stay the night.

Edith place was in full swing by the time I got there. I heard thems a block away. 4 tables was filled with me crew and they saved me a seat at the bar, next to Edith. BM2 had to be on a stool so Etta could bother him. That boy can sure blushed. Come a time and the locals fill the other two. Alfa could be mentioned and Edith didn't flinch. Etta got the most comments. "Knife to hand and thought she'd kill me," one said. That brought up more of Etta and the crew kept it civil, for the locals.

About 8 PM come a knock at the door. Edith opened it to Walbeck, Chips, Armoror, and Donahey. Oh, we all stood to Walbeck. Chips introduced him and Donahey. He said they were there to just say hello. Them at the bar and Etta served them whiskey. Walbeck made some little chit chat to Edith about how the place looked. Chips and Armoror had been there before and gave extra good words to Edith about the place. One drink and they had to attend a social the Governor was having.

Etta kept the pitchers of beer full. There weren't a crew member didn't get a wink and some jokin. She had her names for each. The locals just loved this. They drank more to keep their mouths wet. I kept fillin me glass with whiskey and seltzer water. I need the water as was potent whiskey. I drank real slow. Best was the sparkle in Edith eyes, about to tears from laughter.

Only 4 of mine were to stay overnight. The hostel had guest to the other rooms. The rest went to other boarding places. I got showed me my comfy bed earlier. Her and MaMa must be writin as the second thing was the new, "Water Closet, QMC." Worsh room. Each of us got 15 minutes, on her wash schedule. Brits be like that. Thursday was 4 days ago. We did catchup a rain worshin since then. No, Edith didn't say, "Strip, Soak, Scrub, Wash." She did said, "Clean bodies on my clean sheets." There was no argument from us.

Come 9:30 and Edith said she needed to go to bed. "Up early to make breakfast." It took time for her to get hugs and kisses from the crew. I didn't take that spritzer in the glass after that. I was up this mornin at 4:30, with the waisters, to scrub the deck. Tired I was, head to pillow, and asleep.

Come 5AM I got woken by a nice kiss to cheek, blanket and sheet stripped off, and, "Up, now, to help with breakfast, QMC!" A thought crossed me mind that she was a Bos'n in a former life, for the tone of voice! I got 30 minutes more sleep than aboard ship.

I used me knife to cut up tators and onions to Edith bad eyes. The bangers got cut in half, "To cook faster." It seems all but us sailors had orders in for breakfast. I couldn't touch the pot for cooked oats or any pot on the stove. I could be her server as the guests came down to eat. Oh, somes I thought were locals were guest. Linen over arm, I delivered the plates to the tables she said. Nope, I got no tips.

Me crew and the guests went out the door by 7AM. I sent my crew to gather the others at the pier and back to the ship. Jacket and hat on, I reached my jacket to, "You bring out money and I swear I'll cut off that hand, QMC." I pulled out me personal card to her and, 'It would be nice to hear from you, now and then.' I got her house card from the registry desk.

A point to her card name got, "Passed. He loved London. I moved back here as didn't like the wet and cold." I had to give her a hug and kiss on her cheek. "When will I see you next?" I said, 'Oh, about 30 minutes from now,' to looks. 'A barge of 30 liberty crew will be at the pier about then. Maybe you can find places for them to get refreshments?'

Edith knew GM1 Bush when he got off the barge. The Petty officers divided up the crew to 5 places to satisfy their needs. Some recognized Edith, others, housekeepers of places they'd seen before. I gave her hugs and kisses as I stepped on that barge at 11:30, 22 March, 1898.

We made that North side pier in Norfolk on 28 March, mornin. The jackass tugs put us there. Commodore Griffith and staff come aboard to Captain Walbeck cabin, out, and to the pier. Walbeck gave the volunteers good words. I signed for Squadron.

QM1 Potts had Squadron office ready. Medicals and leaves got logged in and off. Meal chits went to mine and Marines, off. "Squadron had to build a special room for you, QMC!" I said, 'You take it. I'd like my old room, QM1.' He moved to it, bein bigger. I need my hidey holes for stuff. Susquehanna is in Philly for hull work. He's awaiting its return. So is a bunch of her crew. There was just enough room in the barracks for me 18.

I saw Effie last afternoon. Mr. Bish paid the bills, from the letter I gave her. Vie and B had not used her services that much. Oh, it was a cost, bein 2 of thems. Effie cut me a discount for multiple uses. I made an appointment to see Mr. Bish and had to see Ella for the evenin social for my crew 'cause of Rishell words about thems papers, not signed by Commodore and cost.

It is Tuesday afternoon, 29 March, hear at me table. I have resurrected that Possible bag. The crew did it up right last night. I just watched their antics. Come 7 PM and came a punch in me back. I turned to Vie, Rose, and Rishell. I escorted her back to her place, after makin sure the crew was off, sorta walkin. They staggered back to base, led by the Marines. Even the latter was not so good at marchin. Vie and I just walked and talked about times past. She giggled and laughed about the last story we played out. I just kiss to cheek and, "Good night, my sailor." Shush. Potts never discovered one hidey hole. I found an old bottle in it.

I got called into Griffith office 'afore noon. He handed over an invite to Retired Admiral Irwin place on Wednesday, tomorrow, early dinner, informal dress. I signed the RSVP and his clerk went out his door. He and Adjutant just gave me looks. I said, 'Commodore,' and left. I felt a change in the wind, like goin to the Med, the last time. There was an undercurrent, with Griffith, from his looks.

I am off to see Mr. Bish about stuff. Effie place is on the way back. I might catch up some Chinese and go bother Ella. No word from Regina. She was not home when I stopped by. 'Course, I have that Wednesday social with Irwin. Sign this out to you, My Lady.

By Your Leave, Missy,

An Old Sea Dog,

IN THE YEAR 1898, 19 APRIL: SQUADRON

Dear Miss Judith,

Monday morning, 4 April, here at me table. Potts, Wagner, and Burch run the squadron. They have divided up duties as only need one to do the musters. As long as Lt. Olson don't bother me, they can do as they please.

I picked up a paper last Wednesday mornin and came to an article about the USS Maine blowin up in Havana bay. I asked the clerks about this and got, "Where have you been, QMC?" It was old news to thems. You probably heard it afore me as it happened on 15 February.

I guess the Spanish Admiral didn't hear of it on 25 February, when I gave him me flag, or I might just have been in need all three pistols! Them Spanish Frigates must have been unawares on the 3rd and 7th of March, when we entered and left Gibraltar. They saluted us real nice, both times. The officers would have talked about it, if they had known, and Ships Ears Engle would have blabbed. It seemed strange the Governor of Bermuda wasn't knowin of such a thing.

The 30th, last Wednesday evenin, I got to Irwin place and greeted by him. Into the social room as B introduced me to, "Benjamin Thomas." A hand shake got his card. I gave him mine. It was Agnes, Irwin wife, and Robert Sr. and Clara Miller. I waited for Carrie to jump out. I got introduced to Mary. She is somewhere 'tween Vie and B in age and height.

They must have removed some parts of the table as it was just big enough around for us. Irwin sat at the head and Robert Sr. set right to him, talkin. Clara came next. I set Mary next to her. I took the other head of table seat. Agnes to Irwin left and then Benjamin and B. Poor Benjamin got two woman talkin in front of him and about interrupted his eatin. B also talked across so it was a gaggle of talk goin on. Woman conversation.

The social, after dinner, was at the table. Irwin served good whiskey and spritzer for me. He told Benjamin and Mary of some of me ventures, from afore. All the others had heard of them. Ben just listened and sipped his drink. He is my size and maybe younger. A bit stiff for me. Mary got eyes to some and laughs to others. I just said Irwin may over tell some of the stuff.

We got a good cigar in the men's room as the women went off to the tea or coffee. Irwin asked how our ship defeated, "two Spanish ships off Spain." I told you about that. Irwin wanted a play by play version. I used his cigars for ships. Benjamin said, "Why not do like Nelson and just go broadside to broadside." I gave him, 'We would have only given 12, 18 pounders to two ships, and received 20, 12 pounders to our sides. Walbeck set us to give the first ship 12, 18s, and then 12 more to the second ship, Sir.'

Irwin said, "I heard you pulled a pistol on two nephews to the King of Spain." I replied, 'If you give someone your sword, then they can hand it back by handle or blade to you, Admiral. I got it handed back real civil.' I had to say I asked for their swords, 'Politely, after the pistol was put away.' Ben said, "I'd call that reckless behavior."

I don't know if Irwin likes this guy. "Good you are into banking and now concerned with self preservation." He looked at me and, "Brilliant maneuvers. I'll send my personal regards to Captain Walbeck about this."

The carriage ride to B place was sorta quiet. They went out one side to me and Mary the other. I got a handshake from her and thanks for the evening from her. B come around and, "Regina said to bring those two scoundrels to her place on Friday. Bring food." The scoundrels begged off. Rishell did the same. I caught up Regina on this, after seein Mr. Bish. It was a woman thinkin eyes I seen and her odd looks to, "Bring Potts."

Friday, Potts and I set 4 pails to Regina kitchen. They jabbered like old friends. I took some whiskey and spritzer to glass and to the back porch swing. I got shoes to me eyes and, "Some for my glass, QMC?" It was B. I asked about Mary, to a smile and, "She said you were too old, too ugly, and have a dangerous job. I came so you have company." I said no words of Ben. Not me concern and I always like her smiles.

Inside, Potts introduced me to Sarah. Regina had introduced them some time ago. Around that table they were like two peas in a pod. I kept getting a wink from B. Rishell and Rose came to mind.

We had to leave early as, "You owe me a second story, QMC. Vie told me she had two parts to play in hers." I said, 'We can play out the same one. Then you will be one up on her, B.' It ended with the same giggles and laughs from her. I spent Saturday and Sunday evenin at Regina place for meals, with Potts and Sarah, to card games. B had social plans both days.

Tuesday, 12 April and it had been a week of stuff. Bos'n Silvis came by on his way home and caught me up to Admiral Taylor and stuff. Rishell said Walbeck was gonna unload some crew as he was headed to Gasport shipyard for some 2 or 3 weeks work. He still checks Bobbit paper figures and stuff. To the ship, quick, I told Walbeck ifn he did that then just might lose some gooduns to other ships. 'First ask, first get, Captain.' I told him to give them to Captain Saltsgiver signature and have Purser Hitcock pay for their meals. "Thank you, QMC."

That afternoon got called into Griffith office to a big envelope. An invite from Carrie to a formal dinner at Robert Sr. place on Saturday. Nope, just me name. I accepted and I had Rishell write them orders. I took that to Saltsgiver for my personal stuff and back to ship for Armoror Hardis stuff. He gave me a bad look, but it was on them orders.

We took pails to Regina place on Wednesday evening, me and Potts. I went to the back porch swing, with spritzer and whiskey. From the dark comes a woman and, "Eva, I'm invited to supper." I got a nice handshake, eyes up and down, and she went into the house. Regina introducer her to all. Eva and me took to chairs and them folding tables, as the table was full. I can only say my good name was sure slandered by most, to thems laughin. I had to say they were exageratin, 'For your entertainment and to embarrass me, Eva.'

She begged off card games so I got to mention some true things she asked of. She went out once for a bit and back to seat. Polite, I didn't ask much of her. She lives near and knows Effie, who introduced her to Regina. She knew Vie and Rose, "live near." Come just after 9 PM, she shook me hand and off she went.

Carrie card said, "See Effie at 6 PM, Thursday." I got to stand at Effie counter and out came her and Eva. I asked about, 'Dinner at the Chinese place, Eva.' A nod of head and off we went. Effie gave me an odd look.

She knew the routine and filled a bowl. Seated, Vie and Rose came in. I paid for their bowls and got more of me character slaughter by thems two. They did say I was always a gentleman with them. Eva caught that wink of Vie. We went to the wine place, just outside. Eva caught up a bottle as thems two took two and Eva went off with, 'Good night.'

Friday morning, 1 April, I got called into Lt. Olson office about, "The men in the Marine Tent, QMC!" I said he'd need to talk with the Marine Major. 'They were not turned over to Squadron, so not on my list, Sir.' He gave me a list of crew required by Williams, Carney, and Fran. They came in as I saw QM3 Mark, QM2 Bush, QM1 Hood, and BMC Bothel. They just passed through to say hello. Burch, Wagner, and Potts got to tend that mess.

Friday evenin, well, just reread on Wednesday. Eva did bump me for some pocket bottle to her spritzer. I got some reaction from her when I mentioned I taught QM school in Philly for a year. I told her of Weaver and me doin height measurements in the park. Her up, I said the carriage would be at Effie place at 6 PM, to her nod and off she went.

Saturday, best uniform, her hand to mine, we went down that reception line headed by Robert Sr. and Clara, Robert Jr. and Carrie, B and James, who I missed his last name, then Vie with Stewart. Vie just smiled to her arm on Stewart. Carrie took Eva around during social, afore dinner. During dinner me name got slaughtered again, to laughs around, 'cept for Eva.

At the after dinner social I presented Carrie with her arm protectors and gauntlets to Ohhs and ahhs around. She kept closing her hand and punching me, to more laughs around. I put on my full regalia, asked for a chair, 'tween us, and gave her that blunt sword. I took other and pulled belayin pin from me bag. I told of the ships officer practice and showed her how to 'Tink, Tink, Tink' the swords. Carrie about slashed me with her thrashin and givin me mean looks.

B got dressed and we did the same for a bit. I had to have Vie give it a try. Eva to guards and I noticed she was as good as the officers I done this with. She kept tryin to go over the chair to get me. I was fightin with sword in right hand and belayin pin in left. She sure didn't like when I fended off most with the pin. I got a look and, "Fight me without the chair, QMC!" I had to set some rules.

She set her stance real proper, sword out. I flinched the pin at her and she ducked. Oh, I just poked her in the mid chest, to bad her eyes. She asked for a pin. I pulled one from me cloth bag to her sword to me back. That got laughs and, "Never turn you back to an opponent, QMC."

Eva didn't know what to do with the pin. I figured she never used one so I stood square to her and waited. She did Lovelace slash, which caught me gauntlet. She is quick, but off balance, so I put the pin to her side, shoved her some and put blade, easy, to her back, and pushed her away. Oh, the eyes I got. She gave some motion to that sword point my mind saw.

I changed sword and pin. Only me refluxes saves me. I blunted the sword with the pin, cut her side with sword and used it to push her forward. Oh, the eyes of death I got. She did the Lovelace attack. I crossed pin and sword, dropped the pin, and caught up her arm to around her. Sword in hand, I wrapped her other arms to her and picked her up. Oh, I got nice words, for a sailor. In her ear, said, 'Never got angry in a sword fight, Missy.' I put her down to feet and shoved her forward to real mean looks.

I unbuttoned me coat, got the revolver from the left side, cocked it, and shot her with a blank, to silence. Eva didn't know what to do, but her sword tip came up. I shot her with another blank, came to attention, and did that sword salute to me nose, the blade tilted to her, as a sign of respect. I did it a second time, the dip of sword. Well, Eva caught on to this and did the same. We did that sword salute and the room was about blown out as all exhaled. I offered, but no one would take her or me on, without the chair. To Robert Sr. I said, 'Eva and I will take one of your fine panatelas and whiskey on your veranda, Sir,' to no objections.

She poured her own mix, light. It was good whiskey, so I added just a little filler. I lited her and my slim cigar and just leaned on the railing. Her mouth moved twice, questions in her eyes. Out came the gents to ask her questions. Yes, we still had the guards on so polite hands looked at them. It was a delight to see her face lite up.

I got a hand to me shoulder and turned to Carrie. "So, QMC, I hear you tell your stories, in private," with her good smile. 'Some are best told, in private.' Came, "And me?" I gave a wink to, 'I thought you liked wrestling best?' Oh, that got a better smile. She looked to Eva and, "We should save her from the hungry horde." Eva face and smile was to remember. 'Leave her in the sun a bit longer. She is enjoying herself for once, Carrie.'

Eva was quiet back to Effie place, where she wanted to be let out. A hand to hers, out of the carriage, I said, 'I'll be here at 1 PM, tomorrow, to square up with Effie on things.' Came, "No need." I pulled her back some, hand on hers and said, 'Tell Warrant, Master at Arms, Reynolds, I defeated his move, for a second time.' She melted into the dark.

Effie wasn't at the counter when I got there so I looked around, said hi to George, the guy in the shoe department, and Tina, who takes care of the women section. I got to counter as Effie came through the curtains to the back room. "Eva already paid for the clothing I gave her. She don't want to be in debt to no man." I said, 'Understand, Effie,' and gave nice words toward Eva and all I knew of her. 'She is quite the woman,' and more good words. 'But, she didn't live up to Regina formal dress stuff.' Came, "I dressed her myself. Nothing better, QMC!"

'Well, yes, but, her skinny leg stockings didn't match her skivvies, nor her scuffed up shoes!' The curtains parted ahind her and Eva was fit to kill someone. Me! Oh, nice seaman words I got. I went around the counter, pinned her arms around, lifter her, and gave her a little kiss to her lips. Back to her feet and I got poked in me chest to more bad words. Effie shushed her and said, "You two love birds sit, talk civil, or I'll have your hide." She point to a bench, like PaPa did, and, "Sit! Talk quietly!"

I asked for her shoes and got feet hidden under her skirt. 'To have them polished, please.' Her hand under skirt, shoe off, and I gave them to George. I sat and said I'd seen her shoes and stockins when she went into her stance, to fence. I got her eyes and, "Personals." I said, 'You have on brown stockins and tan skivvies.'

'You came up to the curtains and adjusted your skirt, lifted it. I saw your shoes and stockins.' "And personals." I pointed to Tina and said, 'She said you only buy tan ones, never white nor dark.' About then Effie came over and said we should buy something or find another place to park our behinds. I pointed to the ladies section and got Eva looks. We had a nice time talkin that afternoon. Mostly me, of 'afore.

Eva grew up in Philly. Reynolds was a family friend. They used sticks to duel. She said he smacked her in the butt when she did things wrong. He retired and still lives there. She works as an accountant for one of the importers. I said I shot her with the pistol to end the match as I was gettin tired and she was about to get the best of me. That got a raised eyebrow. Come time and I got a little kiss and, "Thank you, QMC. And, what story do I get to act out?" I said them women talk and tell.

Tuesday, 19 April, 1898, and I pick this up again. You say to write when stuff is goin on. Since last Monday I can say, not much, as far as excitement. Not to me. Lt. Olson talked to Commode Griffith about men assigned to squadron. Me and Rishell got called into see him. Rishell has 5 lists of men to track of leave, sick, hospital, in the barracks, and staff. By the time he got done addin, subtractin, and all, he confused me and I know the muster sheet. Admiral asked of those in Marine tent. "Not assigned to squadron, Commodore. Under Marine guard, Sir." "Dismissed!"

I saw Eva most evenins last week. Wednesday, Friday through Sunday with Regina, Silvis, Potts, and Sarah there. Thursday I paid for Chinese. Vie and Rose came in. There was laughs around Eva small room table. Thems drinkin wine, more of my character was destroyed. I had to get even with Rose so brought up about her needin a plumber, to get her voice back. 'So, Rose, Rishell is a good kisser?' She got red, we laughed. No, she never answered.

Socials, ya ask? Formal ones be only once a month. Informal come about maybe twice a month, 'cause of cost. Eva has come to know our loose group a bit better. She stays quiet, but smiles more. She asked about how I know Carrie and B. Maybe I hedged a bit on some direct questions. But, Regina name is tied to all of them. She asked how I knew she smoked. 'In the carriage you crossed your legs and brushed ash off you skirt. You smelled of peppermint. At Regina meals you step out, for a bit, and came back with ash and a peppermint smell.' She just gave a smile.

I'll put this in the mail goin to dinner. I need to wind up Ella as I haven't seen her in a while.

By Your Leave, Missy,

An Old Sea Dog,

IN THE YEAR 1898, 02 MAY: SQUADRON

Dear Miss Judith,

Monday morning, April 25th. Oh, it was week of it. Last Tuesday, I went to Ella place, after dinner, to her bad looks and words. "Ain't seen ya in a while, QMC!" After a couple remarks I could hardly get a drink! Glass to that bar and I got a punch from ahind. I about put a fist to a face and, 'Eva?' A hand to her and she set to a stool. Ella came by and, "Leave him alone, here, and trouble follows." I got eyes from Ella and a laugh from Eva. Thems introduced each other.

Ella gave a wink. "He is a bother, without company, Eva." Eva asked if I was an honest man. "Honest as the day is long. The problem is come night, you have to watch him," got a smile from Eva. Ella sent a runner to Effie, who directed him to Eva place. Ella talked to us when no busy at the bar. Came no better words of me character. I got Eva smile and a Kiss at her door.

Thank you for the letter. Eva? Light brown hair, not blue nor green eyes and bad, when pissed! Younger than B. She be eye to eye in her high heels and lower for her other shoes. Lower again in them flat leather shoes, like when fencing. Each has a different clickin sound. 'Tween Vie and B in build, what with the layers of cloths younz wear.

20 April and I got called into Griffith conference room with Admiral Taylor ahind. Me and Rishell were charged with false musters. "The Marine tent people should have been listed on Squadron muster! You are missing 18 people from morning muster reports, Rishell!" Rishell put that paper to his desk of Walbeck request to house them, temporary status. Came that 'Volunteer" contract to his hand and I got bad words from him. Admiral Taylor just looked on. "Commodore Mast! Brig for Both, Captain Saltsgiver! Irons On!"

Saltsgiver said, "I can only confine QMC to quarters, till a full Admiral mast, Sir. As far as Rishell, only to the Marine tent, until Admiral Mast also. Volunteer orders apply, Commodore." Taylor gave a whisper to the Commodore Adjutant Captain.

Friday, 22 April, 10 AM, we went into that same room and a legal Commander headed the table. Captains, Commodore, and Taylor ahind him. The first page was, "Captain Walbeck assigned his people to Marine Captain Saltsgiver for charges, now dismissed." Next page of, "Captain Walbeck accepted 18 men, to his ship, Volunteers, to be aboard at his need, Gentlemen." Only Taylor smiles at this. "Breach of Contract, Commodore, 4 times, registered against you," and bad looks to me and Rishell. On with, "Dismissed, as you two failed to inform Commodore of his requirement to inspect the men. The volunteer contract has been previously found to be a legal document, Gentleman. The 18 men belong to Walbeck crew, Commodore."

That evenin we took supper with Regina and Silvis, Rishell and Rose, Potts and Sarah. Come a time and I got high heels to that porch. Eva. Bottle to her glass, I lited them panatela cigars, to no words, and just eyes from her. We entered Regina place to good words, salutes to me, and Rishell. I walked her back home to, "In for a glass of wine, QMC?" 'Na, I got to walk and think, Eva.' I got a little kiss and "Tomorrow, 1 PM at Effie place, if you please."

The charges dismissed, Taylor shooed them out, to me standin. Oh, he gave bad words to me and reminded me of the grait thing. Last was, "You are living on the edge of your sword, QMC." Another look and, "Well played, stoke for stroke. I just hope Admiral Palmer finds your, ah, antics, as humorous I do, QMC."

Saturday, I walked into a trap at Effie place. In came Rose, Vie, and Eva, to the bench, shoes off, and to George. I got Eva little kiss and all three showed socks with a hole in the foot. 'Ok,' to 'nother peck on the cheek. Yep, a sucker I was. Thems three padded feet all over Effie place to, no, no dresses.

Rose wanted curtains, Vie needed candles, and Eva wanted some napkins. OK. Effie put each bundle to paper with string around. I had to pay her and George. Oh, we had to visit the wine shop. Two to each. Rose took the packages, 6 wine bottles, and off. So, it was Vie and Eva gabberin as we walked around. Rose came back and now a hen party of talkin. I wondered why I was there, 'cept for money. Vie has the bigger place they drank some of the wine and talked.

Last evening, Sunday, it was a quick dinner at Regina place. It was like the woman were talkin, mind to mind. The table cleared, dishes done, and I got about jerked out the door by Eva. She didn't like any of my stories. She mentioned Vie said I was oblivious to the obvious, but picked up on little stuff. A game, for me.

'Rose picked out curtains. I signaled her to get a set for you, also. You seem to have a new set in your window.' Eva gives this growl sound when peeved. 'The candle is same as the 6 Vie picked out. Nice Napkins,' to 'nother growl. I added, 'You women can't darn very well. The poor socks showed some effort. I can get an oldster here to show how to darn socks, proper.' That got a, "Humph!" On with, 'Effie sent younz back for another pair as was 6 pair for 5 cents.' Game over? No. I had to say what shoes she had on.

So, shoes off, into her room, and 'ahind the curtain. I had to guess, "Shoes, QMC." I already saw the color of the socks she bought and Tina mentioned personals. Came some time, rustlin goin on, and she come out tryin to hunker down. The hem of her skirt gave her away. Plus the shoe soles. Humph!

Second time, she come on tip toes. Her flats make a sound. Her sword first step was forward on her tie, to set a stance. 'Nother humph. Out the curtain and no sound. I got her big grin and, "So, QMC?" She came over all cutesy and turned in front of me. B had a better sense of humor about what I did. Well, just maybe the three words I said started that wrestlin match. No, not I love you. That might have been taken better. Just mentioned her skinny legs and such I saw.

Like with Carrie, I got bit. A dirty fighter, she be. I got kicked when I got her around and so picked her up. Oh, and the bad sailor words to me ears. I let her win 2 of 3 matches as I let her go for arm bites and kicks to shines. At the end of 3, I finally got a smile, kiss, and "Thank you for all, QMC." I had to win the last one.

Over my store bought wine I mentioned I could get her a better payin job. B came to mind. Irwin knows people. Eva didn't like that. "If my boss heard I'd interviewed for it, I'd get fired! How will I live?" I said, 'Marry Me!' That got no good looks. "Never here and still no work, QMC?"

Monday, 02 May, and back to me table. I've been away to Philly. Lt. Olson called me into his office after lunch, last Monday. He had orders for me to sign, to be temporary Ships Master of Susquehanna, till Norfolk and sail on Friday, 29th. I can say we had some words, 'tween us. 'Never on a Friday, Sir,' was one.

Into Commode office and, "Simply sail her here, QMC." I had to mention Shenandoah comin out of Philly, 'Just sailing along, Commodore.' I mentioned her runnin aground, more than once, and jackass tugs down to Dover, Delaware, and ones from the Pilot ship to the pier. Came, 'Express train to Philly,' and lots of stuff. Oh, he had no religion in his words. 'As part of Shenandoah crew, assigned, Captain Walbeck must agree, Sir.' Got more words to that, I did.

Rishell came in and took notes of what I asked for. Potts got called in, as he was QM1 assigned to her. I got Commodores agreement to all clauses, 'cause of unknown Captain, officers, and crew. Ships Masters Paper was me worry. That ship goes aground and them are paper gone.

I took them Telly messages to the base place and the guy just clicked them off on that key. It took time to get a reply, to me hand. I caught up Eva at her work place and said where I was goin and asked if she had an address for her aunt and Mr. Raymond. There was no love loss for her aunt. She married a supply office that Raymond introduced her to. They moved to Portsmouth Navy yard, got her a job, and transferred to Key West Naval station. No tears, just gray eyes and "Stop by when you get back, QMC."

Tuesday, it was a reverse of me gettin to Norfolk, long ago. I ate a big breakfast, trolley to Norfolk, and onto a ferry to Cape Charles. 3 hours of it. At 11 AM we got on the "Express" train. Potts and me just to seats and watchin the scenery go by. I put notes to me pocket tablet. There was only 5 stops and one train change at Laurel, Delaware. We dot first sitting for meals, made Philly station at 6:30 PM, and a trolley to the base.

The Petty Office at the Admin building didn't look up, took our orders and said, "Transit barracks." Me broke hand took his pencil away and I put a finger to the orders. He looks up and I said, 'Single rooms, or Warrant, or Officer berthin, if you please.' Me hard eyes said I wasn't pleased. He didn't like the Tellys I handed him.

It was just our duffle bags to our private rooms and off to the piers we went. Eyes 'atween us, it would take some days to make the ship fit to sail. Oh, the sails was stowed in them yard arms all nice.

It looked like a derelict, what with all the ship yard stuff aboard. It reminded me of Monongahela, afore the base Admiral came aboard. I took Potts to an old bar I knew off base. We had no good words toward the ship and that list grew as we talked.

Wednesday, we stepped aboard her at 7 AM to no officers, some crew about. The Quarter deck watch said most showed up, "About 8, Chief." I asked of Captain and officers. "Oh, about then, Chief. The yard still is in charge of the ship." Monongahela all over. We did a walk around the upper and lower decks. Old Tom, the ships cat, would have left for the number of critter below.

The crew meandered aboard like sheep and the officers came aboard. Me and Potts saluted the Captain and into his cabin. He was a nice guy, Captain Wilson. I showed him me orders, Ships Masters paper, and got, "We'll sail on Friday, QMC, come hell or high water." A finger to the orders and said, 'I think we need to see the Ships Board of Inspection Officer, Captain,' to his bad eyes. I pointed to the orders, smiled, and said, 'The ship only sails when I say so, Captain.' Came his bad words of, "Mast." I picked up the orders and said, 'Captain. I rightfully refuse to be aboard, let alone try to sail it to Norfolk, Sir.'

Potts and me made the pier and this Lieutenant caught us up, asked us to a go back, and see Wilson. I got introduced to the officers. It was a nice meeting till I read me orders and, well, thems didn't like the account I gave of the ships condition, personnel, deck clutter, and condition of ships stove, 'Captain.' I said we should visit the Board of Inspection Officer.

This Captain, Board of Inspection, didn't like me words. "The ship is under control of the Ship Yard, QMC." He didn't like me words about the ship trying to sailin on Friday. Orders to his hand, words read, Masters Paper to his hand and, 'My report, which I have to give to Admiral Taylor, will contain all the details I have noted. I will await word of where the ship grounds, to add to that report, Captain.'

It was about 10 AM that me and Potts was walkin around, rememberin all the stuff from Boot Camp, when we got caught up by the ships Lt. We went aboard to this civilian arguin about work to be done with Board of Inspection Captain. It seems the ship yard was 'ahind in ships work. I will say that Captain pulled out papers, fingers to words, and them ship yard workers ignored the noon whistle for lunch. From the Nav deck, me and Potts saw lots goin on. After ashore dinner, the shipyard workers was like ants on dead bug. We went back to that same cheap place to talk.

Thursday mornin, 7 AM, and there was lots of ants around. Lots of barrels, gear, and stuff was gone. I asked the Lt. to form up the men on the pier, 'Sir,' to lots of shouts, bad words, a whistle, and little order among the men. It took half hour just to get them to divisions of Gunners Mates, Bosn's, Waisters, and supply types. The officers were no help, as they didn't know their men. The Admiral had stripped the ship of men and ordered in new ones. Oh, this was gonna be a sailin to remember.

I called, 'Petty Officers Forward.' Thems was hidin among the sheep and not a 1st Class around to be seen. I wished I'd brought along BM1 and GM1. I told the Bos'n Lieutenant, 1st Lieutenant too set men to Fore, Main, and after masts, 'Sirs.' Gunner, an Ensign, to gun positions. 'Petty officers,' not many, 'to gun numbers, Sir.' Potts got the rest to sort out. Last was a Cooks 2nd and his two people. I asked, 'Ships store aboard?' Three days' worth. I went with him to the provisions building, showed me orders and. "Extra provisions will arrive this afternoon, QMC."

Thursday afternoon and the deck was about clear. I caught up this civilian about the deck he about spit on. I said, politely, "Your damage, my ship!" That Captain from that Board of Inspection must have said something to him. Me and Potts took a quick dinner, back, to them civilian's holly stoning the deck. They did work them holly stones all over, not proper though.

I'd already spoken to the Harbor Master about tugs. Friday morning, after formal muster aboard, was that meetin in Captain cabin, officers around, me center, and I checked of that list. Last was, 'Cook 2nd to make noon meal for crew,' to whispers around. Cook, his two, and some Waisters were raisin dough for bread and lited that stove. It worked. Check list done, I wanted sails set, that I mentioned. 'Half hour, gentlemen.'

The Lead Tug Master and assistant came aboard afore lunch. Over the Captain table he went over the Delaware River stuff. He mentioned all the hazards, bad places, and ship groundings afore. Susquehanna was mentioned, a lot. He and I set the sailin time to 10 AM. A 6 hour pull to Bombay Hook point and then on our own.

Up on deck, afore goin ashore, he gave a bad look and no chance to make the ocean. He had keen eyes of things on deck and most especially the men in formation with strings of dead rats in their hands. I told them at quarters I'd pay a copper for each 10 dead. He eyed me up and down he did. 'I can put this ship in the ocean without sails. Done it before, Tug Master.' After that, well, I'd have to see about that.

Cook 2nd put the freshest barrel of beef to the seepin tub after muster, with tators, and the freshest vegetables to them pots. 'Tween watchin the Bosn's settin sails I asked for, I stopped by his pots. No, not up to squadron Edwards standards, but no bad. The roasted beef smelled good, cookin. With the bread smell comin from the oven, I gave him good words. I told the Waisters to mind the bread!

Bos'n and 1st Lieuy hurt me ears with words and yellin. I went over the signal whistles to start each mast. Twirly, attention. One blow, jib. Blow twice for fore mast. Once for fore top. Two for fore course. OK. Same with the Lieuy for main mast, 'cept three whistles, and then one or two. No, no top gallants for this crew.

I caught up 4 oldsters, not assigned, at forecastle bulkhead and asked if they liked how the sails were set. They gave knuckles to their foreheads and their words. I assigned each to one of the belayin pin boards of the Bow sprint, Fore mast, Main mast, and Aft mast. At each I just said, 'Square them away, ABS.' I got knuckles to head and the sails lines set better. I told Bos'n and 1st Lieuy about this.

By supper time the bosn's were better at sail handlin. I caught up a Bos'n 2nd and made him in charge of the aft mast. I figured I'd only need the spanker, the pusher sail. His 5 men and me oldster set it to me likin. Cook 2nd Stairs meal was OK. Crew ate hearty, from the afternoon workout. Me and Potts did the 'Smokin Lamp Lited,' to listen to the crew conversation. There was no grumblin or such.

At quarters, Saturday, the 30th, at 7:30, I paid off the strings of rats presented. At my request, Captain Wilson, me, and officers inspected the ship and crew, all 85 of thems. That is much less than

120 compliment. Cook Stairs presented the stove and I got a smell of bread and fruit and complimented his meals.

9:30 and them tugs tied up fore and aft with Wilson in chair on the Starboard side, Bos'n to port poop and 1st Lieuy to starboard side. The Pilot said, 'Prepare to sail.' I had Potts and 3 new seaman at the helm. I was at helm indicator and put up me hand to one finger. Wilson gave the order to single up fore, aft lines, and bring in the spring ones. That Pilot looked at me. Done, two fingers up to Wilson, "Cast off fore and aft lines, up the brow." It took just whistle tweets to do this.

In the river, settled with the current, the tugs was givin whistles. A Waister comes up with these little baked things and handed them around. Just bread dough folded over, filled with raisins and apples, baked. Another came up with coffee cups, around. The Pilot Master just gave me looks and he gave good words around from all.

Come Bombay Hook Point at 3 PM, the Pilot Master had Captain look at the chart. There was words around. Him and his Polly Parrot, on the forecastle, get into a tug and gone to, no wind. Wilson called for sails. Ok. I turned to him and pointed to his limp pennant and my flag. 'Would you like to go down river bow on or backards, Captain?' No one likes me humor. Just for the fun of it, I had Potts turn us around in the river, floating backards. Wilson was to have a spell at this, so, I had another at the helm turn us around. The other two at the helm got to do it.

Come 4 PM and came a breeze from the North. I gave a finger to Wilson and came tweets from Port and Starboard poop. Bos'n and 1st Lieuy kept changin their minds on sails. I took a turn of the deck and gave orders to them oldsters. I couldn't stop thems from putting knuckles to foreheads. They liked me pats on their backs.

At 10 AM on Sunday, 01 May, Potts woke me up in the Chart Room. "QMC. Pier is in sight." He'd relieved me at the Chart Table at sun up, around 6. I stayed up all night, with lots of Bosn's and them oldsters. I allowed them to slept where they could. A helmsman bumped me as required, what with the contrary winds. The Bos'n and 1st Lieuy were about useless.

I put a finger to papers on that Chartroom table, pen atop. 'Commodore said you could write in to accept or decline the orders,

QM1. Ship is understaffed and poorly lead.' I got, "Any thoughts, QMC?" Mine was to go to me room, get some good sleep, afore startin that report to Taylor.

The Commodore came aboard with his staff and into Wilson cabin. I stepped off that brow and to me room. I took 2 good drinks of that 'Hidy Hole' bottle and to bed. Uncle Curtis words were there, on me mind. "Oh, the thrill to take a green crew, on a ship headed to the Horn, me Laddie!"

Sign this out to you, 2 May, 1898, as I go to supper, My Lady.

By Your Leave, Missy,

An Old Sea Dog,

IN THE YEAR 1898, 30 MAY: SQUADRON

Dear Miss Judith,

I start this on 9 May, in the afternoon, Missy. Me Log Book is present. Last Tuesday, the 3rd, I got called into Commodore Griffith office to an invite card across to me. He be still mad at me as I didn't allow him to change a word of that report, sailin Susquehanna to Norfolk. He took great exception to that paper of recommendations I gave him to look over. The invite was to B commin out party at Admiral Irwin place on Saturday.

Walbeck got to read the recommendations first, that Monday morning. He signed the report, me recommendations, and signed that volunteer list back to me. "You do know we are at war with Spain and are sailing to the Caribbean, QMC?" I gave, 'Yes, Captain.'

That evening, as agreed, I went to the Chinese place to Rose, Vie, and Eva came in. I showed thems that invite and got, "Can't afford it, QMC." A finger to the invite and, 'QMC to escort, Miss Eva E. Kinter.' On with, 'It seems I, not you, must make sure you are dressed for the occasion, Eva,' to her bad eyes. To Rose and Vie, 'We could hog tie her up, stripper her bare, have Effie dress her, and hog ties her back into that carriage.' Both agreed to that.

Oh, was words to me, back at Eva place. Nope, I turned no cheek to her hand and got bit some number of times and feet stomped as I put arms around her. I allowed her first win, what with hurt feet, bit hard, so I let go for second round. The third ended only when she said, "Uncle, QMC. I'll go, properly dressed." I think she, like B, just likes to wrestle!

Wednesday, the 4th, I got called into Commodore conference room to Walbeck, his officers, Taylor, and Captains 'ahind him. Wagner and Burch were ahind me. I already had words to them and the Commodore, Adjutant, and Olson. Taylor gave me a hand to speak. I went on for, a time of it. Susquehanna was in lots of them. Good and bad.

It came down to Shenandoah was over staffed with capable officers and Petty Officers. 'Admiral, some need to step up, to advance.' I gave a list of names on Shenandoah and another list of

Susquehanna that, 'Stayed to station all night, so we made that Pilot ship, Admiral.' I could give no bad words to any crew member. Even, 'Cook Stairs, Sirs,' got a good mentioned.

Taylor shooed all from that room, 'cept me. He was like one of them caged tigers at Philly zoo, just pacin around that room and finally set to that desk. The Marine Major, at his quarters, should have heard him call in his Adjutant, clerk, and Rishell. "Commodore is by half afraid to make a decision, QMC. You are a whole and half forward with yours."

We took pails to Silvis and Regina place. Potts, Wagner, Burch, Rishell, and me. It was an outside party as the house couldn't hold us all. Cora, Margaret, Sarah, and Rose showed up. Eva snuck up ahind me and got her poke to me back. She has an open invite to Wednesday supper. "Vie got invited to the social." I gave her a grin and, 'So, you and I get to dress her, Regina formal,' to her laugh.

Maggie, Bothel wife, showed. I went to check on them little flags, Bothel was out, and thought she might enjoy the night out. Carrie show them flags off. It cost me more than a penny a flag. "Quality costs, QMC." I got a kiss on the cheek and smile.

Thursday evenin, the 5th, was me sittin on that bench as Vie and Eva came out in dresses to my looks. B was, 'The Show,' for the day. Vie would be on Stewart arm, so she just need a stylish dress. By the t\Third time, to Eva, I asked of shoes she would wear. A mention of Regina formal wear got a growl and out she came in that tan dress.

Friday, 11 AM, there was a formal inspection at Squadron. Me 18 and more lined up to new Marine Lieutenant and Corporal Waltermire. The new Marine to the podium and Wagner came forward. Taylor read him that oath of Warrant Officer. Oldster came forward and gave him a Shenandoah flag. Burch came next to the same and flag. They got three Hurzays.

Griffith got introduced and Taylor, Adjutant, pinned on two stars, for Vice Admiral. Hand up, down, and an Oldster came with Monongahela flag on pole, followed by the rest, to that wood place and three Hurzays to him. It was an evenin party at Regina place for the new Warrant Officers. Cora and Margaret was so pleased at this. Maybe them two scoundrel will now marry them.

Saturday, the 7th, I handed Vie to Stewart at Admiral Irwin place. There was twinkles in thems eyes. Hand on mine, Eva and I went down that reception line of Irwin, wife, Robert Sr, wife, Mr. Williams and wife, Vie parents, Robert Jr. and Carrie, and lots I don't remember. It was an informal, formal thing.

Into the back yard and B got to introduce Eva to all the women. Irwin and I took to the bar, watchin, and talkin. He gave me bad words to my recommendations of the ships, but gave Eva kind looks. It was just a tan skirt, pearl blouse, tan jacket, and straw hat! "QMC, the blue, green earrings, and simple necklace just set her eyes off to that blue ribbon in that simple hat." I said, 'Her smile sets them all off, Admiral.'

We had some time to talk, 'tween us, 'afore Carrie caught me up in this women stuff. Oh, the carnage to me character she did. Agnes, Irwin wife, introduced Eva to the men. It was a fine afternoon of socializing, for Eva. Come that time and Irwin invited Eva and Me, Vie and Stewart to Sunday lunch. "Informal, regular dress, please."

Sunday, the 8th, was another trap I walked into. Oh, Irwin and Agnes greeted us. 'Course, there was B, James, holdin hands. Carrie and Robert Jr. were there also. Irwin had 4 other men and wives for me to not remember. A nice lunch and all, eatin over, Irwin invited Eva to, "Spritzer and whiskey. Some of the men would like to talk to you."

Oh, her to sit at a table and those 4 talkin to her. I was ahind her, listenin. They asked where she worked, what she did, and all. One guy asked what she was paid. Hands to her shoulder and, 'Eva, if one of these men hired you on, today, would you just go to that place and hope to find work.' Her voice said, "I'd need to tell my boss I'd found a different position, QMC. I don't know if I'd be hired on or what I'd do when I got there." That got eyes around that table.

I don't know them gents from Adam. 'Here sits a lovely, independent, intelligent woman with integrity, Gentleman. She tells her current employer she found another job, to go to your office with no assurance of employment.' Me hand into jacket, two coins to hand, to the left, the broken one, and I showed them two gold pieces, back into me jacket. 'Wages for a common woman in you accounting department, down stairs.' I got two other coins from me jacket, to left hand, shown to thems and, 'The minimum cost for a lovely woman, appropriately dressed, as part of you staff, in accounting, Gentlemen.'

Eva kept grabbin me arm. I ignored her and put eyes to them 4 gents. I asked Admiral Irwin for paper, pen, and ink, wrote down the date. 'Employment contract for Eva E. Kinter. Unconditional employment for 6 months, evaluation to increase wages at that time. Advanced wages paid today, for the week. Friday pay is advanced, for the next week.' I gave them, 'She'd always have a smile on Monday morning, Gentlemen.'

Eyes to thems and I said, 'No pennies or nickels, Gentleman. Honest offers.' Irwin kept givin me looks and Eva was white. I got another strong spritzer and water, for me and Eva, as thems 4 talked awhile. Came two gents to the table and signed that paper. She signed as accepted. Me and Irwin signed as whiteness.

I stood back as them two signers caught up her hand in conversation. 'Ahind, I got, "You sold her for a good price, QMC," and mentioned the ladies would like to talk to her. 'Give her moment, B. And ifn your James keeps try to eat left handed, he will starve to death! I guess you two were holding hands, under the table?' That got her squinty eyes, a little smile, a cheek kiss, and she took Eva from the circle of men.

We begged off supper there as, 'Eva needs to check her wardrobe for appropriate cloths, Admiral.' His coach took us back to Effie place and Eva was not happy. I mentioned the company Eva got hired to and, 'She needs two modest skirts and two blouses, Effie.' Eva objected as, "No money to my hand!" Ya, it was in that IOU in Me pocket. Officers and them gents seem to never carry money. Effie was in and out of that curtain room and had to catch her up to some stuff. Done, came paper and string to that package. Effie threw in that straw hat and two different ribbons for it.

We ate Chinese, got bottles of wine, went back to her place with few words, and that package clutched to her chest. Off to the worsh room place she went and must have worshed twice. Her face came back scrubbed clean and pink. From ahind the curtain she came out in old blouse and skirt, with sad puppy looks. "I owe Effie money and don't know about tomorrow to paying her back." I asked if Effie had asked her about money. "No, she just gave me things to try on."

I took that receipt from jacket and showed Effie had her account with a nice credit amount. The back of it showed that $3.00 charge for stuff. I got her eyes and she attacked me as, "I won't be in debt to no man!" Luckily, she'd taken off her shoes! I rolled her from 'ahind, proper, and said, 'Never get mad in a sword fight, Eva.' Me hands touched her sides and them good sailor words got cut short. She was laughin and wigglin. I touched them again to more bad words, but laughin. She is ticklish, like you, Miss Judith. Your father did that to you, time ago.

The scrubbed face and looks said Eva was fearful of the comin mornin. A new situation, after her boss gave her words for leavin, unannounced. I stood many a time to new Capt'n and a butt chewed, yes both of them, for somethin out of my control, mostly. She is frustrated and angry at herself for her situation. Ya can't be mad, giggling, and laughin. For once I was correct!

Set to bare feet, she was like an old hen chicken in a dust bowl and just shook all over. I got evil eyes, that nasty growl and said, lied, 'They paid to me, your new employers, after B took you way.' I held out me hands, like to grab her sides and got, "You wouldn't dare!" I put out 1 finger, wiggle it, pointed it to the curtain, and asked to see her new cloths.

Out of curtain she came in a light brown skirt and off white blouse with lace around neck. 'Nice.' Into curtain, shuffling, out in tan skirt I seen afore, and just about blueish blouse. Effie did have an eye of that style. She twirled around, like afore. I asked about legs, 'To match Regina style, Eva.'

She raised that skirt hem above the new socks, a bit. I got her glad eyes to mine. 'Still skinny, hairy legs, Eva.' I had to remind her, 'You don't want to wrinkle the new cloths!' Came her growl, bad eyes, to curtains, back out in old cloths, and bad language to me ears. She forgot that sword rule so I wrapped her up in my arms, again, fingers to her side, to her laughtin. I only let her go when she said, "I Give, QMC." She didn't mean it and attached again! There must have some "B" in her blood.

There was Eva smiling face there, after our goin ons, with them blue, gray, twinkling eyes. I gave her a string pouch, 'Money to eat.' From me jacket I handed her a little jewelry box. She opened it to silver earrings and a pendant with little sapphires on it. 'Polaris, Eva. The star we shoot at night to give us our Latitude.' I got a nice hug and kiss.

17 May. Shenandoah started on load of supplies last week. On the 11th I invited Warrants Wagner and Birch to watch from the Poop. They kept wantin to jump into this. It took a bit of time for them Petty Officers, they trained, to catch up to that task. Come noon that day and they slapped their backs for a job well done.

We found a horse and carriage at the end the pier. Retired Admiral Irwin. Oh, such nice words to them advanced. "Well done, QMC, for Eva. I'd hate to negotiate with you." I said, 'Your name is on that contract, Admiral. It seems you have another to look after.' I got his grave look and, "Oh, another gray hair to my head." It was a joke. He is partly bold and gray of the rest. He handed $12 dollars gold plus 25 cents interest. Eva advance wages for that first week.

Friday I came off Susquehanna, from watchin the on load, to a buggy on the pier. Admiral Griffith must have been watchin what was goin on. On the ship there was just whistles and barrels goin aboard, and empty wagons passed him. "Seems all is going well, QMC." I agreed. "Admiral Taylor told me you would be a handful." Agreed. "He didn't forget to say you got things done, somehow, QMC. Thank you for the squadron ships flags."

Eva? Only I can whip the smile off her face with a comment. She don't like me jokes. It took two days to find her a desk to set at, proper, at the front of that room. She takes care of some kind of accounts for some customers. Her sparklin eyes say she likes her position.

Eva is settled into her company real well. Monday, Wednesday, and Friday I take meals to Regina place. Tuesdays and Thursdays is Chinese with Rose, and Vie. Last Saturday, 21 May, we got invited to Carrie place for an afternoon of me and Eva crossing practice swords on the lawn. The only thing that saved me was I haven't taught her to use the Belayin pin.

Over a lawn chair, Carrie, B, and Vie used her arm shields and gauntlets to challenge me. It was a fine practice. I paired them three gents, one at a time, with Carrie, B, and Vie. Their escorts must have been their sisters or a cousin. Oh, the words they had for them men bad moves. I guess the woman learned watch the Gents practice. All begged off takin on Eva.

Walbeck wanted to take the ship out for a trial run. Instead, Bos'n Gaston, thems two new officers, and crew, got to practice settin sails, at the pier, 26th of May. Walbeck called for some sails, Gaston tweeted to the Bow sprint and Foresails. 1st Lieuy then tweeted to the Mainmast people. Next came 2nd Lieuy, yes, now two, to me aft mast. The savin grace was BM1 Marshal and BM 2 James callin out good orders. Yes, advanced.

30 May, 1898. Admiral Griffith inspected the Volunteers this mornin of Rishell, plus 12, and me. The Oldsters won't sign but to me. Readers like Rishell. Shenandoah has some gooduns. Potts needed to step up to head of ships enlisted men, to make Chief. Wagner, Burch, and I sorted out what was at Squadron to fill both ships. I got 2 of 8 Boots and most they didn't want. Lt. Olson signed them on to Shenandoah. It is time to end this contract stuff.

Eva and me had a schedule of events last week, as I said, with Regina, Vie, and Rose. We are back to her place, not real early. Eva opened up on stuff, in talk, about the men at work and thems at the afternoon party. I did goose her, after her kiss on Saturday, to a wide smile, and a laugh to remember.

Sunday was just us. Yes, she had to stop by Effie place, to thank her for the stuff, and we walked and talked. So, another damsel in distress I saved? Sometimes, more like an angry wheasel I got handed to pet. Maybe I did rile her up, here and there. I think she was just lonely and needed women friends to be with. Uncle Curtis words where there about good deeds to Davy Jones log and copper to that chest, to get into Heaven. Sister Catherine came to me mind.

We set to sail to the Caribbean, 'amorrow, at 10 AM. To Ella place tonight for farewell celebration drinks with me volunteers. Me belongin's are aboard, 'cept for a small bag. Last night to sleep in a true bed. I have a bottle hidden, for a nip or so to help me sleep.

Sign this out to you, as I go to supper, My Lady.

By Your Leave, Missy,

An Old Sea Dog,

IN THE YEAR 1898, 07 JULY: CARIBBEAN

Dear Miss Judith,

I start this letter on 03 June, 1898. Them jackass tugs got us out into the current and we passed through them Hampton Roads shoals on 31 May, all nice and proper. Capt'n Walbeck sure squirmed in that chair to Starboard side. The Pilot Capt'n said he had to sit there, 'cept to ship water. Walbeck didn't want to move. I ain't sayin anything here. The Poop crew was to stations, as required. There was 4 to the wheel, me at chart table, Mr. Horn, the new Navigator, and QM2 Joseph across. McFeature and the new boots at the helm. No rompin and stompin out orders. Walbeck hates that stuff. It was 3 hours to Pilot drop off point.

Capt'n Walbeck is in a hurry to get South. Him and me have been over this Nassau and the new base at Key West, daily. I said the winds tell East or West, as to which to go to first. I learned that last time here. He wanted to, "See Hatteras Island Light house light." The second day, second time, I handed Rishell my Ships Masters paper to sign into the log as, 'Disagree. Sign them over to Captain Walbeck. He is Ships Master.' Walbeck into the Chart Room and gave it back to me. "I'd like to see it, for once, QMC." The wind weren't bad. 'On a cloud, tonight, Captain,' as was West winds, high clouds, as I showed it to him. We was 50 miles out. Oh, it shines for 25 and the rest is off a cloud.

Warrant Gaston has his hands full with 1st Lieuy Landry and 2nd Lieuy Novak, from the Susquehanna. Me recommendation. It seems I taught them the whistles, "Wrong, QMC." Well, they got us to the Pilot ship. I ain't no Bos'n and sails type. No, not a day sail, and they was tuned to his methods. Admiral Taylor, good to his word, gave me Ensign Horn, "and train him well, QMC!" New Marine Lt. is Mr. Smiets. He is tryin to make Captain with his words to them Marines. I have known Waltermire for a long time. BM1 Marshal and BM2 James are me savin grace. Old crew and the crew likes thems, they do. 'Tween Gaston, thems, Oldsters, and Readers, I could sail to the Horn of Africa and not a worry from me. GM1 Garto, new minted, and Mr. Campbell set a good deck of guns.

He was recommended by Warrant Burch. There were lots in that recommendation I forgot.

By the time we got to Florida, Shenandoah could Tack and Wear real good, pot belled she be. Campbell and gun crew was right on with layin out them 18s, and them 6 pound breach loaders. Hardis was pleased with ships boarding party practice. I took on all the officers, there at the fence, with the line under that thing. Eva and that woman sure got me in practice. Walbeck stepped up to that line and I took that sword from his hand, I did. No, real ones. I made sure I didn't dent me blade. Belayin pin to his, smacked the blade 'afore the guard and off it went.

I allowed him to pick it up and stood straight to that fence. The second time, me sword caught his and the Belayin pin sent it off, to the other side. The third time he does this French style, hand 'ahind. He leaned over that fence a bit much, to thrust. Oh, the side of my sward caught his, and maybe, just maybe, that Belayin pin smacked his hand, a touch. Not a word said as he picked it up and saluted me. Oh, I had to do the same.

The crew watched and said not a word. Around the Smokin Lamp Lited was their usual talk. BM1Marshel, GM1 Barto, and me just got looks. Me new mess mates. They caught up on the crew and things. They have to learn of their elevated positions, in charge of their crew members, different parts of the crew.

Eva, you'd ask about. 30 May, I caught her up at that Chinese place, as we agreed. It saves her a nickel of expense, and cost me for her and Vie. Rishell took a pail to be with Rose. A last night for thems, what they do. We dropped off Vie, who begged off Ella place. I had to introduce Eva to the Volunteers. All gave good words to her. She just might have been a Princess. They are polite scoundrels. She gave bright eyes and smile to each. Came kind words to me ears after. Ella gave her some bad words to them, to her smiles. Ella knew thems well.

One drink and she asked, "Our pardon, for leaving you Gents." Them scoundrels looked around, said, "Oh, Thank ya, Our Lady." I got their winks and nods. She liked the men. "Quiet Seaman." Well, was, till got more beer down! I could name their faults to a man. I figured another trap was in the works.

To her place, ahind the curtain, a rustling of cloths, out in her old dress, and another game of guess. The bad thing was I'd gone to Effie place and set up her account, for things. Effie gave me that list of stuff, just simple items, that Eva had purchased, off her credit. It didn't amount to much. Just items a simple woman would need and value.

So, a bright smile she had to this guessin game. I ticked off that list, from Effie, I 'membered. Some were, 'ahind that curtain. Personal. I got that growl. Attacked! She has "B" blood for wrestlin. Bit, feet stomped, and a wild wheasel I put up with. The only thing saved me is I put fingers to her sides, to bad words, but laughin, and thrashin. I set her on her feet, to bad looks, and mean words. Me wigglin finger got the most laughs from her. I got a good kiss and asked, "You intentions, QMC?" I intended to sail to the Caribbean.

She set some aside of each week wages, for stuff to get later. Credit to her Effie account. No, she watched what she spent. Her room was smaller than Vie and Rose, less cost. I gave Effie some guide lines, for her spendin on my money. Necessities! Mr. Bish gave me some bad eyes to our arrangement. Damsel in distress? No. I already said she was an intelligent, independent woman.

I mentioned her new position and, 'savin some for when you got in invite to a social, at Admiral Irwin place?' By the time I got back I figure 'atween "B" and Carrie, she would have, 'So many Bows around I'd need me sword and pistol, to defend your honor!' That got her smile and twinkling eyes. I said for her to see Effie about formal cloths, to rent. She wanted to be told, "B, second story, QMC." I said, 'No.' We wrestled to best of 3. 'Couse, I lost. It is better than getting bit, feet stomped, and kicked. She giggled and snickered so, I thought her room neighbor would pound on the wall! The first flick of that towel got her attention. She asked for the story.

We made Nassau, de Bahamas, on 08 June. It was the West winds as Bos'n Gaston gave Capt'n Walbeck the bad news as he wantin to hit Key West first. Bein, 'Ships Master,' I got to go with him to visit this Brit Minister. A US Naval officer gave us the, "Situation in Cuba." It seems them costal supply ships, Fran, Carney, and Williams has been providing stuff for them Iron Cruisers down here, supportin the Cuban rebels. A coal ship set there in Key West to give them coal. The Spanish Frigates, and such, were bottled up in a West Cuba harbor. "No need to worry about seeing any, you providing stores to the, ah, Sailing Frigates."

He did give us some times to where they'd be. It was the usual counter clock rotation. There was 4 of thems. Two off South America. One off Puerto Rico and the other under Jamaica, with the usual stops in Cozumel for hull work, and such. So, we just headed into the Caribbean, to find some Frigates, stores to thems, and to Barbados. No.

An East wind got us around Nassau and it had some North to it, so we got around that them Grand Bahamas Island and made it to Key West on 10 June. Right there sat this Armored Costal Cruiser Olympia. It was tied up to that coal ship, with booms over and on loadin sacks of coal. I got invited to be with Walbeck for this Captain meeting. I took Nav, Mr. Horn, along. Officers talk to officers. Me bein Ships Master amounted to that piece of paper.

I stood 'ahind Horn, seated at the table in the "Wardroom." It is not proper for me to sit. Oh, it was the usual officer talk and such. The Olympia Capt'n kept givin me the eye durin this discussion. Came more news of the Spanish fleet and what the Army on Cuba was up to. There was 3 other cruisers supportin Army landins by throwin them big shells at Spanish places. Thems at the table got some wine and sweet breads. I was close enough to the head of that table for this cruiser Capt'n to hear me stomach growl to his ears, then eyes, and, "Captain Walbeck, who is that man behind you?"

I was introduced as, "Ships Master, Captain. Designated as such by Service Squadron Admiral." He never heard of such stuff. Warrant Office only. At least he didn't know me well enough to attach my, ah, varied character. He said Olympia would escort us, "West, past Cuba, and around to the South of the Island." Walbeck gave his thanks for that. That was the last thanks he'd be givin that Captain, as me log says.

On 12 June we up anchored with Olympia. Her flags gave us a station 1000 yards 'ahind her. The bad thing was wind only gave us 6 knots to her 8. Her signal gun to lee said to increase sail. OK. We did. Our speed dropped to 5 as the Aft sails took the wind from the Fore sails. Gaston and Walbeck had some words about this. Me?

I only set the course for the best wind. Gaston and Landry tweeted and back to 6 knots. 'Nother gun to lee, lots of flags up, guns, flags up, to more guns. Olympia slowed and got close enough for Captain to Captain to talk. It was agreed that we would set course and best speed. Olympia would be South of us, closer to Cuba, in case some Spanish ship came into view.

15 June we rounded that island, goin South, so Olympia went East. I saw somes in the high yard arms give them that not good send off. I'd have done the same, 'cept for the officers on the Poop deck. I did see Bos'n Gaston scratch a spot on his rump. Walbeck caught this and Gaston said it was 'cause of the lack of rain we had. Salt in his skivvies. Officers ain't me concern.

The afternoon of the 16th we anchored of Cozumel. No, no Frigate there but Capt'n gave orders for one shore liberty per division. Me and Mr. Horn went ashore in the Capt'n gig to get the Harbor Master permission. Mr. Hernandez wasn't there. Mr. Garcia couldn't say yes. I asked about Sister Catherine, to more arms from him, like when mentioned he Hernandez. I left Horn there to figure this out.

The church yard had three nuns and groups of children around. Sister Catherine got more words in Spanish then I could understand. No, no Pietro. Oh, Pietro name got more hands, arms, and words I still didn't understand. Finally, one little girl mentioned Catherine and, "Fruitos pala nienos." Well something like that, to me bad ears, and a pointed down the street.

Sister Catherine was not to be missed, in a pure white head cover and her white dress stood out from the dirty street, little off color stands, and people. The place is not as neat as Aspra, in Sicily. Her basket over her arm held little. I just watched as she approached each vender and said some words. She is tall, to my eyes in her shoes, straight backed, and like a military figure. Lovely long fingers, graceful with them, seemed to bless each and got no offerin. I tried to sneak up on her. I did get about 10 feet to her back and,

"My knight. I heard you ship was in." Nope, she never turned. "The woman whispered you were behind me. They knew you from last here." She turned and I got her smile. Angelica! I took her basket and went back to the first fruit stand. A Small copper got a fruit. At the next place a larger copper got some more. Big centavos get more than little ones. I learned this 'afore. We had to stop at each fruit place, 3 on the North side and 2 on the South, filled that basket to her nod.

Arm on mine back to the church and she explained how she tried to get bruised or damaged fruit, "as a treat, for the children." Her blessing got nothing as the weather had been bad, they had poor crops, and fruit was not in season. I got thanks for that full basket. 'Course, the children were delighted in the pieces they got. I sat in them low bench seats, knees to me chin, and Sister even gave me a piece of the fruit I bought! "Share and share alike, QMC," to the delight in the eyes of thems children, I saw, and an Angelic smile to me.

I about dragged those 10 to the church at 4 PM. Sister Catherine seated them to a bench, after they did their obligations. I even got her cross of water on me forehead, "Not to tempt God, QMC." A hand to them, into that place, out, and they sat proper. All done, it was lucky the isle was empty, what with them leavin in such a hurry. At the church door I caught up her hand in me left, right over, and closed it. I got her nice smile. 'Treats, for you children, Sister Catherine.' Me 10 left nothing in the poor box. Pietro? He is of age to workin with his father.

The sailor and Marines each got liberty for 6 hours. Only me, BM1 Marshal, and GM1 Garto did Shore Patrol. Marine Lt. Smiets accompanied us. He didn't like us takin, 'Refreshments,' at that quiet place we stopped at. We had to beg off refreshments at each of the 4 places the ship fixed. I only took a fruit from them 2 push cast venders. I reminded the crew of last here, rebuildin the places. Mess mates took some back. Mr. Hernandez spoke well of the crew behavior, as I took the last boat off that pier.

It seems the new water barrels had soaked up more that was thought. There had been no rain, so there was not much in them seepin tubs for salt meat and less for worshin. Come morning brief, all seemed to be scratchin some itch. Doc Stiteler morning report included some strange stuff goin around. I mentioned to Walbeck about this place just 'afore Trujillo, for fresh water.

We stopped at this place called Betulia, Honduras. I'd been there 'afore. There was shoals around that place and a slow stream of good water. It took a day to fill casks. Walbeck was sure walkin the Poop deck at this slow waterin. Marshal had been here 'afore. I left him to that task so I got Walbeck eyes at each turn of the Taft rail. I was workin on the current chart and figures of the Caribbean. Especially that 'tween Cuba and Mexico. Cozumel current I already knew.

21 June, 98, and we made Trujillo. No Frigate was there so off to the East we went. Mr. Campbell got to fire the guns and Hardis had boarding party practice after. I took on the officers, at that line, and fence across. I took on Walbeck last. He and I played "Tink-Tink" for 4 rounds. Nope, I never took that sword from his hand. Shush. He did well, but still don't like me Belayin pin. At least he didn't try to cross that line, like 'afore.

See, after I took his sword from his hands, last time, I took him to see Armoror Hardis. Oh, he is the best at steel I've seen. So, he takes Walbeck right hand and does a firm shake. Then, takes that sword to his hand and I heard Eva growl. Hardis didn't like the handle. He gives Walbeck some wood pieces to grip. After the third one, another handshake, he griped that wood, and gives Walbeck back his sword. Well, bare handed Hardis took it right from him and said, "Wrong grip, Captain."

It took till Trujillo for Hardis to set it right. No exotic stuff, like Talig ivory here, so, he used some hard wood that Mr. Chips gave him. McGraw has some odd wood at hand. Anyway, thems pestered Capt'n the whole way South with fittin out this sword hilt to his hand. It wasn't no glamour thing handle he held, but, I couldn't smack it from his hand. Mine, ya ask? Once in that "Bird Cage" thing, well, it be easier to remove me wrist, 'cept for the gauntlet. Capt'n was sure proud of his fightin skills. He even got me gauntlet once. Shush. Let him hit it.

26 June we found that 1st Frigate 'tween Honduras and Columbia. It seemed to be just circling that midpoint. Capt'n and Purser went to her for talkin. We got close enough to put spar lines over and barrels goin to her. A rope round the forward Cat, line to that barrel, and she took up slack on her line to take it over. BM1 Marshal directed this. BM2 James is comin along. He directed the Aft Cat line.

We made Cartagena on the 28th. It seems that Harbor Master 'membered us. Oh, no need for the "Habla" guy as he understood American real good. Right up 'till orderin stuff. The Silver Liberty guy was right there to help us. It took some time to arrange what Purser wanted. The gig crew didn't mind this wait. I only allowed fruit and water. What he wanted was for the next morning.

03 July and the next Frigate was off Caracas, Venezuela. Well, La Guaira. The town Maggie, Barbados bar maid, said to see the Harbor Master. The Frigate wondered as to how we came up with fresh vegetables and such. Maybe be nice to the local people? Purser and me never said. Only Walbeck and Purser went over to talk to the Frigate people. And, no Silver dollar from Purser. I ain't gonna give him that name of the Harbor Master in La Guaira Maggie mentioned. I'll keep that in me vest book, just in case.

06 July and I was standin 'ahind Mr. Horn at this conference table with the Barbados Brit Governor. A US Naval officer there to say what was goin on what with the Spanish Navy bottled up in Cuba. A 2 master was botherin ships in the Caribbean. No name or country of origin was said. "Most likely a pirate praying on commerce, as the Spanish ships are defending Cuba." I had to cough at that. It might be the same one we shot up a couple times, here. But, we never got close enough to sink it. I could out sail our Frigates, even the Spanish ones.

Maggie gave me an ear full of what was goin on. Shush. She still has a "Boy Friend" on each of the Frigates down here. The Packets brings her letters from them poor boys. They give more details of what is goin on than that US officer did. It seems the Frigates had tried to engage that 2 master, but too slow. The Packets have seen this 2 Master and out run it. They sure gave a mind to what it looks like. They laughed, out sailin it. Oh, I paid a round to hear all thems said of it.

I had BM1 Marshal, BM2 James, and GM1 Barto there to hear this. We was supervisin the liberty party. We had to make sure Engle and Rishell got back to the ship, ah, accompanied. There was just nods and eyes 'atween us, as Packet crew gave more of Pirates notables, to our eyes and small words 'atween us. They mentioned this to Gaston and Gunner Campbell.

One problem was Puerto Rico country was not governed very well. Our waterin hole there was isolated from most towns. Hardis, Campbell, and Chips, Mr. McGraw knew of some little places the Pirates came from. There was a dozen of places on the South American land they could be from. I never knew the Dominican Republic to harbor Pirates. But, I don't know all.

Now, in me letters we have had some problems with that Windward Passage 'tween Haiti and Cuba. What with them Armored Cruisers goin and comin, I figured none would be found there. We need to watch for that lookout atop that mountain on the West end of that island. Dossours point. Such was on me mind, listenin to them Packet ship crew.

Oh, the first half of this Caribbean cruise is done and no problems, other than some winds. I might need you to conjure up an Eastern one for this next round. After helpin fix his sword problem, Walbeck and me be on good terms. We both say little to each other. The second day here so Engle got his snoot full last evenin. Spiel served Walbeck warmed sweet breads and coffee this morning, to choke on. I need Engle to show him how to make proper coffee.

Hitcock is callin for mail close out to that Packet ship. I guess I bent yourn ear enough for now. Sign this out to you, My Lady, 07 July, 1898.

By Your Leave, Missy,

An Old Sea Dog,

POST LOG

To answer your question, no, this does not end the letters to Miss Judith. This sailor is only about half through what we now consider a normal enlistment. The "Oldsters" he mentions might be in their late 60's and still sailing. It was the life they lived, the life they knew, at that time. The same with his "Readers," though they maybe not as old. But many of the men in that era were hardly literate. That was one consideration to be promoted to "Petty Officer."

I considered where to end this volume. It ends on a nice note. Miss Judith would have only laughed, or snickered, at some of his words.

I'm still copying the letters in that box. I do it as I have time and inclination. Mrs. Bracken is trying to hurry me along with this endeavor. She is down to last of those not copied. Maybe we have missed some of them. I doubt it, what with her evil, teacher eyes. Those copied have a check mark next to the postage stamp. That is an old habit. Oh, she knows of this. The bundles are looked through and sorted to her purpose. Don't ask me. I only get handed them one at a time and watched real careful by her.

What a life he must have had. Miss Judith must have cherished them, to keep them.

E.G.'L.

ABOUT THE BOOK

In Western Pennsylvania, in a village, hardly on a map, sits a Victorian house, on a quiet street. The back side faces the local train tracks to the next cities. There in the comfy alcove, facing the rails, sits a young woman, reading a letter. Tea cup on the serving tray, feet under, on the padded cover.

Her correspondent writes such she reads a page, goes to the next, back to the start, through the pages at hand. She is familiar with his writing style. It is reread to snickers, laughs, giggles at a man's life, hundreds and sometimes thousands of miles away. Letter done, tea done, she goes to the kitchen for another cup, snickering the whole way.

Her mother pours her another cup, adds some little milk and asks, "What is he up to now?" The elements of the letter are read out, to the mothers looks. She says, "His mother must not sleep at night, worrying about him." "Oh, mother, it sounds exciting. Ah, to travel." The older woman just looks at her, pats her hand and says, "I'll take our quiet life, here."

E.G.'L.

ABOUT THE CHARACTERS

I was queried on QMC age. He entered the Navy in 1882 at 16 plus years of age. It was mentioned in the first book. He was born perhaps in1866. I could never find documentation of this, other than via the letters. He wrote his first letter to Miss Judith in 1888. That was his second cruise to the Mediterranean. That is the one with the reference to the Triremes. I can only speculate Miss Judith age. He once said she was, "Just flowering." I took that to mean she was around 13 when she received the first letter. I have no documentation on her either.

ABOUT THE AUTHOR

The author grew up in the Western area of Pennsylvania. The small town would have been little different than the sailor in this book. He lived next to his Grandfather farm and would have similar experiences. Time and circumstances cause him to join the Navy. As with "QMC," he enjoyed his duty stations, his work, and the individuals he met. He retired from the Navy as a Senior Chief.

The first letter from the sailor is to be found in, "A Sailor's Tale, Miss Judith 1888-1893 Miss Molly.

Questions or comments are welcome. Contact the Author can be found at eglusko.com.

E.G.'L.

. . .